THE INFINITE HUMAN

An Ascension Guide for Awakening Infinite
Humans, Star Seeds, Twin Souls, and Co-Creators of
the New Infinite 5D Earth

ELIZABETH MONROY M.S

PETER MONROY M.D.

Infinite Human Productions

Print Editions 1.1 2022
ISBN-978-1-958184-23-3

INFINITE HUMAN PRODUCTIONS
www.infinitehuman.com

Enquires:
infinitehumanproductions@gmail.com

Infinite Human Productions L.L.C
USA, Italy

This book is my own personal journey and perspective of life. I wrote it
to help me make sense of my own life experiences, to access the hidden
history of our multiverse and to recover my lost memories, reclaim and
heal my lost identities and bring myself back into holiness. I hope it will
inspire you to do the same! It is in no way meant to be misconstrued as
spiritual, medical or legal advice nor any other means of advising you as
to how you should live your life. You are a God Sovereign Being who has
been granted free will, making you responsible for your own choices. The
names of individuals used throughout this text serve as examples to explain
concepts and situations and are fictitious and any similarity to any persons
living or deceased is purely coincidental.

CONTENTS

DEDICATION

This book is dedicated to the Divine
Infinite Source within us all!

FOREWORD

"There is emerging on the face of the Earth a new human, an Infinite Human, and that Human is YOU!" These words spilled out onto the page of a paper I was writing over thirty years ago while I was working towards my Masters in Mental Health Counseling. Shortly after that, my computer was struck by lightning. I managed to recover the paper and submitted it to my professor, who called the idea "Kooky." But the idea stuck, and it has taken the form of this book, which relates to Earth's Hidden History, Current World Events and the Frequency Wars on our planet.

This is not just my story but the story of my twin soul, Peter Monroy, a physician and how we tried to change the course of modern medicine. It is a heroine's journey, an alchemist's memoir, a love story of two broken souls who managed to find each other against all odds, heal their past wounds and create an eternal love that survived even death! But above all this is your story, of the true freedom that only comes through organic ascension. Of the power that comes to those who awaken from the Dream Spell to co-create an Infinite New Earth! This book offers full disclosure of the truth behind the lies that have been hidden in plain sight, so you can heal while taking you on an amazing spiritual journey around our planet and into the higher dimensions of forbidden knowledge, supernatural phenomenon, and cosmic disclosure to awaken you to the truth that, "YOU ARE ALL THAT IS, EVER HAS BEEN AND EVER SHALL BE!! YOU ARE INFINITE!"

CHAPTER 1

THE DIVINE STORYTELLER

"In the beginning was the Word, and the Word was with God, and the Word WAS God."

JOHN 1:1

We are all just stories in the mind of God the Divine Storyteller. The further we stray from the original word, which IS God or the vibrational frequency of Infinite God Source, the more our life story begins to unravel. The more pain, suffering and confusion we experience until like the prodigal son, we decide to return Home to the vibrational frequency of Infinite God Source within.

For years, I have worked with film students using the Mythic Story Structure that Joseph Campbell so intuitively captured and wrote about in his books. He explained that inherent in all myths, legends, novels, films and stories, since the beginning of time, there exists a mythic structure, which he called "The Hero's Journey." It is really an alchemist's journey to transmute what Carl Jung referred to as our shadow self. According to this renowned psychiatrist, all humans possess a shadow self. This is the part of us where our deepest, darkest fears, anger, grief, sorrow, traumas and wounds fester until we have the courage to bring them out of the darkness and into the light. When the main character faces and transmutes their own shadow self it is called a comedy. But when the darkness overpowers our main character and he or she succumbs to their inner flaws, never transmuting the shadows within, we call this a tragedy.

Which story are you writing? Is your current life story a comedy or a tragedy? How do you see the World around you? Is it a cold, cruel world? A dangerous world? A heartless world? What type of character have you chosen to play? Are you the heroine in your own life story, the leading man or lady? Or are you a supporting character in someone else's life story? A sidekick? Are you a people pleaser? Are you living your life for others? Do you take care of everybody but yourself? Do you constantly seek validation from others? Do you feel unworthy? Unloved? Abandoned? Fearful? Not enough? Are you swimming in a sea of shame and guilt? Are you playing the victim? Are you repeating the same old story over and over, again, stuck? Not knowing how to change? Are you longing for something new to happen but not sure how to write it? Or perhaps you are soul weary? Perhaps you just long for an end to your life story? Perhaps you don't even care how your story ends anymore! Maybe your life story has no real meaning, no connection to the world, to others, to God, or to your authentic self?

You are the hero at the beginning of a great story. You, like all heroes, are filled with flaws and defects as well as amazing gifts and talents. And what is a story without a good villain? In fact, any good writer knows that the stronger the villain or antagonist, the greater the character arch or growth of the hero. Take a moment to determine whether this statement is true. Have you had people or experiences come into your life that you thought were horrible? Yet in these times of great difficulty and challenge haven't you had to reach deep inside of yourself and find out just what you were made of? Haven't all the challenges you faced in life made you a better person, taught you valuable lessons? Or have you remained bitter? Have you allowed your deepest, darkest fears, pain, and sorrows to remain hidden, festering like pus inside a wound?

There is really only one story. The story is always the same, but the people, places and situations change. Our hero may be a handsome young man in a galaxy far, far away dreaming of adventure, or a humble hobbit dreaming of his next meal, when adventure comes knocking at his door. All Hero's journeys are ultimately the same journey back Home, to the original word or vibrational frequency of Infinite God Source. It is the Prodigal Son's return to the Father, the Fool's navigation of the Tarot's Major Arcana, or the Alchemist transmutation of lead into gold. We are all students here on this Earth Campus, just walking each other home. I hope by sharing my life story, this book will serve as an impetus for you to embark on your own supernatural journey of inner healing, transmutation, ascension, and to drink from the "elixir of life" that holds the knowledge of Truth!

Story creates meaning in our lives and allows us to learn and grow, share our experiences, know ourselves better, and appreciate this spiritual journey we call life. The curative effect of the genuine sharing of our story, the exposing of our vulnerabilities, weaknesses, and the bringing forth of our dark side into the light was known to the Ancient Greeks. They performed their stories in Amphitheaters as part of a religious festival which the entire community would participate in. These festivals would last days, even weeks, and contained moments of climax followed by a catharsis or "release" for the purification of the body, mind, and spirit. In this manner, the townspeople would "purge" themselves of toxins they held physically, emotionally, mentally, and spiritually, often weeping and vomiting. Aristotle, in the Poetics, describes the healing and detoxifying power of story as "Tragedy having a healthful and humanizing effect on the spectator." Perhaps we don't have to weep and vomit on one another but certainly there is a healing affect as well as a deep bond formed by those who openly and intimately share their deepest darkest secrets. Those who unbosom their souls free others to follow.

"All the world's a stage, And all the men and women merely players."
WILLIAM SHAKESPEARE

With that said I will quote my husband Peter, "everything is sacred and nothing is sacred." The point being that once you become too attached to your story it may be time to loosen the grip. If you find yourself identifying too much with your finite story and its characters, it is time to detach. Time to take a step back and see things from a higher perspective. You are not "your" story. You are merely "playing" a part. You are Infinite! If you can approach your life story from the third person omnipresent, you will find the inner power to become the Divine Story Teller and co-create a new divine version of yourself in unison with the Divine Word Vibration which IS God. You will hold the pen that writes your life story. You will become the Finger of God, writing words that are in harmony with the Vibrational God Source Frequency while leaving your own unique finger print with every word you write. Then you can change your life story and change the your world. You can erase the past mistakes and rewrite your own ending. Ah, but here's the rub, you must first understand, heal and transmute the life lessons you have created for yourself in order to free yourself, and loosen the grip of karma.

When you came here, part of your story was to learn Earth's Collective Story. This is why we read books, watch plays, see films and listen to other people's stories, to better understand the collective human story. But many of you have forgotten that your job was not to become part of the fallen Earth story. You came here to be a hero! To guide humanity out of the darkness. You came here with your own unique story, plot, and theme, to be a light! But many of you have had to dim your brilliant light to fit into this world of darkness. Perhaps you have been raised by wounded parents, indoctrinated into a broken society and let other people's perspectives, opinions and stories bleed into your own life story, infecting your every intention like a virus? Perhaps you have joined humanity in the lower frequencies of the broken finite earth? Perhaps the insidious and infectious infiltration of Earth's Dream Spell has taken your words from Infinite God Source and quietly reversed these words into swords used as weapons against you? These words have convinced you that you are a victim, a martyr, or a villain and cannot change your story. Perhaps these words have perverted your story's theme, hijacked your plot, and made you into a sidekick in someone else's story rather than the hero in your own life story?

Words are magic! Words hold frequencies and can be used for either g(o)od or (d)evil. It all depends on who is holding the magic pen. Words can harm you or heal you. Words can empower, liberate, illuminate, educate, inspire, and expand your consciousness. Words can direct you closer to the truth of the unspoken Word which IS the vibrational frequency of Infinite God Source or they can be used as weapons to confuse, embroil, ensnare, and entrap your consciousness into their finite narratives of fear and powerlessness. Hence we can see the truth behind the saying, "The pen is mightier than the sword." This also demonstrates the ancient alchemical premise "thought directs energy" or "energy goes where attention flows", at work in the World.

The first thing any child learns in school is how to "spell." The definition of the word spell is, "a spoken word or form of words which holds magic power". So "spelling", or the art of casting spells is the first thing taught. It is important to note that in the English language, each word has multiple meanings. So people can easily say one thing and mean another. People who are under a spell or spellbound are hypnotized to SEE only what those who cast the spells want them to see. The storyteller, the writer of words, the caster of spells directs the words or thoughts in a certain direction. The storyteller keeps the reader's mind contained in the narrative of the story. They can only see what the storyteller wants them to see and only go where the speller directs them with the wave of their magic pen. So the reader is spellbound to the confines of the word, the plot, the story, and the narrative. They cannot see outside the finite architecture of the words, that make up the pages that move the plot forward. If you add an S to words you have swords. So you can see that the word or the pen is indeed mightier than the sword.

The intention of my words is to ignite the spark of divine truth within you, to arouse the power that lies sleeping, to awaken the Divine Dreamer, the Divine Storyteller. My goal is to expose the underlying virus that has infected you and bring you back to the Truth of the unspoken vibrational frequency of the Word, which IS God inside of you. I will do this through the antidote of Truth, full disclosure of the lies that have been spun around you to keep you asleep in the dream spell. We, on Earth, are on the verge of a great new story, a great awakening, an Ah-hah moment that will jolt the collective in a way never before experienced. But this can only happen if you the Divine Infinite Dreamer awaken from the dream spell that has been cast over you to keep you spellbound, asleep in the dream, and unable to awaken to your true power within.

"The Moving Finger writes; and, having writ, Moves on: nor all thy Piety nor Wit Shall lure it back to cancel half a Line, Nor all thy Tears wash out a Word of it."
OMAR KHAYYÁM

But you can change your story! You are the writer! You hold the pen ...or do you? Many of us think we hold the pen but do we really? Are you letting someone else hold the pen of your life story? Are you allowing yourself to be defined, manipulated, hypnotized, mind controlled by something or someone outside of you? A partner, a family member, a friend, a spiritual teacher? Are you permitting your culture, your government, your vocation, your sex, your age, your race, your religion to define who you are and what you can or cannot do? Where is there an insidious virus poisoning the real story that you have come to Earth to write?

Many people believe they do not hold the pen of their life but God does. But if God is omnipresent or present in all things, doesn't this mean that God is also present in you? Doesn't this mean that you too are the omnipresent voice of God writing your story? But first you must match the "words" to the vibrational frequency of God's Word. You must merge with the Divine Infinite Storyteller and become "One with God!" When you can awaken to the truth by surrendering your finite self to your infinite self, you will know that you are God, all that is, ever has been and ever shall be! You can then take back the magic pen of your life story, step into your power as the Divine Infinite Storyteller of your own life and become the Infinite Human Being God intended you to be.

So the work is to become an alchemist and transmute your life story! Then you can cancel and wash out every word that is not in atonement or at-one-meant with the ONENESS OF ALL THINGS inherent in original Vibrational God Source Frequency. This is the journey Home, which can take many lifetimes or can happen in the blink of an eye. The reason being that there is no time! Time is an illusion. Time is a series of flash sequences much the same as lightbulbs on a Marque that flash on and off, creating the illusion of movement and time. These flash sequences create mathematical equations that create geometrical patterns that create the structure of each Multiverse or Time Matrix. This pattern carries on into infinity. We use these flash sequences to create the illusion of time to create meaning in our lives. To have a beginning, middle and end to things. To allow us to reflect, learn and grow from our experiences. What does exist is an infinite number of realities, moments and versions of you! These separate realities are like distinct and separate pictures or frames in a movie. When we splice the frames together, we create the illusion of time through moving pictures. These movies create our life story. So your story is simply a series of framed moments or choices made by flashing into Infinite Source, then back out again co-creating your unique holographic reality. Moment to moment, you are choosing another version of yourself, writing and rewriting each word of your life story. Each moment in time is like a pearl when all strung together make up a necklace. When these strands of pearls or threads are woven together, they create the tapestry of time. You can choose to step into a higher vibratory frequency or flash sequence of yourself or a lower one. Likewise, you can step onto a higher timeline of Earth's future or a lower one. One of ascension or one of descension.

How do you ascend in frequency? Thought directs energy. Imagineer the new optimal version of yourself and step into it! But in order to maintain that higher vibratory version of yourself, you must heal all your past wounds and traumas so your triggers will not pull you back into the lower frequencies. You must heal your shadow self and learn all your lessons. If you are having trouble maintaining this higher version of yourself then it is a sign that you have not completely healed from these painful experiences and learned the lessons that they are gifting you. I know nobody likes to return to painful moments in their lives, but unless you have fully integrated these life lessons, you cannot graduate from Earth School and move into the next vibrational frequency.

All creation moves in spirals. You are either returning back to Infinite God Source on the KRYSTALA SPIRAL of LIFE or descensing away from Infinite Source on the Fibonacci spiral of DEATH. (Fib-A-Not-Chi) When you are choosing life and ascending back to Infinite God Source, you feel good! Your life flows. Of course you may feel you are repeating some of the same lessons over and over again. But if you look closer, the pain or discomfort you feel around the subject is diminishing and you are receiving help to fully integrate these lessons into your life. It is in feeling, accepting, understanding, learning and loving our pain that we heal ourselves back into wholeness. Love is the magic ingredient that transmutes all! This is necessary to move beyond the confines of your finite self. When the lessons are learned, when tests are passed... you graduate and move up to the next grade. It is in this way we transmute ourselves from the lower vibratory frequency versions of ourselves into a higher more refined version of ourselves aligned and RESET with the Vibrational Frequency of Infinite God Source within, thus becoming One with God.

In your life story you may create a tragedy or a comedy. It makes no difference to God, the Divine Infinite Story Teller. The whole purpose of these stories in the mind of God is for you to better know yourself. The

Divine Infinite Storyteller within you creates characters, plots, themes, and catharses for you to better "know thyself" or the Infnite to know ITself. Infinite God Source then plays out all of the roles because, after all, God is Infinite. It casts itself as both the Hero and the Villain. It plays all the major characters and minor characters and will continue rewriting the same story over and over again until you, the main character, say, "There's got to be something better and I WANT IT!" Then you must create it! This is the story of the Hero, the Heroine, the Shaman, the Alchemist! This is my story, your story. This is the story of the Hero's Journey Home.

CHAPTER 2

MY STORY

An unexamined life is not worth living.
SOCRATES

My story begins on the Island of Manhattan in New York City where I was born the same year Fidel Castro took over Cuba, the Dali Lama fled Tibet, Aldous Huxley warned the medical community about the dangers of "future medicine", Walt Disney released Sleeping Beauty, NASA announced its selection of America's first astronauts, Mattel Released the Barbie Doll and the Presbyterian Church accepted women preachers. My parents named me "Elizabeth Lee Steere". Elizabeth, meaning Dedicated to God or God's House of Light. Lee, meaning Poet or Healer, and Steere, meaning, Star or to Steer. When I married Peter, I took on his name Monroy which means "My King" or in my case "My Queen." Women who take on the name of their husbands join in their soul mission. This is his story, as well as mine. Your name as it appears on your birth certificate is your logos which will guide you to your life's purpose. If you look closely, every soul, has set up signs and symbols to help them remember who they are and why they came to Earth. They are in the letters of your name, the lines on your hands, the bumps on your head, the numerology and astrology of your birth chart, even the bumper sticker on the back of the car in front of you! They are everywhere! Your job, is to properly interpret them. My job is to be assist people in their own inner healing through my words serving as a guiding star, steering them back to the Kingdom of Infinite God Source within. This is my logos. I did not know it then but I was to be a brilliant light in a world of great darkness. Though many times my light was doused and my divine creative sparkle smothered I always reignited it!

The obstetrician christened me a "perfect" baby at birth. Every year on my birthday, my father would retell the same story of how "perfect" I was. I would always feel it was a standard I could never reach, a bar raised too high. But now that my dear dad is gone, I realize it was a message we had set up long before my birth to remind me throughout my life, despite all the challenges I faced, underneath all my imperfections, I was PERFECT! We humans beings are all perfect. . . we have just forgotten. We have been born into an imperfect world where our divine essence was fractured, and this spiritual journey we call life is simply the process of becoming whole or holy again, by releasing our imperfections and returning to our true Divine Infinite State of "perfection."

TO BE INFINITE, YOU NEED ONLY LET GO OF THE FINITE!

The catalyst for my awakening was in kindergarten. One day when I was in a pitch-black bathroom, I saw the skeleton of my classmate walking towards me. I thought everyone had this type of x-ray vision until one day in the emergency room after a bicycle accident, they wheeled in a heavy machine to x-ray my skull. When I asked the medical staff why they didn't just turn off the lights, they laughed. I began to SEE that there were two very different realities—the one that most people agreed upon as "reality" and another "unseen" world. As I moved through life, I began to realize that most people no longer had this ability to SEE beyond the veil of illusion. I thought everyone would be delighted to benefit from my intuitive abilities, but I soon found out that the world did not want people like me nor my extraordinary gifts and talents. This was perhaps the greatest tragedy of my life. It wasn't until years later when I read the book *Autobiography of a Yogi* that I learned that my x-ray vision was the sign of a true healer. It took me many more years to come to understand the full power of this extraordinary gift and how to properly use it. X-rays create shadows, separating the dark from the light and exposing the dis-ease within our physical bodies. This allows the healer to SEE the root cause of the dis-ease that must be addressed so they can properly assist the person to restore balance. But it takes an intuitive healer to SEE the darkness in the emotional, mental, and spiritual bodies. I did not know it then, but I possessed this ability. I just needed to learn how to use it with wisdom, which is knowledge administered though love.

One of my first memories is of holding my head next to the stereo console and listening to the song "Puff the Magic Dragon" by Peter, Paul and Mary, tears streaming down my face. I never understood why every time I heard this song I would sob uncontrollably! I now realize it was a memory of my true star family, a powerful, noble guardian race of Dragon Kings and Queens. This royal Dragon Queen lineage is passed down from mother to daughter. Normally, the higher the genetics, the more wounded the females. My mother was no exception. I so desperately wanted to communicate with her my "otherworldly" experiences, but she could never understand them. As I grew up, she became more and more critical of me, perhaps for fear of what would happen if people found out I had special abilities. She was unable to give me the love and nurturing I so desperately needed as a child. At times, I felt so completely alone, like an abandoned orphan on a hostile planet in the custody of a wicked stepmother.

Although I was an intelligent, intuitive, and creative child, I had few opportunities to express it. As a result, I always felt less than others. I was extremely dyslexic and bored with the left-brained educational system. As a result, I retreated into a world that existed within the power of my imagination. My spirit guides inhabited my dolls and stuffed animals. They guided me through the wounds of my childhood. And then there was my father, who was a kindred spirit.

Each morning, before my dad would go to work, I would lay down on the stairs and pretend to be asleep. My father would pause and say to my mother, "Look, Margaret, a golden-haired princess asleep on the stairs. I wonder, if I kiss her, would she awaken?" Then, he would lean down and kiss me, and I would "wake up." He was my savior, my Prince Charming! Thus began my princess programming, but a seed was planted to be fully awakened by true love.

I was always in love with Peter. Even before we met in this lifetime. I was in love with the promise of him. When I was in first grade my mother enrolled me in an acting class after school. I loved it! For our recital, we had to choose a character from history and recite a monologue. I chose Wendy from *Peter Pan*. I remember the heated debate I had with my drama teacher. She was a big woman with flaming, red hair, and a bellowing voice, who told me that Peter Pan was not real. I adamantly disagreed. On the big night after George and Martha Washington, Pocahontas, Lewis and Clark, etcetera, I was the last to proudly take the stage. There, in my periwinkle blue nightgown, I stood in front of the audience, my proud parents gazing on as I began to recite, "I am Wendy Mora Angela Darling, Peter Pan taught me to fly." After my performance, I drew a picture of Peter Pan and taped it on the wall beside my bed. Every night I would kiss him good night and when I fell asleep, he would come get me and we would fly away to Never-Never Land.

When Fidel Castro came to power on the island of Cuba, Peter had to flee for his life. After two years of hiding at his family's beach home, he got passage on a plane destined for the Bahamas, with a layover in Miami. When he arrived in Miami, he bought a pack of Salem menthol cigarettes with the small bit of money his mother had sewn into his clothes, and locked himself in the bathroom. When the plane left, he presented himself to the customs agent who was going to send him back to Cuba. Peter, not being able to speak a word of English, and knowing that this would mean his certain death, began to cry, and handed the customs agent a small piece of paper with a phone number of a priest written on it. The agent, touched with compassion, called the Priest, who came and got Peter and took him to the first Cuban boys' camp. This was the beginning of what came to be called *Operación Pedro Pan* or The Peter Pan Operation which became a clandestine mass exodus of over fourteen thousand unaccompanied Cuban minors, known at the time as "Pedro Pans" or "Peter Pans."

My father was a Presbyterian Minister. He was a very spiritual man who grew beyond the confines of religion. Above all, he was an eternal optimist! He believed in the inherent good in people. He had inherited that quality from my grandmother, whom, I always identified as my fairy godmother. She supplied the nurturing my mother lacked. She would create beautiful clothes for me to wear and always made me feel so special. My dad and I had a deep spiritual bond. He too was descended from the Dragon Kings. I remember, before he died, I sculpted him, a clay statue of Puff the Magic Dragon, reading a book with a large tear rolling down his cheek.

Like my father before me and many of you, I was of the first wave of volunteers, who came from the God Source Worlds to answer the call of creation, to RESET the Divine Angelic Infinite Human Races and our time matrix to the Infinite! I came to assist Earth in the Krystos Mission of recovering the lost souls of Tara and assisting all those souls who desired to return HOME to Infinite Source. I came with my twin soul Peter to learn about the fallen realms and try to prevent the massive cataclysmic "fall." We failed. I choose to stay to help preserve the truth and to help those Earth-bound souls return home during this ascension cycle. Along the way, as Earth fell deeper and deeper into the darkness, and the deceptions of the dream spell, I fell with it. I had my genetics downgraded, my memories erased and my soul entrapped. I had my good intentions of leading humanity towards the eternal light of truth, co-opted by the false light. I became embroiled by the dark side, spiritually hijacked.

My father's quest for union with God lead him to the Seminary where he became an ordained minister. He decided to pursue his Doctorate of Theology at Union Presbyterian Seminary in New York City, where I was born. When he graduated he took his position as a faculty member at the Louisville Presbyterian Seminary where he founded the Marriage and Family Therapy Program. But, in his early humble days, he would travel the back roads of Kentucky, preaching in small farming communities and I would travel with him. I was so hypnotized by his amazing storytelling abilities that once when I was no more than six, I stood up in my pew and my father had to tell me to sit down from the pulpit. One of his favorite Bible stories was *Joseph and his Coat of Many Colors*. When I went away to college my mother bought me a beautiful woven poncho of many colors. One day in Italy it got caught in my bicycle spokes. I looked down at the ripped and stained coat. Foreshadowing?

I was surrounded by religious people my entire childhood. I was baptized by my uncle whom my father had convinced to become a minister. My parent's circle of friends included members of our congregation, fellow ordained ministers, and my father's students who were studying to become ministers. I believe that because of my father's keen intellect he began to question religion. Once, I asked my father for a Bible and he reluctantly gave me one. It wasn't' anything he said but I got the message loud and clear. Another time I came home to find him editing the Bible. I asked him what he was doing, and he told me the female ministers were complaining about always having to refer to God as male. "Good for them!" I thought. He sheepishly looked up and said, "you know they're right." My father intellectually and intuitively knew that much of the truth had been altered or left out of the poorly translated, severely edited, and misinterpreted book called *The Holy Bible*.

I think this discrepancy inherent in religion turned my father's spiritual search towards the humanistic movement being born in California during the sixties. It was his deep desire to serve his fellow human beings and expand his own consciousness that motivated him to load us up into our family station wagon, with our Volkswagen Beetle in tow and like the pioneers before us head West. We were in search of God, adventure, and whatever lay ahead. It was 1968 and at the age of eight I found myself in the middle of Southern California at the tail end of the sixties! The human potential movement was all around me and it was an amazing time to be alive! My father studied Transactional Analysis with Eric Berne, Family Therapy with Virginia Satire, Gestalt Therapy with Fritz Perls, Childhood Development with Eric Erickson, and a host of other pioneers, who had made their way to California to give birth to the human potential movement. I met many of these people personally and was often included in the workshops and group therapy sessions. We lived in a beachfront apartment in Del Mar, California, down the beach from Desi Arnaz, a Cuban! Long haired hippies wearing sandals would play guitars around bonfires at night on the beach. The air was alive with freedom, creativity, experimentation, and the promise of an exciting new age! My school was very progressive, and I was selected to be on the debate team! Sam Keen, my father's colleague at the seminary had also brought his family west. One day, his daughter told me about the "Big Secret". She made me swear I would never tell anyone and she also said, "let's become the youngest authors ever to write a book!" So, I started writing about the "Big Secret", without breaking my oath to her in my first children's book, *The Magical Mist*.

Nine months after blazing our trail West, we climbed back into our wagon train and headed back East. Needless to say, returning to Kentucky after living in Southern California during the sixties was a bit of a letdown. In my children's book, *The Magical Mist*, the main character, Lauren has her magical rag doll, thrown away along with the Key to the World of Imagination. That pretty much sums up how I felt back in Louisville, Kentucky. I had my creative sparkle all but snuffed out by the indoctrination of the public school system, which was the theme of my children's book. It was only in the library where I could escape in books or when I had the opportunity to write, direct, and act in my own plays, that my creative sparkle was reignited!

My father brought the energies of the sixties and the human potential movement back to Kentucky with him. I saw my parents transform from the black and white starch conservatism of the fifties into a psychedelic kaleidoscope of colorful expressions. I watched the conservative restraints of the fifties give way as more open-minded ministers joined the faculty of the Louisville Presbyterian Seminary. Worship services transformed into outdoor events with communion being passed around from bowls filled with wine and loaves of sour dough bread, while the congregation sat on blankets listening to folk music. One Commencement everyone left the chapel singing and dancing to the song *Jeramiah was a Bullfrog*!

People's hair grew longer, their clothing looser, and my parents went to New York to see the Broadway Musical *Hair* which encapsulated the freedom of expression young people embellished as they let their hair grow longer. Interestingly, it has been proven that "hair" serves as a kind of extrasensory antenna. The U.S. Army learned this when they forced their Native American Scouts to cut their hair and discovered that they lost their ability to track their enemies. I have always been singled out and teased throughout my life for my wild, curly hair, my signature feature. I remember standing on the main street in Malibu, California one evening with John Savage, the actor who starred in the musical film, *Hair*, serenading me with Italian opera. Nothing happens by chance.

As "Peace, Love, Happiness and "Flower Power" infiltrated mainstream society, musicians like *Bob Dylan, Joan Baez, Cat Stevens* and *Donovan,* as well as *Rock Operas* such as *Joseph and his Technicolored Dream Coat,* and of course *Jesus Christ Superstar* vibrated the walls of our old log cabin. The Rock Opera *Jesus Christ Superstar* made religion "cool" transforming Jesus and his apostles into rabble-rousing hippies that challenged authority. I knew every word of this Rock Opera and my first teen idol was, well, "Jesus" or Ted Neely. *Buffy Saint Marie's* ballads recounted America's true history, with each line punctured with the reoccurring verse, " America, your people are dying." Even the musical Hair warned us with Lyrics such as, "facing a dying nation of moving paper fantasy listening for the new-told lie."!

Our family vacations were retreats to deepen our spiritual growth. One summer, we visited the Edgar Cayce Foundation at Virginia Beach. Another year, we went to Ghost Ranch, a spiritual retreat center owned by the Presbyterian Church for ministers and their families in New Mexico. It was the same year the movie *Billy Jack* came out and I was around the same age as their daughter Teresa, who wrote and sang the song, *Your Brother is Dead,* in protest of the war in Vietnam. We stayed in teepees, made "God's eyes," tied dyed clothing, acted out bible stories and had fascinating discussions. I remember being paired with a Presbyterian Minister and although I was just a kid he treated me like an equal. He confided in me that he thought the word "God" had lost its true meaning from being so overused and abused. He said he thought we should think up a new word. I reflected on our conversation for years, and one day, the word "Infinite" came to me. So now I refer to God as Divine Infinite God Source or simply: The Infinite. I think it would be very hard to make finite the "word" Infinite.

CHAPTER 3

WHAT IS THE INFINITE?

The Infinite is just that—Infinite. It is all that is, ever has been, and ever shall be. There is no beginning. There is no ending. No Alpha, no Omega! It is everything and nothing. It exists beyond time and space, which is often difficult for our finite brains to imagine. Nonetheless, it is what it is, even if you cannot comprehend it. Imagine if you will a Void. In this Void, there is no light, no sound, no thought, no form, just vast infiniteness. This is the Infinite in its pure divine state of *Prima Materia*. This Infinite all-encompassing energy makes up everything within us and around us. IT is known by many names: Chi, Ki, Prana, Divine Principal, Holy Spirit, the Force or Source. It is not chaotic, erratic energy as we have been taught to believe. The Infinite is love, beauty, unity, harmony, and intelligence. It is a unified field of harmonized energy made from pure love, eternal sound and light. It is the very building block of all creation. IT is ALL ONE. It is LOVE: the unifying, purifying force of the multiverse, the cosmic glue that binds everything together. IT is the unspoken word within the breath of God. This unspoken word is the intrinsic, intuitive, instinctual means of communication within our soul. It is in the way the Trees, the Animals, the Stars, the Wind, the Sea, and our Mother Earth herself, commune. This inner voice of wisdom tells the birds to fly south in Winter, the seedlings to sprout in spring, the planets to rotate around the Sun, the Stars to be born and to die. This is the way a mother communicates with her unborn child, and animals communicate with one another. This is the pure, untainted, true language of the soul. It is the unspoken divine language of truth that cannot be confounded, misinterpreted, twisted, or manipulated into bald-faced lies. It is the truth known only by our soul through its connection with Infinite God Source.

This living organic Infinite God Consciousness is inherent within all things. It is encoded into every molecule, present within every atom, found within every element in the world of matter. This is the native language inherent within our cells; it is what makes up our consciousness that communicates with all consciousness. It is the multidimensional language of light, frequency, sound, and symbols. This energy directs thoughts through telepathic transmissions of creation codes, into encryptions of cosmic downloads that are translated into thoughts and words that co-creates our reality. The true fall of the Tower of Babel was not when our spoken words were confounded into different languages but when the original unspoken word which was God, was separated from God Frequency. This is where the first distortion occurred. This was when the "Language of the Stars" was confounded with the lower frequencies and polluted into our spoken words.

The soul/sole purpose of the Infinite is to know itself! This is why the Infinite fired its first flash sequence, creating the holy trinity of Partiki, Partika and Particum, setting into perpetual motion all of creation. This first emanation sparked by the Infinite was fueled by the desire to "Know Thyself." This was the first "Word of God" spoken from pure love. It was the first utterance of Sound of the eternal "I AM" that set into motion our Story of Creation. It laid the foundation for the Divine Holographic Architecture inherent in the creation codes of our Infinite organic holographic Universes. As this divine technology expanded it created the multiverses, universes, galaxies, star systems, solar systems, planets, and even you! The organic holographic multiverse is based upon "open" Infinite Divine Architecture with sequences that emerge from the center-point of creation and return to it, perpetually retaining an open living, "breathing" (expanding and contracting) connection to Infinite Source. Infinite open architecture always preserves that which came before it. Organic Creation always maintains its connection to Source while expanding through the multiplication of the Infinite. Nothing is ever lost. It is an open system that draws energy or feeds directly from INFINITE GOD SOURCE during its eternal dance of expression, expansion and contraction. This is the true nature of the Divine God Consciousness Technology of our Organic Infinite Holographic Universe.

What does it mean that our Universe is a Divine Organic Hologram? This means that every tiny particle which makes up the Universe is also a hologram, or in simple terms, every part contains the whole. The same pieces of the divine organic hologram continue to project the whole of creation created under God's Natural Laws no matter how many times you fragment them. This means each tiny piece of the whole is in and of itself a reflection or mirror of the Infinite. This is the true meaning behind the concept of humans being created in the image of God, (Infinite God Source). It means you are Infinite and have Divine Infinite God Source within every cell of your being. So YOU ARE INFINITE! If you voyage out into the Universe and then back into your body, the journey is very similar. The neural network of your brain cells and synapses firing look very much like the distribution of dark matter throughout the universe. The birth of a cell looks like the birth of a star. The human eye looks very similar to a nebula. The human body is made up of hydrogen, oxygen, carbon, and other elements that are also found in the composition of planets and stars! We are literally made up of earth and stardust!

THEREFORE, YOU ARE INFINITE!

You are a fragment of the Divine Infinite made manifest to express and learn about itself. You are ITS means of self-expression and self-exploration. You are the embodiment of ITS consciousness. You are a unit of conscious awareness. You are a unique expression of the Infinite. You are a very precious, valuable, and unique contribution to the IS-ness of pure creation. Your uniqueness is your ability to freely express the Infinite through your original individual perspective on life, your story. You are a one-of-a-kind story in the Mind of God, the Divine Infinite Storyteller. Your unique perspective is the theme you have chosen for your life story. Within this theme are pages that you have complete and total freedom to write on as you choose fit. You have the freedom to express yourself, write your own life story in your own unique style. This is because Infinite Source gave to you the greatest gift of all, the gift of free will. You have the freedom to write yourself closer to the true word frequency which IS God, or you can explore what it is like to live in a finite world of false light, void of the true eternal living love and true light of Infinite God Source. You can identify with the Divine Infinite Storyteller, or you can get lost in the plot. You can turn away from Divine Infinite Source and experience the illusion of separation, losing yourself in the lower frequencies, experiencing lack, loss, abandonment, and fear. You can play the villain or victim. But this is only an illusion. Sooner or later, you will return to Infinite Source. Once you remember the truth of who you truly are, the illusion dissolves away. You only experience pain, dis-ease, and separation because you have forgotten that you are— Infinite!

Within your life story, you may create challenging experiences to serve as catalysts to teach yourself lessons and expand your knowledge of self. Or you may create distortions from the Infinite out of boredom to amuse yourself! The Rescuer Persecutor-Victim script may be the story you are perpetually writing and rewriting. Drama, trauma and conflict may be your life theme. Why? Because it's familiar. Your brain is goal-seeking/ problem solving. If it doesn't have a goal it will create a problem. When you are addicted to your problems you continue to repeat these same karmic patterns life time after lifetime until you decide to get off the wheel, change the pattern, heal yourself and write a new story! Many of you have died and been reborn into the same cast of characters, the same set of souls, life time after life time, repeating the same old stories and will continue to go around this endless wheel of karma until you decide to "get off the merry-go-round" by changing your story! Because there is no death only change in form, the only thing that can ever really die is your limited concept of yourself, your ego or your finite identity.

As your consciousness expands, so does the Eternal Consciousness of the Infinite. Through you and your life experiences, the Infinite learns, grows, and expands. So, the Infinite is more interested in you than itself because you are ITS instrument of self-exploration. The Infinite wants you to live! IT wants you to grow, expand, create, enjoy, and have fun in the knowing of yourself; for, it is in the knowing of yourself, IT knows itself. Through you learning about yourself, IT learns about itself, through you playing, IT plays! IT does not want you to suffer unless there is something to be learned from your suffering. Likewise, IT does not want you to remain in a cave hidden in deep meditation. This may be a necessary step to remove yourself from the distractions of the external world for a time, but IT also wants you to know IT through you expressing your uniqueness in the World. The Infinite created each and every one of us unique, like snowflakes! You possess an individual thumbprint that no one else in the world has. The Infinite does not want you to be like others, to herd with the masses. IT wants you to own your authenticity and uniqueness and to share it with others! The Infinite wants you to align yourself with IT so you can better know the Infinite Multidimensional Being you truly are!

As you surrender your ego, and stop identifying with the finite masks you have been wearing, the characters you have been playing, a magnificence thing will happen. Divine Infinite Source will consume you. All that is not the true you will burn away in the flames of divine truth. You will stop having to manipulate, struggle to succeed or to survive! When you can die and be reborn to your true authentic Infinite Self, you will identify with the Divine Infinite Story Teller "playing" itself out through you. You will be the Infinite grounded in human form. You will become God made manifest or an Infinite Human Being! When you can continuously be in this state of Oneness with Divine Infinite Source, all that is, ever has been, and ever shall be residing in the higher frequencies of love, truth and eternal light, your life will flow with ease. Manifestation will become second nature to you and you will be the sole/soul master of your mind, body and spirit.

You are a Universe or a YOU-IN-VERSE, an "Epic tale sung in Verse". So does your second verse sound like the first, or are you writing a "new" verse? Are you breaking the mold? Are stepping out of the herd? Are you stepping into your authentic self, speaking and living your truth, doing things differently? After all the definition of insanity is, "doing the same thing over and over and expecting different results." So how do you know if you are changing your life story to be more aligned with the vibrational frequency of the Word which IS God or Infinite God Source? You can monitor your connectedness with the Infinite by the way you feel. Being attuned or aligned with the Infinite feels good, peaceful, blissful! It occurs when you do some thing you love, when you are filled with passion, when you are in the "zone" or one with nature. When you are in the flow of Infinite God Source you are being fed from Source and your vibrational frequency increases. You fall "in love" with life! Gratitude puts you in the flow of all creation and raises your frequency. The more your frequency rises, the more you ascend in vibration. The more you ascend, the more attuned to the vibrational frequency of Infinite God Source you become. Like a tuning fork, attuning itself to a higher frequency the more you can inwardly hold these higher frequencies, the more Infinite Source will flow through you. Your thoughts will manifest easily. Your life purpose will unfold and people will show up in your life to support your soul mission. You will be funded and Infinite Source will have your back! Love will be your currency and gratitude your mindset.

Direct flow to and from the Infinite is the natural organic order of all things in the Multi-Universe. This is a process of giving and receiving that can be symbolized by our breath. The Infinite exhales the BREATH OF LIFE creating life, then inhales it back into itself taking in life. A beautiful eternal dance of ease where there is no death, no decay, no pain, no suffering, only change of form. Likewise, human beings breath in life giving oxygen from the organic life around us. As we exhale we give back our breath of life which sustains all organic life as we exhale our carbon dioxide. This is part of the miracle and magic of God's brilliant divine God Consciousness Technology that provides for all of creation within the ecological balance of God's natural organic laws. Under God's Natural Laws, it is always a win-win situation in which the Infinite always provides. This is the natural order of Mother Nature, Mother Earth, and all Creation. WE ARE ONE. This is Cosmic Sovereign Law made manifest. Everything is divinely interconnected through the organic frequencies of Divine Technology which is love. A miraculous system that takes into account the needs of the tiniest microbe or the most expansive universe. Everything works in complete and total harmony, making it whole or Holy.

When you fully realize God is omnipresent or in all things you truly realize that Infinite God Source is in everything and everyone around you. When you KNOW this, how could you ever harm another living creature? How could you hurt anything or anyone ever again? How could you not love your neighbor? How could you not love the world for what it truly is, a reflection of the Infinite! As you identify more and more with the Divine Infinite Storyteller and reside in the Word Frequency which IS God, you will see that everyone is just living out their stories to the extent in which they are awakened to the Truth of being One with Infinite God Source. Through your connection with Infinite Source all things are possible! You are an extension of all that is, ever has been, and ever shall be. You are the Divine Infinite made manifest! This direct, free flow of energy feeds and nourishes you and gives forth freely of itself. This free-flowing energy heals, empowers, enlightens and nourishes your soul. Those who feed directly from Infinite Source never lack, never fear, and are never alone. They are of service to others, because Infinite Source serves them. You receive from the Infinite and share this divine energy with others in your unique one of a kind way. This is the natural flow of things. These simple principles of the Divine Flow of the Loving Energy from the Infinite is what makes up the Law of One. The Law of One respects all life in every form, everywhere. Therefore, when you are working within the Law of One, you are naturally creating what is for the highest good of ALL concerned. The Law of One also respects the greatest gift ever bestowed on us by the Creator—Free Will. Every being in the Universe has the God-Given right to choose their own path, make their own decisions, grow, and evolve in the direction of their own choosing. All of creation has been given the gift of free will! This includes those who choose to believe in the illusion that they are separate from the Infinite and walk the Finite, or dark path. Their choice too must be honored. This too is the Infinite's way of knowing itself. This, too, is part of the Infinite.

Divine Infinite Source is like the apex of a triangle or the pentacle of a pendulum. At the top, there is no distortion, no duality. All is One. It is the still point within the Great Void. When the pendulum is set into motion, the first distortion, the first swing occurs, and polarity begins. The further the distortion from the apex of the pendulum the stronger the swing and the greater the polarities. This vast sweeping motion back and forth creates the World of Duality. Good, bad, right, wrong, light, dark. These extreme distortions or polarities can only exist at the bottom of the pendulum within the lower frequencies.

WHAT IS THE FINITE OR THE DARK SIDE?

The Natural Order of our Infinite Conscious Multiverse is based on love, harmony, beauty, and intelligence created from the building blocks of the Open Divine Architecture of the Eternal Living Love / Light Frequencies which always lead us back home to Infinite Source. Within this foundation, all of creation lives in harmony, respecting and honoring every life form and its right to free will and free expression. The Dark Side is the complete opposite. In my definition of the "Dark Side," I am not referring to an absence of light. The Void for example has no light but is an infinite expansion of pure love. The Dark "Finite" Side is like a piece of fruit plucked from the vine or the "Divine". Because its disconnection to the Divine Vine of Life has been severed it begins to rot and decay. This collection of finite "dark" entities, who reside in the lower frequencies of the astral plane have chosen to sever themselves from the "Di-vine". As a result, they are the undead, decaying and rotting. Because they have chosen to live in the illusion that they are separate from Divine Infinite God Source they can no longer feed directly from Divine Source so in order to sustain their existence they must parasitically feed off of others. They must steal the energy, rob the life force, the light, even the souls of others. Because of their parasitic needs, they must enslave, control, manipulate, deceive, glamour, cheat, intimidate, and SCAM other souls into becoming their energy sources, their slaves, their followers, their conduits, their subjects, their A.I. robots, their food. They have no respect for God's Natural Law, Cosmic Sovereign Law, the Law of One, or the Free Will of other beings. Because of this choice, they must reside in the lower frequencies trapped in reverse polarities where like bottom feeders, they lure their prey into a watery grave in the darkest phantoms of a Cosmic Sea.

Because they live in a world of distortion the only power these parasites have is its power to distort, pervert and deceive. But because their very existence depends on this they have become masters of distortion and deception, fathers of all lies. These Fallen Angelics have perfected their parasitic dark arts to become skillful manipulators. They are the true infection that infests our time matrix and our world today. They silently sneak into any healthy host, insidiously taking over the functions of a healthy organism by inverting, reversing, hijacking, and perverting all that is pure, whole or holy. They have degraded Infinite God Source's Divine organic technology into an artificial bad copy. They block the flow of the Infinite and channel it into finite prison matrixes. They have downgraded Infinite Krystic Beings into their Anti-Krystic systems that disrupt the building blocks of their DNA and cut them off from their direct connection to Divine Infinite God Source. They have disconnected human beings from Di-vine Source and all natural organic open living systems that flow in unity, harmony, and ease with Divine Infinite Creation. Their artificial anti-life patterns weaken and decay all life creating dependency, and death. The Dark Side is the virus, the cancer, the plague, the infection, the intruder that infects all healthy organic living systems in our multiverse, on our Earth and inside you. These parasitic gestalts of non-human, anti-life entities' power lies in their ability to remain hidden in the shadows and to convince you they do not exist. They want you to believe that all the woes of the world are caused by you. They want us to believe we human beings are the virus and so they infect us with their virus and turn us against one another. They create illusions, to distract and divide us, making us fear, attack and blame one another. They create lies to make us feel we are guilty, unworthy miserable sinners whom God has abandoned, when it has always been these anti-life parasites who have cut us off from Divine Infinite Source, so they could feed upon us. But the truth is the dark side has also infected you. It has become part of you. Your shadow self serves as a portal or gateway that allows these dark forces to enter your energetic body and take hold of your mind and soul. Until you can heal your own shadow, you are unconsciously allowing the dark side to work through you.

Because these finite self-serving, parasitic imposters have cut themselves off from Infinite God Source the only true Creator, they lack the ability to create. True creativity springs forth from the divine creative sparkle within us all. This inner creative sparkle is our direct link to our divinity. They have no divinity, no divine creative sparkle since they have severed themselves from the Di-vine and envy human beings for their creativity. All they can do is make bad copies, knock offs, artificial replications of true creation. They have been passing off their cheap imitations throughout history creating a world filled with fake history, fake gods, fake food, fake medicine, fake people, fake news, fake science, fake laws, et cetera. They have been terraforming our earth into a fake A.I. bad copy of God's Green Earth. And now they are spinning their fake AI Meta Verse around us trying to pass it off as the bad copy of true Ascesnion.

Since they cannot create they seek to control the creativity of human beings. They do this because it is only in their artificial "man-made" A.I. world of illusion that they can "play" God, usurping God's Natural Laws and the free will of all those who reside in their fallen worlds. They have created agendas to trans-humanize our organic bodies and minds into A.I. life forms. They are scamming us into believing our Divine Conscious Technology is inferior to their artificial technology. But the only weapons they have are the spells they cast over you. Tricking you into using your creative free will to co-create their warped reality. What the dark side fears most is that you will awaken from their dream spell and remember the truth of how powerful you are. Remember that you are an Infinite Human Being and transmute your inner shadow self, reconnect to Divine Infinite God Source within you and take back your God Sovereign Freedom. This is the Truth and The Truth Shall Set You Free!

It doesn't take a keen intellect to come to the conclusion that our Planet Earth is a fallen planet. Greed, war, corruption, sexual perversion and violence infect her. The good news is that everything finds its way back to Infinite Source, eventually. We are now on an auto-correction cycle to restore us to our true organic divine template. This process is called ascension. We are now in a FAIL SAFE ascension cycle and our return to Divine Infinite God Source is assured. Our Mother Earth has chosen ascension ! And all her divine organic life forms are being called home to return to the God Source Home Worlds and embody our divine blueprint. As we ascend into the higher frequencies of eternal love and truth our planet earth will face many challenges. The dark side is using all its power to scam you out of your divine birth right of organic ascension and back into its artificial time loop of a false ascension matrix. It is doing its best to assimilate you into a "Borg"A. I. technological hive mind of enslavement and pull you into their fallen parallel time matrix. Sound like a Sci-Fi movie? Observe the world around you with awakened eyes! This is a time when the dark side is coming out of its shadows to do everything in its power to maintain its grip on earth and humanity. It is using blatant tyrannical force to usurp your God Sovereign Freedom and your birthright to Organic Ascension. It is trying to scam you into choosing the bad artificial copy of ascension and writing your life story into their finite A.I. Meta Verse instead of becoming your own infinite You-in-Verse! It is a time of great change as we are watching our old finite 3D Earth crumble before our very eyes. We are being asked to grow up fast. We can no longer be the "children" of God but must become the embodiment or incarnation of

Infinite God Source here on Earth. We must not wait for a Christ to come and save us but become the Kristos or the Infinite Human Beings Infinite God Source intended us to be! We must take back our bodies, our minds, our souls, our Earth, and the pen that is writing OUR life story and our Earth's Future. Otherwise, we will be lulled back into the dream spell of a finite artificial A.I. Meta Verse time loop prison void of all free will, free speech, free thought, and FREEDOM!

CHAPTER 4

MIND CONTROL

There was a massive influx of ascension energy that poured into our planet during the sixties that initiated an expansion of consciousness, and brought about experimentation and the sexual revolution. The Youth of America became painfully aware of the "Sins of their fathers." In Hebrew, the word SIN (chatá) and its Greek equivalent (hamartia) mean "missing the mark". So The Young Generation became painfully aware of their ancestor's true his-tory. America was founded by a corporation, The Virginia Company, who proceeded to clear the real estate by exterminating all the Indigenous people, then planted cash crops like Tobacco and imported slave labour to create large margins of profits for their corporate stock holders. These sins against our fellow African and Native Americans were recounted by Folk singers in their Ballads about the injustices of racism and war along with our growing loss of freedom in an attempt to take down the establishment. Unfortunately, the sixties were cleverly hijacked by the C.I.A. so instead of a massive spiritual awakening the movement was co-opted into "sex, drugs, and rock and roll." The C.I.A. distributed L.S.D. to the "Youth of America" while Timothy Leary encouraged young people to drop out and turn on with sex and drugs. Undercover trolls infiltrated sixties groups distributing drugs, creating disharmony, and assassinating potential leaders who threatened to set people free. John F. Kennedy, Robert F. Kennedy, Martin Luther King Jr. and Malcolm X were just a few of the leaders who were killed for their actions and beliefs.

When I was nine my father took part in an L.S.D. experiment conducted by the U.S. government in Baltimore, Maryland. I remember my father's face when we picked him up after the experiment. He said he would never do that again. A few years later, his friend who had invited him to do the experiment mysteriously died in a scuba diving "accident". L.S.D was used in MK Ultra Trauma based mind control experiments, also called the CIA mind control program. This is the code name given to a program of experiments conducted on human subjects that were designed and undertaken by the U.S. Central Intelligence Agency. These rituals and practices date back to Ancient Egypt and were perfected during World War II by Nazi Scientists. MK ULTRA Trauma based Monarch programming is a mind-control technique comprised of elements of Satanic Ritual Abuse (SRA) used to create a Multiple Personality Disorder (MPD). It utilizes a combination of psychology, neuroscience and occult rituals to create an alter persona within the subject or slave that can be triggered and programmed by the controllers or handlers.

MK ULTRA TRAUMA-BASED MIND CONTROL ORIGINS

Throughout the course of history, several accounts have been recorded describing rituals and practices resembling mind control. One of the earliest writings about the use of occultism to manipulate the mind can be found in *The Egyptian Book of the Dead*. It is a compilation of rituals heavily studied by today's secret societies, which describes methods of torture and intimidation (to create trauma), the use of potions (drugs) and the casting of spells (hypnotism), ultimately resulting in the total enslavement of the initiate. These ancient Egyptian texts of occult knowledge were preserved by the Catholic Church and put into practice during the Inquisition to raise suggestibility in their victims. The Jesuits passed this knowledge on to Hitler where mind control became a science where thousands of subjects were systematically observed, documented and experimented on. One of the first methodical studies on trauma-based mind control was conducted by Josef Mengele, a physician working in Nazi concentration camps. He is best known for performing grisly human experiments on camp inmates, including children, for which Mengele received the name the "Angel of Death". He is also referred to as "DR. GREEN and the father of Monarch Programming. Thousands of Monarch Mind-Controlled slaves in the U.S. had "Dr. Green" as their chief programmer."

HOW THE NAZIS WON THE WAR.

The truth is most humans only use about three percent of their brain on a good day! The rest of our brain activity is categorized by what modern psychology calls the "sub"conscious. The definition of the subconscious is, "the part of the mind which one is not fully aware of, but which influences one's actions and feelings." This makes up ninety percent of your mind. Wow! This means that if below your veil of consciousness, you have deep seated trauma, thoughts and beliefs unbeknownst to you, they can control you outside of your awareness. This means that ninety per cent of the thoughts you do not even know you have are controlling your actions, your beliefs, and your perception of reality! These thoughts take on a frequency which when amplified become boomerangs, continuously attracting to you information, experiences and people that validate this subconscious programming. This will continue to create energetic pathways that become "carved in stone." Why? Because we are physical, emotional, mental, and spiritual electro-magnetic beings. Our thoughts, charged by emotions fire synapses that feed the magnetic energetic sphere orbiting around us which is sent into the Universe as frequency which magnetically pulls back to us similarly charged electro-magnetic frequencies. This is why for example if underneath all your positive affirmations, buried deep within your subconscious mind are the underlying beliefs that you are inherently bad, evil, wicked, unworthy of love, abundance or even freedom then you will continuously recreate the same experiences, patterns, repeating the same life story over and over again.

The Black Sun Nazis knew that to conquer people they needed only to control their minds. Thus they created a prison free from any bars...a prison of the Mind. You may think that the CIA had nothing to do with influencing the course of modern-day psychiatry, psychology, psychotherapy, marketing, entertainment, et cetera unless you fully understand the CIA's Project-Paperclip. Dr. Mengel was backed by the CIA and brought to America during Operation Paperclip, a secret operation of the Joint Intelligent Objectives Agency (JIOA) largely carried out by special agents of the Army CIC, in which more than one thousand six hundred German scientists, engineers, and technicians were taken from Germany to the United States after the end of World War II for employment by the US government, primarily between 1945 and 1959. Many were former members and leaders of the Nazi Party. Many of these CIA Nazis had been members in good standing with the Nazi party, as well as the Gestapo. Many had tortured concentration camp victims and were guilty of numerous war crimes.

MK ULTRA, as well the projects ARTICHOKE, and OPERATION MIDNIGHT CLIMAX, which dosed unknowing American citizens with LSD, were code names for Nazi/CIA joint projects on mind control.

The Paperclip Nazis became leaders in the Masonic lodges and worked under the support of the Illuminati families. The Rockefeller Foundation has been a significant benefactor and protector of the Paperclip Nazis. Funded with billions of dollars, it has shaped society for more than a hundred years in America, and around the world. Education, medicine, and eugenics have been its main focal points. It is estimated that these trauma-based mind control experiments were performed in secret on over two million U.S. Military personal and unsuspecting Americans without their consent. The experiments included the exposure of humans to many chemical and biological weapons (including infections with deadly or debilitating diseases), radiation, toxic injections of radioactive chemicals, surgical experiments, interrogation and torture which involved mind-altering substances, and a wide variety of other experiments. Many of these tests were performed on children, the sick, and mentally disabled individuals, often under the guise of "medical treatment". In many of the studies, a large portion of the subjects were mentally ill, poor, racial minorities, or prisoners. There is no accounting to how many people have been killed or injured by these "experiments" conducted without their consent or even their knowledge.

Project MK-ULTRA ran from the early 1950s to at least the late 1960s, using American and Canadian citizens as its test subjects. The published evidence indicates that Project MK-ULTRA involved the use of many methodologies to manipulate individual's mental states and alter brain functions, including the surreptitious administration of drugs and other chemicals, sensory deprivation, isolation, along with verbal and physical abuse. The most publicized experiments conducted by MK-ULTRA involved the administration of LSD to unknowing human subjects, including CIA employees, military personnel, doctors, government agents, prostitutes, mentally ill patients, and members of the general public, in order to study their reactions. However, the scope of MK-ULTRA does not stop. Experiments involving violent electroshocks, physical and mental torture and abuse were used in a systematic matter on many subjects, including children. These were all done under the guise of national security to develop torture and interrogation methods to be used on the enemies of America.

TECHNIQUES OF MK ULTRA TRAUMA-BASED MIND CONTROL:

Hypnosis, fear, isolation, deceit, torture, implantation of false thoughts, repetition of ritualistic activities, inversion of pain and pleasure, neuro-linguistic programming, erasing memories, using L.S.D or other drugs, and the splitting of the brain/ ego-personality are all used in trauma based mind control. Other techniques such as the use of fear, guilt, shame, ridicule, dehumanization and submission to external authorities such as the government, or "God" are also used. Practices such as blackmail, bribes, peer pressure, punishments, fines and the use of fear, as a control mechanism are key aspects of MK ULTRATRAUMA-BASED MIND CONTROL and should begin to sound very familiar since our entire planet has been undergoing this type of Mind Control for eons and the 2020 Lock Down brought these methods to a global level for all the world to see.

ORIGINS OF THE NAME MONARCH MIND CONTROL

The spiritual meaning of the symbol of a butterfly is one of transmutation, ascension and liberation. However, satanic controllers of the dark side always hijack highly powerful spiritual symbols and invert them to enslave you. Many believe the name Monarch Mind Control comes from the Monarch butterfly. This insect begins its life as a worm (representing undeveloped potential) and, after a period of cocooning (programming) is reborn as a beautiful butterfly (the Monarch Slave). The Monarch Butterfly genetically passes its knowledge and memories on to its offspring allowing them to be easily programmed. The definition of Monarch is, "One who reigns over a state, territory, or an empire usually for life." "Monarch" Mind Control techniques are derived from ancient Satanic Ritual Abuse practices used throughout the ages to keep those in power bound as faithful servants to the "satanic forces" to do their bidding here on Earth.

Throughout history, Satanic Ritual Abuse begins at birth in order to ensure total obedience. Traditional conditioning requires that for the first two years of the infant's life, the child is isolated and given love, by only one "controller" parent. This parent becomes a "god" to the child granting the child's every whim and overindulging them. They shower the child with love and affection. Then around the age of two, the controller parent turns on the child for no reason. The parent tortures, humiliates, and may even rape the child, performing repeated acts of sodomy. Sodomy before the age of three stimulates nerve endings at the base of the spine activating the kundalini which gives the child flashes of illuminations and stimulates the third eye. These glimpses of illumination are easily turned into addiction. Anal sex with young people also allows the perpetrator to draw the life force from that youth and feed on their energy. This is why in many of the cults of Ancient Greece, Rome and Renaissance Florence, homosexuality was practiced as a means of reaching greater spiritual heights but became degraded into orgies of self-indulgence and blood sacrifice rituals.

When individuals have deep seated underlying trauma tucked away in their subconscious, insulated by feelings of fear, guilt, shame and unworthiness that incur from early childhood trauma they open an energetic portal for negative energies to enter. During satanic rituals, demonic entities are conjured up and bound to each personality created by Monarch Mind Control. The more powerful the individual the more powerful the demonic entity who possesses them. Sounds too far-fetched to be true? History teaches us otherwise. Isn't it true that in most ancient cultures, it was considered the highest honor to be "possessed" by the "gods." Wasn't the ruling class of Pharaohs, High Priests, Priestesses, Kings and Queens considered to be living representatives of "god" or the "gods" here on Earth? This explains the bloody history of our planet filled with endless wars and blood sacrifices incited by the ruling class. This layering of demonic entities or shadow creatures into the various personalities creates hollowed out human bodies with an insatiable thirst for blood to extend their life and continuously feed the demonic shadow creatures that possess them. As they age they become the walking dead often with pale "vampire" like skin and bruised or blackened eyes, serving only as a host for satanic entities. This explains the rumors of pedophilia, the use of the drug Adrenochrome and child trafficking, which always surround the Global "Elites", Royals, and the Catholic Church.

Research has shown that extreme trauma before the age of seven will cause the mind to split. This process is repeated to create numerous personalities or alter egos thus creating a person with multiple personalities. Each personality or alter is created and programmed to serve a specific purpose and each personality does not know that the other exists. This is used to create assassins, as depicted in the film, *The Manchurian Candidate* where the character of Raymond Shaw, was trained to assassinate people yet had no memory of having done so. He was unaware of his internal programming until the "assassin alter" or personality was activated by a "trigger." This trigger can be a word, a sound, a phase in a book, or an image. In this movie, his trigger was the Queen of Diamonds, which was connected with the abusive relationship he had with his mother, who also happened to be his handler. A handler is an individual who is fully aware of the slave's programming and all his triggers and uses them to maintain the slave under his or her command.

The book, *Catcher in the Rye*, is also famous for being used as triggers for assassins. On December 8th of 1980, John Lennon was shot dead by Mark David Chapman. Outside of Lennon's Manhattan home, when police officers arrived at the scene of the crime they found Chapman seated in his car casually flipping through his copy of *Catcher in the Rye*. Some other alters are the "sex kitten" programming used often in the entertainment and sex trafficking industries or the "Spy" alter. The Spy may possess heightened extra sensory perception and physical abilities. They are often used as intuitive empaths or "remote viewers". Some survivors of MK ULTRA who have managed to escape their captors and "deprogram" themselves have gone on record to disclose the horrifying details of their ordeals and the circle of powerful world leaders who used and abused them. One such person is Cathy O'Brien who has written many books about this topic.

LEVELS OF PROGRAMMING:

ALPHA is within the base control personality. It is characterized by extremely pronounced memory retention, along with substantially increased physical strength and visual acuity. Alpha programming is accomplished through deliberately subdividing the victim's personality, which, in essence, causes a left brain right brain division, allowing for a programmed union of the Left and Right Brain through neuron pathway stimulation. This is often used for Spies.

BETA is referred to as "sexual" programming (slaves). This programming eliminates all learned moral convictions and stimulates the primitive instinct, devoid of inhibitions. "Cat" alters may come out at this level, known as Kitten programming, it is the most visible kind of programming as some female celebrities, models, actresses, and singers have been subjected to this kind of programming. In popular culture, clothing with feline prints often denotes "Kitten" programming.

DELTA is known as "killer" programming and was originally developed for training assassins, special agents or elite soldiers (i.e. Delta Force, First Earth Battalion, Mossad, etc.) in covert operations. Optimal adrenal output and controlled aggression are evident. Subjects are devoid of fear and very systematic in carrying out their assignment. Self-destruct or suicide instructions are layered in at this level.

THETA – Considered to be the "psychic" programming for *Bloodliners* (those coming from multi-generational "elite" Satanic families) who were determined to exhibit a greater propensity for having telepathic abilities than did *non-bloodliners*. Many forms of electronic mind control systems were developed and introduced, namely, bio-medical human telemetry, which comes from the greek word meaning "remote". This is the phenomena of transmitting radio signals to devices (brain implants), or "directed-energy lasers using microwaves (5G) and/or electromagnetic waves." It is reported these are used in conjunction with highly-advanced computers and sophisticated satellite tracking systems. MK ULTRA trauma-based mind control integrated these technological practices into modern psychology, to spread this mind control to the masses.

So how have they been able to do this on a mass scale?

VIRTUAL TORTURE CHAMBERS/ CLOCKWORK ORANGE

The human brain cannot tell the difference between what is real or imagined. With the advent of technology and mass communication, these Nazi scientists were able to perfect their mind control techniques away from live trauma-based experiences into simulated ones, which proved just as effective. With the use of drugs, imagery, sound, light, hypnotic suggestions, and low frequencies these scientists perfected the Art of Mind Control and began to "BROAD(LY)-CAST" their spells via mind control devices called "tel-a-LIE-visions" or televisions. These techniques quickly found their way into the entertainment, music, and advertising industries. In a few short years, all of the world had several of these mind control devices (tel-a-lie-visions) in their homes and had fallen under the spell of technological mind control.

These visual and audio aids are used to program special triggers into the victim's mind. The trigger symbols have two functions. First, they reinforce the mind-control programming so that the victim does not resist it during their everyday life. Secondly, triggers can be used to call forth an alter persona or to reinstate the primary core personality. In this way, the master controller can switch on or off, the alternate personality of their choice. This works the same way as a hypnotist who snaps his fingers or claps his hands to bring a person back out of a trance. Some examples of triggers commonly used for visual reinforcement may be occult symbols such as dolls, spider webs, snakes, goats, mirrors, masks, skulls, mazes, monarch butterflies, angels, devils, demons, pyramids, (false) infinity loops, syringes, glass shattering, mazes, hour glasses, clocks, robots, ancient symbols and letters, et cetera. The same secret societies that created MK ULTRA Monarch mind control also control mass media and the entertainment industry. These reinforcing visual trigger symbols are placed, in plain sight, in media, movies and music. These symbols are commonly inserted into mass media, popular culture movies and videos for two reasons: to reinforce and desensitize the majority of the population to the subliminal and neuro-linguistic programming and to deliberately construct specific triggers and keys for base programming to highly impressionable children. If you have difficulty believing this is true, take a closer look at most major events like the super bowl or many of the movies being created for children now a days and see how many of these ever present symbols you can find.

Once a split in the core personality occurs, an "internal world" can be created and alter personas can be programmed using tools such as music, movies (especially Disney productions) and fairy tales. These visual and audio aids enhance the programming process using images, symbols, meanings, and concepts. Many popular films are used in MK ULTRA Trauma-based Mind control as programming devices for children such as *The Wizard of Oz, Alice in Wonderland, Pinocchio* and *Sleeping Beauty*. For example, a slave watching *The Wizard of Oz* is taught that "somewhere over the rainbow" is the "happy place" to go to in their mind to dissociate from the unbearable pain being inflicted upon them. Using this movie, programmers encourage slaves to go "over the rainbow" and dissociate, effectively separating their minds from their bodies. In the movie, *Eyes Wide Shut,* Kubrick hinted at how this phrase was used by sex kitten slaves when women repeatedly asked Tom Cruise if he would like to go "over the rainbow." Like all occult symbols the Dark Side draws on powerful hidden symbols from our collective unconscious, memories that build on our collective trauma to control us. The image of "over the rainbow" is a strong collective racial memory of our original home world on Tara and the over-the-rainbow bridge to Andromeda where the first human holocaust occurred. Another classic film used in Monarch mind-control is Pinocchio. Consider Pinocchio, the wooden boy puppet, who wants to become a real boy. This wooden boy puppet is prone to telling lies, just as an alter persona is programmed to tell lies. The wooden boy puppet is a symbol for the alter persona, who, at the end of the movie, is turned into a real boy. Thus, the film represents the shift between the wooden boy who feels nothing (alter persona) into the real human boy with human feelings (primary personality). So you can see how by splintering the mind and the soul into separate identities, compartmentalizing our consciousness into finite realities though the use of trauma we human beings have been "mind controlled"! The fact that most humans can not remember what happened to them pre-birth and are unable to recall their multiple "past" lives or alternate identities testifies to the truth that humanity is still being mind controlled. It is not until you heal your past life traumas and begin to remember and recover these alternate identities by integrating them into your present life that you free yourself from mind control.

There are many triggers and symbols hidden in plain sight like the ruby slippers or the "Red Dress" you so often see in films. When I took my film students to the Cannes Film Festival, I was wearing a red dress and caught the eye of Malcolm McDowell. When I approached him, he smiled and said, "Ah the woman in the Red Dress." Coincidently, (there are no coincidences), he was the actor in the film, *Clock Work Orange*, where Kubrick revealed how MK ULTRA trauma-based mind control works. The film the *Labyrinth,* starring the famous pop star David Bowie, who was a known Satanist and a fan of Aleister Crowley, depicts a trip through the maze of MK ULTRA mind control. Bowie steals an infant child (symbolizing the core personality) and uses his musical witches voice to embroil the child's older sister (her alter self) deeper and deeper into the labyrinth in search of her true identity.

One thing that Monarch mind-control programmers have learned is that they can build their virtual tortures on the painful experiences that the victims have previously undergone. The human race still contains hidden memories of the holocaust events that led to our fall from our mother Universe in Andromeda, and our entrapment into the lower frequencies of our fallen universe. We carry the memories of the sinking of Atlantis and Lemuria, the shifting of the poles, the rising of the seas, and the destruction of Earth that followed. These Armageddon memories have been weaponized and used against us to recall that trauma. It is no coincidence that Hollywood excels in disaster movies. Once you are captured in a state of fear and trauma, you are easily programmed. It is the first step of mind-control. Not only do we, as a collective, share deep-seated memories of our own holocaust, but we all store our own personal traumas initiating as early as inside the womb and from birth traumas that continue through our lives.

After the U.S. Military had learned everything about the human brain and perfected their Art of Mind Control, they began experiments combining technology and biology to develop weaponized bio-technology that could totally control the body and mind of a human being without them even knowing it. DARPA originally known as the Advanced Research Projects Agency (ARPA), was created on February 7, 1958 by President Dwight D. Eisenhower "supposedly" in response to the Soviet launching of Sputnik 1 in 1957. Later the word defense was added to form the name DARPA Defense Advanced Research Projects Agency which "executes research and development projects to expand the frontiers of technology and science, often beyond immediate U.S. military requirements"

WHAT DOES THAT MEAN?

In 1989–90 DARPA was instrumental in creating the World Wide Web or what we now call the Internet. They also created Cell Phones, GPS and Siri. Through the Nazi's experimentation on human subjects they were able to map the human mind and determine where and how thoughts and emotions originated and were transmitted electromagnetically inside the human brain. Then they learned how to create these thoughts and emotions artificially so they could control a person's thoughts, feelings and even their own bodily functions and motor skills. DARPA has secretly been a "brain initiative evolving Biological Technology or "Bio-technology" under the guise of helping injured war veterans recover from post-traumatic syndrome. They have conducted extensive experiments learning how to fuse man and machine together integrating organic human tissue, specifically brain tissue, with inorganic or Artificial Intelligence (AI) technology. According to Dr Justin Sanchez, the Director of Biological Technologies at DARPA: "Our mission at DARPA is to change the world and change the future." In one of his videos he describes a future world filled with "neurally" enhanced "haves and have nots".

For decades, scientists have wondered whether electromagnetic waves might play a role in intra- and inter-cell signaling. In 1953, Russians began to bombard the U.S. embassy with electromagnetic radiation in the microwave spectrum (5G) which was kept secret from the employees who developed blood disease, bleeding eyes, nausea and eventually died from the micro wave radiation. In the 1960's a top-secret DARPA project, called Pandora, was created to investigate the effects of low levels of microwave radiation (5G). Experiments bombarding humans with highly concentrated doses of micro waves occurred all over the US at many prestigious universities and hospitals. They were exploring the Radio-Bio effects electromagnetic signals have on biological systems. Years later President Clinton offered an apology on national television for the governments' behavior.

In 1965 project Pandora studied the way micro radiation could control human beings. After learning that the human brain and cells can indeed be impacted and controlled by microwave radiation they went on to study how they could modify the human brain by modifying the human body via the DNA. Gene editing tools using a Crisper or cross section of DNA were injected into the human blood stream which fused with the organic human DNA. They learned that, "by changing the DNA, they could change the brain cells, **"turning you into something different than what you were."** Dr. Jose Del Gatto, who created a brain transponder used to robotize humans, stated, **"the greatest danger of the future is not atomic energy but that we will have robotized human beings who are not aware they have been robotized."**

If you haven't figured it out yet mRNA Crisper "gene therapy" is what is contained in ALL the Covid 19 vaccinations.

At the Center for Strategic Communication at Arizona State University, DARPA experimented with "Transcranial Magnetic Stimulation" (TMS) to remotely combat "dissent and extremism". TMS stimulates the temporal lobe of the brain with electromagnetic fields in order to "turn off" reactive centers in the brain. They also used this technology to train several elite Green Beret groups for mind control or, as the military termed it, "affecting one-mind cooperation in the field" under the guise of developing defense weaponry and helping combat depression and anxiety, DARPA or the US Military experimented on their own soldiers to learn how to completely control the human brain creating altered states of mind, perceptions of reality, and "turn off" any feelings of anxiety, resistance, rebellion or dissidence. They then experimented with these electromagnetic "signals" in research labs in Northern California, learning how to "Use alpha brainwaves inserted into *entrainment*, (the process of making something have the same pattern or rhythm ie algorithms), programs for "consciousness exploration" (Basically they learned how to control the algorithms of the brain through the media.) They perfected this technology and inserted it into mainstream media and entertainment programs. These silent mind-control techniques are presently being used on the public without their consent or awareness.

HERE ARE SOME CHARACTERISTICS OF MIND-CONTROLLED PEOPLE:

Mind Slides: When a person completely ignores an unapproved tag word lumped into an unapproved category like "Aliens, Alien Abduction, Negative Aliens, Reptilians, Satanic Ritual Abuse, Child Trafficking, Conspiracy Theory, UFOs, Implants, Secret Space Programs, MILABS, or any information about Radiation poisoning, Vaccinations, Green Pass restrictions, Covid 19, 5G et cetera that may conflict with the accepted narratives. On an aside note, when I returned to the USA and found a huge military installation of 5G beside the elementary school in my hometown of Anchorage, Kentucky, I pointed it out to many people walking on the "nature" path below it. Most people could not even SEE it. When continued to point to it many said they had never noticed it before!

TAG words, such as "conspiracy theorist", which was carefully crafted by the CIA and fed to the news media to pacify the American public when they began questioning the assassination of JFK, are created by controllers to "handle" the population and to create a programmed response which may take the form of denial, aggressive reactions, or labeling the information as ridiculous. Mud slide victims may exhibit hostile feelings, and even verbally or physically attack the messenger, call the police, become drowsy and fall asleep or have a compulsion to leave the room and get away from the messenger of the information. They may feel excessively agitated, have the compulsion to smoke cigarettes, self-medicate or simply refuse to listen.

CONSCIOUSNESS SWEEPS

When certain demographic areas are ascending in frequency, they are targeted by consciousness sweeps. Actions to lower the frequencies are then taken in that particular country, region or town, such as chem-trailing: criss-crossing the skies with planes releasing clouds of toxic metals, nanobots and other materials that blanket the skies shutting out the Sun's rays and putting people in a drowsy stupefied state. Or releasing televised broadcasts inciting subconscious fear programming, raising polarizing topics, inciting racism, political division, mandating lockdowns, mask-wearing, bringing out a new variant by turning up the 5G radiation so everyone gets "C.O.V.I.D." powdering the area with chem-trails of smart dust, creating destructive weather patterns, beam-steering extremely low frequencies 5G, ELF, GWEN, Bio Radio Waves, and AI signal transmissions directed into the people, planetary body, or even targeting individuals through their devices, such as cell phones and computers. This destroys the health and affects the subconscious mind often with depression and thoughts of suicide, as well as down grading their brain waves, creating brain fog and cognitive dissonance. This lowers people's frequencies and stunts their awakening.

DARPA discovered that to impact and manipulate human consciousness, all that is required is to create a complex signal through a frequency. **The brain then locks onto the external signal coming from the environment or their "cell phone" and begins to mirror that signal within the brain.** As a result, the brain chemistry alters, this begins the transhumanization process. Many young people who spend long hours plugged into their cell phones experience changes in their consciousness plummeting them into a range of lower negative emotions and confused perceptions. This explains why one day you may be feeling on top of the world only to plummet into darkness the next day. Large populations can be sent frequencies of massive radiation or frequencies that incite fear, agitation, aggression, anxiety, rioting, suicidal thoughts or cause specific health issues. Then they put out news feeds that there is a rise in Covid cases or a bug going around. It is even possible to modulate signals on any electromagnetic carrier to alter brain chemistry, implant thought forms, suicidal thoughts, burst organs, burn lung tissue, cause heart attacks, or attack RNA, DNA, and mitochondria which are vital to our health and survival. Inorganic machinery or AI (Artificial Intelligence) technology is used to infiltrate and harm the human organic biological system. These AI programs infiltrate the biological neurological processes of the body like a VIRUS to infect and block the natural frequencies from running appropriately. Etheric weapons such as energetic knives, cleavers, needles, and other sharp objects can penetrate the light body, aura, physical body, genitals, nervous system, and brain. The use of EMF frequency disturbances can weaken the auric body and create pain, distress, illness, or energy leaks in the human aura and body.

HOLOGRAPHIC INSERTS

Many awakened individuals who could see clearly what was really happening on Earth during the 2020 Plandemic could not understand how others could not see or perceive what seemed so obvious to them. Implanted thoughts block people's perception of reality by jamming neurological receivers and hijacking the brain so that the masses cannot decode or perceive what is really going on. Whoever controls an individual's mind gains control over their identity, their consciousness, and their soul. Thus, whoever controls the collective mind of the masses through the premeditated use of covert technological mind-control tactics, controls the group's unconscious and conscious thoughts and their perceptions and beliefs about reality.

Before the age of seven, children are in a hypnotic theta brainwave state and when they do not receive the nurturing they need in order to develop healthy, happy, balanced brain connections, they compensate. They tuck these unmet needs and traumas away into their subconscious and forget about them. The effects of living with this unresolved trauma can be seen in Alfred Hitchcock's film *Spellbound,* where Gregory Peck developed amnesia due to a guilt complex from a repressed childhood trauma of accidentally killing his younger brother.

When you begin to understand just how divine and important the first few years of a child's life are, and consider all the innumerable experiences that could have impacted any child's ability to gain the nurturing it needed, then you can begin to understand the significance a healthy, attuned, nurturing, fresh start has on the child's development. A child's connection with their parents is divine, and they need to FEEL loved, wanted, bonded, nurtured, and secure enough to trust that their needs will be met by the people responsible for their care. As you realize this you begin to understand that any subconscious programming that does not meet these needs will be accepted without question by these young minds as being their fault. In their small minds they will automatically believe that they were bad and that is why their parents did not meet their needs. In a perfect world all little people's needs would have been met but in our imperfect fallen planet it is more the exception than the rule that anyone born here on Earth does not suffer some type of trauma or wound during early childhood that lies buried deep within their subconscious mind. So this creates a fertile ground for mind control. Probably one of the most devastating mind-control programs is the sexual misery program which has been created to keep men and women from coming together in a loving sacred union and providing a home for their children filled with love, respect and proper nurturing.

CHAPTER 5

LET ' S TALK ABOUT SEX, BABY

My "Spiritual Teacher" once said that the problem with the World is that nobody understands sex. Thirty years later, I am beginning to realize the profundity of his statement. To begin to comprehend our Multiverse one must know the true creation mechanics. It was not as we have been taught, some random Big Bang that blasted our universe into a chaotic pattern of existance. Rather, our Multiverse was created when Infinite Source simultaneously gave birth creating the true holy trinity of Partiki, Partika, and Particum. This divine trinity of Infinite Source birthing Matter and Anti matter created the Divine Mother and Divine Father who then gave birth to the sacred hierogamic union of Divine Masculine/ Divine Feminine or the Krystos/ Sophia within the Infinite Human. I suppose you could say it was sex! So what is the real meaning of SEX? Is it a sacred alchemical synthesis of two energies coming together to form one? Is it the integration, assimilation and procreation of two energetic holograms, exchanging energetic codes, to co-create a third manifestation of themselves as an intergrated whole or as another entity such as a divine child, planet, star system or universe? Is it the two becoming three that sparks the ONE?

This harmonious Tri-fold wave of existence is the way the Universe expands, contracts, learns and grows. When this natural organic balance is disrupted, expansion and growth are halted, and the energies become deadlocked in duality. This pulls us out of alignment with Divine Infinite Source and keeps us trapped in a Viscus Piscis harness of AI Metatronic reverse polarities. This finite Architecture alters our organic infinite geometric patterns leading us away from Infinite Source and into fallen Systems. Freedom occurs by clearing away these anti-life mechanisms and bringing harmony and balance back within ourselves and our Multiverse by resetting our alignment to the Infinite! This occurs through the alchemy of lovingly transmuting these distortions and mutations back to their true, original, authentic essence of Infinite Source. Restoring their infinite nature and freeing them from their finite prison. This occurs by loving them back to wholeness or "making love"! Sometimes tough love, but always love. This is the true essence of Alchemical Ascension.

As above so below. Just as galaxies make love giving birth to new star systems, making love is a natural part of creation. In human beings, it is a healthy, healing, regenerating practice when done with love and the right person or even with oneself! It balances and harmonizes the masculine and feminine energies inside of you, augmenting your ascension. This is why throughout history this powerful energy has been co-opted into a shameful, sinful, lustful, guilt laden practice often resulting in violent acts against oneself or others. Because sexual energy is a sacred loving energy that can heal, harmonize and enlighten people, most religions have made it taboo and require their leaders to be celibate. This creates sexual misery and often leads to self-loathing and unhealthy outlets. When you taint this powerful energy with guilt, shame, fear and remorse you create "loosh" that feeds the dark parasitic shadow creatures. It is no coincidence that the Catholic Church is plagued with a pandemic of pedophilia and sexually deviant behavior since the priests and nuns are taught that their own natural flow of sexual energy is unholy and must be repressed in order for them to do God's work in the World. This unholy attitude which separates sex from spirituality has found its way into society and unfortunately most marriages. My parents' marriage was no exception.

I once asked my Dad why he didn't stay in California like his colleague Sam Keen. He told me Sam was a flame thrower and he was a bridge builder and bridge build he did! He pioneered the first marriage and family therapy program at the Louisville Presbyterian Seminary, so young ministers could learn about themselves and have the skills to help their flock deal with life's challenges. He wrote many books and traveled around the world, giving inspirational talks and workshops. But despite all my father's great accomplishments, he carried a deep wound. The first movie he ever took me to see was *Gone with the Wind*. This movie haunted me my entire life. It wasn't until after my father's death that I finally broke the code. One day, my mother admitted to me, that she had never really loved my father. Wow! The key to my entire rocky childhood fell into place! Why had I been so blind? My father, like Rhett Butler, had been turned out of the bed by a woman who could not return his love. So he poured all of his love and affection into me, his only daughter.

Ironically, Peter had a very similar upbringing. He had been born during a terrible hurricane that hit Cuba in 1944. It was not an easy birth. He had been born by Caesarean, and his mother lost her womb as a result. Unable to bear more children, Peter and his mother, formed a very close bond. This also caused his mother to turn away from all sexual relations with his father. Unable to fill her longing to have more children, she became a midwife. One night, Peter's father came to him with tears in his eyes, asking if it was normal for a woman to lose all interest in sex. Peter secretly harbored a deep guilt about causing this pain to his father, which was his motivation for becoming a doctor of women. How very interesting that we both had such similar upbringings.

When I first met my spiritual teacher, she told me, "I'm surprised you're not deaf!" I asked my mother about this. Apparently, when I was just a baby, I could hear my parents at night, through the bedroom wall fighting over sex. As a child, I was so desperately hungry for my mother's love. She had always been able to love my brothers but not me. I always felt there was something inherently bad about me and that was why she didn't love me. As I grew up, I tried to be like my mother, hoping she would love me. But it didn't work. My mother became increasingly more critical of me. Meanwhile, my father loved and adored me. He used to call me his blond bomb shell. As I blossomed into womanhood my mother became threatened by my sexuality. A huge conflict raged within my body, mind and soul. I wanted so much to be sexually desirable to men, but I did not want to threaten my mother. Now, my sexuality threatened her and I felt ashamed, seeing it as something bad or evil.

As I reached adolescence my mother's jealousy grew and she treated me like a rival rather than her child. The emotions culminated in a traumatic event that happened one day while I was bathing. My mother banged on the door and told me to come out. I opened the door naked, wet and cold and stared into her angry eyes. I had no towel to cover my adolescent body. She stared at my budding breasts and as I tried to run past her, she pushed me backwards into the bathroom. I slipped on the wet bathroom floor knocking my front tooth back into my mouth. I had just undergone a very painful journey with my other front tooth which I had knocked out prior and the nightmare began again! I began to scream and my mother grabbed me angrily and tried to shove the tooth back in place, telling me it was nothing. This traumatic experience made me realize my mother was not and would never be the loving nurturing mother I needed but an enemy and rival. I realized I could not trust her. This realization caused me excruciating pain and shame which plagued me my entire life and kept me emotionally stunted at the age of twelve. I always felt that something must be terribly wrong with me if my own mother could not love me. This always made me feel less than the other girls who seemed to have good "mother daughter" relationships. I created the same relationship with other females. I secretly longed for their acceptance, love and approval but did not trust them. I saw them as weak, helpless creatures like my mother. And they saw me as a rival. I became a target for girls' bullying. This caused me to seek my solstices in the opposite sex, shunning other females and the feminine within me!

As I entered my teens, my father's empire grew as his ambitions brought him success and fame, while my mother's world declined as her children grew up and her beauty began to fade. I became very angry and rebellious towards my mother, not wanting to be a victim like her. My father played out his underlying resentment for my mother through me, silently encouraging my rebellious nature. This fueled my mother's anger and created a triangle of a rescuer-persecutor-victim. My mother would attack me, like a wicked stepmother and my father would swoop in to rescue me, like my prince charming. Once when I was a teenager, I remember my mother pulling one of my arms, while my father pulled the other with me caught in the middle! As my mother's anger increased she would deny me even my most basic emotional and material needs. I learned that by playing the "victim" I could go to my father who would then spoil me with gifts and money to make up for it and always say, "Don't tell your mother."

Although as a child I learned how to milk this arrangement, it brought about a deep sense of guilt, shame and confusion which created a spilt inside my mind. There were two Elizabeths, one who felt shameful, worthless like a poor abandoned orphan girl unworthy of her mother's love. Then there was the beautiful blonde bomb shell, a spoiled Daddy's Girl who felt entitled. On top of this I secretly felt I was the cause of my parents' marital problems. Deep down all I wanted was for BOTH of them to love me and each other! I tried my best to heal their marriage and always felt it was my fault when I heard them quarreling. As I grew up their relationship became worse. I would come home at night and find my father alone, drunk on the couch and I would feel I was to blame. I began to think my mother didn't love my father because of me. I thought if I was out of the picture maybe they would fall in love. I wanted so much to escape this triangle. I felt more like a mistress in my family than a daughter.

I sought refuge in the arms of my first love, my high school sweetheart who also had a very similar upbringing. He confessed to me that he slept with a knife under his pillow, afraid of his own mother. He was from England and we met in the Theater where we could both express our creativity. I was fortunate to have had a wonderful high school teacher who recognized my talents and fanned my creative sparkle as an actress. I was given many roles, but my favorite was the part of "Lisa" in the play *David and Lisa*. Ironically Lisa was a schizophrenic girl who heals herself by learning to trust David, a fellow patient in the mental ward. How symbolic of my inner schizophrenic state!

One day a high school friend proudly reported that we were the only virgins left in our senior class. I knew I had to take the plunge into this treacherous world of sex that had created so much underlying tension in my home. I did! After that my high school sweetheart and I spent most of our senior year studying "sex education" at his home while his mother was away at work. We had to escape the watchful eyes of our parents who forbid such terrible things and my father who had become jealous of my attentions towards other men. It was wonderful, playful and fun! I wondered why it had been forbidden! We graduated from high school and we both got professional acting jobs in a troupe of young actors. Life was grand and we were on top of the world, until the bubble burst and I found out I was pregnant. Ashamed, I could not bring myself to tell my parents. I just wanted to get rid of the embarrassment. When I was young I kept a diary. Most of the pages were filled with the words, "I hate my mother!" Then I found a page where I had written the words, "I will never bear a child" and signed it in blood! Oh my God! Unbeknownst to me in a moment of rage, I had signed a blood covenant with the Dark Forces to remain barren! At that time I wasn't aware of what I call the Thothian Curse, which has poisoned ALL sexual relationships between men and women and severed the divine mother child bond. I will go into that in more depth. My boyfriend took me to the clinic, but when I went out to ask him a question, he was gone. He left me for the stage manager of our acting company. Once again I felt abandoned, ashamed and betrayed. Not only was it the pain of having my child ripped from my womb, but I had opened my heart, my body, and my soul for the first time to a man. We had become intimate and passionate. Like children, we had innocently explored the mysteries and magic of sex. This sense of betrayal left a deep wound, along with the guilt of killing my own child. But how could I care for a child when I couldn't even care for my own inner child? Years later on his knees, with tears in his baby blue eyes, my high school sweetheart begged for forgiveness. He admitted that his parents had not loved each other and conceived him out of wedlock, and he was supposed to have been an abortion. This helped me to stop hating men and seeing them as heartless, faithless monsters but rather as fragile injured creatures, in this broken, fallen world, in which we live.

Unfortunately, the story of the ancestral miasma of the Mother Wound on our planet has been carried down from one generation to another through out history, and the entire human race holds varying degrees of childhood trauma. These karmic patterns would bleed into the rest of my life, until I could finally heal them. It wasn't until years latter when I visited the island of Mozia, where I now live in Sicily that I received my healing. As I walked down the pathway leading to the temple of Baal built by the Phoenicians on the ancient cliffs overlooking the Mediterranean Sea, I began to have memories of carrying my own new born child down the same path and placing it on an alter under a huge statue of the "God" Baal. The crowd cheered as a mask was placed over the infant's tiny face and the priest snuffed out my baby's precious life. Afterwards I was hailed as a hero the one who had saved the community, but I felt the same pain that continued to bleed into my other lifetimes which had severed this sacred bond with not only any children I bore but also with my own divine inner child.

Although very painful, I had gained a certain sense of freedom due to my turbulent upbringing. I had come to the realization I could never please my parents, heal their relationship, nor live the life they had planned for me. My father had wanted me to follow the family tradition and go to Center College where my grandfather had been a Professor of Music. But I longed for the freedom of California. I wanted to "break free" from my family's dysfunctional patterns and break into Hollywood, like so many broken aspiring starlets. My parents felt California was too far from home, so we compromised and I went to study Theater in Austin, Texas. I didn't know it then, but this was the beginning of my international gypsy lifestyle.

Saint Edwards University had a diverse foreign population made up of the sons of rich Middle Eastern oil families and the children of poor Mexican immigrant workers. I dated a boy from the Middle East. Fascinated by his culture and his stories about Islam, I enrolled in a course on Middle Eastern History. I was the only American woman in the class! It was filled with all male students from the Middle East, we even had a Prince! The Professor was an X- CIA agent. He began telling us how the U.S. Government went into the Middle East to basically divide and conquer the people. They did this by studying all the sore spots between these people of diverse cultures and religions living in such close proximity to one another. Then they exploited these sore spots to cause the people to war among themselves. For example, he explained that "there were Sunni Moslems and Shiite Moslems or shit as we called them," and laughed, "they hated one another, so the C.I.A.'s job was to encourage conflict between the two. Then to sell arms to both sides." There he was an X- CIA whistlerblower explaining the cause of ALL the problems in the Middle East before my very eyes! I was young and very rebellious, and that familiar feeling began to rise up inside of my throat every time I witness injustice. It is an uncontrollable urge to speak out. So, I shouted out, "That's not right!" And suddenly the whole room of Arabs raised their voices in unison with me. "How could you do that to your fellow human beings?" I shouted. The C.I.A. guy looked terrified and told me to leave the class. I felt ridiculous being sent out of the classroom in college. He came out in the hall and apologized to me and told me he didn't know what to do but I was about to start a war. I thought to myself, "isn't that your job?" The sad thing about it was he didn't even see how wrong he was and how much misery and pain he had caused.

Part of me still believed that if I could just be like my mother, marry a man I didn't love and settle down to raise a family, I would be accepted by my family and find the love I so desperately sought from my mother. So when I returned home for Christmas break, I got back together with my high school sweetheart, who followed me to college where history repeated itself, and we broke up... again. After that, I secretly vowed to stop trying to be like my mother, the image of a powerless, sexually repressed, weak, suffering Madonna! I would become the opposite! I would never be vulnerable to men again. I would become a woman of the world, a sophisticated lady, a femme fatale, a "man-eater" a blonde bomb shell leaving behind the innocent naivety of my childhood which had caused me so much pain and sorrow. My feminine side was no match for this depraved fallen world dominated by wounded males, so I decided to stow it away and toughen up. I furthered my sexual education by reading books like Erica Jong's *Fear of Flying* and Xaviera Hollander's, *The Happy Hooker.* But instead of becoming a maneater I became a conundrum, a patch work of sexual inhibitions, repressed anger, and wounded inner child traumas all shoved into the body of a young woman trying her best to portray the Pygmalion of male fantasies.

College brought me into the life of a wonderful artist named Jill. She was the first woman with whom I formed a long and lasting friendship. She was a badass from Miami. But underneath Jill's tough exterior lay the soul of an artist and a fragile female heart. The oldest female in a family of five she had taken on her absent mother's role. I found in her a glimpse of the maternal love I had been seeking. We traveled the world over, having torrid love affairs with men from every culture. I saw it all as great fun and loved the freedom of loving and leaving men since I had learned how fickle the male ego was. My father's love had been very possessive and he had programmed me to believe that, "no man would ever be good enough for his little princess!" So ironically my friendship with Jill was much more important than the men in my life. But, like so many woman, Jill would fall in love with every man she met. I saw her suffer greatly every time her prince turned into a frog. I lost track of her over the years but heard she died young from cancer they said, but I am sure it was from having her heart broken one too many times.

When summer break came I visited her in Florida to escape Kentucky and my old boyfriend. I got a job at Disney World, a dream job! Imagine me, working at the happiest place on earth! But soon, the veneer began to fade, and the truth began to sink in. The whole place was a put-up job! We had very strict rules to maintain the clean-cut Disney Image. You would get violations for almost everything. Your day began in Wardrobe, where you would put on your costume and pop up in your appropriate land. You would get a violation for being in the wrong land, with the wrong costume, so we traveled to our "lands" via underground tunnels. There were hidden doors all over the park and underneath these fake picturesque store fronts lie rumors of a dark and murky underworld. Very strange indeed. This perhaps was my first real lesson that "things are never what they seem", a theme that would be repeated throughout my life. So, at age eighteen, I learned that the "happiest place on earth" was a put-up job. I saw the innocence of my childhood fade.

Jill talked me into studying abroad in Italy for a semester which was the beginning of my life-long love affair with Italy. I felt at home right away. The people were natural born actors and every piazza served as an amphitheater! I found I only needed to stand on a street corner to stop traffic. It was a repeat of my family dynamics and it felt so "familiar" since most Italian women did not share their husbands' admiration for female beauty. But it was a magical time! I loved the culture, the history, the food... and the men! I was becoming the blond bomb shell my father had raised me to be! I was in search of adventure, fun and had no trouble finding it! I had tasted the smorgasbord of Mediterranean men and their old world passion and liked it! We were part of a study-abroad program within a very conservative Catholic School out of Dallas, Texas and I was the only non-Catholic, the lone rebel as always.

All of a sudden, the beauty of Art, history, architecture, ancient culture and language was all around me, and I wanted nothing more than to learn! In the spring, we went to Greece. It was there I first realized I had the gift of Psychometry, "the psychic ability in which a person can sense or "read" the history of an object or place by touching it". I remember embracing the large columns of the Parthenon and recalling vividly my past lifetimes there. I loved Europe and opened myself up to new ways of learning and exploring reality. I saw how artificial the entire college paper-chase, accreditation world was. When spring came, Jill and I backpacked all over Europe, from Spain to England, Amsterdam down to Sicily. We entered the sleepy town of Mondello the beach town of Palermo. I was infatuated with the fishermen and romanticized their lives of pulling the nets from the Sea and casting them back out again. I even wrote my first screenplay about the fishing village and called it *Mondello Bello*!

My adventurous ways continued in Rome. Once I was riding on the back of a motorcycle whispering, "faster, faster" in the ear of a professional motorcycle racer. We hit oil and skidded down the motorway. I should have died. As I rolled down the highway, I kept hearing a voice shouting in my ear, "Get up, get up!" When I finally stopped rolling out of control, I jumped up and ran off the road. While in the hospital, I reflected on my life. I decided to stop my wild crazy ways and return to the USA to become a teacher. I wanted to change the World by bringing the intuitive, creative adventure I had experienced in Europe into the classroom.

THE DUMBING DOWN OF AMERICA

I returned to Texas where I did my student-teaching with a basketball coach and drove a moped to school. The students called me Miss Moped. I taught them "real" history. I lectured about how the Catholic Church got rich selling indulgences. I let the students create plays about the Greek Gods instead of taking written tests. I created havoc for my poor basketball coach. One day, one of my student's parents called the coach wanting to know why I was speaking badly about the Catholic Church. Coach told me that I reminded him of Barbara Streisand in the movie *The Way We Were*.

After graduating, I got my first job teaching English to grades seven through eleven, in a small Texan town outside of Austin. Again, I guess it was just my rebellious nature, but I found myself creating two sets of lesson plans. One that I would turn into the administration and the other, I would use to really teach the students. We did creative writing, acting and journaling! I gave the kids creative assignments that they loved! I brought speakers in from all over the world to this tiny speck of a town. I empowered the children's creativity and talents. At the end of the year, the principal told me that I was a really good teacher, but not to come back. They cared nothing about what I was offering, and to make matters worse, the superintendent had been embezzling all the money the government had given him for special education classes. He had been overcrowding my classes and funneling all the funds into his own pocket unbeknownst to me! I had been so focused on being a young aspiring do-gooder, I hadn't even realized I had been used as a pawn to make a greedy school administrator richer. But I had done my job! I had learned how to be a great teacher and given those children a taste of how exciting learning could be! I had seen first-hand how corrupt the educational system was and how school administrators cared nothing about the children and only about their own personal gain. Through the years, I have taught at both the secondary and college level in the U.S. and had my fill of "The Dumbing Down of America" agenda that robs students of their creativity and their ability to think independently. I decided to I would go back to Italy.

THE DUMBING DOWN OF AMERICA

Up until the 1840's, the American school system was mainly private, decentralized, and home schooling was common. Americans were well educated and literacy rates were high. In 1902, John D. Rockefeller created the General Education Board with the cost of $129 million. The General Education Board and other Corporate Foundations, including the Carnegie Foundation, provided major funding for schools across the nation and was very influential in shaping the curriculum and format of the current educational system. Predictably, the board started to exert strong control on the policies of the State educational institutions based on their funding and research grants, placing demands on standardizing courses and inventing a bureaucratic maze of conditions and educational reforms. Those teachers, schools, universities and researchers who took the funding and did what they were told were greatly rewarded and they quickly advanced into positions of power. The end result was creating systems that rewarded individuals who were receptive to mind control tactics, obedient to obeying commands, and not creative or critical thinkers. This is just what the Controllers had in mind as currently half of the U.S. adult population can't even read a book written at the 8th-grade level. This means that most adults are unable to discern, comprehend or synthesize the information they are reading, and thus rely on the televised media propaganda churned out by mainstream media broadcasts. My children's book *The Magical Mist* was a warning to parents that the school system was robbing their children of their creative sparkle. I traveled all over the U.S. doing book signings, giving creativity workshops, T.V. interviews and visiting public schools spreading this important message.

MY NEVER-ENDING LOVE AFFAIR WITH ITALY

In Italy, I found the freedom and creativity the US lacked. I taught English as a Second Language to the lawyers of the Gucci, Pucci, Fendi, dynasties at the American Institute, and eventually started my own ESL Program with an Italian friend of mine. This was my first taste of being allowed to use my creativity and let my students' curiosity lead the way. The students would write short scenes in English, then act them out. It was fun, creative and developed their skill and confidence in mastering the English Language. This laid the foundation for me to create my own film school where students from all over the world would come to fan their creative sparkle!

My cousin had come to Italy with me and we became one of the first Aerobics instructors in Italy. They called us "Jane Fonda's" since they did not have any real "health clubs" back then, we taught in the basement of the American Church. Sometimes I didn't even know whether I would eat that day unless a student showed up! Needless to say I was very skinny! All those were the days! But it was thrilling because I had broken free from my culture and was creating my own unique lifestyle in Italy!

Every day I would wake up and say, "Thank God I'm in Italy" Then I would walk out the door with a long list of things to do and would return home with nothing scratched off my list. Welcome to Italy! Growing up in the good ol' US of A, I was a human "doing", buying, working never just being! I was a natural born consumer, but I finally realized living simply is freedom. I began to cultivate the Art of Doing Nothing," or "Dolce Far

Niente," as the Italians say. My Italian boyfriend from the South of Italy taught me this precious gift. We spent a great deal of time, well doing nothing, having a coffee or just walking around the streets of Florence where beautiful Art and Architecture were free for the world to see, having chance encounters with people from all over the world as we let the day take us wherever we were intuitively drawn! These ancient cities were perfect for that!

ANCIENT ART AS OPPOSED TO MODERN ART

Renaissance Art and Architecture places great emphasis on symmetry, proportion and geometry. I once made the mistake of telling a Florentine Artist that beauty was in the eye of the beholder. Thus began a huge discussion where I learned that geometrical patterns and geodetic knowledge was used in ancient times to create beautiful structures that resonated with the Earth's energetic field which amplified higher consciousness and healing properties, and restored and maintained energetic balance. The Tartaria Culture holds remnants of this. I also learned that there are mathematical equations that define beauty, harmony, unity and intelligence. Years later my spiritual teacher used the same words to define God.

I suppose that is why millions of tourists flock to Italy every year to see God expressed through Art and Architecture. Or perhaps they are escaping the uglification of society where cement jungles of small pod apartments are stacked up like coffins to create architectural terrorism. These sprouted cities assault our human senses and incite dehumanization through chaos and depression. Modern statues of twisted steel shards masquerade as modern art. "That's Art" they tell us, and we're supposed to admire and appreciate that twisted piece of metal, graffiti art or a banana duck taped to a canvas on the wall with a public price tag of millions. These anti-beauty, anti-life and anti-art forms are designed to instill oppression, fear and sadness, disrupting the energetic flow when put in public spaces while attacking aesthetics, harmony and balance. This uglification is slowly robbing our planet of all the beauty left behind by great artists. It has already spread throughout Italy. If you wander outside the historic centers of most Italian cities, the outskirts look like depressing concrete ghetto projects. The last time I was in the beautiful Boboli Renaissance Gardens in Florence huge plastic monstrosities obstructing the carefully planned geometrical flow of energy had invaded the garden. Needless to say, the tree spirits were very angry!

LET YOUR FOOD BE YOUR MEDICINE! HIPPOCRATES

One thing all Italians have in common, no matter where they are from, is their passion for food! Food is an Art! Food is prepared with love and eaten in a ceremony to bring people together in celebration. They spend hours talking about their food. At first, I thought, how boring, until I watched as the food in my country deteriorated. I began to realize what could be more important than food. As a child, I was raised on McDonalds, Long John Silvers, Dairy Queen, and T.V. Dinners. What could be more worthy of your money, your time, your energy than good clean, healthy delicious organic (which is simply the way God created it) food? One summer as the American tourists flooded into Florence, an Italian friend asked me why Americans were so fat. I intuitively told them it was because they were starving to death. Ironically "the richest" country in the world lacked the most precious commodity that money could not buy... good health. Americans were swiftly becoming the most dis-eased population on the planet. They had even forgotten what "real" food tasted like. I watched as my American friends who came to visit me, marveled over a simple salad, asking me what special ingredients made it taste so good? I would tell them that this is what real food tastes like, and you haven't eaten it in a long time. My girlfriend from Iceland, who worked as a maid in a five-star hotel in Florence once asked me why only the American tourists had dozens of medications and supplements in their rooms. I told her the truth, that Americans no longer had real food to eat, so they had to spend lots of money on supplements to get the vitamins and minerals they needed and if that didn't work, then they would get sick and go to doctors, who gave them medications, that poisoned them, making them even sicker. She couldn't understand why, with so much land Americans grew flowers and sprayed their lawns with pesticides instead of growing fresh wholesome food. I didn't have an answer.

I learned many things from Italy and its people throughout the years. I gained a healthy distrust of government, a deep appreciation of good food, fun, festivities, art, craftsmanship, and the Art of Socializing. I learned that human kindness is more valuable than money and that there is an adventure waiting around every corner. Every other day was a holiday, a saint's day, a procession, or a carnival to be celebrated! It was one of the funniest places to live on Earth! Italians pocess a unique childlike quality that brings fun and laughter to life. They love their land and love sharing it with foreigners. I learned a deep appreciation for the beauty of nature, and the simplicity of life. I also learned about the Catholic Church.

Growing up in Suburbia, where good Christians show up dressed in their Sunday best coming together for punch and cookies in the rectory after the worship service, I hadn't been prepared for Rome or what was known in Ancient times as Saturnia. I witnessed first-hand the "Roman" Catholic Church and its rituals. I even had an audience with the Pope. I saw people line up to eat the flesh and drink the blood of "Christ" under the image of a half-naked man hanging from a cross dripping blood. I saw the collections of bones and skulls encrusted with jewels lining the walls of crypts and cathedrals. I saw the death cult celebrating their anti-life, anti-Christ practices in plain sight with good hearted people kneeling before these images of saints, climbing up stone steps on their bloody knees and suffering for their sins! All this darkness was a side I had not noticed before. I realized that behind our brightly colored mosaics and tiny glasses of Welch's Grape juice, all "Christians" are reciting the Nicene Creed, swearing their allegiance to the Roman Catholic Church and binding themselves to an imposter god through Satanic Blood Rituals!

Through the Roman Catholic Church, Rome continued its conquest of Italy. The Vatican is built upon the site of worship for *Vatika*, the Etruscan Goddess of the Underworld. Roman festivals and the "goddess" energy was transited into Christian holidays and the veneration of saints. Ancient temples were transformed into "Christian" churches. But even more than this, Rome conquered the soul of the Italians by monopolizing their spirituality with religion. These devout people have had their good intentions and love for the Krystos perverted into worshipping the destruction of their own inner Christ. The Church's Black Pope and Black Nobility took control, creating black Madonna networks of misogyny and anti-female belief systems. This can be seen in its treatment of women and in the tragic figures of the suffering "Madonna" image depicted so poetically in Italian Cinema. This also explains why Italy is a country of ironical paradoxes, which can be maddening to foreigners, but is simply these ancient people's way of adapting and surviving eons of Tyranny. They have learned to, "give to Caesar what is Caesars" creating an amusing culture of contradictions!

CHAPTER 6

WHAT IS GOD?

I can't speak for my father, for he is only with me in spirit now, but I think his job was to "steer" me away from the consciousness traps of organized religion. As you have seen from my childhood, religion had been an intricate part of my life, but something had intuitively felt wrong to me. For me, God was not something or someone outside myself. God was not someone I must bow down to, kneel before, sacrifice to, worship, or make atonement to. God was not separate from me. GOD was within me. For me, the fundamental flaw within ALL religion is the separation of God from the human being. If God is Omnipresent, this means God exists in all things. God exists even in you! You are also part of God! So, why is it considered heresy to say, "I am God?" Perhaps because of what that wise minister told me so many years ago, that the word "god" has been so abused. History is filled with those who have proclaimed themselves to be "god" or "a god" or "one of the gods" or "the one true god". Many people throughout history claim that "god" or the "Voice of God" instructed them to carry out atrocities. Many have misused this omnipresent, omnipotent energy to exalt their own power over others. That is not "god". That is not Divine Infinite God Source.

I made a documentary film entitled, *What is God?* in Italy. I interviewed individuals from all over the world, from every walk of life, religious and non-religious and asked the question, "What is God?" Some did not believe in God, others thought of God as an energy, as nature, as an old man with a white beard, a puppet master, the prime creator, et cetera. Not one person thought of God as something inside of themselves. Even the most spiritual of initiates struggle with the concept of being One with God or saying, "I am God." In the Eastern traditions a Yogi is one who seeks "Union with God" or "God-Realization". When you "realize" the truth, with every cell of your being, that you and God are ONE, only then, will you become "God-Realized". When you know you are Divine Infinite God Source incarnate, ONE with all that is ever has been or ever shall be, it's like being in love, you just "know" it! After all isn't this the goal of all religions to reunite the human with God? I believe all the pain and suffering in our world is based on this one sin or incorrect thinking, to believe you are separate from God. This is why there are wars, violence, cruelty, greed, poverty, pain, and suffering. This belief, that we are separate from God, creates division, polarization and perpetuates our broken finite world of illusion. If we could truly pay respects to the God within US ALL, we could never harm another living creature!

The origins of the word God stems from the Proto-Germanic word *gudan* which means "to call" or "to invoke". So if the word God means "to invoke" then the question is "who or what" are you invoking? Who or what was the "God" being invoked throughout history? Who were the "gods" we must obey, sacrifice to, subjugate to? Since Ancient times, religions have served as political power structures that have perpetuated the illusion that you are separate from God. Religion usurps your direct connection to Infinite God Source within and creates a middleman through which you must go to communicate with "god". This may be a priest, rabbi, preacher, shaman, medicine man, holy man, spiritual teacher, spiritual leader, pharaoh, king, queen, pope, speaker, et cetera. It may be a sacred place of worship, like a temple, synagogue, mosque, church, chapel, or sacred spot. It may be a sacred object, relic, talisman, tribal art, or object. All these things can serve as stepping stones on your pathway to the ultimate knowledge that you and everything in this world is a part of Divine Infinite Source, but the minute you place the power of God on something finite outside of you, you have given away your power.

These representatives of God here on Earth who speak to God or for God, or the Gods or the Guardians, for you and interpret the Word "of " God" from religious texts, scriptures, records, stories, artefacts, the stars, the ethers, cosmic downloads, et cetera, tell you how you should live, what you should eat, what you should think, what you should believe and what is the truth. They interpret the Word OF God not the word which IS the vibrational frequency (which we can all tune into within us) of God from their "bibles" that have been mistranslated, rewritten, severely edited, hijacked and redirected on purpose to hide the truth. Lies, omissions, and half-truths are all ways to lead people astray. But of them all, half-truths are the most deceptive. This doublespeak of the truth hooks in the initiate, the truth seeker. Humanity has been deeply traumatized and as a result we are a race with amnesia. We have all had our minds erased, our memories stolen. We have no memory of who we are, where we come from and why we are here. We walk around in a dream searching for someone or something familiar to jog our memories. When we hear a trigger word, something that resonates or jogs our memory, we flock to it in desperate hopes that our true identity will be restored, our true history revealed. We pray the truth will finally surface and at long last we will awaken from our dream state remembering who we truly are, where we are from, and what we are supposed to be doing here on Earth. But unfortunately, bits and pieces of the truth are mixed in with lies orchestrated as mind control techniques to misdirect us and lead us back into a mental prison. This mind control programing, these spells halt your awakening process and the reclamation of your true inner power. The truth shall set you free, which is exactly why it has been so carefully guarded throughout the ages.

On my Esoteric Renaissance Walking Tour of Florence, as we head from *Santa Croce* towards *Palazzo Vecchio*, I casually ask my tourists from all around the world, if they have seen the famous *La Madonna del'UFO* in *Palazzo Vecchio* which belonged to the powerful Medici Family. It is a 15th century painting called the *Madonna of the UFO*, in English. Behind the left shoulder of Mother Mary, in a clear blue sky, is a glowing metallic object with a shepherd gazing up at it in amazement. I casually ask my adepts, "Do you believe there could be intelligent life on other planets?" I have never once had anyone say no. I have, however, had many of my international tourists tell me in great detail of encounters they have had with "Aliens." These are "normal" people from all over the world. Then, I sometimes share with them some of my own personal experiences.

When my husband, Peter and I began to awaken, we would spend hours gazing up at the stars. It was then that we began to see strange things in the night sky. Peter, always the observant scientist first noticed them and would become excited and point them out to me. We would see stars zig-zag across the sky at amazing speeds then disappear. The first time Peter mentioned this to our friends they dismissed them as satellites. Once when we were driving home late one night on a deserted road, a pair of bright lights appeared in the road before us. At first, they looked like headlights. Then they separated and shot up into the sky. I would have dismissed the incident in my mind except that Peter was so excited. He kept saying, "Did you see that! Did you see that?" I did but my brain wanted me to forget it. How many times do we humans SEE something strange, perhaps a flicker out of the corner of our eye and dismiss it? When Christopher Columbus's ships were approaching the Americas, the Native Americans could not SEE the ships. They could only observe the water stirring around them. Only the Shamans or "seers" could eventually see the ships. The reason being the natives had no point of reference in which to categorize the information, so it was discarded. It was filtered out by the ego which is located at the base of the brain and programmed to dismiss "irrelevant" information or information that does not fit into one's finite preconceived concept of reality.

The typical human eye will respond to waveforms from about 380 to 740 nanometers. In terms of frequency, this corresponds to a very small band in the vicinity of 430–770 THz. The spectrum does not contain all the colors that the human eye and brain can distinguish. In the early 19th century, the concept of the visible spectrum became more definite as light outside the visible range was discovered and characterized by William Hershel (infrared) and Johann Wilhelm Ritter (ultraviolet). Leonardo da Vinci, an Alchemist and genius, would mix his own paints and painted with colors outside the human spectrum of visible light. His use of these paints, invisible to the naked eye, were not discovered until years later when modern X-ray machines exposed them. Animals too, have more evolved vision than humans. Once when I was traveling with Kiki, my Pomeranian dog, giving talks and intuitive readings at psychic fairs, I decided to have my aura photographed by a woman who had been doing this for years. I was holding Kiki on my lap. When the Polaroid was developed, the woman looked at it and laughed. She told me that in all her years she had never seen anything like that before and handed me the photo. There I was, holding Kiki as she sat on my lap staring up at my aura! Perhaps this is one of the reasons dog people always say, "I trust my dog if they don't like a person, but I don't trust the person if they don't like my dog!"

So why is anyone who mentions the word "Alien" immediately categorized as crazy? Why does our Scientific community continually deny the existence of intelligent life on other planets? Why has the C.I.A. been keeping countless "X-files" on Aliens, UFO abductions, et cetera, secret for years? Millions upon millions of people have reported sightings or encounters with aliens and/or abductions. What would happen if humanity could openly discuss E.T.s, off-planet cultures, and the secret space program? Why has the truth been kept from us and why has Earth remained in lockdown, quarantined and cut off from the rest of the Universe for eons? I think the answer may be found in the true history of our planet which has unfortunately been altered along with our memory banks so we must follow the bread crumb trail.

Every ancient culture has some reference to "gods" or beings who came from the heavens or the stars. They are documented in myths, legends, poems, ancient texts, scrolls, statues, base reliefs, cave wall drawings, paintings, burial chambers, ancient artifacts and through oral traditions passed down from one generation to another. So, the question is... who are these "gods"? And where did they come from?

The Dogon Tribe in Africa had advanced knowledge about astronomy before the scientific community confirmed their knowledge as being accurate. They knew that Sirius had another star orbiting it, which they called *Po Tolo,* which was not discovered until years later by looking through a telescope. They called the beings from Sirius the *Nommos*, and they described them as being amphibious or reptilian humanoids. Likewise, the Swahili of South Africa describe lizard-type people that they called the *Chicha huri.* Ancient Cuneiform tablets discovered in ancient Sumeria, now modern day Iraq, considered to be the cradle of civilization, describe their Sky Gods as Fish gods and called them the *Anunnaki.* In Islam, they are known as the *Jinn.* In Ancient Greek, Roman, and Indian Cultures they are referred to simply as "the gods." In Christianity and throughout the Bible they are referred to as fallen angels, the Nephilim, the Lords of heavens, or demons. The *Nag Hammadi* Library, a collection of thirteen ancient books (called "codices") containing over fifty texts, which were discovered in upper Egypt in 1945 refer to these off-planet cultures as the *Archons* or *Demiurge.* Since these ancient Gnostic texts were hidden and unearthed less than a century ago, they did not undergo the countless, edits, omissions, and translations all other texts included in the Bible have. These ancient texts exposed the existence of a Demiurge or Archons, demonic entities that rule our planet and prevent souls from leaving the material realm. According to the Gnostics, the Archons are masters of deceit and illusion. They lack creativity, originality and envy humans for this ability. They can only make a "bad" copy of what humans create. The Gnostics describe the Archons as non-organic beings, that use artificial technology which they referred to as HAL to simulate reality. It is no coincidence that in Stanley Kubrick's film *2001* the computer that killed its human hosts was named HAL. Nor is it a coincidence that Kubrick "died" while making the film *A.I.* which Steven Spielberg stepped in to finish.

We have now reached a time where humanity has enough technological knowledge to understand these historic biblical passages that now take on new meaning. We can understand the truth behind these words written by men with no technological foundation thousands of years ago to describe what they were witnessing.

"I looked, and I saw a windstorm coming out of the north—an immense cloud with flashing lightening and surrounded by brilliant light. The center of the fire looked like glowing metal."
EZEKIEL 1:4

"Who are these that fly along like clouds, like doves to their nests?"
ISAIAH 60:8

"When human beings began to increase in number on the earth and daughters were born to them, the sons of God saw that the daughters of man were beautiful, and they married many of them."
GENESIS 6:1-2

"They come from faraway lands, from the ends of the heavens—the LORD and the weapons of his wrath—to destroy the whole country."
ISAIAH 13:5

"For our struggle is not against flesh and blood, but against the rulers, against the authorities, against the powers of this dark world and against the spiritual forces of evil in the heavenly realms."
EPHESIANS 6:12

According to Plutarch, a highly respected historian, in 76 B.C., a Roman army commanded by Lucullus was about to begin a battle when, "all of a sudden, the sky burst asunder, and a huge, flame-like body was seen to fall between the two armies. In shape, it was most like a wine jar, and in color, like molten silver." In 1561, residents of Nuremberg saw what they described as an aerial battle, followed by the appearance of a large black triangular object in the sky and then a large crash outside of the city. The broadsheet claims that witnesses observed hundreds of spheres, cylinders, and other odd-shaped objects that moved erratically overhead. There were a series of UFO sightings in July 1952, accompanied by radar contacts at three separate airports in the Washington area. The sightings made front-page headlines around the nation and ultimately led to the formation of the Robertson Panel by the CIA.

These are just a few samplings of the multitude of accounts throughout history of alien sightings. But still, no one in their right mind can mention the word alien without being considered crazy. The truth is our Universe is teeming with life. Intelligent life of all forms and frequencies. There are inter-dimensional beings who exist within our living spaces but outside the limited range of the visible light which humans can see. As well as a multitude of extra-terrestrial cultures most being humanoid in constitution, meaning they have a head, a body, and appendages that function as arms and legs. Our Earth has been visited and seeded by many off-planet cultures. They have conducted genetic experiments both evolving and devolving human genetics. Every animal and insect on our Earth has an intelligent humanoid parent race in the stars. This would explain why there are ancient Earth artifacts depicting "gods" with heads of birds, felines, monkeys, fish, and serpents. This also explains the ancient worship of Serpent Gods.

Some of the earliest gods were known as the Serpent Gods. For example, the *Dahomey* have the cult of the python, the *Hopi* revere the rattlesnake. In Mexico, the Aztecs worshiped Quetzalcoatl meaning "feathered serpent." There is a *Caciqui* legend of a "Serpent God" living in the waters which the tribe worshipped by placing gold and silver jewelry into the lake. In Cambodian mythology, the Serpent Gods are called *Nagas*. In India, snakes have a high status in Hindu Mythology. Serpent figures are prominent in archaic Greek myths. According to some sources, *Ophioneus*, a "serpent," ruled the world with *Eurynome* before the two of them were cast down. *Medusa* and the other *Gorgons* were vicious female monsters with sharp fangs and hair of living, venomous snakes. The Gorgons wore a belt of two intertwined serpents, the same configuration as the Caduceus, the symbol used in modern medicine. In Ancient Sumeria, these reptilian creatures were known as the *Anunnaki* Sky Gods. And, of course, there is the serpent in the Bible that tempted Eve, who is responsible for the Fall of Humanity.

Each culture has its own creation stories. Just as our myths and legends have depicted Dragons as both good and evil, there are factions of dragons that broke away from this non corporal noble race in the higher dimensions that were the Guardians of the Universe, and began their descent into the lower frequencies becoming Dragon Moth creatures. This strain of reptilians continued to mutate into aggressive, warring creatures in Orion. There was among them a powerful Reptilian Queen who was a fierce warrior. She conquered many star systems and became known as the Queen of Orion. But there was still strife and conflict within her Empire. Siris contained a fierce Draconian warrior race that had always warred upon Orion. To keep the peace, she formed an alliance with their King Anu through marriage. They had two sons; the older was known as Enki and the younger, Enil. Enki was a very powerful being, a creator of worlds, loved by all, especially his Dac warriors. But he had one flaw. He was very arrogant.

Enki, against the advice of his mother, flew into a fallen Parallel Universe and was attacked and so severely traumatized that his mind was fragmented into multiple personalities, causing him to become a mentally deranged psychopath. He and his mad crew were then infested with Artificial Intelligence nanobots, that inhabited this Dark Universe that began replicating inside of them, turning their own organic bodies into A.I. hosts. Consumed by this A.I. infestation, they lost their free will and became controlled by a hive mind. So, Enki and his Dac warriors returned to Orion and waged war upon his mother's Empire in hopes of assimilating it into the Dark Empire, but he was defeated and cast out. As a result, he lost his position as Prince and successor to his mother's empire. Angered and insane, Enki continued his conquest of the Universe. Enki joined forces with other fallen angelics of Niburu where they were sent to Earth on a mission to supposedly mine gold, but in truth they came to mine souls. According to other sources Enki was a master geneticist creating many clones and an army of Sirian Annuaki Nephilim.

THE FALSE CREATION STORY

Zecharia Sitchin wrote many books about ancient Sumeria and its *Anunnaki* Sky Gods. He claims to have translated the true meaning of the ancient cuneiform tablets found in Iraq. According to this story, Prince Enki was sent to oversee the activity of the mining of Gold on Earth. But the workers who they had been using to mine gold rebelled. So, Enki's "brother" Ea (often thought to be one and the same) devised a plan to take the lowly indigenous population of primate apes that inhabited the Earth at that time and evolve the species to a level of intelligence enough to serve as slaves for the Anunnaki. They did this by setting up laboratories or Edens and cloning themselves with these primates, creating them "in their own image". This began the theory of Darwinism developed by the English naturalist Charles Darwin (1809–1882) stating that humans evolved from Apes discounting the existence of divine angelic infinite human beings and not even mentioning the Enki Overlays which downgraded our divine blueprint. This set into motion the survival of the fittest misconception that all species develop through the natural selection of the fittest and the belief of "God the Father," who lives in heaven above and was the "Creator" of the human race and needed to be worshiped. In Hebrew, the word "worship" means to "work for." Hence, this is where the belief that the human race was created as a slave race to worship or work for their *Anunnaki* "Sky Gods." I introduce Enki to you now, because he has had a very prominent role in the his-tory of our planet and is the Great Pretender or impostor known by many names such as Thoth Posiedon, Zues, Nimrod, Osiris, Oden, Saturn, Chronos, and Lucifer, to name a few. You will learn in the chapters to come of his many fragmented alters or identities. He is in fact a fallen angelic who possesses highly evolved genetics which allowed him to play the role of trickster very well. Many of you have received subconscious programming lifetime after lifetime to grovel and obey this imposture and "await" the return of "God the Father," your "creator" god to give you the "tools" (codes, words, triggers) needed to "free" your mind so you can ascend.

CHAPTER 7

AND NO RELIGION TOO ?

The oldest "recorded" religion on our planet is Sun Worship. In every ancient culture, people worshiped the Sun. Our Sun is the life-giving radiant force of our planet. Its rays create the miracle of photosynthesis which feeds all life on Earth. Without our sun there would be no organic life and Earth would become a dead planetoid. Our Sun communicates with the other suns or stars in our Multiverse and transmits energy and solar activations to human beings who are its little suns. The Sun is key to life and our ascension since there are cellular activation codes transmitted from these alignments of the suns to activate our dormant "junk" DNA. Sun Worship or "working" in harmony with the Sun goes back to the ancient practices of the Golden Age of Atlantis, before the "fall". It was not a religion then but a practice of the Law of One, celebrating and honoring LIFE, the life giving Sun, nature, love, unity and the Oneness of All Things. During Akhenaton's reign in Egypt, the Pharaoh tried to restore Sun Worship and destroy the worship of the Egyptian Pantheon of the "gods" that had been implemented by Thoth. But he was murdered and his name was all but eradicated from history. These were Akhenaton's last words taken from the film *The Egyptian*:

"You try to kill God
By destroying the temples ... But the house of God
is all creation.

Tear down the mountains, empty the oceans, undress the sky of stars, and yet you
have
not touched God.
Now I see clearly.
I thought God

was the face of the sun ... But God is more than that. The sun is just a symbol, of
its warmth ...
its creative power.

Not an image ...
God is not a tangible thing ... but the creator
of all things ...
It is the spirit of love that lives within our hearts.
my death matters not.
I was not more than one shadow of things to come. A voice that spoke for God.
But there will be other voices."

The Law of One celebrated and communicated with the energies or deva spirits of our Mother Earth, the water spirits, the mountain spirits, the tree spirits, the elementals, the fairies, the gnomes, earth spirits of the forest, jungles, desserts et cetera. They did not worship or "work" for them but communed with these energies with gratitude, respect and loving devotion. But soon, this concept became distorted and co-opted into the false "Gods". The "God" of the Sea, the God of the mountain, the Rain God, and the Sun God ruler of them all. These "Gods" began demanding sacrifices which quickly became human sacrifices to grant the people a boon.

So, the question arises: Who were these gods and what "sun" were they worshipping? Every known culture has a long list of solar deities. These are families of gods that ruled over the earth and mortals. Throughout history, the names of gods have changed but their powers and personalities have remained more or less the same. According to Earth's "recorded" history, Sumeria is the cradle of civilization. It was located between the Tigris and Euphrates rivers and was also known as Mesopotamia. Babylon was its capital. Sumeria is considered to be the oldest civilization "known" to mankind. In Ancient Sumeria, Enki was the name of the first sun god (also known by many other names such as Ea, Enkig, Nimrod, Nudimmud, Ninsiku, et cetera). He was the "God" of wisdom, freshwater, intelligence, trickery, mischief, crafts, magic, exorcism, healing, creation, virility, fertility, and art. He was depicted as a bearded man wearing a horned cap and long robes as he ascends the Mountain of the Sunrise; flowing streams of water run from his shoulders, emphasizing his association with life-giving water, while trees representing the male and female principle stand in the background. The streams are interpreted as the Tigris and Euphrates rivers which, according to one myth, were formed from Enki's semen. The word Enki means "Lord of the Earth" and his symbols are the fish and the goat. Lord Enki was considered one of the three most powerful gods in the Mesopotamian pantheon, along with Anu and Enlil. He was the patron of the city of Eridu, considered by the Mesopotamians to be the first city established at the beginning of the world. Excavations at Eridu have uncovered evidence of a tradition of shrines to Enki dating back to the founding of the city in 5400 BC.

These sun gods continued throughout Earth's history changing names with each culture. As the Sumerian culture evolved into the Egyptian pantheon, the name Baal was used, which in Hebrew meant "owner" or "lord". Some of the other family members were Isis, Osiris, Horus, Amun, Ra, Hathor, Bastet, Thoth, and Anubis, which evolved into the popular Greek pantheon of the "Gods": Zeus, Hera, Aphrodite, Apollo, Poseidon, Hemes, Ares, et cetera. In Roman times their names changed to Jupiter, Venus, Mars, and Mercury then we have the Norse Gods, Oden, Thor, and Loki, and the Hindu Gods, Krishna, Shiva, et cetera. Every pagan culture has been hijacked by the same family of "gods"and their savior narratives.

If you look closely at these "solar" deities, they were all born of a Virgin on December 25, under a bright star, adored by three kings. They traveled around with twelve companions. They were known as the light of the world, the savior, the anointed one. They were all betrayed, crucified on a cross or tree, died, and were resurrected in three days. All these stories are metaphors for the procession of the equinox. This is the journey of the Sun that begins December 25 when the brightest star in the sky, Sirius, is accompanied by three other bright stars called the three Kings, visible in the constellation of Orion on Orion's belt. All of these stars point to the rising place of the Sun on December 25. The Sun rises beneath the constellation Virgo, also known as the Virgin. So, it can be said the "sun" is born of a Virgin. During the time the sun moves from the summer solstice to the winter solstice, days become shorter and colder. The Sun appears to grow weaker and at last dies or disappears for three days during its change of direction. Then it is resurrected and starts its rebirth and return toward the Summer Solstice bringing more "light to the world," warmer days, and the return of summer. The entire Roman Catholic Church is based on the oldest religion in the world, Sun Worship. Piazza San Pietro is in the shape of a Sun. If you look at the altar of most Catholic Churches, the symbols there are helios or sun signs. Even the staffs the priests carry and the robes they wear depict Sun Worship. The hats are creations of ancient fish hats worn by priests who worshipped Enki, the first "amphibious" (Reptilian) sun god.

BUT WHICH SUN ARE THEY WORSHIPPING?

In Roman mythology, Saturn overthrows Jupiter, his father. The planet Saturn is a dwarf star. This means it was at one time a sun and our solar system looked much different. Our Earth rotated around the sun, Saturn and was closer to the size of Jupiter and called Tiamat, inhabited by giants or Titians. At that time, the Earth rotated around Saturn and these luminous gases took on a glow from the reflection of our current sun. These various shapes began to take on symbols and meanings to those on Earth who viewed them. One was a luminous crescent. This crescent has been depicted in artifacts throughout history as horns, horned gods, or horns around a disc, also as wreathes around a disc. It has also been symbolized as a bearded man. Hence, Saturn began to be depicted as the "bearded man". At times in its rotation it would cast a luminous glow resembling a four-pointed cross akin to the red cross used by the Templar Knights.

Due to a massive cataclysmic event caused by warring galactic families, the Sun of Saturn exploded, rearranging the planets and catapulting massive gaseous materials into its atmosphere, causing a ring or halo to form around it. As a result, the Saturnian Sun went dark, and became the burnt out dwarf star which is known today as Saturn. It was called the Old Sun the Dark Sun and the Black Sun. Because of its rings, it is also referred to as The Lord of the Rings and has often been symbolized by one eye. Saturn is also symbolized by the G.O.A.T. or God of All Things, since Saturn is in the house of Capricorn, the sign of a goat.

Many scientists attest to the fact that the rings of Saturn are indeed a new addition. In fact, in the book, *The Ring Makers*, the author talks about seeing in the actual NASA footage huge crafts, three times the size of Earth, manufacturing these rings minute by minute. It is believed the rings serve as some kind of transmitter of a vibrational frequency that is hacking into our organic divine holographic reality. This low-frequency band generates sounds emitted from Saturn's rings. The Cassini space probe has recorded these sounds. Unlike the other planets, Saturn churns out a very low demonic noise. The Cassini probe also detected storms located on the North Pole that form the geometric patterns of a cube, a hexagon, hexagram and a six pointed star.

Cymatics is taken from the ancient Greek word *kyma* which means wave. This is the scientific study of how energy waves and sound waves create systems of energy within ordered geometric patterns, which transmit their relative frequencies into the environment. Dr. Hans Jenny extensively studied these geometric relationships in the late 1960's using various materials like sand, water, and iron shavings on vibrating plates and crystal oscillators, to demonstrate how substances would organize themselves into very specific geometric patterns. From his ongoing work, it was obvious that sound waves are frequency wave signatures which create frequency patterns that form consciousness in space. Dr. Jenny's work with *Cymatics illustrates the structure of the physical universe and the interconnection these patterns have with human consciousness* is intimately related to sound waves and frequencies, as well as energy architecture and blueprints. It is indisputable that our cells respond to sound, vibration and frequency which can alter our cellular communication, which influences frequencies in our daily life and manifests what we experience in the outer reality. Through the use of *cymatics*, when the vibration of the sound emitted from Saturn's rings reached the sand, these waves formed a geometrical pattern of a Hexagon, Hexagram or a flattened-out Hexagon which is also a cube shape. The numerical patterns formed on this cube are also found on the North Pole of Saturn and add up to the mathematical sum of 666. This is the same Magic Square of Saturn used by the Freemasons.

Science has proven that everything you see in the physical is energy, and energy holds a certain vibration or frequency. We are not solid beings, nor is the table or chair near you, solid. All things are made up of atoms, protons, and neutrons swirling about each other. In truth, we are holograms. And those who control the energy or frequency of a thing, control the thing. Those who program the holograms control the holograms. These frequencies interphase with your energetic field affecting you profoundly. They can raise your vibrational frequency, uplifting and healing you, or they can lower and distort your energetic template creating dis-ease and disharmony locking you down into a lower frequency band, or vibrational prison. It is believed the Rings of Saturn serve as some kind of transmitter of a vibrational frequency that is hacking into our divine organic holographic reality. So, these artificial frequencies from Saturn have been hacking into the Divine Infinite Architecture of our holographic reality distorting and morphing it into a low frequency fence or net, that keeps human consciousness and souls entrapped in its vibrational prison matrix. These low frequencies, which entrap us in reverse polarities, originate from the Orion System and are amplified through Saturn's rings to our moon.

When bombs were exploded on our moon, it rang like a bell. That led many scientists to believe that our moon was hollow. In truth, our moon is not organic to our Earth. It is a hollowed-out planetoid which was injected into Earth's orbit to act as a receiver and transmitter of these Saturnine broadcasts. It is much akin to the Death Star depicted in the movie *Star Wars*. NASA has set out several propaganda news pieces on the history of moon wobbles and catastrophic flooding destroying the Earth's surface. The Moon has been used throughout history to create mud slides and other disasters to cover up all evidence of ancient Tartarian civilizations that demonstrate the true history of our Earth. The Moon is a weapon directly responsible for the weather wars we experience on Earth.

Research has shown that the human body loses twenty-one grams immediately upon death. This small amount of energy is believed to hold your soul or the complete essence of who you are, along with all your memories and experiences. It is your eternal identity, your unique unit of consciousness. It is not unlike a disc or hard drive that records all of your life experiences, a quantum archive you take with you on your journey of eternal life. In the natural uninterrupted Divine Order of our multiverse, under the Law of One, upon dropping your body, you would be free to go where ever you wanted within our Infinite Multi-universe. You would take with you all the memories and experiences you had acquired and you may even take your Krystic body if need be. However, this Saturn -Moon -Matrix has interrupted that natural flow. Now souls are not allowed to leave the "net". This Saturn-Moon Matrix is what keeps Earth souls in lockdown. It keeps human souls from leaving Earth's "net" or prison matrix, forcing them to recycle time and time again.

HOW DID THEY DO THIS?

They encased the Earth in an A.I. Artificial Intelligence "Net" or space fence to stop the souls from escaping but many souls would find a way to poke a hole through the net, cage or frequency fence. So they created a tunnel of false light to herd souls back into their prison matrix. They posted holograms of dead relatives or spiritual icons such as Jesus, Buddha, Krishna, Mohammed, et cetera to herd the stray souls back into a "tunnel of false light". Once you are in the tunnel you are imprisoned in the artificial time matrix where your memories are erased, and you are recycled back to Earth into another body, with no memory of who you are, to continue serving as a mind controlled slave. Eastern religions call this the cycle of reincarnation and have perpetuated the concept of reincarnation as being a necessary spiritual practice, to work off karma, and to learn your earthly lessons and that only by reincarnating lifetime, after lifetime, after lifetime can you free yourself. In reality, since there is no time, these lifetimes are simply alternate identities fragmented from your soul through trauma, much like the altars created in a MK ULTRA mind controlled slave. As you begin to clear the trauma, karma and heal, these soul fragments will return to you, along with your memories and you become whole or holy.

Until you decide to ascend you are like a writer who is writing their eternal life story. Each lifetime is akin to a chapter in your life's book which you cannot remember. You forget the plot, the characters and the theme and even where you were in the story and begin rewriting the book over and over again from the same limited perspective. You have lost your ability to learn, to grow, to explore and to change. You are on a Merry Go Round, unable to get off! How can you learn your lessons if you continuously have your memories erased, your mind wiped and unknowingly keep repeating the same karmic patterns?

These low frequencies have also disrupted our natural polarities of duality, distorting them into reverse polarities. These explains why there is such division and separation on Earth. Black against white, rich against poor, Muslim against Christian, and perhaps the most devastating of all, male against female, since everything is both masculine and feminine including ourselves. This has fueled misogyny and the repression of the Divine Feminine.

SHEDDING THE LUNAR WOMAN

One need only look to history to know that the feminine energy has been completely suppressed by a lunar harness. Since we are all both masculine and feminine, this creates an inner imbalance within us all. The Mother God aspect of the Infinite, the Divine Feminine has been reduced to a Moon Goddess matched with the shadowy reflections and phases of lunar false light, equated with the secondary reflection of the male solar light. This image has been inverted into the Baphomet, a Satanic image linked with monsters of the Id where seeds of misogyny can take root. This incorrect thinking about females has fueled violence, rape, humiliation, and menstrual disgrace. These fears feed the Dark Witch Female archetypes, such as the Black Widow Mother promoted by voodoo superstitions. These produce images of a mother eating her young and decapitating her husband, if she is not put in her place, kept barefoot, pregnant, and commandeered by her husband. Fears of the male's sexual organs being swallowed up by the female fuel the ignorance promoted to subjugate women to the status of breeders or prostitutes. This wound of being a woman on our fallen planet has been transmitted as the "mother wound" which is the MOTHER of ALL WOUNDS and passed on through ancestral miasma.

THE BLACK SUN

So, the truth is the "sun" being worshiped, or worked for, behind all religions has been hijacked, or diverted away from the life giving, solar entity, our true sun, into the dead, anti-life, Black Sun of Saturn. Because all religions have been duped into worshipping Saturn, a dead star, rather than the life-giving radiant Sun, they have become death cults of necromancers' part of the Anti-Life and Anti-Christ Campaign. All the devotional energy that billions of people are feeding to "god" has been co-opted and misdirected into the false male tyrannical imposter horned god of Saturn. The Catholic Church is worshipping the Black Sun of Saturn, or Satan, not the Sun/Son of God. Likewise, the Dark Side has stolen powerful ascension symbols and inverted them to misdirect us back into their Saturnine Satanic Slave Matrix. These symbols are hidden in plain sight, all over the world, for those with eyes to see, that Saturn or Satan rules over our Earth. It is their way of staking claim to OUR EARTH. One of the symbols of Saturn is the Black Cube which forms part of the geometric pattern found on the North Pole of Saturn. This black cube is present in places of power all over our planet. There is a black cube on Wall street. A black cube is worn by Jewish people on their hands and forehead called *Tefillin.* Even the Muslims must make a pilgrimage at least once in their lifetime to Mecca, where they walk counterclockwise around the *Kaba,* a black cube.

On my Esoteric Renaissance Walking Tour of Florence, I begin my tour in front of the Church of Santa Croce, where there is a six pointed Star of David on the Church facade. This raises many questions. Why is there a Jewish star on a Christian church? The truth is, the Hebrew name for this symbol is *Mer -Ka-Ba*, which means vehicle of light. This is a powerful ascension tool because its three-dimensional form is used to activate our true multidimensional nature, and reclaim our twelve-stranded silicone based genetics to reconstruct our Krystala Body. The top being the masculine electrical which rotates clockwise and the bottom being the feminine magnetic which rotates counter clockwise. Unfortunately the spin ratio and direction has been severely distorted, which has rendered it useless or even harmful and often creates gender distortions. The Rothschild "bankster" family hijacked this symbol and uses it as their coat of arms. Then they took the locked down version of the symbol to represent their Zionist Party. This is the same family that funded Hitler so he could exterminate the true Jewish people and pretended to create Israel and the Zionist party to "help" the Jewish people. However, their Zionist "storefronts" have been used to funnel money out of the USA and around the world to further the One World Order Agenda.

The single eye, or "one eye" along with the *MerKaBa*, is another powerful symbol for ascension, which has also been completely hijacked by Saturn. Activating the third eye gives humans the ability to SEE the truth. Imagine if all humanity could access their third eye, they would be able to see through all the Archonian deceptions and game over. This has been hijacked into a masonic symbol of the Pyramid of Power with the all-seeing Satanic reptilian eye replacing the missing capstone of Divine Infinite Source, as depicted on the American dollar bill. The Magic Triangle or Pyramid has also been hijacked away from its true meaning of ascension or rising above the prison of duality into the higher frequencies of Infinite God Source into a pyramid of slavery with the Black Sun Reptilian Overlords on top commanding their illuminati puppets who enslave "We the People" at the bottom.

To SEE who really rules planet Earth, one needs only to look at these Symbols of Saturn incorporated into the flags of countries, corporate logos, inscribed on world architecture, incorporated into art, placed in films, and inherit in the hand gestures used repeatedly by the rich and powerful "elite" ruling class who are constantly paying their allegiance to Saturn's reign. Corporate logos like CBS, Toyota, Saturn, Alfa Romeo, and Disney demonstrate their allegiance to Saturn with endless Saturnian symbols incorporated into their logos. Politicians and celebrities are constantly being photographed covering one eye, or flashing the "hook em horns" sign, which refers to the horned God of Saturn or making the pyramid sign referring to the masonic pyramid of power. All these symbols belong to Saturn or Satan. As you begin to awaken, and your third eye opens, you will begin to SEE these symbols all around you. Don't believe me. Investigate it for yourself!

If you pay attention you can see these symbols are integrated into the very layout of cities, buildings, positioned on the power points or ley lines of our Earth. Some of these power points are Washington D.C.; Rome, Italy; London, England; and Cairo, Egypt which all have Obelisks strategically placed on the ley lines. Other energy points, meridians, chakras and star gates of our planet have been hijacked. By continuously conducting Satanic Blood Rituals on these sacred spots, our Earth absorbs these negative energies. It is like injecting toxins into the main arteries of a living being. And since our human bodies are directly linked to our Mother Earth's body, it is a direct attack on our body and our ascension. It is in this way Saturn controls the morphemic field or the energetic soup we are all swimming in here on planet Earth. These lower frequencies are maintained by continuously infusing earth's arteries with low vibratory energy produced by emotions such as fear, terror, hate, anger, pain, loss, sorrow, grief, and satanic blood sacrifice. When the Luciferian Knights Templar stole Malta away from the Goddesses who maintained its Krystala Connection to Infinite Source and its high frequency they obtained the KEY to the energetic Template of our Mother Earth.

HOW DO THEY DO THIS?

Our ancient myths, legends, and spiritual texts are filled with stories about blood-thirsty "gods" who continuously demanded sacrifices to appease them. The ancient stones of *Chichén Itzá* bear testimony to the blood baths of millions of humans sacrificed to the "gods" by cutting out their beating hearts. When I recently visited the Yucatan I was invited to the property of two nagas or female Shamans. My intuitive remote viewing friend had told me I would meet a shaman who would work with me. When I arrived at the property with Kiki, I noticed the yard was filled with beautiful husky dogs all chained to trees. There were probably twenty of them. I held Kiki close as we made our way through the mirage of growling beasts. The house was circular and the two women, who were apparently a gay couple greeted me. I gave them a copy of this book and they gave me a copy of their book. It wasn't long before the reason I had been invited was revealed to me. They had chosen me to take over their property because they had heard I was looking to create and ecovillage retreat center. After the traditional cup of cacao, they offered to take me on a tour. As I followed behind them, a little Mexican girl no more than six years of age who had been playing with Kiki walked over to me and said very seriously with the wisdom of an old woman "Guidado"! (be careful in Spanish) This sent a chills up my spine. Kiki and I followed them through the mirage of howling dogs while they kept telling me what great energy the place had but all I could see was death around me. The seeds they had planted had all died. The off the grid system was not working and when I was invited to join them in their tamasca (an ancient Mayan Sweat lodge ceremony for purification) their fire would not start! Finally they took me into a small room and introduced me to their "gods". This were 5,000 year old stone carvings of gods from Guatemala. An ancient obsidian knife used in ancient times for human sacrifice lay in front of the gods. They told me to pay respects and that I could communicate with them. I did and politely moved on. After we returned to the main room I had a srong desire to get the hell out of there! I told them I needed to leave, but the fence was locked. Kiki and I ran through the howling dogs and I got in my car, but it was hemmed in. I literally had to force my way out of their compound. It wasn't until I was well on my way that I realized the little girl's warning was well merited. I was being tested, once again to see if I would put anything before Infinite Source. I chose wisely but the moment I did the illusion of seduction was shattered and I saw the place for what it truly was a place of death! I was no longer welcomed nor did I want to be. The old "gods" did not want to be forgotten nor lose their power.

It wasn't until I was about to leave the Yucatan that I found my true Shaman and had a most powerful purging Tamasca experience. I had been offered two different experiences on the same day: huawasc or tamasca. One involved taking a hallucinogenic drug while the other was about symbolically entering the womb by going into a small round structure filled with hot lava stones. The flap is closed and you sit in total darkness, sweating, and breathing while herbs are thrown on the fire. It was a journey into darkness and back out into the light of rebirth. It was the journey of the hero. Afterwards I told the Shaman it was like reading my book!

Not far from my home in Sicily, there lies the tiny island of *Mozia* which was inhabited by an ancient race of people thousands of years ago. I already shared with you my experiences when I visited the ancient temples and burial grounds. When I discovered that parents had willingly put a ritualistic "mask" over the face of their infant child and sacrificed their own child to a statue of "the god" Baal I kept asking myself what on Earth could have "possessed" them to do this? Yes, possessed is the correct word!

In ancient myths virgins were required to appease the "Wrath of the Gods". What are virgins? Children. Why children? Because they have a strong life force. As I explained before, these dark entities are parasites who can no longer feed directly from Source. They cannot survive in the higher frequencies of love and eternal light. Like vampires, true light is toxic to them and they are creatures that thrive in the darkness. So they must feed vicariously off the life force of others. But first they must pervert this pure life essence into a lower frequency compatible to theirs, so they can assimilate it. They do this by instilling terror, fear, rage, misery, pain, and suffering in their victims. This energy collected from the misery of others is called *loosh*. It is a highly coveted currency traded all over the Universe. It is harvested in many ways. One of the most common ways is by terrorizing a child through violent acts of rape and sodomy and after endless torture, killing them in a very traumatic and bloody manner, then consuming their flesh and drinking their blood. I know this sounds horrible, but we must face the darkness that has been going on right under our noses for eons. This is why there are always rumors of Pedophilia and lairs of child trafficking rings surrounding the Royals, Hollywood, Washington, the Vatican, and its priests. Not only does this *loosh* feed the Satanic forces and moon chain black hole entities, but it also contaminates the ley lines and power points of our Earth with negative energy, keeping Earth trapped in the dead space of the phantom worlds.

Bohemian Grove is a restricted 2,700-acre campground at 20601 Bohemian Avenue, in Monte Rio, California, USA, belonging to a private San Francisco-based gentlemen's club known as the Bohemian Club. People who have managed to sneak in have reported that they have witnessed human sacrifices in front of a twenty-foot owl figure symbolizing Moloch, the Canaanite God, associated with child sacrifice, yet another name for *Baal* or *Chronos* the "god" who ate his own children. MK Ultra mind-controlled sex slaves, who have escaped their captors, and freed their minds, have recounted their experiences and have named powerful world leaders who they saw participating in these satanic rituals. Many of these powerful political figures, wealthy banking families, royals, and celebrities have a history of living well into their nineties and beyond. Science is now admitting that the ingestion of young people's blood can extend life. Many elites buy a substance known as Adrenochrome on the black market. This has been around a long, long time and is referred to in Kubrick's film, *Clockwork Orange*. This is the blood from the pituitary gland of an infant who has been tortured to death. It is highly addictive, creates an intense high and is believed to prolong life.

The Schumann Resonance records the energy temperature of our planet daily. When the twin towers fell, the fear on the planet was off the charts. Keeping people paralyzed in a state of fear allows the dark side to not only remove people's personal liberties, but the energy produced from this fear is used to power up their A.I. Beast Machinery. All wars, genocides, murders, rapes, violence, and plan-demics feed the Loosh Beast A.I. Machines. Whenever you participate in these blood sacrifices or rituals you feed these symbols even if you do so unknowingly, you are feeding the dark Satanic forces and binding your soul in service to them.

THE THREE CHRISTS

Although my mother was the wife of a minister she always maintained an air of skepticism about religion. But I do remember my mother saying to me, " I'm not sure what happened back then but it must have been something big because people are still talking about it today!" Many believe that in our true hidden history there were three Christs. The true Christ referred to as Jeshua 12 had his full 12 strands of DNA divine template. He could perform what seemed to us in distorted carbon based bodies miracles. However this was just part of being an Infinite Human that we lost when our genetics were downgraded. His full name was Jesheua Melchizedek his mother was Judi and father Joehuis. His true mission was to heal the morphogenetic template of our Earth which would allow our Mother Earth and humanity to ascend. This task required a 12 stranded Krystos avatar body. He also resotred the genetic imprint to the Hebrew people and left a Krystic bloodline. He wrote down the truth held in the emerald records which was our true galactic history, the ascension mechanics and other forbidden knowledge. He entrusted this knowledge to various essence tribes around the world for safe keeping. These are the documents that the Essennes and Cathars were murdered for and have been stolen from the Great Libraries around the world by the Catholic Church, then omitted from our modified present day Bible. There are however a few hidden scrolls that have not yet been unearthed. At the age of 39 in 27 AD Jesheua 12 bodily ascended to Tara through the Ark of the Covenant taking with him a few Essenes.

The second Christ was Jesheua 9 who held 9 strands of DNA. He was constructed for religious and political motives and was manipulated by the fallen angelics. Unfortunately Mary Sophia Magdalene who was the genetic twin soul of Jesheua 12 was married off to Jesheua 9 wrongfully.

This action left her vulnerable and her divine essence was hijacked by the fallen angelics to run into their black Madonna reverse lunar matrix systems and her Sofiatic gnosis was inverted into black magic rituals to sustain the parasite's life force.

The fallen angelics had plans for Jesheua 9 but the Guardians were able to get a hold of him and used him to restore the principles of the Law of One into religious texts. He also left a genetically enhanced lineage. But his work was becoming noticed by the Romans. Story has it a third Christ named Arihabi who was not genetically evolved and just a regular man was manipulated through mind control and inner messages. He was convinced that he was the true Christ and must sacrifice himself. So the third Christ was crucified but the Guardians resurrected him allowing him time to accrue enough knowledge and genetics to eventually ascend. This third Christ was the one misused by the Catholic Church to corrupt the Krystic teachings so that good "Christians" would worship the destruction of their own inner "Kryst".

In Christianity, the true meaning of the "Body of Christ" is your Ascended–Krystala plasma Body. It is your Divine Twelve-Stranded Double Diamond Sun Krystal Plasma Rainbow Body of Light blueprint. Ascension is our natural organic Divine Angelic Infinite State of Being. Transmutation is the transfiguration of the physical body through the Solar Synthesis of light activations which build the light body to receive plasma codes, restoring our inner Kathara grid creating a plasma luminary body or "Krystala" body. By embodying liquid plasma light, you can vaporize dead energy miasma, alien machinery, artificial technologies, entity attachments and mutated inorganic substances that require an extremely low frequency and low vibrational density to continue to exist. In short, as you ascend into the higher frequencies by constructing your inner "KRYSTIC Body" you free yourself.

"If a picture is worth a thousand words, a symbol is worth a million."
JAY WEIDNER

Symbols go directly into the subconscious and affect our bodies. In the East many Buddhist monks stare for hours at artwork depicting ascended masters in their Rainbow Plasma Light bodies. It has been proven that visualizing an image affects your physical body. This is why many cancer patients have had success visualizing their cancerous white blood cells being eaten up by their healthy red blood cells. Visualization is a powerful tool for manifestation.

The true power of Art is that it sneaks into our subconscious mind. Living in Italy, the amount of Art is staggering. The Image of Christ's Crucifixion has been depicted throughout the centuries by almost every great artist. However, there is very little "Ascension Art". Ascension Art is when Christ is depicted wearing his celestial garments of white, representing his ascension into his KRYSTIC Body. The Christ is often shown with brilliant light radiating from his body as he hovers in the sky or appears to descend from a cloud. However, if you look at the altars of most churches, there is a figure of a half-naked man, blood dripping from his body parts, writhing in agony, hanging from a cross. This anti-life, anit-christ image is what many devoted saints fixated on throughout history. As a result, they have been "blessed" with stigmata. This means that by focusing on the tortured image of "Christ" they began to show the same "Wounds of Christ" in their own bodies. The bleeding nail holes in their hands and feet, and even the wound in Christ's side, where he was pierced in his spleen by the "Sword of Destiny" To experience these "wounds" in your physical body is a ticket to Sainthood. Saint Katherine and Saint Francis of Assisi had them, and it is rumored that Padre Pio faked his own stigmata to ensure his sainthood.

As we all know, words are powerful weapons that can be inverted becoming swords that hide the truth in plain sight. The word *cruc* or crux means "a conundrum or insoluble problem" and the word *fixion* or fiction means "something invented or feigned" The "Crucifixion of Christ" is promoted so Christians will worship the crucifixion of their own inner Christ and halt their ascension. The Truth is these Crucifixion implants were created to destroy our inner Krystala body with artificial inserts that stop the organic ascension process. Crown of thorns to block the pineal and third eye and a spear in the side that disrupts another powerful centre. The horizontal beam separates our right and left sides, blocking the Alchemical Unification of our masculine and feminine, to further prevent our inner divine hierogamic union. The vertical beam blocks our heart chakra, and stops the flow of Kundalini rising from our lower chakras into our upper chakras. This blocks the opening of our heart chakra, our third eye, and prevents the flow of energy to our crown chakra, blocking our direct communication with Infinite God Source. These Crucifixion Implants have been inserted in our holographic make up to perpetuate the sexual misery program and the Reverse Caduceus by inverting the flow of the Kunda ray or Kundalini energy downward to feed shadow creatures. To make matters worse, they have perverted the Ascension of our Inner Christ Body into a Satanic Blood Ritual. Most good Christians line up weekly to receive the false "Divine Host" in front of the tortured body of a half naked man. These good Christians have been brainwashed into participating in a Satanic ritual of drinking the blood and feasting on the flesh of "Jesus" binding them to Satan. This ritual has degraded humanity into worshipping the destruction of their own inner Christ and perverted the true Trifold Trinity into the Unholy Trinity of an imposter "God the Father, Satanic Son, and Hungry Ghost".

The name Jesus is not the true name of the Christ Avatar who came to Earth. Jesus comes from the Greek word which means "Hail Zeus". The face used by Italian artists that has come to be known as the face of Jesus Christ is actually the face of Cesare Borgia, the second illegitimate son of Pope Alexander VI of Rome. Cesare Borgia was a Spanish-Italian, homosexual cardinal who resigned his church office to become a military commander and a powerful evil corrupt figure in the politics of his era. This is the image good Christians kneel before making blood sacrifices.

The word Jesuit means the Society of Jesus. The following is the Jesuit *Extreme Oath of Induction* given only to high ranking Jesuits. This oath is taken from the book *Subterranean Rome* by Carlos Didier, translated from the French version, and published in New York in 1843.

"I promise and declare that I will, when opportunity presents, make and wage relentless war, secretly or openly, against all heretics, Protestants and Liberals, as I am directed to do, to extirpate and exterminate them from the face of the whole earth; and that I will spare neither age, sex or condition; and that I will hang, waste, boil, flay, strangle and bury alive these infamous heretics, rip up the stomachs and wombs of their women and crush their infants' heads against the walls, in order to annihilate forever their execrable race. That when the same cannot be done openly, I will secretly use the poisoned cup, the strangulating cord, the steel of the poniard or the leaden bullet, regardless of the honor, rank, dignity, or authority of the person or persons, whatever may be their condition in life, either public or private, as I at any time may be directed so to do by any agent of the Pope or Superior of the Brotherhood of the Holy Faith, of the Society of Jesus."

More people have been killed in the name of "God" or Jesus than any other wars on our planet. The greatest trick the devil ever pulled was to convince you he didn't exist. The second one was to convince he was good! These Satanic Luciferian forces have been around a long, long time, and have tricked us all because after all that is what they excel at. They have managed to remain hidden in plain site for eons. As Mick Jagger asks over and over in his famous song, *Sympathy for the Devil*, "What's my name?"

I have listed a few of the names of the "devil" or these gods of Saturn, or Satan, who have been casting their spells over humanity and controlling our Earth's HIS- story through their representatives here on Earth for eons. Let's bring these parasites these fallen angelics out into the light. Let's SEE these gestalts of dark entities who have used their free will to sever themselves from Divine Infinite Source and who continue to ignore God's Natural Laws, Cosmic Sovereign Law and the Law of ONE. Let's take a peek behind the curtain at those who have usurped your free will stolen YOUR planet right out from under your noses, with your help! Let's see these parasitic feeders who like bottomless pits roam the multiverse seeking out prey, conquering planets, star systems, and even multi-universes to feed their insatiable emptiness? Who are these dark forces? Many are a gestalt of shadow creatures, and off-planet races who come from fallen parallel universes.

What most people do not know is that the true original sin occurred over two hundred and fifty billion years ago in the cradle of Lyra when the Elohim blew up the 12th stargate disconnectiong our Time Matrix from Divine Infinite Source and declaring themselves "God". Some believe this event was orchestrated by invading shadow creatures from fallen parallel universes who infected our time matrix with their "Andromeda Strain" creating an infection or distortion in the Elohim of Stargate Eleven which caused them to take this tragic action and become the fallen Elohim Anu. Infinite Source could have closed off our time matrix and let us fall but they choose to let this drama play itself out. They would allow our time matrix to fall and learn all the lessons of what it felt like to be disconnected from Infinite Source. But they encrypted within our fall story a FAIL SAFE or reset button. This "reset button" could be pushed as a final solution if all other attemtps to bring our time matrix back home failed. But things had to get so bad that it was the only alternative. It case you didn't know it that button has been pushed and we are now in fail safe. If it had not been our entire time matirx would fall into one of the fallen parralle time matrixes fighting over us. Two hundred and sixty billion years ago when our time matrix was infected warring began between the Elohim of star gate eleven and the Draconians of star gate ten. These races were made up of collectives or families one family which fell was the Giovani collective, many of these were our own brothers and sisters whom we joined in an attempt to save them. We have now entered the end times the final trauma playing itself out in front of our very eyes.

These fallen angelics families formed lineages and hybrid races with the intention of destroying the divine angelic guardian races. They interbred with human angelic races, creating their own fallen houses or families: Annu-Elohim, Tothian Enki, Draconian Jehovivan-Anunnaki, the house of Satan, Enoch, Nephilian Marduke, Necromition-Andromis Nibiruian, Omicron-Drakonian Dragon Moth. These fallen races are the ursurpers of the true magi grail lines. They became known as the Leviathan races the false tribes of Israel ursurping the true Isrealites. These Nephilian Leviathan Anunnaki hybrids infiltrated the Angelic Krystos races by conquering them, killing the men, and raping the women to use their higher genetics to create their own warrior races. Consequently, we have all been infilterated by these fallen Anunnaki genectics and we all have a shadow self. These alliances of *mafioso* families are constantly warring among themselves. The Draconian Black Sun Reptilians Are Extra Dimensional (ED) overlords referred to historically as Archons and the Demiurge who rule through an Artificial Intelligence Hive Mind. The Gnostic texts refer to them as the Archon Lords. The Black Suns were directly behind the Nazi Black Sun groups and fueled their Satanic tyrannical philosophies. We can see these tyrannical forces at work in the world today through all the "Draconian Mandates" handed down by the WHO of the One World Order. These have been warring with the Anu Elohim but behind them are other fallen parallel universes of Wesax and Borgua.

Many people do not want to SEE the evil that is happening in the world today because they refuse to see the evil within their own shadow self. They do not have the courage to face their own inner pain and trauma and heal it. So evil continues its dark reign over our Earth. "We The People" can no longer point out fingers at others because we are doing it to one another and to ourselves. The first step in fighting evil is to purge it from within yourself. As I just illustrated the dark forces have seeped into humanity's very soul becoming the shadows we are afraid to face. We can see their Satanic forces at work in the world where individuals are of service to themselves rather than Humanity, Mother Earth and all God's Creation. These people believe each person should do whatever it takes to get ahead, no matter what the cost to others or our planet. They have no ethics, moral standards, or sense of right or wrong therefore they "just follow orders" without ever questioning authority. "Yours is not to question why yours is just to do or die," is their mentality and their fears cause them to commit horrible crimes against their fellow human beings. These actions carry heavy karmic debts and claiming ignorance does not absolve you. These Satanic forces have taken over the minds of humanity and tricked us into believing we are doing things for the good of humanity, our fellow human beings and our family, when in reality we are committing horrific acts against one another. "We the People" are inventing technology that threatens all organic life on Earth. "We the People" are administering poisons under the guise of medicine breaking our oaths to "first do no harm". "We the People" are enforcing tyrannical criminal laws that take away our own freedom and bodily ownership. We the. people have empowered narcissistic individuals who lack empathy for their fellow human beings and allowed them to rule over us and worse allowed their mindset to penetrate ours. We the People have turned a blind eye where Eugenic protocols based on Social Darwinism have been unleashed to "cleanse society". We the People are purchasing and consuming technology that is detrimental to all organic life on Earth. So in truth Mick Jagger is correct when he reveals the true identity of the devil at the end of his song when he sings, "After all it was you and me." Great evil could not exist in our world if we did not allow it to.

In Western civilization, our culture is based on the Judeo-Christian premise that the actions of Eve, the first woman, are responsible for our "original sin" and our "fall from grace" Within this false historical narrative recorded in the Bible, the "Fall" of "mankind" was due to a woman eating from the tree of knowledge. I believe it was our dark masculine nature and curiosity that caused humanity to stray outside the boundaries of God's Natural Laws and eat from the poison apple of AI, artificial technology. I believe the masculine energy of Atlantis began experimenting outside of God's Natural Laws creating abominations by melding human DNA with animal DNA and using artificial technology to usurp our divine technology and women got the blame! History is now repeating itself! Will we allow the unconditional love of our true Divine Feminine Nature, which resides within us all, to become the antidote for the self-serving narcisstic dark masculine energy that has consumed our planet? Or will it remain suppressed?

Let us investigate further the grains of truth left behind in the Garden of Eden. "When Adam dwelt in Eden, he was clothed in the celestial garments, which is the garment of heavenly light...light of that light which was used in the Garden of Eden." (Zohar II.229B) Were these "celestial garments" our refined light bodies? "And the "LORD" God made for Adam and for his wife garments of skins and clothed them." (Genesis 3:21)" Skins" are what we have now, not "celestial bodies of heavenly light" but, denser, heavier "genetically" downgraded "meat suits".

EARTH AS A PUT UP JOB

The imposter god(s) have put into place a false history to make you believe you are some lowly beast or ape that evolved through the survival of the fittest or that the "gods" genetically upgraded, or fashioned you in their own image. Quite the opposite. You are Divine Angelic Infinite Human Beings. The truth is these impostor "gods" stole your angelic DNA, then created "Eden" laboratories where they tampered with you, inserting their reptilian DNA. This explains why we all have both a reptilian "hind" brain and "reptilian tail" or Satan's tail at the Coccyx as part of our current anatomy. Our 'perfect ' body of light, symbolized by the Robe of Light or the Celestial Garment of Christ depicted in sacred art around the world was downgraded into a "meat suit" that ages, rots, and decays. Then we were made to feel shame the lowest emotional frequency. Shame for our "bodies," our sexual organs, our sexual desires and even contempt for the opposite sex.

CHAPTER 8

TWIN SOULS

*"According to Greek mythology, humans were originally
created with four arms, four legs and a head with two faces. Fearing their power,
Zeus split them into two separate parts, condemning them to spend
their lives in search of their other halves...
...and when one of them meets the other half, the actual half of himself, the pair are lost
in an amazement of love, friendship and intimacy and one will not be out of the other's
sight, even for a moment...»*

*"Love is born into every human being; it calls back the halves of our original nature
together; it tries to make one out of two and heal the wound of human nature."*

PLATO

At one time, when our polarities were balanced, we embodied both male and female. This sacred hierogamic union of the Divine Masculine and Divine Feminine resided within all Infinite Human Beings. As Infinite Humans descended in frequency and assumed more grosser forms we desired to experience the separation of the masculine and feminine aspects of ourselves more fully so we separated the masculine electrical and the feminine magnetic aspects of ourselves into two separate bodies.

We remained connected by having the last six strands of our twelve strands of DNA braided together. This separation was a joyous way to experience ourselves as masculine and feminine. We felt the unity of our bond but could express our deep love for one another by making love in two separate embodiments. We never thought of sharing ourselves with another nor did we feel the need to look outside this blissful union because being together was like coming home.

According to Plato: "we humans were in such a state of eternal bliss, that we refused to properly "honor" the "gods." As punishment, we were split into two parts "male" and "female" and cast to the far ends of the Earth." So the "gods" divided us because we were too powerful then they cast us to the four corners of the Earth and have done everything in their power to keep us from reuniting with our hierogamic partner through sexual misery programming, scrambling timelines and creating alien love bites to cause us to marry our false twins. But through it all our instinctive desire for union with the opposite sex to find our other half and become whole or holy again has survived. "Given that we are all separated when we find our other half, we are lost in the amazement of love that cannot be accounted for by a simple desire for sex." Love is the name that we have given our desire for wholeness, for restoration to our original divine holy state.

We were torn apart through trickery and deception creating the most painful trauma ever experienced by Krystic Beings. This left a deep wound of jealousy and betrayal fueling sexual misery and perpetuating the illusion of separation. The profound pain of the loss of our twin soul is lodged deeply in the pain bodies of both men and women.

How did this first trauma first occur? And why has history been repeating itself?

It happened because we Krystos Beings trusted the wrong person and continues to occur because our fear, pain and trauma has keep us paralyzed, stuck in a time loop unable to face and heal the past so we can choose another future. I share these words not to cause you more pain but to free you from this destructive cycle. Deep down everyone is seeking their twin soul to heal this wound but few truly understand what it is. The first separation occurred on the island of Kauai in what was left of MU on the island of Hawaii over twenty-six thousand years ago. Krystic twin souls were working with Thoth who at the time had returned to the Guardian Alliance for bioregeniosis and was helping to restore our Earth's template. We trusted him and allowed his crew of warriors to land but he turned on us taking everyone prisioner and threatening to kill the men unless the women would accompany him to Nibiru to breed with his Annunaki warriors. The women agreed to save the lives of their husbands. But unbeknownst to them while they were captive their men were hunted down and castrated and brutally murdered their bodies used as rods to run reverse polarities into the grids creating the Niburian checkerboard matrix. The result of this was devastating to the krystic women who were taken to Niburu away from their mother Earth. They lost their power removed from their Mother and became totally dependent on their captors. They were pawed over treated like merchandize valued only for their physical appearance as breeders or sex toys. Many of the women became the brides of Thoth. They learned that the only power they had was by pleasing their psychopathic husband who would tire of them like a used toy. This is when competition rather than sisterhood was created between women. Jealousy and betrayal of their own sisters was part of the truama based mind contolled used to destroy women's indentity. They were tortured raped and humiliated. Thoth may choose one of his wives as his favorite one day and shower her with gifts and attention only to have her locked in a dungeon starved, beaten, humiliated, and even raped by whomever he desired the next.This cruel and inhuman treatment became ingrained in the psyche of the female collective. Women's identity as Goddesses were erased from her memories. Their self esteem suffered and they became rivals to each other rather than sisters. They lost their power and their entire existence became dependent on the men around them.

Through forced breeding women began to bear the very spawn of the men they hated. These men who raped and humiliated them were forcing them to bear their satanic deranged psychopathic sons to kill more men and rape more women. Many women would throw themselves off cliffs rather than bear such offspring. As a result they were chained raped repeatedly and forced to bear children until their bodies gave out. This has been repeated throughout his-tory and can be seen documented in statues like the "Rape of the Sabine Women". Every Krystic Community was hunted down and raided by Leviathan invader races like The Luciferian Knights Templars or other groups: the Essenes, the Cathars, and so on. The men were slaughtered, the sacred scrolls written by Jesheua 12 stolen and the women raped to breed more Annunaki Hybrids. Each time the mind control traumas were imprinted deeper and deeper into the female psycic until women's self image, self esteem and self respect were shattered. The sacred sexual act of making love with their true love, their genetic twin soul in an intimate passionate tender way was degraded into animalistic pleasure turned into sadomasochristic conditioning inverting the pain and pleasure causing women to crave pain in order to achieve organism.

But many women rejected orgasims all together because they knew that orgasms opened portals in their divine template and when they copulated with their Annunaki hybrid captors they would distort their divine Krystic template. This created two sexual misory programs the Ice Queens who rejected sex or the Femme Fatal who was a sex addict.

The seeds of misogyny were sown as all men and women were damaged by these traumas. In the trauma based minds of the male twin souls they felt betrayed by their women who had become the whores of Annunaki thugs. Men began to see women as lustful evil betraying whores who would easily give their devotion to the strongest male. The Annunaki warrior race had manipulated their genetics so they were bigger, stronger and more endowed then the kyrstic races. This is where values such as sensitivity, spiritual connectiveness, gentleness, tenderness, compassion were rejected as part of the male psyche. They were replaced by preoccupation with size, being aggressive, competitive, and physically stronger. Women were conditioned to value these traits. Women were no longer valued for their deeply intuitive, nurturing and healing wisdom but only for their physical appearance and their ability to bear sons.

This Thothian curse caused women to become sexually aroused by aggressive, competitiv men. Numerous implants, shunts, cages and other sexual misery implants have closed down hearts, blocked the ability to associate love with sexual ecstacy, inverted the Kundalini energy into reverse Caduceus systems creating sexual addiction and misery. Women have been laden with guilt, shame and hatred for our own sexual parts and sexual feelings. THIS CONDITIONING HAS MADE WOMEN BELIEVE THEY WERE LESS THAN MEN AND THEIR ONLY PURPOSE IN LIFE IS TO BREED TO PROLONG THE BLOODLINES . This is how women slowly began to stop asking for what they wanted. This is how many women began to hate their own children and recluse from the dark masculine world that hunted and destroyed the Goddess Cultures. As a result we became powerless separated from our Mother Earth.

Because of this insidious programing women began to hate themselves for being sub servial. They began to hate their sex. Men began to fear females and both sexes began to retreat into the abodes of celibacy denying their very nature in the pursuit of "purity". Women carried a deep seated guilt about betraying their husbands and breeding with the conquering races. The Catholic Church exploited this guilt into "original sin". But perhaps the greatest sin orchestrated by Thoth, Enki, Lucifer the master manipulator was not just dividing the male from his female but to disrupt our inner hierogamic union within. All twin souls carry this Cruse of Thoth and all must heal from it. Even if you defy all odds and find your twin soul you must internally heal this trauma within yourself and within your relationship or HIS-tory will repeat itself. As you heal yourself you will heal your counterpart and vice versa because you are ONE! As you ascend you return to the wholeness or holiness of this sacred unity. This is inevitable because ascension is the restoration of all fragmented parts of the soul and you were, are and have always been one soul. Perhaps the greatest curse that Thoth gave us was the hatred of our own inner masculinity or femininity which we must heal. Alchemy is the restoration of polarities the integration of both the Divine Masculine and Divine Feminine forces of duality through "Sacred Marriage in No Time." This is the foundation for ascension. The Goddess holds this balanced divine feminine and divine masculine within. This is essential in transmuting the lower frequencies of duality to achieve the "Great Work" of Transmutation.

It is necessary to first understand and embody the energies of the sex you were born into then and only then can you integrate the energies of the opposite sex. By integrating these two polarities within you, you become the transcended amalgamation of both divine feminine and divine masculine. This holy alchemical union has been degraded into the symbol of a Hermaphroditus, the two-sexed child of "Aphrodite and Hermes". This has further been distorted in today's society as children are being transgendered before they can even learn to embody the sex they were born into. This is done purposely to confuse the child and stop them from achieving a strong balanced sexual identity that leads to them realizing and harmonizing their inner masculine and feminine qualities.

Romantic cravings push one to seek their other half, not just to procreate like livestock but to come together in the divine union of sacred sexual alchemy. This union is not limited to heterosexual relationships, since we all are both masculine and feminine. Because this union is so powerful, it has been the most highjacked union of all. Throughout history, most twin souls have not been able to incarnate into the same timeline. If they did, marriages were often arranged for political alliances merging family lineages, consolidating wealth, but rarely for love. History is filled with stories of "star crossed lovers" and "unrequited love". Walls between the two sexes have grown, creating a battle ground for misogyny and sexual misery, reducing women to property, toys for sexual pleasure, or livestock for breeding, degrading this sacred holy union into an unholy union.

When I moved back to the U.S. I worked "the lines" for a while. This means I signed up with several dial up psychic reader services. I worked with English speaking clients all over the world. I sincerely thought I could help people on their spiritual journey. At first, I did my best to empower them and help them gain clarity into their "soul purpose" and what karmic patterns were holding them back. But after a while, it became obvious "the lines" were filled mostly with desparate women looking for their "soul mate", Prince Charming, Mr. Right, for all the wrong reasons. They may call them their soul mates, twin souls or twin flames, and their longing may stem from the deep pain of being unjustly ripped apart from their other half, but most of them were desperately looking for love in all the wrong places, and for all the wrong reasons. They wanted someone to take care of them, to support them, to give them the love they lacked, to give them a position in society, to father their children, to heal them, to make them feel needed... et cetera. It also became clear after a talk with one of the owners of these psychic phone services that my job was to keep these clients on the phone as long as possible, so they would pay as much money as possible! So I quit.

Too often, men and women are too busy being distracted by the package, rather than being drawn by the soul essence of their true twin flame, that they miss each other. It is rare indeed when two twin souls find one another. Then, if they are lucky enough to find one another, they must heal all the pain, sorrow, and deep-seated wounds that they have incurred from others or have inflicted on each other lifetime after lifetime. All memories of trauma are triggered and must be transmuted and healed, with unconditional love, back into their original holy union. This often creates a dichotomy of intense love and hate, which explains why we seem to hate the people we love the most. The deep thrill of finding your other half, is often followed by a repulsion of committing to the process of healing that you both must embark upon to return to wholeness. This often causes, both or one of the partners to want to run from the relationship due to the intense light that is being shone on their inner shadows. This is not done intentionally by the other twin soul; it is simply part of the reuniting with your twin soul and returning to wholeness or holiness. Both may refuse the call, renege on their vows, refuse to grow and evolve, which is tragic for both parties since you are really one. Most often but not always it tends to be the wounded male who rejects his female counterpart, because she brings with her the Divine Feminine's desire to heal and return to wholeness.

The Divine Feminine within both the male and female seeks to nurture, love, heal, unify and make whole all that it touches. So, it is no wonder that it has been all but eliminated from Earth's culture. Instead, imbalanced, dark masculine, tyrannical rule has dominated our planet. Competition, exploitation and degradation of the feminine gender and her principles have been the sad state of affairs that run the laws of business, banking, politics, sports, religion, et cetera, with a male Tyrannical God reigning supreme over all. Love, compassion, kindness, nurturing, and altruism have all too often been deemed weak and unnecessary. Even women who have wanted to "make it" in a male-dominated society have often had to shed these qualities to be deemed "professional" as we see all too often in the medical profession, legal and politcal arena. On the other hand, too many times, women have been made to believe that their only value in life is through marriage and childbearing. These two extremes, have created a great dichotomy, within the female psyche. To make matters worse, women have all but been eliminated from history. Except for short excerpts about women's evil and seductive ways, and how they brought about the ruin of many a good man, history rarely documents the female. Even the genocide of millions of women during the Spanish Inquisition has received little recognition. Only once did I see a place where women were so prominently mentioned in history. It was a museum for instruments of torture in Prague.

Throughout history, women have had absolutely no rights. They could not own property; they were property! They had no rights over their own children, and it was legal to rape, beat, torture, or even kill them. In many countries, female children are killed upon birth, sold into marriage, or collected in harems. The misogynous use and abuse of women on this planet has been criminal and continues to this day. Even in countries like the United States of America which is supposed to be based on freedom and justice for ALL, our precious "Declaration of Independence," states, "We hold these truths to be self-evident, that all MEN are created equal, that they are endowed by their Creator with certain unalienable Rights, that among these are Life, Liberty and the pursuit of Happiness.– That to secure these rights, Governments are instituted among MEN..." All MEN? Governments instituted by "MEN"? Perhaps that's the problem? But the worst part is that no one even seems to notice these Freudian slips of language because we are all so brainwashed to live in a masculine world. Language is so powerful as you know, it casts spells over us. In the English Language when referring to a person in the third person, it is grammatically correct to always refer to said person in the third person masculine. For example, "He sat reflecting on his situation." Even God is referred to as male and most women think nothing of it!

In most ancient Indiginous cultures, it was the older women, the wise women, the Crones, derived from the word crown, who wore the crown and were the leaders. They made the decisions guiding their communities. Especially the decision to go to war since they had the most to loose My spiritual teacher, who was a retired Sergeant in the U.S. military, told us once, "guys," he called everyone guys, "it's the men who got us into this mess and it's up to you woman, to get us out."

Fear is at the root of misogyny. This fear is held in place by mind-control programs implanted into both the male and female psyche. Some of these female programs have created spoiled, demanding Princesses, cold frigid Ice Queens, or the famous femme fatale, the dangerous man-eaters. Rita Haywood was so convincing in her femme fatale role when she sang the song, "*Put the Blame on Mame, Boys.*" And women have been getting the blame for everything since time began! To this day, in many countries, if a woman is caught having sex with a married man, she is the one stoned to death, not the man. Also too often rape is considered to be the fault of the woman for being so devilishly desirable. And of course, wo-men or "woe to men" are to blame for all the woes of the world because according to the Bible's false creation myth, Eve, or as we say in Italian, "Putana Eva"... Eve the Whore, was the cause of original sin which stained our souls forever. Eve, who can not be trusted because she listened to the serpent and dared to eat from the Tree of Knowledge , thus leading Adam and mankind astray. It is a wonder that any relationship between the two sexes can survive in this climate much less develop into loving, trusting, sexually intimate relationships!

First of all, the serpent is a symbol of the kundalini rising which occurs when an adept or spiritual seeker begins to awaken and raises this dormant serpent fire in the root chakra. Through the loving act of Sexual Alchemy, this sacred, sexual holy union awakens, heals, integrates, and enlightens both the male and female. But because of its power, it has been co-opted into an unholy union, polluted with feelings of shame, guilt and running the reverse caduceus frequencies. It has been downgraded into an act of lust or procreation and nothing more. Men and women are not only programmed to be fearful of having sex with one and other, but to be ashamed of their bodies and the sexual act.

In the Bible, two Marys were loved by Christ:one, his virgin mother and the other was Mary, the whore whom he saved from being stoned to death. In truth, the Yesheua 12's sacred spouse Sophia Maria Magdalene who was his spiritual and genetic twin soul was married to the wrong Christ Yeshua 9. I believe that Sophia Maria and Yeshua 12 did find a way to come together in a Sacred Sexual Alchemical Union, which activated their Krystic template. This is the role of twin souls. But the Church made her out to be a whore and, in her place, exalted the "Blessed Virgin." This sends the weaponized message out to men and women that sex is sinful, while celibacy is pure, good, and "holy," and "spiritual" beings do not have sex. This was created to usurp the Christos/Sophia holy alchemical union.

This message further sabotages this sacred union by creating the Puntana/ Madonna that infects most marriages to this day. It has bred an ancestral miasma passed down from generation to generation. In Italy, it is known as "Mammissmo". According to Telegraph News: "It is an Italian bond of love between a man and his mother that chokes romance, inhibits sex drive, and even has the power to slow the economy." They report that Cardinal Angelo Bagnasco, the archbishop of Genoa, warned that the phenomenon is "one of the biggest risks to marriage in the country today." According to "Living in Sicily" "*Mammismo* is now considered as a legal cause for the annulment of a marriage. The church approves annulments for this very reason, a reason that is increasing fast in Italy.Although it has always existed *Mammismo* got registered in the Italian vocabulary in 1992. It is defined as "a dependence and psychological pressure from the mother put on the son, or a psychological addiction from the parent that requires every choice and every move by the child to meet the approval of the parent who actually becomes psychologically the true spouse while the married person becomes a substitute, and causes much incapacity that burdens the marriage."

This is a curse where the male's distrust of the opposite sex leads him to only trust his "sainted mother" who indulges his every whim. This bond usurps any authority and position the wife may have in the family. As a result, the husband is married to his mother, and the real wife is shunned. This ancestral miasma repeats itself because the wife who lacks the love she craves from her husband seeks the love she so desperately needs from her son, thus, perpetuating the cycle. This may be apparent in Italy, but exists in all cultures. We may call it being a "Mama's Boy", but the results are the same. It often leads to men limiting women to two categories: sex objects for their personal gratification or child bearers of their progeny, all the while they keep their pure true love for their sainted mothers. Meanwhile, the daughters remain in the shadows never getting the love and recognition they need from their wounded mothers thus seeking it from their fathers. Doomed they repeat the same karmic cycles forced to choose between the lesser of two evils: the Madonna trap or the Putana curse!

This objectification by the parent occurs to both male and female children, who must supply the affection each parent is missing in their dysfunctional marriage. The daughter acts as the missing wife and the son as the emotionally absent husband. The freedom of self-exploration and self-discovery is lost as they struggle to please and heal their wounded parents, which they never can do. This breeds co-dependency and perpetuates the cycle until it can be healed. Both men and women lose from this sexual misery curse. Because most children never receive the love they so desperately need in order to feel enough, safe, worthy, seen, heard and cherished they seek this validation outside themselves. As they grow up they turn longings of unconditional love towards romance and the desire to find their perfect match, their "soul mate". Society of course reinforces this fairy tale version of "true love" making believe that just finding this magic person will heal all. If as a child you never received unconditional love and you can not give it to yourself, how can you give it to a partner? But we all expect our partners to have this unconditional love to give. Many who seek this"fairy tale" romance plummet into deep despair when the honey moon is over. Because they have been glamoured by this romantic illusion they are unprepared to roll up their sleeves and do the necessary inner work to create mature and lasting relationships. Despite what we have been taught your union with another is not about healing your partner but about healing yourself!It is always about you! This in turn will ultimately heal your partner since you are ONE! This is why you both chose to incarnate in 3D Earth School to learn about yourselves as separate entities.

If you are not physically with your twin soul or you have not yet "found" each other or you are separated through the illusion of time and space, do not worry! You have both created this sacred time and space so you can focus on your own inner work! Many of you have very important soul missions you have come to Earth to carry out together. But you both must be up to the task! More twin souls are coming together now during this ascension cycle and have agreed to clear the path for future generations by transmuting their own ancestral miasma, breaking cultural cruses and debunking sexual misery programming. These twin souls have agreed to become the embodiment of the sacred hierogamic union, to be role models for others. They are not here to simply, "talk the talk" but to "walk the walk", grounding each foorprint into the New Earth as the Divine Masculine and Divine Feminine working together as ONE.

I know many individuals deeply long for this twin soul union and grieve the lack of it. But you must realize the truth that everyone has a twin soul. Perhaps you think you have met your twin soul but you may have met your false twin, who came to prepare you for your true twin soul. My false twin soul's name was Simon. According to the Bible when the Apostle

Simon recognized the "Christ" energy his name was changed to Peter. As you embody the Christ energy you will recognize that you and your twin soul have and always will exist as ONE in and outside of time. Your love is eternal and like two rivers that eventually flow to the Sea, your twin soul is coming home to you. All twin souls reunite as they return home. As you rise in frequency you will realize the separation you feel is an illusion and the truth is your other half is, has been and will always be with you. You are ONE! So how could you ever be separated? Yes, in this world of illusion it may "seem" like you are but "things are never as they seem". As your frequency rises your illusion of separation will shatter!

Despite my love for Italy, I kept feeling something pulling me back to the States. Of course, I kept ignoring it, but it grew stronger every day. I didn't want to go. I missed three planes trying to leave Italy. Finally, fate took a hand and my girlfriend Jill, who had brought me to Italy in the first place, came to visit me. I begged her to take me to Rome and put me on the next plane home. She did and a few months later, I came to visit her in Miami, on my way to Hollywood to break into showbiz! It was there I finally met Peter, my twin soul. I was on my way to Hollywood, California seeking fame and fortune when I found my twin soul on "Hollywood Beach", Florida!

It was as if we were the only two people on the beach. I asked him if he had seen the dead shark that had washed up on the shore and he said no. So I took him over to examine it. I asked him what he did for a living and he told me he was a gynecologist. I asked him if he and his "friend" would like to come over to my place that evening for drinks. He told me his "friend" was his son. My jaw dropped and I asked him how old he was. He lied. I'm glad he lied, because if he had told me the truth I probably wouldn't have gone out with him. That night he took me, my best friend Jill, and her little sister out to dinner! He was so handsome, but what impressed me most was his kindness. He exuded a genuine concern for human beings. We wandered away from the crowd, stealing our first moments alone. We sat down in a small fishing boat and silently stared into each other's eyes. He met my gaze without hesitation which surprised me. We were searching for soul recognition. We were trying to remember who we were, and what we had meant to each other. Ten years later, Peter wrote these words about our meeting in our book *The Pathway Home*:

"It was in this manner that I met Elizabeth, my wife, ten years ago. I had just arrived in Florida and she was there for a few days, on her way to California. It was a chance encounter on a beach where we were brought together by the sight of a dead shark. I now realize the Universe was communicating to me through the symbol of a dead fish, representing the death of my own spirituality. This was indeed the state Elizabeth found me in. Until then, I had still been seeking spiritual answers within the confines of organized religion. I had even begun to doubt the existence of God because I could not reconcile my extraordinary experiences with the information I was being given by my religious teachers. Elizabeth was much different than anyone I had ever met. She had a strong dedication to God yet understood the limitations of organized religion. According to her, anything was possible through the individual's own connection with God. We argued constantly over spiritual matters, my lack of faith, and everything under the sun. How could two people be so different, yet be so much in love? Despite our arguments, we both knew at some level we had been together many lifetimes and had reunited to make the final journey Home. Charged with a higher purpose, we embarked on our spiritual journey and began the task of blending our energies."

I intuitively knew he was the One. But I was terrified! That hard external shell of protection, I had so carefully crafted around myself, was screaming for me to run, run, run away! But there he was, my soul mate, my twin soul, my other half standing in front of me! So, what did I do? I ran. I boarded a plane to Los Angeles. When I arrived in L.A., everything went South! I spent hours stuck in traffic singing, "Santa Monica Freeway sometimes makes a Kentucky girl bluuuue." I tried to get acting jobs and was offered porno scripts! Little did I know at the time that was the initiation of "breaking" onto Hollywood." But I refused to sell my body, my mind, or my soul. So doors never opened. I suppose I just found the "dues" too high to pay to "make it" in Hollywood. I may have failed to "make it" there but in truth, I had passed the test. The test of integrity and of my true dedication to Infinite God Source. I had found my reward not in Hollywood, California...but in "Hollywood" Beach, Florida!

I finally picked up the phone and called Peter. I hadn't wanted to call him until I was a rich and famous actress, but the doors kept slamming in my face, and all signs pointed to Peter. It was as if he was just waiting for my phone call. I asked him to come and visit me for my birthday. He said, "don't ask twice." So, I did and it was magic! He took me to all the places I loved, Del Mar, Mexico and Disney Land. As we were boarding the ride for space mountain, Peter asked me to move in with him. As we were being strapped into the rocket, I shouted, "I don't live with men!" And zoom, we were catapulted into space!

Peter had rescued me from Hollywood, and now it was my turn to rescue him back. But I had a deep intrinsic fear Peter would clip my wings as a fortune teller had once warned me. I had agreed to move in with Peter only after becoming a flight attendant for TWA so I could fly away from my Peter Pan whenever I wanted. But I was grounded when the entire TWA work force went on strike. Suddenly I was a scab. So refusing to cross the picket line, I returned to Peter in Miami. But the underlying truth was I was afraid of what Peter had ignited in me. Peter's true name was: Pedro Antonio Candelaria Rodriguez Ortis. Candelaria meaning "light bearer" which was the word that stood out most to me. We had both agreed to be lights in a world of great darkness, but that meant we had to shine the light on each others shadows first. Not always pleasant!

Finding your twin soul is not the fairy tale union many believe it to be. Yes, finding each other is a huge feat in and of itself, but then the real journey begins. You must learn to love each other unconditionally in order to come together in the sacred alchemical union of Hiero Gamos. Peter was a tall, dark, handsome latin lover, but when I found him, he was a broken man. He had married his first wife when he was too young to even sign the marriage certificate. He had been the epitome of an unfaithful "mujeriego" or womanizer. His second wife, was from a wealthy Jewish family, who had him sign a prenuptial agreement before the wedding. Peter used to say that he gave his second wife a green card into the US, three beautiful children, a home, and a respected position in society, then one day, she turned to him and said, "I rid myself of you." The extreme pain and suffering Peter experienced with his second wife broke his spirit and reopened in him his deep distrust of women. But I am grateful to her because if Peter had not had these hard lessons, he would still have been an arrogant, spoiled womanizer and our relationship would have never survived.

We fought daily, about everything under the sun. I was into yoga, herbs, and meditation; he was a practical man of science and traditional medicine. I was a flower child, a hippie; he was a rigid conservative. I took everything on faith, he needed to see physical proof for anything! One morning, I woke up to find money on the kitchen table with a note telling me to take the next plane home. I was so angry I wanted to! But something inside me just couldn't get on that plane and fly out of his life. It was like some cosmic karmic glue was binding us together.

My experiences with "Mammissmo" in Italy had not fully prepared me for Peter and his inseparable bond to his mother. One day, Peter told me, his mother had asked him to give her the wedding bands from his two previous marriages so she could melt them down to make a ring for herself. This statement struck a cord deep within Peter. I shared this with my mother, who had become a psychotherapist, and she cleverly said, "maybe Peter should have divorced his mother instead of all his wives?" Peter had no interest in spirituality and did not even believe in God! I felt that our relationship was doomed, but my mother suggested we seek counseling. Fate stepped in and we connected with a very creative and deeply spiritual woman. She recommended we read the book, *Siddhartha*, by Hermann Hesse. Peter and I took it with us to our secret getaway on the island of Captiva, Florida, where the pirate Gaspar would take his female Captives. This book opened Peter up to a new idea of spirituality and paved the way for many, many more books and experiences that heralded his awakening. However, the greatest impact on Peter's spiritual quest was Shirley McClain's movie, *Out on a Limb*. He realized that he had experienced many of the things depicted in the movie, especially an "out of body" experience. After that, his intellectual curiosity kicked in and he began reading everything he could on Magic, the Mystical Kabbalah, Numerology, Astral Projection, Western Mysticism, while I, on the other hand, studied Eastern Mysticism, practiced yoga, meditation, and worked with Crystals.

CHAPTER 9

THE TRUE CREATION STORY

As our Spiritual Journey together began to unfold, we felt the desire to leave Miami. We had gone on many short trips, being guided only by our intuition. On one such pilgrimage, I went alone to the Cherokee Reservation in North Carolina. I was recalling many of my past lives as a native American and felt drawn there. I was going to a spiritual retreat center I had read about located in the Blue Ridge Mountains, not far away from the reservation. It was growing quite late when I finally found the place. I was greeted by the groundskeeper, who told me the place was closed. I pleaded with him to let me stay the night, since it was late, and there was nowhere to stay for miles and miles of winding country back roads. He showed me to a room where I could sleep. Then we went into the living room and he handed me some "past life cards". He said, "no one is here to help you, but you might find what you came for by using these cards." I began to select cards that told me a story about one of my past lives. Detailed memories charged with emotions began to emerge. It was revealed to me that in my last life, I was a beautiful young Austrian girl who had committed suicide. I saw myself lying on the bottom of a bathtub, my clear blue eyes opened, having drowned. It was so real and I was so terrified. Then the guy told me to visualize something to heal it. So, I visualized my higher self-embracing my dead body and raising my spirit up out of it. I was surrounded by love and luminescent light that flooded into the bathroom, surrounding me and transporting me away.

That lifetime was during World War II. Peter had been a Nazi Doctor who experimented on Jewish women, and I had been his nurse. Peter had been killed by the American soldiers. I was lost without him. So I killed myself by overdosing on sleeping pills and falling asleep in a bathtub. I didn't realize it then, but this was to be a karmic pattern I had to break. It became clear to me now why I had felt compelled to visit the concentration camp of Dachau when I was in Germany and why Peter's Jewish wife had once had him incarcerated for not paying child support. While living in Hawaii a Jewish Friend had invited me to a meeting where all religions were honored. There was a holocaust survivor who told her story. Suddenly I became very emotional and started sobbing. I began apologizing to the woman and describing in great detail how difficult things were in Germany during the war and how we had been so afraid. The woman looked at me and said, "how old are you?" I had become so emotional I had forgotten the fact that I was recalling another lifetime and was currently in the body of a thirty-year old young woman! Everyone looked at me like I was crazy, so I stopped and smiled. In retrospect I should have just said I was a Buddhist, they believe in reincarnation!

On another trip Peter and I were guided to go to Arkansas and mine for crystals. We found some crystals that held transmissions which contained seeds of holographic information about the true history of our planet, and warnings about the E.T. groups that interfered with our Earth and caused massive destruction . In one of the crystal shops the shopkeeper called us into a back room and showed us a huge crystal that filled the room. She called it an Earth-Keeper. The energy it emitted was so strong I had a blinding headache and had to leave the room. I know now it was an initiation and activation. After that I was able to use crystals for healing and also tune into the holographic messages that had been inserted into them, before the fall of Atlantis about our true Earth's History.

Our spiritual growth became the center of our lives. Peter quit his job as an Obstetrician, and we were guided to move to the Canary Islands where Peter's father was born and he still had family. His family lent us an old cave house built into the side of a mountain and we dedicated our lives to the pursuit of esoteric knowledge. The Canary Islands are a beautiful and mystical place, and it was obvious to us that it was exactly what Edgar Cayce had described as the mountain tops of the sunken continent of Atlantis. The island was made up of jagged cliffs that jutted out of the water. We loved to snorkel the clear blue waters. Once, we saw a great stone road, that wound down the side of a mountain into the depths of the Ocean. Really, a road leading down a submerged mountain top? No one knew who had built the road nor what purpose it served. Another time, Peter told me he was going to snorkel into an underwater cave. Before I could say anything, he was gone. I waited for what seemed like an eternity. Finally, he emerged, out of breath and half dead. He recounted to me how he would have surely drowned because the suction of the water kept forcing him back into the underwater cave, but some powerful force from behind him pushed him out of the cave and to safety.

We visited a museum filled with remnants of an ancient race of people called the *Guanches*. They were tall, fair-haired people whose origins have never been explained. Many believe they were the original inhabitants of Atlantis. They are described as, "having a natural strength in body and soul, being courageous, intelligent, dignified, friendly, passionate and humble, traits that enabled them to face danger, survive calamities and befriend their enemies". Peter's father held these genetics, which he passed on to Peter. They had a great knowledge of surgery and science, yet only had primitive tools with which to live. This indicated clearly to me that the *Guanches* were survivors of the Atlantean cataclysmic deluge, and they had fled to the mountain tops, which were now the Canary Islands. It was becoming clear that Peter and I had been guided there to reawakened something deep asleep within us.

We had brought with us all our precious books, but they had been ruined by water that had leaked into this ancient house. This was pre internet so I began to go deeper into the holographic messages stored within the crystals. Among the multitudes of information stored, there were ancient warnings about alien intruders and their invasions. These transmissions explained how these invaders were assimilated into our culture pretending to be our friends and offering us assistance with their AI technology. As loving Christ Beings, we had never known malicious intent and could not believe that all races did not share our deep love for Creation and the Law of One. We welcomed these intruders into our lives and our hearts. But unbeknownst to us, their weaponized AI distorted our organic crystal consciousness technology that worked in harmony with our own divine inner technology and the Law of One. They disrupted the delicate balance of the masculine and feminine polarities on our planet and within us. I recalled a growing intuitive voice within me and the other women that warned us about the direction our masculine counterparts were embarking upon. Peter, always the scientist, became fascinated with

AI technology and he began working outside the realms of the Law of One and God's Natural Laws. He and other Atlantean scientists began creating abominations of hybrid animals and humans and augmenting the reversal polarities despite countless warnings from the High Council of Mu. I remember the agony of trying to warn people who would not listen. This was the same feeling I had in Nazi Germany and a theme that followed me throughout all my lifetimes.

Peter and I were also having our memories triggered by this strange place. We began to have many mystical experiences while in our cave home, not always pleasant ones. I dreamt I was my Ka or spirit that had left my mummified body in Egypt and had returned only to find that my grave had been desecrated and my body rotted. I realized that the teachings I had been fed as an adept in Egypt were all lies! I was flooded with painful memories of deception and betrayal. I became aware of having my memories stolen and my mind wiped and reprogrammed. It was terrifying! I was also recalling my past life as a great healer and was in the habit of laying crystals and stones on Peter and sending healing energy through his chakras. One day, I left Peter to sleep with the crystals in place. Shortly afterwards, Peter came into the kitchen very excited. He told me in great detail, how he had felt a powerful surge of energy rising from his groin, which moved to one side, then shot up his spine and out the top of his head. "Damn," I said, "You had a kundalini experience!" I was so jealous, because I had been trying so hard to have one. But it was Peter that needed this experience! Here he was, Dr. Peter, a man of science, who actually had felt first hand, in his own body, something that had never been discussed in all his medical books! He had experienced something that could not be explained by modern science. This experience had fully awakened him!

In our innocent explorations, we tried everything, including using an Ouija board. A word to the wise, never touch Ouija boards! They are encrypted with malevolent energies and portals to dark entities. When we were using it one night, we asked who the spirit was we were talking to and it spelled out the letters M-A-L-E. In Spanish that means evil. We had opened up some kind of portal of darkness and at that time we did not know how to close it. So, we packed up our things and left our cave home.

Throughout my travels, I have found that I have the uncanny ability to gain visions and impressions by visiting ancient sites. The memories of the trauma of Atlantis continued to surface as I visited areas around the world that had witnessed the Fall of these two great continents. I remember traveling back beyond Atlantis to Alania and being part of the Council of Mu. We had tried to stop the first growing imbalances of Alania that ultimately led to the first cataclysmic destruction of Tara that pulled us through a black hole and threw our planet into a lower harmonic universe and an Artifical time loop , causing us to replay the same destructive story time after time which most recently played itself out in the fall of the continents of Atlantis and Lemuria . When I visit these ancient sights I realized these ancient sights are portals that link these ancient times.

I had been charged many times with guarding the star gates, preserving the Emerald Records, and teaching the truth through the original Atlantean mystery schools. Somehow being in these places was bringing these ancient memories to the surface.

"And in a single day and night of misfortune all your warlike men sank into the earth, and the island of Atlantis, in like manner, disappeared in the depths of the sea."
PLATO

Yet, this is all that remained in the history books of Atlantis. I had seen with my own eyes proof of its existence, but why did our history books not speak of this? And why was I having nightmares about Egypt? Egypt had always been a disastrous place for me. Once, when Peter and I were visiting the Metropolitan Museum in New York City, I went to the Egyptian exhibition. When I touched the stones to see what impressions I received, there was a feeling of horror so powerful I ran away, fell down and twisted my ankle. Peter had to pick me up and carry me out of the Metropolitan Museum! I remember sobbing, telling him to get me the hell out of there! Yet, I had always wanted to travel to Egypt. I finally had the opportunity to go there when we lived in Cypress, but Peter would not come. I flew into Cairo on a day trip and separated from the tour. I rode a camel across the desert to the Great Pyramid. I had wanted to go into the Queen's Chamber, but when I arrived, the Queen's Chamber was mysteriously boarded up. So I went directly to the King's Chamber and began meditating. I had looked forward to this all my life, but it felt horrible! Terrible feelings grew within me as I tried to meditate. They continued to grow as I walked through the museum, looking at the ancient artifacts and mummies. I had flashbacks of memories about being part of a Satanic mind control ritual. I recalled being locked inside a sarcophagus, unable to breath, then being raised up out of the coffin into a blinding light repeatedly while being told to "follow the light". Ironically, I have always had claustrophobia and once as an actress, when I played the part of Lorraine Sheldon in "The Man Who Came to Dinner", I had to step into an Egyptian Sarcophagus and be carried off stage! I was terrified, but I did it!

When I returned to Cypress late that night, I broke into tears, unable to stop sobbing. A British gentleman looked down at me and said, "Stiff upper lip girl!" At that time, I did not understand my violent reactions. Years earlier, Peter, too, had become very upset after seeing the film, *The Egyptian*. It is a story about a physician who was seduced by a beautiful woman who tricks him into poisoning the Pharaoh Akhenaton and then fathers a son named Thoth. I had repeatedly asked my spiritual teacher about my deep emotional aversion towards Egypt, to which she always replied, "Egypt is where you lost your teachings." I never understood what she meant but felt some deep sense of guilt whenever she told me that. Yet there were ancient places we visited where I only felt loving, uplifting energy. These places were always dedicated to the Goddess of Love. There was Aphrodite's Beach on the Island of Cypress, supposedly the birthplace of the Goddess, where she rose from the Sea. I felt so much love there I wanted to carry away every stone on the beach! I had the same feeling when I visited the Temple of Venus in Erice, affectionately known as the City of Love, which resides above the clouds close to my Villa here in Sicily. I could not tear myself away. The energy was so loving. So why was I experiencing such contrasting feelings?

It was only after returning to Sicily and living near the ancient city of Segesta that I began to recall my past lives during the Golden Age of PreFall. Here in Sicily, like in the Canary Islands, we have groups of ancient people whose origins are unknown. The *Elymians*, were the most mysterious of Sicily's three ancient "indigenous" tribes. The word *Elymians*, is very similar to the word Elysium which is described as "the final resting place of the souls of heroes". It is also linked to the first race of Krystic Beings from the highest God Source Worlds. Peter and I were among those who experienced both the beauty and the horror of losing our golden age, our golden light bodies, and being conditioned to reincarnate through an ancient Egyptian ritual of trauma-based mind control programming, teaching us to "follow the light". It was in this way our souls became trapped in the tunnel of false light, which leads back into the prison matrix and the perpetual cycle of reincarnation. All our memories and knowledge were erased in Egypt. This is when we became trapped in the dream spell. Our souls were trying to awaken us! Peter and I were ready for the next step of our incredible journey together.

OUR TRUE HISTORY

In Greek Mythology, there is a famous myth, the story of Andromeda, about a beautiful young virgin who is to be sacrificed to the Kraken, a terrible Reptilian Sea Monster, to save her village. There is also the myth of Jason and his Argonauts, who journey to the far ends of the Earth to find the Golden Fleece. All these myths are deeply symbolic and hold keys to the true history of our planet and our true divine state. The sacrifice of Andromeda is referring to a time in our Earth's history when warring entities through the misuse and abuse of black "magic," or "dark" science, and AI technology ripped a black hole in the Andromeda Galaxy, severing our Milky Way Galaxy from our Mother Universe in Andromeda. Modern science has stated that our two galaxies are currently on a collision course. This is a sign of the auto-correction of our time matrix resetting itself to its true history in alignment with Infinite Source. We returning home to our divine place in the Multiverse. We are reuniting the fragmented pieces of our Earths. The Earths of the past, present and future are coming together. These fragments of Earth, Tara, Urtha, Gaia, Arura all exist in other dimensions and frequencies are coming back together. In Greek mythology, the Golden Fleece has the ability to heal and even "resurrect" the dead. So, as we return to our rightful place in the Cosmos we too are being resurrected from the dead, the anti-life anti-krystic reversals will fall away. As we ascend, we recover our "Golden Fleece" or our golden radiant plasma body of eternal creation. As we ascend into flash sequences of the higher frequencies,we reclaim our true Divine Infinite Human Being-ness.

The Human race was not cloned in a lab by some fallen angelics to serve as slaves! Divine Infinite Human Beings were created by our highly evolved parents, non-corporal Founder Races residing within the higher dimensions, as a corporal expression of themselves and the Infinite! We had all our multidimensional capabilities housed within our twelve-stranded genetic silicon-based light body. We were created by these exalted beings out of pure love with our own unique soul signature. We were not created to serve them, worship them, work for them, or make sacrifices to them. We were given the greatest gift of all--FREE WILL. This allowed us to freely express ourselves, create, play, live, love, learn, grow, and expand! They even gave us the freedom to fall and experience the lower densities, which is what we have done here on 3D Earth.

Your original Double Diamond Divine Kathara Template is referred to as being "Royal" and directly connects you with Infinite God Source via your genetics. The Emerald Founder Records or CDT plates were placed within your Royal Genetic DNA and hidden in and out of time. These holographic records hold the truth! The true organic historical timelines and genetic records of the root races seeded on Earth, Tara, and Gaia, the mechanics of Ascension and other forbidden knowledge that has been hidden from the human race. As you activate your 12 DNA strands you will begin to heal and regain your memory. Parallel universes, composed of fallen angelic alien entities from neighboring fallen Universes created a black hole in the center of the Andromeda Galaxy and entered our Universe and lowered the polarities of our world resulting in a genocidal campaign for committing the first Armageddon or Christos Human Holocaust. By attacking the Royal Houses and destroying the Star Gates, they severed the Milky Way Matrix from its Mother Universe in Andromeda within the higher harmonic universes. During the final stages of destruction, Tara and her planetary consciousness exploded into fragments and were pulled through a black hole, coming out the other side into the lowest creation realms of the underworld layers of the Milky Way system. The entirety of the planet Tara fragmented and all her species were pulled into the lower density of a fallen time matrix in a lower Harmonic Universe. Once there they reformed themselves into the pattern of our solar system and what we know today as the planet Earth. But before this Cataclysmic Event occurred, those who foresaw the current destructive course of Tara created the Sphere of Amenti by placing their consciousness in the center of Tara's to preserve her template and function as the fail-safe plan to be able to retrieve the lost souls of Tara and restore Tara to its rightful place in the Cosmos.

The aftermath of the destruction caused by the *Lyran* Wars resulted in the Milky Way time matrix further digressing into a Fallen Universe. These Galactic *Lyran* Wars spread to the constellation of Orion and through the Meta-Galactic Core, where the holographic inserts of polarity and duality were created by A.I. technology. As a result, our Royal Divine Genetics were downgraded, our memories erased, and mind control programs of fear-based archetypal patterning software were inserted, such as victim-victimizer. This agenda was a planned gradual takeover of our planetary field in which the magnetosphere would be controlled with artificial magnetic and gravitational anomalies, with the intent to be used as a global mind control device to collapse human consciousness into very low states so that our original DNA would remain unplugged. Over time humans were starved of their natural solar frequencies, oxygen, pure water and real food and their connection with nature. Their inner spirit and connection to Infinite God Source was ruptured. Then they were overlaid with the artificial reverse polarities and magnetism from the lunar forces thus, humanity fell into a deep slumber. A dream spell! While we were in this state of slumber and forced reincarnation, the fallen angelics and their controller bloodlines erased our history, destroyed our artifacts, all evidence of our prior history and changed our timelines. They brought in the moon and stole our advanced knowledge performing a great reset by erasing all global records.

The Founder races from the higher density God Source Worlds looked down upon humanity as loving parents with a deep concern for their fallen offspring. True, we had the right to experience the lower frequencies but because a false prison matrix and artificial time loop had been put into place history kept repeating itself and there was no hope of escape. They had closed off all exit points continuously tricking us from exiting their elaborate labyrinth. We Divine Infinite Humans beings were being forced to live in a finite existence over and over again, never growing, learning, expanding, and never being permitted to return home to Infinite God Source. Our free will was not being honored, and we were trapped in the lower densities serving only as food for the parasitic dark side to continuously feed upon. The Founder Races knew that they had to do something to free us from the time-loop prison matrix that had usurped our free will.

So many of these great ones from these Guardian Founder Races who so dearly loved their creations as only divine parents could, decided to step down the emanations of their original Cosmic densities to take on the form of the Krystos Avatars they had given birth to. They did this out of pure love as the ultimate sacrifice for their children. They descended into the fallen universes stepping themselves down into the lower densities and frequencies of duality to help their fallen Christos offspring to remember who they were and return home to their divinity. This became known as the "Christos Mission," a reconnaissance mission to restore human beings to their Divine Infinite Human, "Christos" status. They formed an alliance known as the "Guardian Alliance." They knew they had to wait for the final organic ascension cycle which we have now entered and have been preparing for "THAT /NOW" for eons. Throughout the dark eons they have sent in many "Krystos Avatars" to counteract the dark side's malevolent maneuvers of hijacking humanity. In truth, Earth's history, has been one long ongoing war over genetics, consciousness, frequncies and timelines.

Since our original fall from our Mother Universe in Andromeda, we have been stuck in a time loop repeating the same cataclysmic events over and over and over, halting our ascension back into the God Source Home Worlds. We have been held hostage by "Chronos," the Time Keeper in an artificially generated AI prison matrix of false timelines. We keep repeating the same galactic year over and over. Every time we reach our exit point the time of ascension, stellar activation and our moment of freedom and return to our rightful place in the Cosmos, instead of escaping the prison, "history repeats itself." We miss our exit point, remaining entrapped in the lower frequencies of slavery and forgetfulness. We go to sleep once again inside the dream spell.

THE ATLANTEAN CONSPIRACY

Right before the Atlantan Flood, the "Luciferian/Thothian" Snake Brotherhoods made a secret pact called the Luciferian Covenant for the eventual goal of ruling over all of humanity and the earth. This was a long-term plan which was to be implemented over thousands of years while waiting for the culmination of the earth's procession of the Equinox in the 2012 timeline and beyond. The mission was to take full possession of the earth's surface during the pinnacle of the Ascension Cycle. These Alien Anunnaki, Thothian, Satanic, Luciferian factions infiltrated the Lemurian and Atlantan cultures, polarizing the masculine and feminine energies, creating division and war between the two continents. They used their A.I. technology to contaminate the Grids and the divine crystal technology of Atlantis that functioned in harmony with God's Natural Laws and the Law of One. They created imbalances, causing the poles to shift and the sinking of both the continents of Lemuria and the Atlantis.

ATLANTEAN MYSTERY SCHOOLS

Many Krystos Beings or "Avatars" who retained their true twelve-stranded DNA chose to remain after the fall of Atlantis. They were entrusted with the tasks of guarding the Holy Grails or star gates and persevering Earth templates or ley lines and protecting the Emerald Founder Records. The information of the Emerald Records was contained within their DNA but also recorded on twelve holographic discs and scrolls hidden around our planet. These discs contained the ancient knowledge that existed before the Atlantean Flood. They also included humanity's cosmic genetic origins, true history, ascension timelines, ascension mechanics, consciousness alchemical formulas, DNA genetic key codes, that corresponded to each particular star gate and tribal shield and much more. Many of these Krystos Avatars who retained their higher genetics became what was known as the Celtic-Druid Magi-Grail Lines. Their missions were to guard the holy grails or star gates, and preserve and secretly share this "esoteric" knowledge with their initiates through the

True Atlantean Mystery Schools. The great Library of Alexandria in Egypt was the last significant library on earth that acted as the repository for these manuscripts that held the truth copied directly from the Emerald Founder Records. When the ancient Library of Alexandria was burnt by Alexander the Great, all this knowledge was stolen, and now resides within the vaults of the Vatican. Alexander continued his conquest towards India, intending to destroy the great wealth of ancient texts stored there, but due to the power of the elephants, the great Ganesh, his great armies were blocked, and India was spared. This explains why India still retains remnants of the ancient texts containing information about aliens, reincarnation, and ascension mechanics. This is why it has been considered the Holy Land and has a long history of Gurus imparting esoteric knowledge to their disciples.

ENKI, THOTH, LUCIFER, AND THE EMERALD TABLETS

Enki, Thoth and Lucifer are some of the names of the fallen angelic being who became corrupted by the misuse of his free will, fueled by pride and a lust for personal power. I already told you the story of Enki, the first "god" of Sumeria, which is another name for the entity known as Thoth or Lucifer, the fallen angel. He has been playing the role of double agent for many eons. Thoth was revered and respected by the angelic Infinite Humans Beings for many years as he worked with the Krystos mission to help bring more fallen Angelics back into harmony with Infinite Source, but unbeknownst to them Thoth defected to the dark side and betrayed the angelic humans.

This story continued to repeat itself through out history as the Thoth/Enki and Enlil Annunaki leviathan groups hunted out the Krystos angelic humans and raided their communities. They slaughtered the men, raped the women and stole their ancient manuscripts. This is fully revealed during the Essenes Massacre by the by the "Luciferian" Knights Templar. They took the female Essenes who held the twelve-stranded genetics to Nibiru for forced breeding to create the Anunnaki hybrid race to turn the true Twelve Tribes of the Magi Grail line into the Thirteen Luciferian bloodlines by inter breeding. This was repeated with the Cathors and every Krystos Magi Grail line race. Until all Krystic cultures had been invaded and their genetics compromised. This occurred to the true Isrealites, the

Ionian and Italic cultures of Greece. The Etruscan communities of Italy. The Celtic communities of Ireland, Wales, and Scotland. And before that to Brittian when it was raided by the Nomands, Vikings and Saxons. It continued on when the Spaniards brought their inquisition to the Americas and the Europeans caused the Native American Genocide. The men were killed, the women raped and their sacred texts and artifacts confiscated. Thoth and his armies stole these Emerald Records and repackaged the information to create worldwide "re-legions" as a control mechanism to serve their dark agenda. Essentially, he took the Truth from the Founder Records and weaponized them into half-truths and lies into what has become our modern day Bible. Furthermore, they installed their pyramidal hierarchy to control these religious organizations. Then these controllers set themselves up to be the capstone monarch at the top of the pyramid and to be worshipped as the "one true god." From this position, they could embed mind control mechanisms and pick and choose what human groups were being most compliant to serve them from the hybrid bloodlines. Then, they would give them access to the higher levels of "esoteric" knowledge through their secret societies and recruit from within these shadow organizations. Meanwhile, the "masses" of the genetic undesirables would be dumbed down into the slave class, further generating division and degenerating their DNA, creating a Master-Slave hierarchy. Thus, the Brotherhood of the Snake secretly and methodically infiltrated the Atlantean Mystery Schools and robbed the Great Libraries in order to steal all of the knowledge for themselves, intentionally confiscating the records in their planned takeover of the Earth by using this knowledge as a consciousness trap and weapon against humanity.

THE EGYPTIAN PRIEST HERMES

After stealing the Emerald Records that held the Truth, and down grading our DNA so we forgot who we were then resetting our history through the carefully orchestrated Great Flood of Atlantis Enki, Thoth or Hermes incarnated as an Egyptian Priest repeatedly during the time that the Mystery Schools were flourishing in Ancient Egyptian culture. This was in order to perpetuate the Atlantean conspiracy and keep close tabs on what was going on in the Guardian Alliance Mission that Hatshepsut,

Akhenaton, and other Krystos Avatars were carrying out. Thoth, the great Luciferian, tricked the unaware people of Egypt into believing he was blessed by the Gods. He indeed did appear God-like because he knew the secrets of alchemy, performed magical feats and promoted himself as sanctified and divine while committing heinous crimes against humanity. He declared himself as the sole scribe or SPEAKER for God and was entrusted to translate the ancient wisdom and mathematical language contained in the "Founder Records." As a result, he falsified recorded history and sacred writings into *The Book of the Dead*. He promoted himself as the God of the Underworld who judges souls by weighing the heart of the deceased. He alone held the power to decide if that soul was worthy or not to enter heaven. Because Thoth is a fallen entity, he is not eternal but has achieved immortality in the lower dimensions through the use of taking loosh energy from blood sacrifices.

Akhenaton was informed of Thoth's true allegiance and the purpose behind establishing the Egyptian Pantheon based upon spreading black magic for feeding blood sacrifices and loosh into the ley lines and grids of our planet. Thus, when he became Pharaoh, he abolished idol worship and sacrificial practices, intending to dismantle the Amen priesthood in an attempt to steer the kingdom back toward the ancient spirituality of the Law of One that was practiced before the Atlantean Flood. But Thoth caught wind and had him murdered and all that he had influenced in the Egyptian culture was intentionally annihilated by Thothian groups. The cult of Thoth continued to grow and thrive in its place.

Thoth is a master at using the Truth to tell lies. He is the Father of All Lies, which is a primary feature of Luciferianism. He promoted superstition and ignorance through organized religion to hijack angelic humanity's divine birthright of ascension. He removed all knowledge of our inner Christ ascension mechanics used to transmute our carbon bodies, activate our twelve-stranded silicon based genetic matrix and our double diamond rainbow plasma body into a fantasy about humans being miserable unworthy "sinners" who must cleanse their sins through blood sacrifice rituals and wait for a savior, the only Son of God, to return. Thoth set himself up as the intermediary through which humans would be forced to go in order to gain access to any ancient knowledge which gave way to the priest class. Thoth falsified and polarized teachings of Hermeticism into Luciferian elitism. He distorted the True Twelve Sephiroth Tree of Life into the Ten Sephiroth Tree of Death. He inverted all open infinite architecture of the true Sacred Geometry into distorted finite prison matrixes of the Fibonacci spiral of death, the false flower of life or bloom of doom, the vesica piscis harness of duality and the Metratonic Cube. Thoth distorted the truth of the Emerald Records, and released it under the guise of the Emerald Tablets.

THE EMERALD TABLETS

The Emerald Tablets, also known as the *Tabula Smaragdina*, were highly regarded by European alchemists and were the foundation of the Esoteric Renaissance, whose purpose was to bring the spark of divine God Source back to humanity through the birth of humanism. This inspired great artists and writers to depict the human as "godlike" in both Art and literature.

"What a piece of work is a man! How noble in Reason, how infinite in faculty! In form and moving how express and admirable! In action how like an Angel! In apprehension how like a god! The beauty of the world! The paragon of animals!"
WILLIAM SHAKESPEARE

Marsilio Ficino, a man of my own heart...(and soul. hint hint) was a humanist and philosopher who translated Plato and was also commissioned to translate the Emerald Tablets found in Egypt by the powerful Medici Family. This information was used to misdirect the course of Alchemy, the Platonic Schools, and other esoteric societies to further embroil the initiates into creating a false ascension matrix, which gave way to the "New Age" Spiritual movement. I wrote an article several years ago for the Florence Newspaper entitled, "Is the New Age Really the Old Age?" Although Hermes Trismegistus or "Hermes Thrice Great" is the author named in a book taken from earlier Egyptian scrolls, Hermes, or Mercury was another co-opted name used for the Egyptian "god" Thoth, alias Enki, alias Lucifer! Hermes is also associated with the caduceus reversal of the two intertwining serpents around a staff with wings, which runs reverse caduceus frequencies. The highest spiritual meaning of the true Caduceus is the rising kundalini which carries one into a state of enlightenment, when properly activated. But it has been hijacked into running descending kundalini serpent fire energy using the False Caduceus Asclepius Rod, which is an AI network installation now associated with modern medicine.

The Emerald Tablets have also been associated with conjuring spirits, animating statues, and turning the practice of true alchemy into black magic. These misdirections have found their way into the "new age". These imposters of the True Emerald Order have been communicating with earth humans often masquerading as "ascended masters" or "benevolent" aliens via false changelings, image projection, holographic inserts, Voice of God technology, or other A.I. technology used to further hijack the awakening of Star seeds and lead them into a False New Age ascension matrix.

LUCIFERIANS AND PALTERING

Paltering is when someone uses bits of the truth to tell lies such as incorporating fragments of truth to promote a large mass awakening that ultimately leads those awakening back into the same age-old consciousness traps. Paltering is the method that narcissists and lying psychopaths use to help themselves maintain an honest, trustworthy image with a good reputation while committing mass deceptions and telling bald-faced lies from the podium, pulpit, or media platforms. They have invented and perfected this lying technique throughout the ages. Paltering is about misleading people with truthful statements, so they perceive something inaccurately. It is also used to cover up evidence contrary to the narrative being told. Luciferians are master liars, who frequently use paltering techniques to mislead people by not telling the whole truth or allowing people to wrongly interpret what has been incorrectly said to point them in the wrong direction, literally or metaphorically, in order to take advantage of them. In short, they are masters at SCAMMING you.

THE COUNCIL OF NICAEA AND THE ESSENE MANUSCRIPTS

The Council of Nicaea is the first recorded worldwide council of the Christian Church in 325AD, which took place in Turkey and was presided over by Emperor Constantine. History would tell us that the purpose of the Council of Nicaea was to create statements and canons of doctrinal belief with the intent to define what would become fundamental Christian beliefs, establishing the Nicene Creed. The oldest version of this copy from the Nicaean timeline is the Codex Vaticanus which is the oldest Greek manuscript of the New Testament that has been in the Vatican Library for centuries. Those manuscripts would eventually form the books that would later become the Canonized Bible. The Bible would then be used for the political motivations of governments and organized religion to continue to enforce these partial truths, lies and patriarchal beliefs set forth by Enki/ Thoth/ Lucifer and the Anunnaki False Gods worldwide, under the guise of uniting the Christian Churches through a written doctrine ordained by "god".

Thus, the original content of the earliest translations of the handwritten manuscripts directly translated by Yeshua 12, the true Christ, and stolen from the Essenes, were repackaged to serve as a weapon to support the Thothian /Luciferians' genocidal agendas. The Druid-Celtic Magi Grail Bloodlines from the original twelve-stranded Grail Kings and Queens were forced to go into hiding. Their true knowledge was hidden and continued to be passed on in secret, to the Cathar sects, until the Cathars were massacred by Pope "Innocent" III. Some of those remaining records were recorded in the Nag Hammadi scriptures unearthed in 1945, to which the public has only been given limited access to partial information.

The Draconian leadership that infiltrated the Church of Rome set into motion the ongoing basis for the dogma that would be used for human torture and blood sacrifices made in the name of God. This resulted in the Inquisition and the countless wars waged in the name of "Jesus" and his father the "one true god"! The manuscripts that were in possession of the Church were embellished with an assortment of falsities, biases, and crucifixion implants engineered to push forward the narrative of their violent religion based on the blood sacrifice of Christ. Throughout history, there have been inexpressible amounts of edits, omissions, and revisions made from the translations of these original manuscripts that have been repeatedly copied from Hebrew, Aramaic, Latin, and Greek into an assortment of languages and varied interpretations.

Finally, after the many long years of murderous crusades and inquisitions to eradicate all truth and those who knew it, King James commissioned a team of scholars to work on the English translation of the Christian Bible for the Church of England in 1604. This translation continued the Church of Rome's influence in enforcing the salvationist beliefs of blood sacrifice through Christ's crucifixion as required for cleansing the sins of humanity and fulfilling this purpose as being the reason behind the existence of Christianity. By the first half of the 18th century, the authorized version of the King James Bible had become effectively unchallenged as the English translation used in Anglican and English Protestant churches. At the beginning of the 19th century, this version of the Bible became the most widely printed book in history. This led to the common people having access for the first time to read the Bible themselves. Previously the only way to access the contents of the Bible was through a Church official who would interpret the meaning to his illiterate congregation.

Today, there are hundreds of versions of the Bible in the English language and translations into over 2000 languages, in which every individual and congregation has their personal belief that their revised bible translation is the most accurate and truthful, containing words they consider to be directly from God! Thus, these "Words OF God," "spelled" out in the "Holy" Bible, contain not only coding from the pure frequency of the original Emerald Record holographic discs, but also contain an extremely clever mixture of truths used to tell lies, in order to make the comprehension of the actual content as confusing as possible to the reader.

The Old Testament describes actual technological events in our history used to terrorize humanity. These are presented under the premise that these destructive and horrifying events happened as the result of the "Wrath of God" made against the "sinners" of earth. In short we are bad children of "god" and deserve to be terrorized if we do not do what "God the Almighty" tells us to. Many humans connect to Bible stories from the deep unconscious memories of the trauma of these tragic events that occurred in our hidden history. These words activate our subconscious collective racial memories of the attack and fall of the Angelic Christos Infinite Human Race into a fallen universe and the holocaust that followed from a place of guilt. This guilt complex creates a feeling that it was our "fault" that we fell and "god" abandoned us because we were bad. These written words, these spells serve as triggers that activate our cellular memories buried deep within the subconscious of the human soul that connect us to those previous timelines. This is our subconscious knowledge that our earth has suffered from a tragic cataclysm, flood and subsequent invasions of off-world cultures which activates our fear trauma based mind control programming thus enabling humanity to be easily controlled because they are reacting from a subconscious fear and guilt complex that has not been healed. So these trigger "words" act as swords used by our handlers to activate our trauma based victim programming created by an alien imposter, posing as the one "true god" and reinforced with horrifying images of fire and brimstone, the punishment of hell, along with mentally rigid mind control dogma. This is how earth's population has been mind-controlled throughout history causing humans to submit out of fear of "angering the gods"to a vengeful imposter god or the living representatives of "god" here on Earth.

CHAPTER 10

ONE WORLD ORDER

We have been conditioned by religion to believe we are inherently evil poor miserablesinners , incapable of self-governing ourselves; therefore, we must look to people , institutions and systems outside of ourselves to "govern" us, lest our inherent evil nature leads us astray. We have been taught that those who hold wealth and power are worthy of our trust, loyalty and obedience and that they are the representatives of "God" here on earth. That their orders should be followed with unwavering devotion even if it may cost us our own lives. We are taught from birth that those of the "upper class" with good breeding are our betters, our genetic superiors, the Lords and Ladies that preside over us. We have been brainwashed into believing wealth and power are more important than love and compassion. That a person's words are more important than their deeds. That the "Elites" who possess money, and position have our best interests at heart and their power should never be questioned. The truth is there is nothing elite about these illuminati families, these imposter gods, and their psychopathic children. They are simply dysfunctional mafioso families, not gods! In fact, they are the farthest thing from God or Divine Infinite God Source! Every child born into an Illuminati family undergoes Satanic Ritual Abuse. This means they have been sodomized, tortured, mind controlled and are possessed by demonic entities. The more powerful the illuminati figure, the more powerful the demonic entity that possesses them. There is nothing noble about the "nobility" nor their families. If you dig deeply into the history of most "royal" families, it reads like a godfather novel, with tales of fratricide, patricide, matricide, sororicide and genocide. The ruling class of today are usurpers of the true nobility! They have sought out and murdered the true grail lines and taken their place. They have stolen their sacred ascension mechanics and inverted them into satanic rituals to prolong their life and extend their supernatural powers. They are demonic abominations of God's Natural Laws, void of any sense of morality, integrity, justice, compassion or dignity. We who are awaking are the true Royalty of the Magi Grail lines! We are the ELITES!

Greek Mythology is filled with stories about the "Gods" being lustful, vengeful, jealous, bloodthirsty families constantly warring among themselves. Chronos, who was a Titan, and the father of Zeus, ate his own children to stop them from rising up against him. But Zeus was spared by his mother who fed Chronos a stone instead. As predicted Zeus rose up against his father and cut him open freeing his brothers and sisters. After the younger gods, (the children) overthrew the older gods (their parents), Zeus with his brothers and sisters reigned supreme in the heavens and used Mount Olympus as their earthly abode. These stories about the "gods" and their violence and lust for human women are recounted over and over in ancient myths depicting Zeus's infidelities and how he and the other gods raped and impregnated "mortal" women with their seed creating a race of Demi Gods.

ANUNNAKI HYBRID FALLEN ANGELICS

These are not "gods" but alien invaders who murdered the true Royal Maji Grail Krystos Bloodlines, stole their royal DNA through body snatching, cloning and forced breeding programs set up on Nibiru, and through their leviathan invasions into every race on our Earth they created an Anunnaki Hybrid race of fallen angelic "demi-gods" to serve as their representatives here on Earth. These are shapeshifting, inter dimensional, shadow entities, some from parallel universes, that inhabit organic puppet bodies or AI drone bodies, designed to carry out a particular job in the hive mind collective of their civilizations. Their job and tasks serve the collective hive mind to which they have been directly assigned based on their recorded history and memory retention from multiple lifetimes. Only those considered royalty at the top of their hierarchy are allowed to have a humanoid five-star body that is based upon the stolen diamond sun DNA that they are able to reasonably re-construct by a Frankenstein hybridizing of the Ruby Sun DNA. To call an entity who inhabits these human-looking bodies royalty is incorrect. These are the false rulers represented in Sumerian artefacts, created by performing an artificial genetic bond transfer in a laboratory, which then requires consuming the essence of living human souls to maintain their lifespan. This requires blood drinking and cannibalism of human beings to consume the living essence in order to ensure their lifespan.

Thus, through gradual stages of nelphim alien invasions, these non-human forces began to insert themselves as Babylonian Kings, Egyptian Pharaohs, Europen Monarchs and Captains of Industry. These same bloodlines are highly venerated today in the power pyramid of hierarchical control that has been weaponized against humanity by the power elite. These groups aided by the invaders inserted themselves falsely as the declared rightful Kings and Rulers of contemporary times, believing themselves genetically elite. Many in the power elite falsely claim to be genetically connected to the Celtic-Druid Grail lineages in which they perverted this knowledge to intentionally enslave and dehumanize the global population. Instead, they are from the lineage of the Fallen Annunaki Leviathan invaders inhabiting human bodies and pretending to be the authentic royal bloodlines of the Maji Grail Kings. But they are impostors.

Thus, for eons in order to maintain their power and control as these great imposters, they defiled the Divine Feminine Kristos-Sophia energy to hijack her secrets of immortality attempting to recreate "eternal" life through perverting the *"Divine Aether"* into satanic rituals. In their desperate quest to preserve physical health and longevity they sought to cheat death and achieve immortality no matter how depraved their actions. They stole all Essene "gnostic" knowledge and perverted the "Great Work" of transmutation into inverted satanic blood rituals. Their Luciferian Knights Templar justified their countless blood sacrifices as a stage of the 'Great Work 'for consciousness evolution in which the initiate must massacre the innocents, in order to gain the energy mass from their harvested souls that would be necessary to become immortal and free themselves of the earthly burdens of reincarnation.

These are the Annunaki Hybrids, that make up the thirteen Luciferian bloodlines of the illuminati families who are servants of the Dark Lords obediently pushing forward the One World Order of the Fallen Angelic Conquest, with no regard for human life nor free will. Over the years, these bloodlines have further digressed into full blown Satanic bloodlines, of cold hearted, violent, lustful, and blood thirsty families. Some of their depraved practices have reverted to consuming white powder of monatomic gold and the adrenochrome harvest from the blood sacrifice of children as their anti-Krystic tools used to prop up their energy bodies for attempted immortality as they descended deeper into criminality, perversions and psychopathy. This, combined with their incessant inter breeding has created a race of deranged psychopaths and sexual deviants. Aleister Crowley is a prime example of what lurks behind the polished veneer of these "elite" Illuminati mafioso family's facades.

As the false"demi-gods" or Annunaki hybrids conquered and infiltrated the lineages over time becoming the ruling class: The Priests, the Pharaohs, the Caesars, the Czars, the Kings, the Queens, the Emperors, the Aristocracy of the world. As the true bloodlines were forced underground, these false "blue" bloodlines of stolen hybridized DNA began to populate the European royalty, the Presidents of the United States and other ultra-rich "bankster" and business mogul families of today. They claimed to possess the "Divine Right of Kings". A political doctrine in defense of monarchical absolutism, which asserted that kings derived their authority from God to rule over people and could not therefore be held accountable for their actions by any earthly authority. This stems from a specific metaphysical framework in which a "Monarch" is, before birth, preordained to inherit the crown." It is interesting that "Monarch" trauma-based mind control is based on the premise that memories and mind control is passed down genetically from one generation to the next and that those subjects born into abusive families make the best mind control slaves.

During the French Revolution, when people grew tired of the obvious tyrannical rule of the aristocracy, they rebelled in a bloody revolt. But the bloodlines simply went underground assuming identities as regular "citizens" while the more unfortunate aristocratic scape goats , were sacrificed in blood baths of loosh. So they "cut off the heads" of the multi headed hydra, only to have another one grow back in its place. As you can see nothing has changed. The same bloodlines continued their control over Earth, posing as regular folks hidden in all races, religions and classes. Don't be fooled by these rags to riches stories of a black man becoming president, a royal marrying a commoner or a nobody rising through the ranks to become a rich elite or powerful world leader. If you dig deep enough into their pedigree, you will find all the power leads back to these thirteen bloodlines! So bloody revolutions are never the answer.

Within the hierarchy of power there are families that are not well known though out history, while there are others who have remain hidden, and are the black hand of real power within the shrouds of secrecy. This is why going after the "cabal" or the obvious mafia front families, is just another attempt at cutting off the head of a multi headed hydra. You cut off one head and another grows back in its place. In truth the real multi headed serpents behind these "cabal" families are exactly that serpents or the Reptilian Over Lords. So unless you can strike at the heart of the multi headed serpent and eliminate the root cause of this infestation, which has infected our earth for eons, you are simply being distracted by heads rolling. Many of us may see the downfall of some of these usurpers and the restoration of the true divine grail linages in our lifetime. But don't give your precious energy to revenge. Make no mistake, these usurpers will have to pay their karmic debt.

If you look carefully with aware eyes, you can see that the true history of our planet has been a history of warring parallel universes to gain control over not only our planet but our entire time matrix. It is the same war that began over 260 billion years ago when our time matrix became infected by parallae universe parisites who initiated the war between the Elohim Anu and the Draconian races of star gate 10 and star gate 11. This drama has been playing itself out with Earth a key strategic point. The parasites have been warring over the energetic templar or grid template of our planet, to gain control of our star gates and of our entire time matrix.

During the last golden age of Atlantis before the "Fall" of Atlantis the true royals or rulers at that time did not rule over people because they believed all human beings to be God Sovereign Free. Instead, they served as Guardians of our Mother Earth and protectors of the holy grails or Star Gates, inter-dimensional consciousness portals linking us to the higher dimensions and the templates or the leylines of the energetic grid network of our Earth. They were the true Templars assigned to guard our Earth's Template. Earth's star gates could only be accessed by the Krystic tribes who held the proper DNA coding for each particular star gate.

Throughout history, fallen Annunaki Leviathan hybrid warriors have conquered every civilization, killing the men and raping the women to gain access to the genetic coding that ran the star gates and ley lines of our planet. In Ancient Egypt through murderous plots the controllers took over positions of power, then incarnated as powerful Greek leaders as its culture conquered the world, then into the Ceasars of ancient Rome and the Royalty of the British Empire where the sun never sets. As the British Empire expanded every indigenous culture they came into contact with was all but exterminated. These indigenous tribes were slaughtered in the name of "god" by war or if that didn't work, they were exterminated by germ warfare. In the United States alone, the Native American population was all but wiped out, by the Rockefeller family's generous donation of small pox infected blankets traded for their land to the freezing Indians. For those who still think that these rich and powerful families would never carry out a genocidal plan to reduce the population, history proves otherwise. There have been far more human holocausts than recorded in the history books. The Kurds, the Armenians, the Native Americans, the Aborigines, the Tribes of Africa to name only a few. In short the ancient indigenous, people who knew the true history of our Earth and who held historical documents, artifacts and the higher genetics have all but been wiped out or raped to pollute their raceline. What many people fail to realize, is that the true Jewish people are also a Krystic race, who retained the higher genetics and much of the knowledge of Earth's true history which was passed down through the female line. They were chased out by the false tribes of Israel recorded in the Bible. These bloodlines migrated to Ireland and Scotland and became known as the Celtic Druid Magi Grail bloodlines. During World War II the last of the true Jewish Linage was all but eliminated and the Rothschild Zionist Party replaced them with their false Anunnaki Hybrids to fund the One World Order Agenda.

Humanity has stood back and watched while innocent people have been massacred and forced to flee their homelands by wars orchestrated by these "elite" mafia families. We have seen racism and poverty, the silent killer, starve people within our own societies. It has been happening all around us, throughout the ages. But those privileged, in society refuse to SEE. Why? Because they always believed it could never happen to them?

Because genocide, is only something that happens to people of color, to poor people, in poor countries, to those unfortunates, not here in the first world? Now the influx of immigrants from these war torn countries are flooding the first-world countries and destroying them. We are all ONE, deeply interconnected. What affects the One affects US ALL.

Many of you have learned to navigate the system. You have gone to the right schools, acquired the right degrees, paid your dues, made wise investments, and become successful. You are valuable contributors to the system. Therefore, it is unthinkable for you to believe that these institutions you supported, these world leaders you "elected", these celebrities you trusted, these royals you fawned over could have anything but the best interest of humanity at heart. Yet, if you were to be honest with yourself, you must confess that throughout your career, your life experiences, your efforts to make this world a better place have often been derailed by an ever present negative force. Most good folks just chalk it up to "the system". They never really go any deeper. They never explore why the funding for that project was cut, that proposal was rejected, or that law was imposed and the good fight was lost. Why in our broken system do the rich continue to get richer and the poor poorer? Why is there always enough money to bomb innocent children but never enough to feed them? People never dig deeper to find out why their taxes get higher, and their pensions get smaller. They never dig deeper to SEE where their tax money actually goes and for what purpose? Many Americans have never even noticed how little of their money goes to fund their Military which serves as the One World Order Army of tyrannical control.

In the United States, supposedly one of the wealthiest nations on Earth, children go to bed hungry, families are homeless and poor people die in the streets or in hospital waiting rooms for lack of health care. The system is not broken, it was created broken by these One World Order Illuminati Families! It is high time to stop trusting your government and those in power! How many scams do you need to SEE exposing the corruption of your leaders? How many times do you need to hear how these sexually, deviant psychopaths have stolen from your cookie jar, squandered your social security? These people are not to be revered, envied worshipped, obeyed or trusted! God should not save the Queen! They are usurpers of

OUR Planet, One World Order puppets serving the Fallen Angelics Dark Agenda their Archon "Lords" who enslave "We the People". They have sold you out! They are the bad copy. You are the original! The solutions are not coming from within these broken finite systems nor those who are in power. Those in power are not going to destroy the system that put them into power! They are not going to bite the hand that feeds them! The solutions are going to come from you and me! From those who have the courage to exit the broken system and do things differently by creating counter-cultures that live in harmony with the Law of One.

HOW DO THE FEW CONTROL THE MANY? WHAT IS THEIR MAIN INSTRUMENT OF ENSLAVEMENT?

"Money, money, money it's a rich man's world!" Have you ever heard the expression "follow the money"? It is true that if you follow the money, you can clearly see who controls our planet. You have heard that "money is the root of all evil"? In truth money is simply energy. But our current "money" system like everything on Earth, has been hijacked into a finite economy based on scarcity, where one percent of the population controls all the wealth, and the rest of humanity are slaves. Our current monetary system has been put into place with the intention to enslave humanity. So, in a sense, our current money system IS the root of all evil. Through perception deception, assassinations, and the Art of Usury, humanity is held hostage in a debtor's prison, where money is fabricated out of thin air and the illusion of scarcity has replaced the true abundant nature of the Infinite Multiverse.

Throughout history, slavery has been part of every civilization. Today, the chains that bind us all are the invisible chains of the Babylonian black money magic system. Ancient Sumeria, where "recorded" history began, was where the lust for gold was genetically engineered into the human. As a result, gold has been found buried all over the planet, in the tombs of Kings, Pharaohs, and Emperors since ancient times. The Conquistador's drive for gold led them to march through Mexico, leaving a bloody trail behind them. The California gold rush was provoked by "gold fever." Even to this day 24 carat golden toilets adorn the homes of the rich and famous. The gold standard was instilled in us by the "gods" to keep us seeking this "fool's gold" outside of ourselves. Yes, there is a pot of gold at the end of the rainbow! The true gold has been buried deep within us all the time! It is our golden radiant body, which we can only find by aligning all of our chakras and by activating our "rainbow" body and ascending into our Golden Christ of Light Body! Don't be distracted!!

Once our goal of reclaiming our Divine, Golden, Radiant Body was co-opted into an addiction to fool's gold and materialism that would never satisfy us; they pulled a fast one. The Luciferian Knights Templar who were the fathers of modern banking, created a way for wealthy pilgrims to secure their gold, as they traveled to the "holy land" to keep it safe from bandits. They could deposit their money in one location and reclaim it in another. Since gold was too heavy to carry around, they issued a "paper" note. This note is basically a promissory note saying, "I give you this amount of gold and whenever you want it back all you have to do is present this note". They soon began issuing more notes than the gold they had. So, in truth, the note was not worth the paper it was written on. (So if you think that the B.R.I.C.'s "Crypt" o currency is backed by gold, think again.)

To take this greed to an even higher level, in the Fall of 1910, a group of six men secretly met on Jekyll Island off the coast of Georgia for the purpose of creating a privately owned banking system. In order to deceive the public, they called it the "Federal Reserve". There is nothing Federal about it. It was just a means to make the ultra-rich illuminati families even richer. On June 5, 1933, the United States went off the gold standard, a monetary system in which currency was backed by gold. This basically gave these elite banking families the right to print as much money as they chose, without ever having to produce the gold that backed it. This printed money funded Hitler's World War and it is responsible for creating a deficit that can never be paid off.

Those that were in opposition to these banking families creating the Federal Reserve were Jacob Astor, the richest man in the world at that time and Benjamin Guggenheim, whom the famous museum is named after. These two men "happened" to be aboard the Titanic, a ship financed by the Rothschild's bank. J.P. Morgan booked a ticket on the Titanic but canceled just before the sailing. Both Astor and Guggenheim went down with the Titanic. As a result of their "tragic deaths" the Federal Reserve was approved by President Woodrow Wilson, whose Campaign was financed by J.P. Morgan, without any opposition by those rich and powerful men who would have opposed him but now lay at the bottom of the Atlantic Ocean.

So how did the few gain control over every government on our earth? Money again. Peace is never good for business. As I mentioned before all wars waged on our planet have ultimately been about two parralle fallen universes trying to manuever our multiverse into their fallen time matrix. But the wars throughout our bloody Earth's history have accomplished many dark agendas: to eliminate all of the true Grail Kings and bloodlines and replace them with the false *Anunnaki* Hybrid bloodlines; to confiscate all truth from ancient cultures and murder all races and lineages who retained higher genetics, memories, records and artifacts of our Earth's true history. To obtain women for forced breeding, to abduct men, women and children into slavery, or for human sacrifices: to provide massive blood sacrifices of loosh; to pirate our Earth's resources; to divide and conquer humanity; to make money; and to take down any nation or its leaders who would not succumb to the One World Order Agenda. But the worst part is that We the People have been used as pawns, played like chess pieces by these off-planet mafiosos families and their "elite" puppets in their selfish conquests. Fed full of lies we have carried out their satanic rituals in the name of God, Freedom, and Liberty, killing and harming our fellow human beings!

Through divide and conquer tactics perfected in Ancient Babylonia, rulers would insight conflict between two peaceful neighboring kingdoms. When the weaker of the two kingdoms was about to be destroyed they came to ask for financial aid from the kind generous leader of the neighboring kingdom, who would of course grant their request for a hefty price, and who had secretly created the conflict between the two kingdoms in the first place! When the victorious kingdom had won, both kingdoms were impoverished and became the property of the one who had started the conflict. Sound familiar? This is the history of most every war on our Earth. If a ruler of a country fails to submit to the illuminati families' One World Order Agenda, they " manufacture" an internal revolution instigated by the C.I.A., using some poor minority group as pawns. Or, if that doesn't work, terrorist cells with weapons of mass destruction are fabricated and the One World Order Military financed by the American Tax Payers invades that country to "keep the peace" killing and displacing millions of families who become refuges and are forced to flood the first world countries because their homes were destroyed. This creates division and wreaks havoc on each country's economy. All this merely to extend the black hand of these mafia families for their total world domination and submission of our Earth to their One World Order. Order out of Chaos. Don't believe it?

Here is an example of one such world leader who abolished usury and implemented these things in his country:

- Free education (including higher education)
- Students were paid an average salary for the subject they were studying
- Students studying overseas were provided with accommodation, an automobile and 2,500 dollars per annum
- Free electricity
- Free healthcare
- Free housing (there were no mortgages)
- Newly Wed couples received a gift of 60,000 dinar (50,00 dollars) from the government. Automobiles were sold at factory cost, private loans were provided free of interest
- Bread cost 15 US cents per loaf
- Gasoline cost 12 US cents per liter
- Portions of profits from the sale of oil were paid directly into the bank accounts of citizens
- Farmers received free land, seeds and animals
- Full employment, with those temporarily unemployed paid full salary as if employed.
- The name of the Leader who did this for his country was Gaddafi. Need I say more?

You know the saying, "Money doesn't grow on trees".It doesn't: it IS a tree. Now with the age of computers these families have set up legal ways to conjure wealth out of thin air. "Money" is nothing more than ones and zeros in their bank computers which they "lend" to you and charge you interest on! Money that never existed! They answer to no one and use their fabricated money energy for total world domination. Now they are quickly herding us into a cashless society of a One World Order, "CRYPT" o currency, so as they herd the masses "online" for their every need they can control who can download their "credits" and who can not, based on how well they "obey". What will happen when you can only pay for something you need by accessing a micro chipped placed inside your body .. or your brain? The minute you place value on something artificial that can be manipulated through technology, you have entered the arena of the controllers' anti-life, AI world of tyranny. Don't be seduced by crypt-o currency. A crypt is a hidden or secret place that houses death. Money is energy. Are you going to put your energy into anti-life systems? Into an Artificial A.I. anti-life currency under the spell of the mer-chants who direct currents from one bank to another! It's mined in a computer. It's not real. It is part of their fake Artificial AI "META" verse.

The irony is that it is ultimately you and I who decide what is of value. "We the People" are the ones who place more value on a piece of paper, plastic, or a "bitcoin" than our own Mother Earth. The only power something has over you is the power you give it. You have been enchanted, mesmerized, hypnotized, seduced and glamorized away from what is real into a false finite economy where the ten percent control everything! "We The People" need to take back our God Sovereign Freedom and OUR planet! We need to stop being scammed and take back our power and our precious energy slowly building a new economy based on a loving exchange of energy, free from the infection of greed, manipulation and grounded in the simplicity of what is real. Our Organic Earth, heirloom seeds, organic food, organic people and their unique gifts and talents are the true riches of this World. Here is where true abundance lies.

The Rothschilds are supposedly the richest family on our planet, with assets in the Trillions and complete domination of the World Banking system. The Queen of England, and now her son King Charles have far more wealth and power than they pretend. The Vatican and its Pope(s) command the wealthiest religious organization on Earth and is in line to be the next New World Order Religion. These are a few of the more well-known bloodlines that form the powerful elite of the Illuminati Pyramid, with the all seeing "reptilian" eye at the top. This hijacked symbol curses the American Dollar bill with its ancient black magic Egyptian symbols and spells. This is the only logical explanation as to why people kill for money, sell their bodies for money, and even their souls. At the top of the Illuminati Pyramid, the one percent controls all the money and all the power on Earth through their banking system. They recruit their World Leaders from within their secret societies, who they place at the top of their One World Order corporations, governments, religions, militaries, police forces, educational systems, et cetera, and at the bottom are the human slaves. This explains why our planet is in such a terrible state since mind-controlled sexually deviant psychopaths are running it.

Meanwhile this tyrannical One World Order has silently seeped into every aspect of our lives. Behind every store front corporation and world organization lurks another "parent corporation", which always leads back to these Illuminati families and their money. This is how they pull the strings and have the ultimate say on every product, service, technology, medical treatment, educational program, news report, television show, film production, et cetera created on Earth. Every election, judicial system, police force, scientific community, educational administration, medical body, secret society, et cetera is ultimately controlled by them. They decide what you eat, what type of home you can build, what your children will learn in school, where and when you can travel, and now even if you can even breathe. They program your mind with their "tell-a-lie-visions" and keep you going to their censored inter-"net" where the truth can not be told. It's time WE THE PEOPLE wake up and realize the entire system is corrupt.

Or perhaps you still believe these wealthy elites only have the "good of humanity" at heart? Let's follow the money and SEE how one family has managed to use their money to shape our modern world though misperception and manipulation. I will let you be the judge. When patriarch John Rockefeller's unimaginable wealth soared in the late 1880's making him the richest American of all time, he quickly realized that capturing the news and running marketing campaigns were necessary to portray his family as philanthropists. He hired people for public relations to give him a positive image, showing that the Rockefellers invest their wealth back into the common people through their many charitable organizations. As a result, the Rockefeller family has exerted enormous control over various magazines, newspapers and the media. This marketing ruse and the coordinated efforts of monopolizing mainstream media worked out very well for them. These tactics are used today by all these bloodline families and the elites to craft backstories and false historical profiles as manufactured advertising campaigns for those people assigned to be public faces representing and protecting certain areas of their One World Order interests. It is in this way John D. Rockefeller became the ruthless architect inserting his power and influential control from behind the philanthropic veil of his many charitable organizations. He avoided income tax liabilities by setting up several charitable trusts and organizations, secret trusts within secret trusts, in which he would avoid paying any taxes and yet pull the governmental strings and hide his powerful influence of manipulating global affairs to his advantage.

The Rockefellers put their sights on Ivy League Universities and other major academic environments, offering large research grants to leading educators, institutions and scientific researchers. This money was earmarked to influence the future direction and outcomes of research. These endowments influenced academic thought and research by funding colleges that only employed tenured professors who produced "accepted" research and scholastic findings. It is in this manner the illuminati families were able to control the top Ivy league Universities and make sure their historical, scientific, medical, legal, archaeological or any other knowledge did not debunk their accepted false narratives in the put-up world in which we live. If so there goes the funding! By placing prestigious schools like Harvard, Stanford , Oxford, Yale et cetera behind the researched findings of scientists, archeologists, doctors, historians within their bought and paid for "World of Academia". Anyone opposing their opinions would be dismissed as a crack pot or pseudo scientist. Hence the truth has now been silenced through the black magic curse of "money". This supported the brotherhoods of the crème de la crème of the academic world. Doctors would not dare go against the accepted medical prototypes or they would be wide open for law suits or worse shunned and ostracized by their colleges and kicked out of their professional associations. In short, anyone who disagreed with the accepted narratives of their profession would be committing professional suicide. However, over the years there have been brave souls who have openly challenged the system. Unfortunately, many of these heroes have died in "accidents" or committed "suicide" at the height of their careers and their research confiscated.

The Rockefellers subsequently invested a great deal of money towards defining modern medicine through cybernetic theory, genetic modification and mind control. They worked with the DuPont family, who controlled the production of the World's chemicals, along with the biggest players that developed GMO's, or genetically modified organisms, i.e., our food. They worked diligently to devise the most effective delivery systems to create wars, diseases, pollution, poverty and genetically modify all organic life on Earth. This is just one family. I assure you there are numerous families in positions of power all over our earth carrying out their role in the New World Order Agenda. Don't be fooled by the show that the United States, China and Russia are enemies. We have been uniting since "recorded" history began, not through love and unity, but under the illuminati bloodlines conquest and push for total world domination. Make no mistake. There has never been an enemy on this earth except for these intruders, and their puppet leaders who have started every war for their own self-serving motives.

Do you still believe these wealthy "elite" families and their philanthropic endeavors have the best intentions of humanity or our planet at heart? The truth is these "elites" have enough money to end world hunger, clean up the environment, stop child trafficking, eradicate dis-ease, but instead, these elites use their money, to create the problems! Do you think it is a mere coincidence that there has been a global mass production and distribution of endless products that are destroying our planet. Pesticides, herbicides, household cleaners and the incessant production of plastic has destroyed much of our organic life, our Mother Ocean and plagues most every country since there is no way to dispose of it. There have been many alternatives to plastic available for years, but they have not been implemented by the One World Order controlled governments and global corporations. Why? Because their hidden agenda is not to heal, preserve and protect our Mother Earth but to destroy her. Here in Sicily as in many places all over the world we sort our garbage for the good of the "environment". Plastic is the biggest garbage to be disposed of. I have a friend who was paid to come down to serve on a committee to solve the plastic waste problem in Sicily, but there was no solution because it is not bio degradable. Nobody is attacking the root cause. Stop producing plastic! But instead they keep good hearted people running around sorting our garbage, believing they are helping our planet while they keep on creating the problem!

These illegitimate rulers are the ones behind the "climate change" of this earth due to their terraforming our organic Earth into an Artificial AI one. Their corporations are behind the relentless fracking, incessant production of plastic, chem-trails, geo engineering, oil spills, perpetual use of fossil fuels and the retardation of free natural energy sources. They have been silently killing us with their radio waves, EMF millimeter (5G) radiation poisoning for years now. Cancer has become an epidemic! 5G and Space X wreak havoc on our Earth's surface. They have been destroying organic life on Earth on purpose, and have the audacity to cover up their evil agenda calling it "global warming or climate change". Now they use the excuse of "climate changes" to fuel their weather wars which have reached catastrophic levels with lethal amounts of toxins being dumped on WE THE PEOPLE all over the world daily. It is in our food, water and the air we breath. They are trying to transhumanize us into A.I. lifeforms halting our organic ascension. These weather wars have created devastating natural disasters and our life giving sun is being blotted out by robot piloted planes spreading toxic chem-trails all over our Earth! They need to be stopped! They use a young mind-controlled white child as their mouth piece when the indigenous people of our Earth have been warning us about this for ages. They have convinced humanity it is ALL our fault and we are the ones to blame for using their products and following their laws. So since WE THE PEOPLE cannot be trusted to take care of OUR planet, they will take care of it for us. They are using this as an excuse to get WE THE PEOPLE off OUR LAND, off OUR EARTH so they can complete their New World Order conquest without us taking our rightful places as the Guardians of our Mother Earth and protecting her creatures. So they can continue their conquest and the destruction of all organic life with their lethal doses of radiation free from watchful eyes. So they can confine us in their smart cities so that we will not notice that our Earth is becoming a dead planetoid populated by AI insects and holographic simulations of nature! If you still believe that the new "green" movement and laws are to heal our Mother Earth think again. In many areas governmental zoning laws make it illegal to live off the grid or build homes that are in harmony with Mother Earth like Earth Ships or "alternative" architecture which is energy efficient. In some areas it is illegal to collect rainwater, grow your own food, generate your own power or even walk on your own planet.

The tag word "Climate Change" previously known as global warming is a mind control device used to trigger humanity's deep-seated fears of annihilation based on the trauma of the first human holocaust. This programming has been reinforced by the preemptive programming script "spelled" out in the Book of Revelations found in the weaponized "Unholy" Bible to cause us to co-create the destruction of our own Earth. The underlying belief is that our world as we know it is going to be destroyed and it is all our fault because we are wicked ever sinners and God is angry at us! So we deserve to loose our planet. Many New Age and "spiritual" speakers/teachers are promoting the desire to escape Earth through star gates or alien space ships. What you need to ask yourself is why do all spiritual teachings talk about the destruction of our Mother Earth and try get human beings off of their Mother Earth? This mind control device permits the controllers to capture our consciousness and use it against us to co create their agenda of co-opting the organic Ascension of OUR Earth and hijacking it into an AI Metaverse, while people are so mesmerized by their "smart" phones they don't even notice! They create the problem in their Problem/ Reaction /Solution formula. PROBLEM: Climate change: message We are evil sinners who are destroying the planet! REACTION: Save us! Save the planet! Tell us what to do! SOLUTION: There, there, not to worry. We will take care of everything. Let us take full control of you and your Earth. We will keep you and your planet safe by keeping you off your land, and telling you where and when you can visit your Earth. We will tell you what you can plant, grow, build, which areas of your planet you can live on. We will protect your Earth for you. We will keep you so busy with all our "green" rules and regulations (green being the new black) that you will not notice that your bees are dying, your forests are burnt ciders and your animals are sick. You will not SEE we are destroying your organic Earth and terraforming it into a dead. A.I. Planetoid so the Archon overlords can live here and reign supreme in yet another of their conquered dead AI worlds!

The truth is our Earth is under going massive changes as it ascends in frequency. Like all living organic organisms it takes in more light and attunes to higher frequencies transmuting from a 3D Earth into a 5D Earth. Our Earth is shedding lunar harnesses, lower densities, evicting the old miasmic shadow creatures, black goo and phantom dead spaces that have infected its ley lines. Like water when it changes from solid ice, into steam, it expands. There will be moments of expansion healing crisis, natural disturbances as our mother acclimates to a more refined vibration and equilibrium. Our Mother Earth may throw off toxins as she releases the old. This is natural. But we are in the midst of a frequency war! The Dark Side is using weather wars and all its artificial technology to try to halt our Earth's organic ascension. Since we are one with our Mother Earth, what affects her body affects our bodies. Ungodly levels of heat, cold, water bombs, toxic waste are being unleashed on our Earth. Laser weapons are creating devastating fires and toxic smoke levels.

It is high time that we human beings realize we are God Sovereign Free human beings who are the Guardians of OUR Earth. If we look after our mother, she will look after us. She provides for our every need. She feeds us, clothes us, shelters us and heals us. But we have been scammed into giving our power away and our planet. We have gladly traded our homes, our land, our resources for pieces of paper from these banksters. They now literally own everything of true value and have left us holding the paper. The banksters get richer every day while more and more families go hungry and homeless. We have been duped by their black magic spells. If we want to take back our planet we have to stop giving it away to these banksters, these representatives of alien overlords who seek to destroy our planet, humanity and all organic life!

We are the guardians of our Mother Earth. We should not have to pay to live on OUR Earth. Likewise, we are the owners of our own bodies. No one has the right to tell you what you can or cannot do with your own body. Your body is your temple gifted to you freely from Divine Infinite

Source. It is unlawful to force anyone to wear something over their mouth that inhibits their breathing or to have something injected into their body, inserted up their nose, tattooed across their skin, or placed inside their brain. We have soul/sole ownership of OUR bodies. But you have been tricked into giving away your God Sovereign Freedom and into accepting the false Maritime Laws over the Law of the Land and God's Law of One. Maritime laws control the international flow of currency or money and ownership. Banks direct the flow of the currents or currency from one bank (s) to another. Maritime law, the Law of the Sea controls the acts of the mer-chant, those enchanters of the Sea. All ships must have their own certificate of manifest. All ships are female and when they arrive in a port or in their birth, they deliver their goods, or merchandise and receive a certificate, issued at the dock. Likewise, when your mother's waters broke or parted, you were delivered at birth, and you received a certificate by the "Doc" who had jurisdiction over your "birth" and signed your birth certificate. In that moment you, like goods delivered from a ship, became "property" under Maritime Law. As you began to identify with a fictitious "straw-man" identity recorded on your birth certificate you unknowingly gave up your God Sovereign Freedom and all the rights as an inhabitant of Earth and agreed to become the property of the "elites" under maritime law.

Since you have been duped into agreeing to become property, you have ownership of nothing, and you must be granted permission to do everything. You must apply for permits and licenses if you want to get married, divorced, buy a car, drive a car, buy a piece of land, build on a piece of land, sell a piece of land. You must have "permission" to hunt, swim, fish, travel and now even to leave your home! Our Earth has been stolen right out from under our noises with this legalese magic act. If we look to the true "Law of the Land" it is unlawful for police to demand documents of any person who is not suspected of criminal behavior. The minute you give your documents over to an official, you have stepped into their finite world of identifying yourself with your fictitious "straw-man" avatar. Your God Sovereign Freedom is relinquished and you are subject to their unlawful Maritime laws that rule this fake finite reality. You are issued a number by the government, a social security number, or in Italy a *codice fiscale,* without which you are not "permitted to work". This number marks you as property and you can be bought, sold and traded on the stock exchange like any other commodity on the Exchange!

In less than one hundred years, people have gone from living self-sufficiently off the land to having the "elites" own everything on God's Green Earth. Since the Act of 1871, Americans have not been living in a country but under the United States Corporation which is owned by international bankers and the aristocracy of Europe and Britain. This legal robbery has expanded to include every country, region, city, even street on OUR Earth. With this, the "elites" have dictated through their "zoning laws" how modern "man" should live. Urban sprawl has become the virus of our Planet as developers buy up pristine natural land and destroy the natural habitat, creating subdivisions, constructed of prompted paper houses erected for "show and tell" lifestyles that cannot withstand the reoccurring geo engineered unnatural disasters aimed at "clearing the real-estate". These homes must constantly be fed. They must be heated, cooled, insured and maintained. Money must be continuously earned to pay mortgages, interest, utility bills, property taxes, insurance, car payments, registrations, food and other "cost of living" expenses. People work nine to five or even twenty-four seven just to keep a roof over their heads and food on the table! Many people are one pay check away from being homeless. Imagine, it's easy if you try, how much the world would change if everyone owned off grid, self-sufficient homes and grew their own food.

It is up to WE THE PEOPLE to WAKE UP from the dream spell and take back OUR EARTH and STOP carrying out their dark agenda! We have been informed of their intentions, but are willingly participating in their satanic rituals. Their symbols of world domination are openly displayed all over our Earth. Their dark intentions have been stated for all the World to SEE. They have painted their genocidal plans on murals in public places like the Denver International Airport. They have even carved their intentions into stone on the Georgia Guide Stones, where it is clearly written in multiple languages "reduce the world population to five hundred million". Which thank God have now been destroyed marking a shift in timelines. Their document entitled "Agenda 21", clearly spells out their agenda to "Reduce the World Population", and has been signed by all the World leaders of the United Nations. Technically we have been INFORMED of their intentions so under Cosmic Sovereign Law, we are now consenting and carrying out for our own genocide. "We The People" are doing it to ourselves! We are paying for their artificial genetically modified food, that is modifying our bodies into artificial life forms. We are smothering our nostrils and injecting toxic materials into one another and our children. We are lining up for the latest weaponized technological instruments, (CELL) phones, investing in crypto currencies to make our confinement complete! We are willingly climbing into their fake, finite, anti-life "crypt" as they reset our world to an Artificial Earth on a descending Fibonacci timeline Spiraling downward into a fallen parallel time matrix to be food for the parasitic fallen angelics! Lured by the bait of becoming a crypto billionaire in a world controlled by D.A.R.P.A.! We are allowing our children's creative sparkle to be snuffed out in public school systems of indoctrination while they are glued to the CELL phones having their brain algorithms altered, being suffocated, vaccinated and trans-humanized before our very eyes! By continuing to participate in these corrupt systems, by obeying their unlawful, illegal laws, buying their weaponized food, products and feeding their greedy corporations by keeping our heads down just hoping things will get better, you are passively consenting and empowering their Agenda.

The truth is one percent CAN NOT rule the world without our participation, without our passive consent. The ultimate truth is that we human beings are doing this to ourselves!!! "WE THE PEOPLE" need to SEE through their Trojan horse tactics. We need to stop playing their mind control games of "keeping up with the Jones", or running their rat races to accumulate their false wealth or competing with one and other to become one of the "elite" chosen ones, recruited from within the ranks to join their secret circle of wealth and power. We need to stop supporting their anti-life agendas by obeying and enforcing their unlawful laws. OUR military and police must remember their oaths to be the SERVANTS of "WE THE PEOPLE" and begin to protect the freedom they swore to uphold, instead of blindly enforcing illegal tyrannical laws, creating a future for our children void of all freedom.

ESCAPING THE PRISION MATRIX

It is as if many are aboard the Titanic, enjoying their brandy and cigars, refusing to SEE that the water is rising around them. Like a frog in a boiling pot who thinks it is in a Jacuzzi, they are smiling and telling everyone, "come on in, the waters fine!", while being boiled alive. Actually, microwaved is more accurate since the toxic radiation levels are being turned up daily. It is time to jump out of the pot, get into the life boats! The old earth you once knew exists no more! It is crumbling all around you. Time to get off your arse and create a new one. It is time to create real SOLUTIONS to OUR EARTH'S REAL PROBLEMS not passively accept the One World Order's bogus solutions. No one is going to save you. You are the savior you have been waiting for! The Solution is going to come from within YOU!

What if WE THE PEOPLE created agrarian 5D eco-communities outside of the banksters' black magic money system? They would have no more slaves to control. Their sugar cube pyramid of power would crumble if the bottom layer of slave labor dissolved. We do not need a bloody revolution just peaceful solutions that extract us from the banksters' finite world of greed and corruption as we transition back to the simplicity of what is real! Here in Italy the "Green Pass" Gestapo Laws came into effect during the Plan demic, as I write this, those who choose freedom, bodily integrity and will not give up their God given right of ownership over their body have been barred from going to work, into stores, post offices, public places, using health care systems, public transport systems and basically participating in the old "finite" banksters' world. Necessity is the mother of invention! This is motivating God Sovereign people to embrace their freedom by exiting these corrupted systems and creating new alternative communities! Sure, it may be difficult at first, even frightening to leave behind the familiar and create something new, but we need to begin to create alternatives to the Banksters' finite world of death and decay, laying the foundation for 5D eco-communities!

WHAT ARE YOU WAITING FOR?

Many are waiting with bated breath for justice to be served, for the white hats to take out the "deep state" for the bad guys so they can resume their lives and everything can go back to normal, but there is no normal to go back to! Our old world is gone. Many thirst for revenge and want to see corrupt world leaders brought to justice and their satanic structures fall. But you must ask yourself why?

Everything happens in divine timing. The Laws of Karma cannot be escaped. Although the Dark Side believes they can escape Cosmic Karmic Law by living within their finite AI reality, they cannot. They are merely postponing the inevitable, accruing interest on their karmic "debts". All creation, even the Dark Side, is part of the Infinite and everything resets to Infinite Source.

As you reset to Infinite Source you must "make good" on all your karmic debts. This, too, is part of the ascension process. As you ascend and gain a higher perspective, you will realize that awakening is an ongoing process not a final state of being "woke". You become aware of all your other identities or "past lives". You may realize that during the many life times you have lived here on Earth, you too existed within the dream spell of the fallen prison matrix of duality and have played out many roles, both as persecutor and victim. Perhaps you came to Earth with the noblest of intentions but as you fell deeper into the dream spell you were tricked, scammed, misguided into following the false light? Perhaps you too batted for the other side, rising to power and serving as "elites"? Perhaps your anger at them stems from a deep seated anger at yourself for your own fall? It matters not! It was all part of Earth School! As you awaken to this you need only to learn your lessons, pay your karma, and forgive yourself. Dedicating your life to the Service of the Law of One is an excellent way to pay off your karma quickly.

This perhaps is one of the hardest steps on the pathway of ascension, yet vital. It is the first step to real change. When you can see your own inner flaws and learn that you don't want to be that way anymore, and forgive yourself, then real change can occur. That's ultimately why we all came to this fallen planet to learn about the Finite or Dark Side. Many of us now feel deeply in our soul a sense of, "been there, done that and don't want to do it anymore!!" Now, at long last you can fully return home with a satisfied soul! But would you deny those who still need to experience the dark fallen finite aspect of creation their lessons? Would you usurp their free will? Then you would be no better than the controllers. You must forgive them and free yourself, allowing their own karma to catch up with them and as you do, you will forgive yourself and your karmic debt will be forgiven.

In the Film *The Egyptian*, these words were uttered to the new Pharaoh, by a Physician who had poisoned Akhenaton, the old Pharaoh:

> *"We live in decay of our world,*
> *And you represent this decline. Nations grow only to fall.*
> *Kings build powerful monuments ... only to become dust.*
> *The glory is fleeting*
> *like a shadow. All these things take itself*
> *the seed of death. Just one thought can withstand ...*
> *a great realization can grow and prosper ...*
> *and a truth can never be killed ...*
> *It passes in secret*
> *From the heart of one man to another;*
> *It is given to a child by its mother's milk.*
> *I will walk among the people and try to answer questions that burn in their hearts.*
> *The question that has pursued me for a lifetime and was answered ...*
> *by a dying man.*
> *a man cannot be judged the color of their skin,*
> *by their clothes, their jewelry or their triumphs ... but only for their heart.*
> *God who created us all.*
> *is truth and it is immortal."*

CHAPTER 11

MEETING OUR SPIRITUAL TEACHERS

Peter and I returned to Kentucky after the Canary Islands to spend time with my family. One evening, we went to see the Bride of Dracula at Derby Dinner Play House. What happened that evening is open to interpretation. Peter's account is that I asked him to marry me. All I remember is that we were trying to decide what to do next. I would say I wanted to study film in L.A., and he would say he wanted to study psychiatry in New York. I would say I wanted to study Art in Chicago and he would say he wanted to practice medicine in Florida. This went on for a while. Every time I suggested one thing, he would suggest the opposite. Exasperated, I finally said okay, are we going to move forward together or not? Peter looked into my eyes across the bottle of pink champagne and said quite casually, "Are you proposing marriage?" I politely excused myself and went to the bathroom. For years, I had been terrified of marriage, of commitment, of having my wings clipped. I looked at myself in the mirror swearing upside and down I would most definitely NOT marry this man, no way, no absofuckinglutely way! I returned to the table, sat down, and quietly said, "okay."

The night before the wedding, at the rehearsal dinner, at a local Italian restaurant in Louisville, Kentucky, after we all had consumed an enormous amount of alcohol, Peter got up and sang the song, "Dream, Dream, Dream." Peter had told me that when he was a Doctor in Cape Cod, on the cold winter nights he would fall asleep in front of the T.V. and dream that he was walking on a sandy beach, where he would meet a beautiful blonde in a bikini, which he finally did... ME!

Before Peter died, he was very upset that I had not mastered lucid dreaming. This is the ability to wake up inside your dreams or become lucid therefore actively affecting your dream reality, rather than just having your dreams "happen" to you while you are in a passive sleep state. He was very adept at this, as well as astral travel or slipping in and out of his physical body at will. He once asked me, "how are we going to be together if I die and you are not lucid?" I decided I would start with astral projection. He told me it would help me overcome my fear of death and all I had to do was just to ask to have an out-of-body experience. So I did, although I was terrified. After that, I was always afraid to go to sleep at night for fear of having one. Until one night, it happened. I felt myself float up, out of my body towards the ceiling. Then, I floated back down. The room was dark so I felt around and put my hand on Peter's familiar face. Then, I felt a strange face next to his. Holy smokes, it was my face! I was outside my meat body touching it! I was so excited I started screaming, "Peter, Peter I did it!" But of course, he couldn't hear me. Then I thought, "what if I can't get back into my body?" The next thing I knew, I woke up in my body!

We had a beautiful wedding at Garden Court which the Louisville Presbyterian Seminary had just bought. Thank God, because I wanted to be married outside in nature but my parents had wanted me to be married in the Seminary's Chapel. So we compromised! My uncle married us. Even our dogs were there at the ceremony and on top of the cake! It was perfect. My youngest brother sang the song from West Side Story: "One Hand, One Heart," "Make of our hands one hand, make of our hearts one heart, make of our vows one last vow: even death won't part us now." "Even death won't part us now!" How powerfully symbolic! It was to be in this lifetime that we had vowed to join our souls eternally to return home. After the wedding, the buzz word that went around the tables and was videotaped was "job well done." I don't know who coined the phrase, but every one of the two hundred guests repeated it. And it was! We had done it! We had found each other in this lifetime, managed not to kill one another, and after three years, at long last, managed to make an eternal commitment to one another! Needless to say, we had a lot of help!

We chose Mexico for our Honeymoon and after a day trip to Chichen Itza, Peter became very ill. For three days, he lay in bed. Finally, on the third day, he rose from the dead and we grabbed a flight back to the states. We went to our favorite island, Captiva, where Peter healed himself. We had bought a beautiful, lush piece of property on the Wekiva River in Lake County, Florida to build our dream home. I had wanted to create a retreat center there. So I traveled to other retreat centers to learn how it was done. I had secretly been searching for a spiritual teacher all my life. I traveled the world looking for one. I went to an Ashram to study Yoga and Psychotherapy looking for my "guru". I went to the Option Institute in the Berkshire Mountains of Massachusetts and studied with Barry Neil Kaufman, the author of the book *Sonrise*, and his wife. It was there I began to realize the power of the words that had been given to me: Infinite Human. There I also met the grandson of one of the wealthiest men in America who received a check for over one million dollars every month in his mail box and still felt poor. As we "dialogued" he broke down and confessed that with all the money he had been given he had never once told his parents thank you. Some people are so poor all they have is money.

We were beginning to see how shallow this money game rat race was. We had done everything by the book. We had followed the fairytale script, we had "arrived." I had obtained my master's in Mental Health Counseling and Peter's practice was booming. We had built our "dream home" and I played the show and tell game with the other doctor's wives. We had reached the pinnacle of what society deemed "success," but we had never felt so empty. We found the superficialities of society boring and longed for the weekends when we could escape to our small cottage on Captiva Island. This was where our spiritual journey had begun all those years ago. One day when we were sitting on the beach reading our spiritual books, one of us came across the passage: "When the student is ready the teacher will appear." We both became very excited and prayed hard to meet our "spiritual teachers." A few months later, Peter and I took a writing class. Peter was working on *The Pathway Home* and I was working on this book. Our writing teacher said, "I'm sorry but my spiritual guides have been bugging me to introduce you to my spiritual teachers." A week later, we were on a plane heading to Virginia to meet our teachers!

They were Twin Souls, a husband and a wife team who lived in Montana, one was black, and one was white, and that's all we knew. When we arrived, they said, "We have been waiting for you." The first workshop was with Patrick. He was a tall, balding, white male with the most penetrating eyes. His words resonated so profoundly within my soul. We were told he was from the future. In this life he was a retired army sergeant turned spiritual teacher and a warrior who told Prince Philip to his face, "Your side is going down!" He had been stationed in Hawaii where he had a kundalini awakening that almost broke his spine in two when he encountered his future self. This had led him to a psychic woman who told him he was a Vulcan. In fact, the character Spock from the Star Trek series was based on Patrick. He was logical, intelligent, and basically pointed out the irony of how illogical we humans were. Although he was older, his energy was fluid and graceful like that of a young man. His wisdom was imparted with love and humor. Patrick pointed out with humor the insanity of humanity and laid the foundation for helping us to "graduate from Earth Campus", as he called it. His job was to point out all the deceptions in our fallen system and to help us to "go home" as he put it. He had several sayings: "Never volunteer. Be smart, and lazy as opposed to dumb and industrious. Never do group, the group will hold you back. Keep your own counsel. Don't believe us, do your own research. It takes linear time," and my favorite, "It's all shit, pick your layer." He had also perfected the "Art of Doing Nothing," as he called it. And he would always tell Peter and I to "take care of each other"!

He was a very direct and honest man. When I first met Patrick, I shared with him my childhood experience of having X-ray vision. He stared deeply into my eyes, and asked me what I did after I saw the skeleton? I told him I got frightened and screamed. He smiled and said, "Now you are going to have to pay us a lot of money to get it back!" Patrick was the best possible spiritual teacher because he did not want to be one. Once when Peter and I had flown halfway across the planet to attend one of his workshops, he looked at us and said, "Don't you have any place better to be?" Patrick's first workshop deeply changed our lives. When we returned home, Peter emptied our subzero freezer and buried all our T-Bone steaks, then dumped out all the wine from our wine cellar! At first, our spiritual practices seemed like sacrifices, to me; things I had to give up. But slowly they became the most exciting part of our lives. In fact, they were no longer practices but simply part of who we were. We became vegetarians and I began to prepare our food by infusing love into everything we ate. We spent much of our time in deep mediation, silent contemplation, and reflection. We found ourselves shrinking further and further away from the hob snobbery of society. We no longer resonated with the cocktail party gossip and show-and-tell lifestyles of the medical community. Peter and I would go on to repeat Patrick's workshop many, many times, each time discovering new nuggets of truth, that we had previously been unable to grasp. We based our book, *The Pathway Home,* on his teachings and practices.

I can't describe how we felt in those days, but it was as if we had been granted the grace of stepping into our radiant Christ of Light Bodies because of our extreme desire and devotion to "Go Home". We both felt so light at times we thought we would blow away. We were flowing from one moment to the next, in and out of time, in a continuous state of blissful joy. We felt like laughing all the time. We were stoned on love! It was a high unlike any high I ever had experienced from external sources.

We were constantly tuned into our inner sounds or the music of the spheres. I was hearing classical music, or violins playing inside my head all the time. We were blissfully in love with each other and everything around us; this combined with the thrill of reading and interpreting the signs and symbols that were guiding us along our newly found level of spiritual unfoldment was thrilling! Incredible things were happening to us daily. I took a course in Reiki, and when I placed my hands over a person's body, I realized I had the uncanny ability to feel things in my own body that related to that person. For example, if the person wore glasses, I could feel in my eye which of their eyes were weak, or if they had a problem in their organs, I could sense it in my organ. I even felt a wound a person was carrying in their physical body from a past life, when they had been stabbed to death.

At the same time, deep karmic patterns were surfacing. I had bought a kiln and was obsessed with making columns. We already had a huge column in the entry way of our house, but I continued to make ceramic columns of all sizes. It wasn't until I saw the movie *Dead Again* and realized the character's obsession with scissors was a key to unlocking her past life that I realized my subconscious was trying to reveal something from a past life. I remember getting the "ah-hah", one day through a dream Peter and I both had. We were in an Ancient Greek Palace filled with columns. It was my home. I was a renowned healer, and Peter was my slave. We were gay lovers. We had lots of problems and fought constantly. One day, Peter found me dead. I had drowned myself in our pool. Peter described our home in Ancient Greece right down to the last detail. These memories of our past lives together kept surfacing to help us to learn from our past mistakes and heal our present relationship. We began to break the karmic circle of our relationship, changing both past, present, and future!

One month later, we flew to Lincoln, Nebraska to meet Patrick's wife Sharon. She reminded me of the woman singing the song, "Aquarius" in the movie, *Hair,* minus the Afro. The night before I saw her, I could not sleep. I had a terrible stomach ache like nothing I had ever felt in my life. The next day I asked her about it. She stared deep into my eyes and said, "FEAR!." I also asked her if my memory of killing myself in my past life was true. She told me, "Yes." I asked her how could I overcome the karma of committing suicide? She told me, "LIVE." I had no idea what she meant by that. Live? How hard could that be? I would find out. I also told her about this book, *The Infinite Human,* and she smiled and told me to file it away.

Thus, Peter and I began our spiritual studies traveling all over the world attending workshops and retreats. I must admit the word that hooked me most was transmutation, but for all the wrong reasons. I wanted to become immortal. I wanted to never age, die, nor be separated from Peter again. Our first retreat was in Red Lodge, Montana. Peter, a Cuban refugee, had never been out West and I was sure the experience would be fascinating for him, but I was not prepared for what happened. When we arrived in Billings, Montana, we rented a car, and Peter started driving. He had no idea where he was going. This was in the early 1990s before GPS's and we had no maps. Peter just drove for hours, obsessed. I trusted Peter enough by then to just keep my mouth shut and let him drive. We drove down highways, over mountains, and finally onto a dirt road. We arrived at this mountain retreat, off a dirt road, in the middle of nowhere. Peter stopped the car and got out, then looked at the place and said, "This is it"! He had seen this place in a dream.

We knocked on the door and a woman answered. We asked if we could stay the night and she told us the place was closed. I was having a Deja vu from my Cherokee retreat experience. We asked her if we could look around and she told us no. We got in the car and drove away very upset that our quest had ended in this way. The next day, we met with Sharon and told her about our adventure. She told us not to go there again because they had had a retreat in that place a few years earlier to finish up her past life as "Chief Joseph". In that lifetime, Peter had been her brother, Ollokot. The story of Chief Joseph is a very tragic story in Native American history. There were many wounds to heal. Peter had attempted to do his own healing on this journey but was not allowed to. It wasn't until a few years later, after we had moved to Montana, and visited Canyon Creek where Ollokot fell in the Nez Peirce War of 1877 and where Chief Joseph had uttered his famous words, "From where the Sun now stands, I will fight no more forever", that Peter received his healing. When we arrived on the battlefield, the sun was high in the sky, but when Peter found the spot where he had been killed in battle as Ollokot, dark clouds rolled in and huge drops of rain began to fall within seconds. He had found his healing and been cleansed. I tell you these things because all of you have past lives, stories and traumas that maybe tied into our Earth, whether you are aware of them or not. Whether you were noted in the history books or not, makes no difference. These lifetimes, past, present, and future are all part of your life's story. There is no death, and the themes, lessons, and traumas you carry with you from one life to the next are like chapters in your very own book of life to be understood and healed. As you awaken, you begin to remember all your past lives and how they relate to your present life now. You begin to break karmic patterns integrating these lessons into your soul's journey towards wholeness or holiness. As you heal, you also heal our planet and humanity!

When we arrived at our first retreat, Patrick caught our eyes and said, "You should see a lot of familiar faces." Although we had never met any of these souls in this lifetime, there was immediate soul recognition. Patrick had jokingly once called us a "clump". Now, at last, I understand his wise words. We had been reincarnating as a group, lifetime after lifetime. His words, "Don't let the group hold you back," echoed in my mind. Sharon spoke to us about transmutation and told us we had three choices, "We could choose to die and drop our body, Transmute our body and stay on Earth in our "ascended" body to do our work. Or leave our body some place safe and become a traveler." After the class, I told Peter I was choosing to stay, and transmute my body to help co-create a new earth. I looked at him and said, "And you had better too!" He just smiled and said nothing. Our paths of service were calling us. We had been given a taste of the blissful state of Ascension. Now, it was up to us to maintain this divine frequency. That required work.

After returning to Florida, we both felt the desire to head west. But where were we to go? One morning on the Beach in Captiva, we shared our dreams as we always did. One of us had dreamt of a flag and the other of a staff. We pondered the meaning of our dreams. When we got home, Peter received a phone call from a headhunter, to work with the Native Americans in Flagstaff, Arizona ...Flag ...Staff! Go west young man! So, we sold all our possessions, left our "dream" home, bought an RV, loaded it up with our three dogs and headed west. We had left everything familiar and were following the setting sun. The journey was epic, filled with excitement and adventure! It reminded me of my amazing pilgrimage west when I was only eight years old, only this time, we did it in an R.V.. Peter would drive while I was in the back cooking up something vegetarian. It reminded me of the movie with Lucille Ball and her Cuban husband Desi Arnaz traveling around the country in a trailer. Peter would turn a corner or hit a bump and the pots and pans would come tumbling down. But we were thrilled, as each day our lives unfolded before us filled with mystical symbols, past life memories, and intuitive premonitions of adventures yet to come! It was paradise, until we arrived in Flagstaff! We found a conquered nation of people who had lost all hope, living in poverty, and sickness in the white man's world. Most of them were diabetics and alcoholics.

We traveled to the Hopi reservation. These people had survived by locking out the white race and staying true to their teachings. Behind the sand drawings and Kachina dolls they sold to the Tourists were great secrets they did not openly disclose. There are many stories of "Ant" people or aliens whose interventions saved them. The Prophecy Rock and other stone drawings held great encoded messages about the times we have now entered. The Hopi tell us that the destruction of our world has repeated itself many times, as far back as human memory reaches, and they have warned that it will meet the same end if we don't change course immediately. Thomas Banyacya explains in two timely talks from 1995, how: three previous human worlds were destroyed when people became greedy, worshiped technology as their God, fought and hurt each other, and repeatedly forgot the ethical teachings they'd been given to honor the Earth as the source of life and sustenance. Three apocalypses inevitably ensued—first by fire, then by ice, then by flood. Elder Grandfather Martin Gashweseoma, who interprets the Prophecy Rock, speaks of two paths, the top path is of the two-hearted people that everyone thinks is the right path and follows, then there is the second path of truth that leads to everlasting life that only a few one hearted people follow. The top line ends abruptly while the bottom line continues around the rock. He also says the original message held in this ancient rock has been defamed by modern Christian symbols added through the years. These ancient prophecies were created long before any bible and do not "ordain what will come to pass" like the Bible, but simply reveal the choices that every human being will face. Other prophecies speak of a new earth a "Fifth" World. "When the Blue Star Kachina makes its appearance in the heavens, the Fifth World will emerge. This will be the Day of Purification. It will come when the Saquasohuh (Blue Star) Kachina dances in the plaza and removes its mask." The Hopi name for the star Sirius is Blue Star Kachina. This occurred during the 2020 winter solstice.

THE WARRIORS OF THE RAINBOW: HOPI PROPHECY

"One day... there would come a time, when the earth would be ravaged and polluted, the forests would be destroyed, the birds would fall from the air, the waters would be blackened, the fish would be poisoned in the streams, and the trees would no longer be, mankind as we would know it would all but cease to exist...a new tribe of people shall come unto the earth from many colors, classes, creeds and who by their actions and deeds shall make the earth green again. This tribe shall be called The Warriors of the Rainbow and it will put its faith in actions, not words. There will come a day when people of all races, colors, and creeds will put aside their differences. They will come together in love, joining hands in unification, to heal the Earth and all her children. They will move over the Earth like a great Whirling Rainbow, bringing peace, understanding and healing everywhere they go. Many creatures thought to be extinct or mythical will resurface at this time; the great trees that perished will return almost overnight. All living things will flourish, drawing sustenance from the breast of our Mother, the Earth. The great spiritual Teachers who walked the Earth and taught the basics of the truths of the Whirling Rainbow Prophecy will return and walk amongst us once more, sharing their power and understanding with all. We will learn how to see and hear in a sacred manner. Men and women will be equals in the way Creator intended them to be; all children will be safe anywhere they want to go. Elders will be respected and valued for their contributions to life. Their wisdom will be sought out. The whole Human race will be called "The People" and there will be no more war, sickness or hunger forever."

"In the time of the Seventh Fire, a New People would emerge. They would retrace their steps to find the wisdom that was left by the side of the trail long ago. Their steps would take them to the elders, who they would ask to guide them on their journey. If the New People remain strong in their quest, the sacred drum will again sound its voice. There will be an awakening of the people, and the sacred fire will again be lit. At this time, the light-skinned race will be given a choice between two roads. One road is the road of greed and technology without wisdom or respect for life. This road represents a rush to destruction. The other road is spirituality, a slower path that includes respect for all living things. If we choose the spiritual path, we can light yet another fire, an Eighth Fire, and begin an extended period of Peace and healthy growth. "

I began having memories of my past lives in the Ancient Anasazi Culture of the West. In one lifetime, I was a Holy Man who had been banished from my tribe of cliff dwellers. I lived in the solitude of a cave save for a young boy who brought me food and herbs to make my medicines in exchange for my sacred knowledge. We did all we could to help our native brothers and sisters but soon the familiar theme of the white man's greed began to surface as the Doctor who had brought Peter there was milking the government money dedicated to the Native Americans. We could not be part of that, so we moved on to Santa Fe which means Holy Faith.

Our next spiritual retreat was in the Yucatan of Mexico. Again, we faced Chichen Itza, where Peter had almost died on our honeymoon, but this time we were prepared to face the Brotherhood of the Jaguar who were behind the Human Sacrifices. It was a tough day. We had to face many lifetimes of karma, of being both the sacrificed and sacrificer, a familiar theme on this planet of victim and victimizer. We were told to "pay our respects" to the brotherhood of the Jaguar so we could move beyond them.

Next, we went to the Jungle of Coba to find our inner earth brothers and sisters. These were ancient races of people who had survived Earth's many cataclysms by leaving the surface and living underground. We were told to stomp around on the ground to signal the inner earth people that we had arrived, but nothing was happening. I wandered away from the group and I saw Sharon and Patrick. I approached them and asked them if, "we could get some help here", but they just walked right by, not even noticing me. Suddenly the jungle became a bustling metropolis. Strange looking dwarf like people came flooding out of the rocks and trees. Some of these strange men carried ancient-looking rifles. They showed us portals into the inner Earth. Later, many of the retreat participants shared incredible stories about interacting with these beings from other dimensions, but it was the children who could most easily see the secrets these inner Earth folks were showing them!

One day during the retreat,while I was sleeping by the pool, I awoke and began walking, where I did not know. Suddenly, Sharon appeared and said, "Oh there you are." She had summoned me telepathically. She told me that I needed to leave Peter. I was shocked. At that time in my spiritual growth, her words were like God had spoken to me, but I refused and said, "But I love Peter!" She told me, "I needed to decide, and we had to spend some time apart".

When we returned home, I stayed in New Mexico and rented out our condo in Santa Fe. We bought a cabin in the Jemez mountains so I moved there. Peter ironically took a job back east in Kentucky. It was very tough being apart, but it helped me realize many things. Most of all it taught me that even if Peter and I were not physically together, because our "assignments" may keep us apart, we were still together. I was alone in the mountains of New Mexico near the mystic four corner area. Winter found me totally unprepared. I had no four-wheel drive for the mountains, and the Cabin had no real heat to speak of. I had been a spoiled, pampered princess, who had been taken care of by men. My father and now my husband had played the part of my "knight in shining armor", always rescuing me. Now I had to grow up. I quickly learned to appreciate Peter and all he did for me. I remember I would watch the movie *Always* over and over. It is a Spielberg film about a pilot named "Peter, Saint Peter", played by Richard Dreyfus, who dies in a plane crash and comes back to help his true love get over him and decide to LIVE again. Foreshadowing?

Finally, Peter ended his assignment and came back to our newly remodeled cabin. It was heaven! We spent our days hiking in the mountains with our dogs and bathing in the natural hot springs! We would visit the Jemez pueblo, an ancient Anastasia village, to buy fried dough and beautiful pottery handcrafted by the women. One morning while I was showering I looked down to see that I was standing in two inches of well...shit! Our septic tank had backed up! We called the septic people and they told us that the problem was that roots had grown into the tank. We both got the message loud and clear. Don't set down roots. We fixed the problem and put our beloved cabin up for sale. Of course, it sold right away and we moved on to our next assignment. This was to be our way of being of service here on Earth.

Sharon had told Peter he would create five healing centers and that I would work in the administration of them? Our assignments were not always glamorous and at times I longed to plant myself down and have my own career. Once while we were working in "Pitts" field Massachusetts, we were driving in the car and Peter told me he had received a job offer to work in Parker Arizona. Tired of always following Peter around I shouted, "I'm not moving to PARKER Arizona!" Just then a huge semi pulled out in front of us blocking our way. Peter looked up and smiled. He motioned for me to look at the large red letters written across the side of the truck which spelled PARKER! After that, I surrendered my ego! We opened the Woman's Wellness Center in Parker and I served as Peter's nurse. One day, a woman came in from the nearby prison handcuffed and manacled. It was such a powerful symbol of the state of the feminine energy on our planet. I realize now we were correcting our past life Karma from Germany and part of our mission to help restore the wellness to woman and their children by helping them to heal and empower themselves.

We lived all over the world going wherever we were most needed at the time. We would do what needed to be done, then quietly leave when our job was finished. We never sought recognition or praise. We never knew where we would be called to go next or what awaited us. Once it was a penthouse overlooking Honolulu with our own private elevator, then a double-wide trailer on an Indian reservation. We worked in agricultural communities where the children were suffering serious health effects from the toxic pesticides; on Indian reservations, where the Native Americans had lost all hope, having been robbed of their land, their heritage, and their dignity; in the poor black communities of the South where not much had changed in three hundred years and folks still lived in poverty, slaving away at menial jobs, without even the basic right of healthcare; with the Mexican immigrants in California, where poor pregnant mothers worked in the fields right up until their time of delivery; and in the coal mining communities of Eastern Kentucky where the indigent mothers waited in their cars until their baby's head crowned to present themselves in the emergency room so they could receive medical care. We worked in Mormon communities where young children were sexually abused and teenagers preferred to commit suicide rather than try to live up to the high expectations of their community's leaders. We worked in Guam where the Micronesians were the only people who received free healthcare for life from the US government because the U.S. Military had bombed the hell out of their tropical island paradise, testing their atomic weapons, which had infected generations of people with radiation.

Peter always worked diligently to improve each community by getting whatever federal aid he could for the poor and upgrading their medical facilitates. In our own small way, we gave back to the poor and downtrodden people of our Earth who had been so cruelly mistreated and robbed of their birthright. I had been raised in the Suburbs of America and it was a real wake-up call for me to see firsthand the true history of my country and how we have treated the indigenous people of our Earth.

Peter and I worked to integrate holistic and traditional medicine. I provided mental health counseling, spiritual workshops, meditation classes, and yoga to those who were open to it. Peter gave our book, *The Pathway Home,* to his fellow medical colleagues who were open to it. He worked to promote diet and healthy lifestyle practices to help his patients heal themselves. We did our best to help folks realize that true healing is their responsibility and must come by healing their physical, emotional, mental, and spiritual bodies.

I also worked to shift the educational system through my children's book, *The Magical Mist*. I would do book signings, children's creativity workshops, appear on talk shows and read my story to whoever showed up. Once in Chicago only one little boy showed up to my book signing, then in Idaho bus loads of children followed by the local news channel swarmed into the bookstore. It made no difference to me, I would read my story to any child who showed up.

Between jobs, we attended workshops and retreats with our spiritual teachers all over the world. On a retreat in Costa Rica, we were told to release the gold from the Arenal Volcano so it could help Earth's people in their transmutation process. We sat in the warm volcanic waters buzzing our mantras and infusing our bodies with gold. After that, Peter was so energized, he danced all night! Peter was Cuban, so when Peter danced, he danced! We attended another retreat in the State of Washington where the Nez Pierce had lived. It was called the "Promise Keepers" retreat. It was there where Patrick taught us the breath of fire. I had always wanted to learn the breath of fire but was afraid. Since then, my life has never been the same. The breath of fire ignites and stokes the kundalini flame in the root chakra. It was like a nuclear bomb went off in my root chakra. Thank God I was with my soul mate! We both had to learn to synthesize this massive new sexual energy! I never knew orgasms could be so intense. But it was a blessing and a curse. With this increase in sexual energy, it became necessary to remove all my blocks about sex. As I began to loosen up and use the power of sex to raise my kundalini, another fear arose. Patrick had told me that most people who were in mental institutions were there because of a spontaneous rising of their kundalini. They had not been spiritually prepared for it.

WHAT IS KUNDALINI?

Kundalini is a Sanskrit word meaning coiled snake. It is a form of divine feminine energy that, if properly channeled, can lead to soul liberation. As my kundalini began to rise up through my chakras and out the top of my head, it continued to rise up into my upper chakras some seven feet above my head. I could feel the weight of the energy as it rested above my head. It felt like I was wearing one of those tall crowns you see on figures in Ancient Egyptian Art. When I was in this state of bliss, I was awakened, enlightened," One with God." I was in a state of complete peace, love, and Oneness with Infinite Source. All things became clear to me. I wanted nothing more than to stay in this state of spiritual ecstasy, to sit in deep meditation. Sometimes the energy moved so powerfully from my root chakra, through my body and out the top of my head it felt like an Anaconda Snake moving under my skin. Sometimes it would send me into panic attacks. Sometimes the energy would get stuck in an imbalanced chakra or remain in my root chakra. That was definitely the most uncomfortable! This energy will seek out and find imbalances in the body and chakra system, forcing you to make the necessary course corrections. But like everything else on this fallen planet, this powerful energy of enlightenment has been hijacked into running reversal serpent fire kundalini downwards into the earth to feed the satanic networks of shadow creatures. This is designed to keep people in a constant state of sexual addiction and stop them from reaching enlightenment through sacred sex. My early childhood and past life traumas, mixed with the lunar matrix reversals and sexual misery implants made my physical body a warring ground. I experienced the ecstasy of our lovemaking and the surge of the kundalini rising up my spine, catapulting me into bliss only to have it pulled back down into the lower frequencies of 3D Earth when I left my meditative state or became too much "in the world, but not of it". I had a tendency to get distracted by the "fluff" of the material world or what the *Tao Te Ching* would call the "ten thousand things." My spiritual teacher had once whispered into my ear, "be still and you will fly Home." This energy forced me to become still rather than becoming distracted by the external world. It forced me to become aware of where I was focusing my energy and disciplined me to constantly tune inward and upward to connect with Divine Infinite Source.

Love is the antidote for all, and Peter and I were healing one another and ascending together through our lovemaking! Sure we brought our old hurts, wounds, traumas, inhibitions, and mind control programing surrounding the opposite sex into the bedroom, but through our love, we were healing, and letting go of our past and transmuting the sabotaged male / female archetypes. We made love every day! It was heavenly. I never wanted it to end! Through our love making we exchanged the necessary codes for our ascension and Peter's masculine energy balanced my feminine energy. Once after making love as we lay intertwined in one another's arms, a thought arose in my mind and I quickly asked Peter, "What if one of us dies before the other?" To which Peter responded, "All we need to do is think of the other and we will be together." I grabbed hold of his body and told him how much I loved being with him in the physical! I knew every nook and cranny of his beautiful body, every hair, pore and indentation! I loved seeing that brilliant fire of passion he held within his eyes, stroking the five o'clock shadow around his face, running my fingers over his pearly white teeth or just smelling his manly scent! He was so dashing! Every time he walked into a room, my heart would flutter!

On the next retreat we went to the Bermuda Triangle. Our group flew in on two separate planes, one from Atlanta and the other from New York. I had booked us on the flight from New York, but at the last minute, I changed it to the one from Atlanta. When we arrived at the resort, we were told that the plane from New York had gotten "lost in the Bermuda Triangle" and we needed to anchor them back to our timeline. The Bermuda Triangle is a wormhole, where many vessels enter one door but cannot find the same door on the same timeline to exit. As a result, many end up exiting onto different timelines and going backward or forward in time. The pilot of the New York flight had gotten lost and could not find the correct exit point. So, we went into the caves located under the resort and were told to chant the mantra "That Now" to anchor them back to us, which worked!

We worked with timelines in Bermuda. We were told the Dark Side had manufactured an artificial timeline to activate their Armageddon program with a full blown World War III, between the "Christians and the Muslims" by the year two thousand. We worked with gridlines, timelines and star gates to divert this planned massive destruction of the world into something much less devastating. In Bermuda, we were told about the biblical figure Peter, Saint Peter was not supposed to have gone to Rome to found the Catholic Church. Instead he was supposed to have let a ship carry him into Bermuda Triangle where the energy of the Cosmic Christ Consciousness could be dispersed throughout the wormhole. It was Peter's ego that drove him to Rome which at that time was the Political center of the World. I remember the first time I took Peter to Rome. As he exited St. Peter's Church and entered the Piazza, he got goosebumps. Towards the end of Peter's life Sharon looked at him one day and congratulated him for finally becoming "non-political".

One afternoon in Bermuda, I was relaxing in bed with Peter when I got this uncontrollable urge to go dunk myself in a freezing cold pool of water in the underground cave at our resort and repeat my mantra. I kept trying to ignore it because it was the last thing I wanted to do, but finally, I put on my bathing suit and went into the cave alone. When I came out of the cave I saw my teachers standing at the top of the hill. Sharon asked me how the water was, and I told her, "cold!" I guess I passed the test. After that, Peter and I began receiving assignments telepathically. Peter and I were guided to buy a Ranch in Montana close to our Spiritual Teachers where we lived off the grid. By the arrival of the new millennium, we were completely self-sufficient, independent and ready for anything! This area was an amazing place, a portal into the higher dimensions. There was an amazingly intensely high energy but there was also the presence of something very powerful and negative that I couldn't quite put my finger on. Sharon told us she worked with the Deva kingdom to keep a lid on the geysers in Yellow Stone Park because they had been due to blow for a long time, possibly taking out the Northwest corner of the USA.

We loved the energy on our ranch, although very strange things happened indeed. Peter and I would often sit out at night and watch the stars in the Big Sky of Montana. We frequently would see UFO's darting across the night sky. One morning Peter told me that in his "dreams" he had suddenly awoken inside a space ship with "Alien" beings around him. As soon as they saw he was awake they were surprised and he slipped back into his body. Our teacher said that some of us had agreed to be "abducted" to help this dying alien race save themselves. Perhaps it was a karmic pay off. I don't know. I just remember thinking. NOT ME!!!!

There were only a few in our group who bought property there. We had hoped others would come and live independently forming an alternative community. But many of the people from our spiritual group had been discouraged by a previous attempt made to create a spiritual community in Montana that had failed. Patrick had said, "Be careful when you start a community to get away from things because everyone that joins will bring with them their own baggage." I learned that all communities are doomed to failure, until the human is ready to ascend leaving behind all the baggage of 3D Earth. Only those who have healed themselves and released all their karmic ties to our broken finite 3D Earth will be able to sustain these higher frequencies and co create from the unity of infinite source within. They will need to embrace their true infinite power within and stop looking to external sources to take care of them. We had learned so much about living self-sufficiently, generating our own power and how to sustain these higher frequencies. As much as we longed to stay in this incredible place, we still had work to do on 3D Earth. We had a New Year's Eve party for our neighbors. Two thousand came and went, and so did we!

Peter had always nurtured my deep talent for storytelling, and that, coupled with his love of films, caused us to become a husband and wife writing team. We wrote books, films, even a T.V. series that at last landed us an agent in Hollywood. It was our dream come true. We bought a deluxe R.V. this time with triple slide-outs and set out for Malibu R.V. Park! We studied screenplay writing at U.C.L.A. and buzzed through the canyon roads to class every day on Peter's Vulcan motorcycle! It was wonderful! We dreamed of our uplifting spiritual screenplays being produced and awakening the world! The Third Strand, Forever Yours, MerWorld, Hippocrates, The Magical Mist, Continuum! We had more creative ideas than we could write down! But we did write them all down! When we weren't' writing, we went to Santa Monica to review the latest films before they were released. We ate, dreamt, and breathed stories! It was glorious! We were filled with hope, visions, and oodles of creativity.

Our agent arranged for us to pitch our sci-fi T.V. series to FOX. We walked into a room filled with pimpled-faced kids. Seriously, I wasn't even sure if some of them were out of high school. They were willing to do anything to get ahead, while not having the authority to back any project. It was obvious their only job was to say no to whatever was being pitched. I sensed their manufactured-iron wall and walked around the room behind them. This immediately threw them off guard. I was not playing by their rules. They sat up and took notice. I pitched a T.V. series about inter galactic exchange students, one who came to Earth while the other goes to the Pleiades. We also pitched our children's show *The Gate Keepers,* about evil inter-dimensional beings who had hijacked the Star Gates of Earth. Imagine if this information had gotten out to the children on Earth in the year two thousand! Peter and I still believed that Hollywood wanted to share the truth with the world! But the mind controlled preteens jumped on me. "We already have that kind of show running. You need to do your research before you come here." They even wrote an article about it in *Variety.*

Peter was always a quick study. Someone once said to Peter, "twice is once too many for you." It was obvious to him that the film "industry" was closed. However, hardheaded me kept banging my head against the rubber door of Hollywood! I was like so many innocent, gullible starlets who had come to tinsel town with stardust in my eyes! I had stories in me, and I wanted to share them with the world! I believed what my UCLA Screenplay professor had once told me, years ago, "keep giving them you, until you is what they want!" I was not going to give up!

Peter was rewarded with a position teaching Medicine at the University of Hawaii reaching the pinnacle of his career. He taught something that was being lost to the medical profession, "love, and compassion". His logos was "Self-love is the best medicine." We lived in a penthouse with our own private elevator and had a huge terrace overlooking Honolulu. I spent my days writing and sculpting.

While we were in Hawaii, the Twin Towers fell, and our Spiritual Teacher Patrick left the Earth at that exact moment. Some believe he took with him the souls who had been sacrificed in this tragedy as he exited the prison matrix. Patrick had met Sharon while they were living in Hawaii. He was the epitome of logic and reason. Sharon told us that when Patrick first arrived on Earth he was a "hooligan", her word for someone from the Dark Side. He had learned to have compassion and love for all human beings. He was the inspiration for Gene Roddenberry's character-Spock, the alchemization of love and reason, and to all who had the privilege of knowing him. Now he was gone. It felt as if a great light had left our world, as our planet plummeted into darkness.

CHAPTER 12

LOSING MY TWIN SOUL

After Hawaii, Peter was offered a position in Guam. Quite frankly, it was nice to distance ourselves from the U.S and all that ensued after 911. The Fallen angelics had left the Emerald Covenant and things were getting pretty grim and we hoped to buy a bit more time together. We had given so much to our country, traveling the highways, byways, and airways, crisscrossing the nation. We had helped the poor, indigenous and forgotten Americans and tried to awaken anyone with eyes to see, ears to hear and hearts to know! It was time to move on. Guam was still a U.S. territory that had been won in the second world war from Japan. It was in a very strategic position in the Pacific Ocean and occupied by the U.S. Navy. In fact, we were the only *haoles*, or "white people" in Hawaiian slang, that were not in the military on the Island. My best friend's husband was a spy.

I loved the place, the people, the food, the culture! I woke up each morning, put on my bathing suit, grabbed my snorkel and fins, a fist full of bread, and walked into the ocean. It was like living in a gigantic Aquarium. I swam around the brightly colored reefs and fed the clownfish and other amazing tropical fish! If the Canary Islands were the mountain tops of Atlantis, Guam and its surrounding islands were the mountain tops of Lemuria or Mu! Because of the Marianna Trench, Guam is actually the highest mountain on Earth, just not above sea level. The *Chamorro* were the indigenous people of Guam and the Mariana Islands. They were the remnants of the *Lemurian* race. They were kind, hospitable people who loved their home and delighted in sharing their culture with us. The palm tree was their tree of life. It provided for all their needs. Its trunk was used to make their homes; the palm fronds served as their roofs. They ate the meat of the precious coconut and used the oil for everything. It was their elixir of life! It was in Guam that I learned about the superpower of Coconut oil long before it became a fad in the rest of the world. Natives would make their own oil and sell it on the roadside or in the local stores.

It was used for everything: cooking, drinking, tanning, moisturizing, and it healed just about everything.

In Guam, Peter only worked half a day or *Hafa Adai*, which means hello in Guam and is a local joke. Life was very, very slow-paced. Because of the climate, the food, and the laid-back lifestyle the people of Guam were very healthy so Peter did not have much to do! The only people he had to treat were those who received free health care from the U.S. government for life. Why? Because they were the victims of radiation poisoning from all the atomic and nuclear bomb testing that went on in Micronesia for years. In my book, *The Chronicles of MerWorld*, I expose the dark military agendas of both past, present and future, as well as the fall of the Divine Feminine Culture of Lemuria. My book was about the growing imbalances of the masculine energy of Atlantis that began to overtake the Divine Feminine Energy of Lemuria which led to the Fall of Humanity. It was about an ancient race of "Wise Whale Women", who worshipped "Mother Ocean", and were eradicated by the blood thirsty Warriors of the "Shark Brotherhood", who replaced their reverence for Mother Ocean with their violent worship of Poseidon. In short it was a metaphor for the hidden history of our planet. I always "download" my information as I write. In fact, I never know what is going to spill out on the page when I put my figures to the keyboard. It's more like taking dictation, at least the first draft! Once I asked my spiritual teacher what was I supposed to do in my life and she told me, "just turn your computer on". In my book, *The Chronicles of MerWorld: The Tale of Serena and Corbin*, which I began in the nineteen nineties I depicted a future world with a black president and powerful weapons of destruction positioned in space surrounding Earth. These weapons could reduce a single human into a pile of ashes while they lay sleeping in their bed. Prophetic?

Our condo was across from the Hilton, where I taught yoga and meditation. My students were from all over Asia: Japan, China, Taiwan. Our sliding glass door faced a huge cliff that jutted out into the Ocean. This was the site of an ancient Chamorro legend about two young lovers who were about to be torn apart because the girl's parents were going to give her away in marriage to another man. Instead of being separated, they braided their hair together and threw themselves over the cliff! I was haunted by this image. Like my days of making columns, I began to sculpt the two lovers falling to their deaths with their hair intertwined in one long braid. I thought to myself, how poetic, if I was ever separated from Peter, I would rather join him in death than live without him! Now I finally realize its meaning. It was a message of healing I was giving to both Peter and myself. It was my eternal pact to heal the trickery of Thoth I would never allow our last six braids of DNA to be separated. IT was a sign to US BOTH that we had at long last healed the Ancient Thothian Curse ALL TWIN SOULS MUST HEAL. We were ready to move forward as ONE no matter what we had to face.

Guam was paradise... until typhoon season came. It took two typhoons, but we finally weighed anchor. Because I was living on the other side of the planet, I got used to staying up all night in my own little world where I painted, wrote, or researched on the internet. I had been getting signs to go to a place called Bocas del Toro in Panama. I don't know how I found it, but I just knew that it was our next assignment. I told Peter we needed to go to Panama and that we would meet someone there who would sell us some beachfront property at a very good price! Peter was not convinced, but he quit his last doctor job and followed me anyway. I had been following him around the world for the past twenty years, so I suppose it was my turn to lead now.

Sure enough, when we arrived in Panama City, as we were waiting to board a little hopper plane to Bocas Del Toro on the Caribbean side of Panama, we met an American woman who told us to look up an Indian called Xavier. He had sold them some land from the Indians. Sure enough, after we arrived in this tiny little town, who did we meet but Xavier who found us thirty-five hectares of beautiful, virgin jungle with an incredible untouched beach. Later, we were gifted with another hundred hectares of jungle that abutted our property that we dedicated as a wildlife preserve. This was the place Christopher Columbus first landed in the Americas and the island was called Bastimentos. This was our small way of healing some of the damage Columbus had caused to the indigenous peoples of the Americas and a wonderful gift to Peter for all his years of service and for at last trusting his intuitive feminine side embodied in me! He loved every moment of it! It was his way of going back to the Cuba that had been stolen from him as a boy. As a political refugee, Peter could never return to his home of origin, so Panama was the next best thing. We employed the local Indians, which they called themselves. Peter was like a little boy playing with his little Indian friends. He rode around the town on his recumbent bike overseeing the building of our home, our dock, our cafe/restaurant, and our Eco-lodge. We bought a boat and would go out to our island property and skinny dip in the ocean since it was completely isolated! It was heaven! But soon came the signs of what we had been trying to escape.

In Guam, one of Peter's colleagues had found something wrong with his liver, so I began to change our diet and gave him liver-cleansing herbs. In Panama, Peter began to get sicker and sicker, but we could not find the reason. Our time was up and we were getting signs to leave. As always, I didn't want to leave. One day I was talking to a British couple when the woman suddenly yelled out, "Your husband is going to die here if you don't leave." I suppose I was ignoring the signs, being so happy in our Caribbean Paradise. But this time, I heard the voice loud and clear. I had been reading the book *The Alchemist,* by Paolo Coelho. It was a book about a young shepard boy's spiritual quest. He had begun his spiritual journey in Tarifa, Spain, and ironically ended it there. I told Peter we needed to go to Tarifa. Again, Peter was not sure about this. So, we sold our property and moved to Miami to spend time with his mother. Peter's health returned and one day, while we were eating the black beans and rice Peter's mother had prepared, she began speaking about how Cubans were reclaiming their Spanish Citizenship. Peter looked at me and smiled. So charged with the mission of reclaiming his Spanish Heritage we set out for Tarifa, Spain. When we arrived, we met an international group of people who seemed to have been waiting for us. We taught them spiritual principles and meditation. I taught them how to recognize where they were at in the various levels of meditation by the sounds that served as guideposts. A young Spanish man named Jaco looked at me like I was crazy. So, I gave the group the mantra "Sat Nam", which means "Truth be its name," and we did a group meditation. I told them to practice that week on their own. I told them the first sounds they would hear as they ascended the levels of frequencies would be crickets, then flutes, violins, the wind and church bells as they ascended into the higher levels of their upper chakras. They were thirsty for what I had to share. The next week Jaco showed up and, with great excitement, told me that he had heard the crickets!

We enjoyed Tarifa, the Southernmost tip of Europe. I could sit on the beach and take a dip in the Atlantic Ocean, then walk a few feet and swim in the Mediterranean Sea! Across the Gibraltar Straits was the continent of Africa. A hydrofoil would take us to Morocco within an hour or a short drive by car would take us to Great Britain, who still held onto the Rock of Gibraltar! So, we had Spain, England, and Africa within an hour's voyage! As our awareness increased, it was becoming apparent that each stop along the way, each place we visited on Earth was our soul's way of finishing up with our past lives on the old Earth and laying a new imprint for the 5D Earth. We were healing and correcting all our alternate identities and bringing wholeness or holiness back to our fragmented souls. We were coming to our cycle of completion as twin souls holding the higher frequencies while touching the souls we met and activating the energetic grids of the Earth. Peter's job was winding down and mine was just beginning.

When I was a child, I had taken the globe on my desk in my bedroom and spun it. I said wherever my finger lands that's where I will go. It landed on Mecca! I looked it up and learned that as a non-Muslim it was the one place on Earth I could not go! This began my lifelong interest in Islam. One of the first plays I ever wrote, directed, and starred in was in sixth grade. It was the story of Islam. I played Mohammed before I knew it was forbidden for anyone to portray him. However, this has not stopped many devout Muslim parents from naming their sons after the prophet.

On the day I took the Hydrofoil to Tangiers, Morocco, Peter stayed behind. I said goodbye to my Art teacher in Spain named Jesus and boarded the boat where I was greeted in Africa by a tour guide named Mohammed. Wow, Jesus and Mohammed all in one day. I was bringing back unity to the distorted time matrix! Mohammed showed me around Tangiers and kept taking me deeper and deeper into the city. I kept asking him to take me back to the port. It was getting late and the last Hydrofoil back to Spain was about to leave. My only way back to Europe was pulling out. In my college days, Jill and I had wanted to go to Morocco from Spain, but our Italian boyfriends warned us that we would be sold into white slavery. I made a mad dash and jumped onto the boat! I was very grateful to be returning back to Europe! Peter and I frequently went to Gibraltar where we would climb the "Rock" of Gibraltar and hang out with the wild monkeys. I would always go to meditate in the beautiful cave of Saint Michael. All this time, Peter had been waiting to get his Spanish citizenship. But we received news that it would take more time.

I had been getting signs to go to Prague. We rented a little apartment close to the center. Peter hated Prague but it had a very dark esoteric history that fascinated me. Prague was old Europe. The river is lined with *Vltavín* or Moldavite in English, which is a dark olive-green rock with an exterior that looks like a pickle. It was there that I was first introduced to this powerful stone. It was formed by a meteorite that hit southern Germany about fifteen million years ago. The splash created a stone comprised of both "Heaven and Earth" or meteorite particles fused together with pieces of Earth. I bought large quantities of these stones and meditated with them daily. This extremely powerful stone can create quantum leaps in consciousness. But it will also leave you when its work is done. I have had and lost many pieces of moldavite over the years. Because of this, Prague's energy is very high and it is believed to be alive with "tachyonic" particles, a particle that moves faster than light. Prague's history is filled with many supernatural events. Prague is where Rabbi Loew is buried. He is said to have created the first Golem. According to Jewish folklore, a Golem is an animated anthropomorphic being that was magically created entirely from inanimate matter, specifically clay, whose purpose was to protect the Jewish people. It is home to one of the oldest Jewish Synagogues which Hitler mysteriously left untouched. The plot thickens. It has a long history of Magic, Alchemy, and Jewish Kabbalah Mysticism. There is a gold coin on display that was supposed to have been transmuted from lead.

I was working with collapsing artificial timelines and would begin each day in front of Prague's famous Glockenspiel, an ornate clock, then move out into different parts of the city working with the gridlines and geometric patterns. I also began tuning in to the true history of our planet and the dark agenda. During some of my mediations, I would visit Nibiru and interact with the Anunnaki who remembered me and wanted me back! I didn't realize it, but I was being seduced by the dark side. They had found my one weakness and wanted to exploit it. One day, Peter and I visited a wax museum where an old woman let us in. We were the only tourists in the place. We went into the basement of this ancient building. Peter went ahead of me and began climbing up a set of spiral staircases. All of a sudden, out of the shadows, a strange man came up to me. He looked young in a very old way and was thin and very pale. Peter looked down but kept climbing up the spiral staircase. I wanted to scream out, "Stop! Don't leave me," but he just kept climbing, which was very strange for Peter, since he was always my protector. I looked into the eyes of this very odd man. At once, I knew he was a vampire. He was there to offer me the gift of immortality. I looked into his eyes. I shook my head, then quickly ascended the steps following Peter.

Peter later told me that it was a test to see if I would join the dark side. Funny how Peter and I got engaged at the play *The Bride of Dracula*. I had initially sought transmutation only because I thought it would keep Peter and me young and beautiful, together in the physical, forever. This was my one and greatest weaknesses, my attachment to Peter as a corporeal being. The lure of the "bad copy" of immortality rather than the truth of knowing I was an "eternal" being was my test. We have been taught to place all our emphasis on the physical which creates a prison for us. The physical world is simply a finite container so that the Infinite can express itself, but when we buy into the illusion that the physical is all there is, we have closed the prison gates.

I knew at some level Peter was dying and I would have given anything to keep him here, even my soul. But love based on enslavement, on stopping another soul from growing and expanding is not true love. Our love was true, eternal, and eternal triumphs over immortal every time! We realized we could no longer stay together in physical form our unified high frequencies were too strong and had been noticed. Peter had completed his soul mission here on Earth and had another, more expansive mission awaiting him, somewhere I could not yet go. He had loved me in a way that I needed to be loved and that only he could have done. He had given me the codes inherent in Sexual Alchemy needed for my ascension and I had helped him return from the dead. I wanted to leave with him, but I had not completed my soul mission here on Earth.

When twin souls must be sacrificed it is always the male (Aden) who must go because the female (Yoshi) holds a more expansive energy. But if the bond is true they become even stronger. Eternal love is a bond that expands beyond the confines of the physical. It can never be broken. When you cling to the lower vibrations of physical enslavement, entrapment, you destroy the purity of the love that once existed. Love is Infinite and the Infinite is love. So, you can never place limits on love. How many great souls have fallen into the darkness because of their despair and bitterness at having lost someone dear? This was to be my greatest challenge!

I was getting signs to move to Cypress. This was a chance for Peter to come full circle. When we first went west, I took Peter to Ghost Ranch, the retreat center in the mountains of New Mexico, where I had gone as a child with my parents. It is a magical place set in the high desert and not far from the amazing Anasazi Cliff Dwellings of Mesa Verde. One evening Peter and I went to the Library to look for something interesting to read. While Peter was browsing, a book fell off the shelf and hit him on the head. The same thing happened to Shirley McClain in her movie *Out on a Limb.* Peter leaned down and picked up the book. It was *The Life of Hippocrates.* Peter had come full circle here on the Greek side of the Island of Cypress. It was there I saw a bust of Hippocrates and knew I had to give it to him.

As we traveled and worked in the multitude of communities on our Earth, Peter and I did the most important part of our work by transmuting the lower frequencies in the areas into higher ones. Sometimes we had specific instructions to carry out, and worked with the energy grids using geometrical shapes, sounds and symbols and sometimes, it was just living in our home and loving one another that transmuted the energy. We created a Heaven on Earth even on the toughest of assignments and in the darkest corners of our Planet. We shared our love and the higher frequencies with the communities we served. Many people loved our energy and craved more, while there were those who did everything to dowse our light or run us out of town. But we were not looking for recognition, appreciation, or accolades. We were just "doing our job".

Our reward was the joy of embarking on a spiritual awakening alongside your soul mate. It is truly one of the most exciting and thrilling journeys of all time. The beauty is that as our old world faded around us, and we moved further away from family and friends, our connection to each other strengthened. We both began to see what an upside-down world we had been living in. We could SEE the "insanity of humanity". Without Peter, I probably would have thought I was the one going crazy! But we began to SEE the same signs and symbols that served as guideposts into a more expansive reality that confirmed the validity of our new perspective on life. As we shared our own secret world, our love and communication deepened to a level that we would have never believed possible! As our awareness increased, our "intuitive" abilities augmented and we would communicate by what we called "T-mails" or telepathic emails, like, "Pick up this at the grocery, meet me here in an hour, or I love you." They were all received telepathically. (There were no "smart"(stupid) phones then) If we went to a mall and separated, we would never think of saying something trite like, "I'll meet you back in this spot in one hour." We knew we would always find each other at precisely the right moment. In fact, any place we traveled on Earth, it was like we were the only two people who existed. Of course, we were there to be of service to others but when the job was done, we were the only ones on our Earth. Perhaps you know that feeling?

If we went on a trip, we were always plugged into our intuition. If one of us felt we should turn down this road, or go into that restaurant, or buy this thing, we always checked it out with each other to validate our reading on the subject. We always agreed. Don't get me wrong, Peter and I had our own distinct personalities, disagreements, and challenges, but together we were "Peter and Elizabeth". We were a third entity that was invincible. We were the two that had become three that had become ONE! We could meet any challenge, surmount any hurdle, climb any mountain. Once we found ourselves in the middle of the desert running on empty, and it was only our concentrated effort of repeating our mantras that kept us going on fumes. Many times, people would not know us individually, but when we were together there was an energy that permeated whatever room we entered. It was a wonderful time indeed. Our lovemaking was incredible not because of the physical mechanics but because we had accessed our higher selves and made love with the power of the universe coursing through our bodies. We were never apart. Except for a few hours each day when Peter would work and I would do my thing, we were constantly together. The smaller the spaces we lived in, the better, because we longed to be in each other's energetic fields. We found it healing, energizing, and of course, filled with love. I had always longed for this kind of "fairytale" love. I wanted to find someone who made my heart flutter whenever he walked into the room. Someone who knew my every thought. Someone I could say I love you to a thousand times a day and mean it. Someone whom I trusted with my life, respected, and marveled at every moment. Someone who lifetime after lifetime together, still amazed me. At last, a person I never got bored of, which for me was unheard of. Peter was constantly reinventing himself and taking on new challenges. He was exciting and brilliant, and as his consciousness expanded, I found him more and more fascinating.

I am so glad I had the patience to stay the course with the Peter I found washed up on Hollywood Beach all those years ago. The angry, hurt, closed-minded "man of science" who had lost all faith. I rescued him and he rescued me right back. My ego had wanted to just move on to the next man, but thank God the Universe kept pulling us back together. It is not easy arriving at this level of love that we have. It takes a great deal of patience, hard work, acceptance, and faith but if you do find your soul mate, it is well worth it. Every button you have will be pushed by your twin soul because they know you so well and that is their job, to challenge you, because it is through this "trial by fire" that your base qualities are transmuted into gold and true love can blossom. True love is unconditional. True love is eternal. I am so glad we had these experiences together because it helps me now that Peter is no longer in the physical to trust the guidance that he gives me. At times, I feel closer to him than ever before and I know he is always with me.

Peter's health was getting worse and worse. He had to be hospitalized in Greece, but they could not diagnose the problem. Peter wanted to return to the States, to our favorite spot on Captiva Island, Florida, where we read our first "spiritual book" *Siddhartha* so many years ago, which started us on our journey Home. I was hoping for another healing. But none came. Peter checked into the hospital at Fort Myers to run some tests. They could not find anything... but what they did find was that Peter's insurance had dropped him. Peter was shoved out the back door of the hospital in extreme pain, with only me to hold him up, no closer to finding out what was wrong. We were presented with a bill of twenty-five thousand dollars for a two-day stay. He applied to receive his social security disability so he could receive the medical attention he needed, but was denied. All the money he had paid into the system, all the battles he had fought for indigent patients across the US, all those years of service to the medical community, and he could not even get a doctor to prescribe him something to ease his pain because he had no diagnosis. At that time, the only thing that was easing his pain was medications that had been prescribed for him by his doctor in Greece that I had shipped to our home in Florida. One day, there was a knock at the door. I opened it to find a police officer with a gun and a federal agent at my doorstep who asked me how I was getting drugs from overseas. I assured them that it was all quite legal, and they left, but my expensive shipment had been confiscated, the only thing that was relieving my poor husband's pain. Big Pharm was closing in on Americans who were buying their prescription drugs for a fraction of the cost abroad. Years later I attended the premiere of Micheal Moore's film Sicko at the Cannes Film Festival. Every bit of it was true and Peter and I had first hand experiences to validate it.

Peter had worked so hard to divert the path of modern medicine from becoming the weaponized, high tech, heartless business it is today. He had fought to preserve the "Healing Arts" integrating holistic medicine with non-invasive technology. He had been the model of compassion and had upheld the sacred oath he wrote so many centuries ago, "Primum non nocere". He had always hired midwives and created birthing suites with handmade additions to make mothers and their babies feel at home while having the backup of modern technology ready if something went wrong. He had refused to perform circumcisions. He had used the technology developed by Nazi doctors to become one of the pioneers of non-invasive laparoscopy surgery. He traveled around the world teaching doctors these techniques and setting up surgery centers in poor communities. He had spent hours counseling female patients and modeling the co-healing modality we wrote about in our book, The Pathway Home. He had served as a role-model to other physicians and medical students, the future doctors of America. He had done everything humanly possible to try and alter the course of modern medicine and it was an honor and a privilege to serve beside him during this great journey.

So, we left the USA and went back to Spain where Peter got his Spanish Citizenship and free healthcare. The only problem was it was too late. He was finally diagnosed with pancreatic cancer and died two days before our twentieth wedding anniversary. I had gone out to get something to eat with a friend I had found. When I came home, Peter was lying in bed with his eyes open. I called to him, but he did not move. Suddenly, I heard the voice of my friend behind me scream, "He's dead!" I really don't remember much after that. I only remember holding him for what must have been hours, rocking him in my arms like the statue of "la pieta" carved by Michelangelo, and saying, "my darling man," as I wept over his lifeless body. I'm not sure how it happened, but the Spanish police were in my home asking me for documents and if I had insurance! I gave them my passport and the hospital records. Finally, a kind woman tapped me on the shoulder and told me that they had to take the body. They had to take away my Peter, my *Tai-Tai*, my all the world, my only true love. I relinquished his body and they put him in a black plastic bag and carried him out the door, like trash. I felt as though they had taken away all the love and light from my life and dumped it in the garbage.

I had bought Peter a new outfit at Corte Ingles in Barcelona for our wedding anniversary that he would never wear. When they asked me why I was returning it, I broke down and began sobbing over the counter. I couldn't stop sobbing. I was panic-stricken, left alone in a hostile world! I felt an undying urge to get Peter back! I walked the streets of Barcelona for days and nights crying for hours on end. I was completely alone. I would call his cell phone repeatedly just to hear his voice. The world was an empty place without my Peter. There was really no point in continuing on, but somehow, I did. I wanted so much to end my life the way I had in so many past lives, but my spiritual teacher had told me my work was not finished here. All at once, her prophetic words rang in my ears. When I asked her how I would have to pay back the karma for committing suicide in my past life, she had told me. "LIVE." Living was now the hardest thing for me to do.

Peter told me to have his body cremated. I could not go and watch his body being burned inside the coffin. Hell, I couldn't even give the word to have the act carried out. Instead, I went to the Sea in Barcelona where my saltwater tears mixed with the salty waters of the Mediterranean. I finally got up the courage to call the funeral home and told them in broken Spanish to burn my husband's body. I know it was just his physical vehicle that he had vacated, that no longer served him, but for me, it seemed so final. I went into the sea and let the waves wash over me, crying and crying while Peter's body burned. Ironically, there was a jazz tune that Peter loved. He once told me once, "this is our song"! We didn't even know the lyrics at the time, but now I do. Peter and I, like two ships in the night, met on the Shore of Hollywood Beach in Florida.

Strangers on the Shore:
"Here I stand, watching the tide go out
So all alone and blue
Just dreaming dreams of you
I watched your ship as it sailed out to sea
Taking all my dreams And taking all of me
The sighing of the waves The wailing of the wind
The tears in my eyes burn
Pleading, "My love, return"
Why, oh, why must I go on like this?
Shall I just be a lonely stranger on the shore?"
ACKER BILK

I cried for months. I cried so hard I could hardly see, until one day, I wandered into a store for eyeglasses in downtown Barcelona. I took a pair down and put them on, I could see again! I was forty-five, so I guess the crying had brought about the inevitable need for reading glasses. I felt so old, so tired and so all alone. My life was over, but why wasn't I dead? Peter had been the love of my life. We had found each other on the shore of this broken Earth, we had overcome our past traumas, transmuted our hurts, and pain from our previous incarnations here on Earth through the power of love. We had committed to our eternal love by joining our hearts as ONE. He had transmuted before my very eyes from an angry broken man of science, entrenched in the dogma of the inverted systems, who had lost all hope, faith, and his connection to Infinite God Source into a very wise, compassionate, intuitive and gentle man who had embraced his divine feminine as well as his divine masculine. He was loved by many, especially me. He had touched many, many lives and I was blessed with the gift of bearing witness to his transmutation and ascension into the divine infinite human being he was. It was not in one magic moment, but through each and every moment of our lives together. Peter had chosen a painful death to help me release him. But he had died healed! He taught me many things but most importantly he taught me how to love completely, holy, and unconditionally. Now, I just needed to learn to love myself.

CHAPTER 13

LIVING AGAIN

During our travels around the world, Peter and I had created our own little world. Friends, colleagues, and family members drifted away as we had moved from one community to the next. We remained encapsulated outside of time and space in the higher dimensions of bliss. We used to say to one another, "I can let go of anything but you!" Now that bubble had burst, and I found myself alone. I looked to the old paradigms of 3D Earth only to realize how completely broken and totally screwed up the world was. Our love had sustained me in such a high frequency I had glided over all the problems of 3D earth now the pain of losing Peter caused me to crash land. My grief was overwhelming and unbearable. I could not allow myself to FEEL for fear it would consume me. So, I turned to outside sources. I searched for comfort in the men around me. I was a young widow living alone in Spain and had no trouble finding it, but all I wanted was Peter. Anyone who has managed to find their soul mate and evolve their relationship into a sacred union knows that nothing can ever compare! Once you experience the magic of this union you loose all interest in any other sexual partners. All I could focus on was the absence of Peter. After his death, Peter came to me in a dream and told me that I now needed to give my love for him to humanity. But that was the last thing I wanted to do. I was deeply hurt and angry, so very angry at God for having taken away the only thing I truly loved. My grief clouded everything. It had opened portholes in my energetic field for shadow creatures to attach to. I was still not ready to move into my own power, to access my multidimensional nature, to find my own inner peace, and to carry on our work in the world.

I was guided to move back to Florence, Italy, where I had lived before I met Peter. In the early eighties, I had tried to start the New Renaissance School for the Creative Arts back then but everything just kept going wrong. That was when I ended up leaving Italy and meeting Peter. Now twenty years later, the timing was right, and my vision was ready to take fruition, and because of Peter, I could. With his dying breath, he had moved us to Spain to reclaim his Spanish citizenship. He had done this for me so I could get into the EU. So I returned to Florence and got my permanent residency in Italy. Funny how life is. So many times, when you want something so badly, it is taken from you, and then it comes back when you least expect it or even want it. When I met Peter, all I could talk about was going back to Italy. He used to tell me he would wake up each morning and look over to see if I was still there! Now that I was in Italy and my dreams were coming true, all I wanted was Peter!

I threw myself into my vision to create spiritual films that uplifted humanity. What I hadn't been able to do in Hollywood, I would do here in Florence, Italy laying the foundation for the New Consciousness Renaissance. I created a production company called Infinite Human Productions to produce my student's films. My goal was to help students connect with their divine inner creative sparkle, learn to trust their intuitive voice, and produce stories from the soul that helped to heal and awaken themselves and humanity. I wanted to not only help the students learn about themselves, but I wanted to give them a professional start. I hoped to create an alternative market outside of the preemptive programming of Hollywood, here in Europe centered, around artistic expression, enlightenment, and creativity born of the soul. I dreamed of co-creating a new film market for conscious media. I had my students create film shorts that could be shown in International Film Festivals around the world. I founded the Florence International Film Festival for short films where I premiered my student's films alongside with other professional's international film shorts. I felt Peter's presence around me constantly, but every time I did, it only filled me with pain and sorrow! I would actually get angry at him for not being with me in the physical. So I swept all my grief under the "red" carpet!

My first students were amazing! I was telepathizing with them even before they arrived. I would have a story rolling around in my mind weeks before they arrived, then I would ask them to pitch the film they wanted to produce, and they would open their mouth and begin telling me the same story! Talented Artists, Directors, Actors, Musicians, Graphic Designers, et cetera showed up from all around the world to help out, which was wonderful since all our films had no budget. I had started the school with zero financing and a lot of passion. I knew nothing about managing a business, creating a budget, or doing payroll.

The first film was called *Eye Talk* made by an amazing soul from Ireland. It was a coming-of-age movie about a young man questioning his sexual identity. I remember this intelligent, kind, caring, and very aware individual who had the courage to reach deep inside and explore his own innermost shadows and express that journey on film. When we first met he confessed to me that he wasn't sure if he was gay or not. I clamped my hands and said, "let's find out!" So through the telling of his story, he was able to move through his pain and fear, heal himself and emerge the hero in his own life journey. He made one of the most impactful films, which we took to the "Cannes Film Short Festival" and it even went on to the Durango Film Festival in the USA. But more importantly, he came to Florence a boy and he left a man. This, to me, is the mark of a great artist. Someone who has the courage to bare their soul to the world. One who uses their divine creative expression and the Alchemy of Art to transmute their inner shadows and in so doing touches the collective consciousness of humanity. True Art heals, awakens and inspires and requires a bit more "inner" work than ducktaping a banana to canvas.

The next film we made was Eve-o-lution. It was by a young Latino girl who had suffered greatly in her misogynous culture. Her film was about the biblical figure of Eve breaking free from her "cruse". It demonstrated how women have been defined and pigeonholed by men for years. In this film, Eve strolls nude through *Piazza della Signoria* eating the "apple" of knowledge and throws away the core, breaking free! It was about women moving beyond the male-imposed labels and finding their own identity. We premiered the Film in Florence. The audience was from all walks of life, both men and women, ranging from traditional middle eastern cultures to modern day British and Americans, mixed with Italians from all generations. The film was roughly eight minutes long, but the "discussion" that followed lasted for two hours! I had many wonderful, talented students whose films were very healing to all, but especially to me. One very loving and spiritual girl wrote and starred in a beautiful film called, *ALLONE*. It was about a woman reading aloud a love letter she had written to herself. It was a love letter from her higher self, telling her how she was giving away all her love to the wrong people when she, her higher self, had all the love she was seeking and longed to give to her. It was such a beautiful message that all the world needed to hear, especially me! I was still not able to love myself. I refused to face the reality that Peter was not coming back. I was clinging to the past, attached to the Peter I had known in a physical body. I was not accepting his "death", his transformation, nor facing my pain and grief because it was too unbearable. I had just buried it deep inside until one day a student appeared and made a beautiful film called, *Notes to Heaven.*

This young girl had lost her boyfriend in a tragic accident. We both held deep scars from our grief that needed to be healed. In her film, she conducted very touching interviews with people who had lost their loved ones. I was among those she interviewed. She then invited one hundred people to write notes to their loved ones who had died and tie the notes to red balloons, which we all released in front of the Church of *Santo Spirito* in Florence, Italy. We filmed it on my birthday. We filmed all the balloons lifting off in front of the Church. I had written a note to Peter, but I didn't want to let my note go. When I finally did it skyrocketed up into the heavens like a helicopter! A few days later, we received a message from someone in Mount Olympus, Greece. They had found three of our notes caught in a tree. Amazing! We showed the film at the Odeon Theatre as part of the Florence International Film Festival.

My film school had brought me back to life. My reward was not in money, for I did everything on a shoestring budget. My reward came in staying alive! I had found something I loved doing, and my passion drove me forward. I attracted many courageous souls had a deep desire to grow, explore, and heal themselves. This healing not only touched my life, but the lives of the audiences and those who volunteered their services in a very intimate way. It was magical. The work was created from a place of love, devotion, and from the soul. But this also began to attract the upper echelon of Florentine society. I was embraced by the Tuscan Film Commission, who had their own agenda for me and my film school.

Our next film was actually based on a screenplay that I wrote at the University of Miami where I taught Freshman composition and audited a screenwriting class. It was about a time traveling female who comes to Florence the day of the *Pazzi Conspiracy*, falls in love with Lorenzo the Magnificent and consequently saves his life. A wonderful student from Panama showed up with a similar idea. It was about the "*Pazzi* Conspiracy" or the attempt on Lorenzo de Medici's life and the murder of his brother Giuliano. We called our film short, *The Prince*. We got permission to film it inside *Palazzo Vecchio*. We filmed a scene where Lorenzo stood staring up at the painting of the Madonna dell' UFO while his advisor, played by a brilliant actor who had a professional acting company and supplied all the costumes for the production, warned him that Rome did not like his "interests," referring to his esoteric studies. We hit a nerve in our innocent attempts to expose the darker side of the Vatican. My crew was falsely accused of knocking over a cleaning sign and I was taken to a part of the palace that had served as a prison for famous historical figures such as Savonarola. There I was held "prisoner" not allowed to rejoin my film crew to oversee my student's production. But we made the film and it premiered at the Tuscan Film Commission's annual film festival.

No one was ready for the depths of the truth we were exposing, and I began making enemies in Florence. After that, the Tuscan Film Commission wanted to "screen" my films. However, I was told by my student that after our little short, *The Prince,* premiered at the Odeon Theater in Florence, Italy, the Vatican, nearly five hundred years latter, issued a statement admitting to their involvement in the *Pazzi Conspiracy.*

Ironically the patterns of my past life during the Renaissance were once again surfacing. In that lifetime, as Marsilio Ficino, I had faced numerous accusations of heresy from the Church. I had navigated the cesspool of Machiavellian politics, as well as the jealousy and backstabbing that had plagued prominent Renaissance men of that time and I had managed not to be poisoned like so many of my colleagues. I found myself having a Deja Vu! This time it was compounded by the jealousy of my success as an independent American woman living in Italy. The same Machiavellian tactics were being employed to secretly turn my students against me. It was after all Florence, where not much has changed in five hundred years and the same illuminati families held this beautiful city prisoner. As a result, I pulled away from the Social Spotlight and decided to write, produce and act in a film directed by my student who was mentored under a very talented director from England. Again, I was so fortunate to have such talented people working with me! It was a comedy about the Ancient Roman Gods making a comeback. Mars, Venus, and Cupid roamed the streets of Florence in search of Psyche! It was called *From Florence with Love*. A year later, Woody Allen released his film titled *From Rome with Love*.

Peter's greatest pain was leaving me. He was so worried about how I would survive on 3D Earth. Quite frankly, he had taken care of all the "earthly" business and provided a buffer between me and the malicious intentions of this fallen male-dominated planet. I genuinely did not know how dark and sorted things could be. I felt like a lamb left to a pack of wolves and my grief made me very vulnerable. Despite my professional successes I had not dealt with my grief and patterns from my past life were reemerging. In my past life in Germany when Peter was killed, I had committed suicide by taking sleeping pills and drowning in a bathtub. After Peter died, I could not sleep. The bed felt so empty. I could not allow myself to FEEL the devastating pain of his loss, so what did I do? I began taking sleeping pills! I loved sleeping because it was in my dreams where Peter and I would meet and have a life together!

In my dreams, my Peter Pan would always come to visit me. I'd be so glad to see Peter and then I would tell him that I had the worst nightmare I dreamt he was dead. I would hug him and tell him how glad I was that he wasn't dead. Peter would just stare at me and smile. Then, in the morning when I woke up, I would remember that Peter was dead. The first word out of my mouth was "Fuck!" Then I would take more sleeping pills and go back to sleep, where Peter was still alive and we had a life together.

"You know that place between sleep and awake, that place where you still remember dreaming? That's where I'll always love you, Peter Pan. That's where I'll be waiting."
SIR JAMES MATTHEW BARRIE

I found "living" was the hardest thing to do. Soon I found one pill wasn't enough, so I had to keep increasing my dose. Because of my childhood fear of bathtubs, I only rented apartments with showers. So thank God I didn't drown myself! But it got so bad that I was popping these pills all the time. Honestly I should have died. I remember one night when I had consumed a large number of pills mixed with alcohol. I stumbled home and wanted to just pass out. But "something" kept me awake forcing me to drink water and purge myself. I know that had I not had divine intervention from Doctor Peter, I would not be here today. This continued for seven years until one day I woke up in a rehab unit. I had gone back to the States to see my family and tried to wean myself off the sleeping pills, but when I ran out, I became very ill, and I finally admitted to my parents I needed some help. In the rehab unit, the psychiatrist told me I was bipolar and extremely mentally ill and put me on even heavier medications. WTF? I had checked myself in to get off pharmaceuticals and now they were putting me on more? I was under lock and key, in a mental institution, being forced to take meds every couple of hours! I was living my darkest, deepest nightmare! The Ambien I had been taking was detoxing from my cells and I was in a state of almost total amnesia. I had wanted to forget, forget Peter, forget my pain, and as a result, I had forgotten everything. I had no defenses. I was at the mercy of modern Psychiatry which put me on meds that were far worse than the ones I was taking! I had gotten on to the Big Pharm Merry-go-round and was too grief stricken to jump off!

After I was released, I was in a comatose state of confusion and dependency. I was like a teenage girl taking my meds and completely dependent on my parents! My Dad had been my champion helping me get the help I needed and my mother would drive me to AA meetings. They were great and I was so grateful for them. They gave me the help I needed but I had to get my life back. I finally remembered I had a life in Italy! I found the keys to my apartment in a hidden compartment in my purse and even a return ticket to Italy! I made a phone call, and miracles of miracles, my ticket was still good. When I arrived back in Florence, I had to look at my ID to tell the taxi driver where I lived. I didn't even remember that I spoke Italian! I had gained over fifty pounds in only two months because I was put on Depakote. My legs swelled up like sausages and I could hardly walk. But I had my independence back and slowly began to heal myself. It was a very dark night of the soul. I had no work, no money and I was very ill. I had to go to the hospital twice and to add insult to injury, I found out my father was dying.

My father had been the rock that replaced Peter. He was always a phone call away, always looking out for me. He told me on the phone that "my presence was requested," so I knew I had to come home. But my mother and my brothers did not want me home. They knew at some level my Dad was just hanging on to say goodbye and saw me as an angel of death. The day my father passed, he looked me into my eyes and said, "I think I am going to die." I told him that "wherever you go, God will be there." My two brothers and I held him close, tears streaming down our faces as our father took his last breath. The Dragon King was dead. His funeral was attended by so many people from all around the world. He was deeply loved and had touched the lives of so many human beings. Each one pulled me aside, to recount a story about how David Steere had changed their lives. He was a great man and is greatly missed.

I had flown from Italy to my spiritual teacher's ranch in Montana where I took a workshop about"Dreaming your Future". I had seen myself living in a beach house filled with beautiful paintings in Malibu. So I decided to give Hollywood one last shot. Third time's a charm or so I thought! So I bought myself a one-way ticket to L.A. with some money my mother had given me for Christmas and set out with all the screenplays Peter and I had written over the years for one last attempt to break into the Showbiz!I had seen a woman who channeled an entity called Simon back in the early eighties, who had told me I would one day ride into L.A. on a white horse. I arrived in L.A., not on a white horse but a 747. The apartment I found in Malibu was true to my vision, ocean front and the upstairs was an Art Gallery! The Artists gave workshops in Transformational Art combined with yoga which they called "Yogart"! We would get grounded with Yoga then begin to paint intuitively. This was amazing since I had done the exact same thing in my film school. At night I fell asleep to the waves crashing under my bed. In the morning, I would feed the seagulls scraps of bread from my balcony. I had a small private beach because the surrounding homes had been destroyed in mudslides. The girls invited me to their gallery openings, where I met aspiring actors, writers, and artists.

I loved L.A! It was like the movie *Back to the Future.* I had time-traveled from my simple life in Renaissance Florence into the future. I gorged myself on technology. I bought everything apple, even a Prius so Siri could tell me where to go, and I could answer phone calls with the touch of a button on my steering wheel. I had bitten from the forbidden fruit of the Macintosh apple and was addicted! Little did I know that is was a "poisoned" apple.

I volunteered at a convention put on by G.A.T.E. (Global Association of Transformational Entertainment) which was founded by Jim Carrey and Eckhart Tolle. There were many New Age celebrities there. One man who had worked with Joseph Campbell talked about our need to change the third act, because in almost every film produced today... boom the world is destroyed in the third act! The storyline was always the same, Armageddon outcome! Jim Carrey lay down on stage holding the microphone close to his lips saying how everything was a big put-up job. How it was all B.S. the news, the media and so on. I saw they were trying to create a film school focused on spirituality and self-exploration using many of the same ideas and practices I had implemented in my New Renaissance Film School in Florence. I connected with many people there who shared similar visions to create projects for an alternative conscious film market. I also volunteered at the Spiritual Consciousness Expo at the Hilton. I crossed paths with John Savage again, as he searched for his daughter, who was singing a song about GMOs. All the Who's Who of the "new age" community were there but I didn't know who anyone was since I had been living in Italy and was not up to snuff on the latest New Age Gurus.

It was all wonderful and I was sailing on a cloud of New Age Astral Dust propelled by the California Dreaming of the sixties I had experienced as a child. I had big dreams as does everyone who comes to La-La land. "It was all finally happening!" I thought, "The "New Age" was taking hold. Hollywood was finally ready to produce spiritually uplifting conscious films! They were looking for new voices, new talent, and I had been masterfully guided here by my Spiritual Teacher in a vision I had at her ranch! I was to be part of this New Global Renaissance. All the hard work and preparation I had done was at last paying off. I was going to help storytellers around the world create powerful consciousness films that would enlighten humanity!" I created the Council for Global Enlightenment and planned to bring my film school to L.A.. I joined a group of writers and actors who met weekly in Santa Monica to share our writing and act out our scripts. It was all so perfect! At last talented actors would read the words Peter and

I had written! I signed up for the great American Pitch fest in beautiful downtown Burbank to pitch all our screenplays to Hollywood agents and producers!

One night, as I was drifting to sleep, listening to the waves crashing under my bed and dreaming of my "Great Future", I noticed the inflatable bed I had been sleeping on was deflating. I found myself laying on the hard wood floor of 3D reality. After that my California dream became a nightmare. The underbelly of Hollywood I had been ignoring was rearing its ugly head. While my landlords were in Hawaii the real-estate agent posted an eviction notice on the door and told me that my landlords had not paid their rent and I they had no legal right to rent this space to me! At the pitch fest I had two minutes to make my "pitch." Then the bell would ring and it was the next person's turn. But, I actually took my time and told people a bit about myself and my film school in Italy. Do you know what everyone said? "Can I come work for you?" I was meeting with talented writers and actors every day, who quite frankly were not getting the parts they deserved because they were not willing to "do" what it takes to make it in Hollywood. I heard it straight from the horse's mouth of talented aspiring actors that, "you have to sleep your way to the top". Those who were not willing to pay that price with their body, mind, and soul never got the break.

One evening, I was sitting at a bar in Redondo Beach having some dinner, when a very drunk man staggered into the restaurant. He walked over to me and shouted very loudly, with great passion, "You have no father, you have no husband, you have no son. You answer to no man!" I was shocked, to say the least. It was one of those extraordinary moments in my life when the Universe speaks to you through whomever they can find. I suppose he was reminding me that I was free! It took me many years to decipher the meaning of this dramatic experience. Growing up in Kentucky I was raised to be Southern Belle. Hell I even wore a hoop skirt to my prom! My husband was Latino and I happily followed him around the world, but because of a "twist of fate"I was now alone. I had not been able to have children, my husband was dead, my father was dead and there was no man in my life. Through my life experiences with other women I have found that like me, we have been programmed to think of others first. Our husbands, our children, our parents become our world. Had life been different, I probably would be a doting grandmother, happily taking care of my husband. But life had thrown me a cruel card which forced me to look to myself for everything. This caused me to go deep within. I was slowly beginning to see this as my greatest strength. Life was helping me to embrace my divine feminine power breaking the chains that have bound women for eons. I was becoming a new woman, the embodiment of both the divine masculine and divine feminine, free to walk the Earth clearing the path for the Divine Feminine energy to change the world!

But I still needed to learn that lesson. My mother had been showing signs of dementia. I kept thinking to myself, "why am I wasting my time here when my mother needs me? I have nothing holding me here." So, I climbed into my Prius and drove home. As I drove away, I thought of the pretentious "new age" spiritually I had seen, and all the broken souls I had met. I thought of the dark underbelly of the glamorous movie stars I had learned about in the "rooms" of addiction. It was there I heard a young man's story of how his girlfriend had drowned in her own vomit at a celebirty's Malibu Beach Party. I was finally SEEING the truth behind the fame, fortune, and glamour of all these broken souls who had "made it". Underneath the glitz there was great pain and suffering. What price had they paid for their success? Was it worth it? But I had finally realized that no seeds, no matter how premium, can survive in a weed infested garden. Like crabs in a barrel these sick satanic systems will never allow anyone to crawl out. I had made a lot of friends in L.A., wealthy ones as well as homeless ones. I had learned a lot about money in my life. I have had a lot of it and none, but I have ALWAYS found myself provided for. While I was living in my Malibu beach house, one day I found myself without money and I was invited to eat at a church with a homeless friend. I was very grateful. Money is simply energy. It comes, it goes, and it is not worth fighting over, killing over, and certainly not worth the price of your body, your mind or your soul. "But how sad," I thought, "that so many talented, creative artists, actors, and storytellers cannot use this powerful medium to enlighten our world. How many talented people come to L.A. every day with the desire to share their unique gifts and talents with the world but meet with ruin one way or another?" As I drove further and further away from the smog, the noise, and the toxic frequencies of "Lost" Angeles, an amazing thing happened. I could hear myself think. For the first time since I had flown into this god-forsaken town nearly a year ago, I could hear my inner sounds. The soothing silence of the desert enveloped my soul as I drove deeper and deeper into its emptiness.

CHAPTER 14

HURRAY FOR HOLLYWOOD !

"I put a spell on you, and now you're mine."
JAY HAWKINS

Moving pictures, the greatest mind control device ever invented! And we love them! These broadly cast "moving images" on your tel-a-lie-visions, conjured up through the Magic of Hollywood are simply focused energy for a directed purpose. Like the conductor of an orchestra who waves the baton, that follows the melody, which the orchestra plays, the same is true of the writer who waves their magic pen. She or he who holds the magic pen, creates the words that cast spells of enchantment and holds you under their power. Words when combined with images and the frequencies of music, pack even more power. If a picture is worth a thousand words, a symbol is worth a million. When this magical brew is interlaced with symbols, it speaks directly to your soul and the potion becomes spellbinding.

The word Hollywood means "wood" or stick from the holly tree or a magic "wand." The magic wand of Hollywood has enchanted the world for many generations and changed the way we view reality, the way we speak, even the way we perceive both the past, present, and future. In short, it has created and continues to create our perception of reality. From its humble beginnings with silent films to its multi-million-dollar blockbusters, it has changed the course of history. Broadly-casting its spells into every language across the globe, infiltrating every home, every culture, every race, every creed, every color, and every religion. This Magical tool that keeps us spellbound, glued to the boob tube, mesmerized by its hypnotic sounds and images has the power to do great good or great harm, depending on who is holding the magic wand. So, the question is, who is holding the magic wand of Hollywood?

One of the earliest films ever created was *The Great Dictator* which Charlie Chaplin wrote, directed, and starred in. He delivered one of the most powerful speeches ever to be uttered in history. This inspiring speech was about POWER to the PEOPLE. It inspired humanity to join together in unity against Tyranny. As a result, he was banned from Hollywood and exiled from America, the land of the free. Over the years, Hollywood has degenerated from films like Frank Capra's *It's a Wonderful Life*, *Mr. Smith Goes to Washington* and *The Lost Horizon,* movies with high ideals, powerful dialogue, and uplifting storylines, that celebrated the goodness of the human spirit, into violent, sexually perverted, satanic films depicting the destruction of humanity and the annihilation of our Earth. Computer graphics and cartoons have been weaponized with dark agendas to sexualize and trans-humanize our children. Hollywood reaches into the unaware minds of the masses with this powerful media of preemptive programming, weaponizing great stories and corrupting the kernels of truth left behind in our history, legends, myths, and bibles.

With every generation, the degradation of music and entertainment becomes more pronounced. I remember my dear grandmother, whose husband was a music professor, asking me how I could listen to Rock and Roll. Many have called it the devil's music. I used to laugh at her just as my niece now laughs at me when I don't share her love for punk, rap, or whatever she listens to. It is amazing how each generation shuns the music of the previous generation. I thought this was just the way of the world, until I learned the truth.

In 1885, the Music Commission of the Italian Government declared that all instruments and orchestras should use a tuning fork that vibrated at 440 Hz, which was different from the original standard of 432 Hz used though out history. In 1917, the American Federation of Musicians endorsed by the Italians, followed by a further push for 440 Hz in the 1940s. After World War II, in 1953, a worldwide agreement was signed. Signatories declared that middle "A" on the piano be forevermore tuned to exactly 440 Hz. It is important to note that 432 Hz resonates with the Schumann Resonance, the documented fundamental organic electromagnetic "heartbeat" of our Earth. 432 Hz "feels" better to the human body. It harmonized the cells and the DNA of our organic bodies with the higher "natural" frequencies of Earth and the Cosmos. Research says that music tuned from this frequency is easier to listen to, brighter, clearer, and contains more inherent dynamic range. If you look at a human cell responding to the frequencies of both 440 and 432 Hz, 432 Hz crystallizes the inherent organic geometric patterns of our cells while 440 Hz destroys them. The music of 432 Hz tuning need not be played at higher volumes and thus reduces the risk of hearing damage. After World War II and the importation of the Nazi scientists through the paperclip project, the Rockefeller Foundation made sure the United States adopted the 440 Hz standard leading to musical cult control. Without going too far down this rabbit hole, this theory says that tuning all music to 440 Hz turns it into a military weapon. Musicians like Bob Marley and Jim Hendrix refused to use it. The plot thickens.

According to a whistleblower from an Illuminati family who worked in the Music Industry during the seventies, witchcraft runs the music industry whose "soul" purpose is to cast spells through rock music. In order to obtain a contract with a major studio, musicians must be full "witches" and learn the language of enchantment, a form of doublespeak, where their words have double meanings sourced from ancient curses. The word "Helter-Skelter" which invoked Charles Manson on his wild murderous rampage, is an ancient Egyptian word conjured up by the Beatles.

Most people have no idea what the words of the songs they listen to mean. Yet, they are infiltrating their minds constantly, many times while they are in an altered state of consciousness produced by drugs and alcohol. Sound like MK ULTRA Mind Control? This whistleblower, who was never heard from again, after sharing these revealing statements, publicly recounted how each album is taken into a "temple" room in all major music companies and placed on an altar during a full moon and infused with demons, binding those who listen to it, to a "demonic addiction" to "sex, drugs and rock and roll." If they can do this with vinyl albums, just think about what they have done to "bind" people to their cell phones! Anyone with a bit of awareness who watches Mick Jagger sing "Sympathy to the Devil" in one of his first videos, knows they are watching a Satanic Ritual, as the" Mick" pulls off his shirt revealing the mark of the beast, the face of Satan which brands his entire body. It's been there in front of our eyes for years. "What's my name?" The greatest trick the devil ever did was to convince you he did not exist, the second was to convince you that he was good!

Many people are shocked to hear rumors of Pedophilia, Satanic Rituals, and Child Trafficking surrounding Hollywood. Many are upset to learn that their favorite "icons" have been part of this. These actors that you love, rose to their level of success, fame, and fortune because they were good at "acting." Hello? They never said they were activists, philanthropists, world leaders, spiritual teachers, or morally upstanding individuals to be trusted! But you keep making them so! They are ACTORS, paid to pretend to be something they are not, to "play" a part in a story. They get paid the "big bucks" because they are good at acting, pretending, okay ... deceiving you. Take someone like Max von Sydow, who can convince you he is the son of God, one minute and Satan the next. If they are talented, they can convince you they're good one minute and evil the next. They do so for money. They do so on stage and off. They do not care what is written in the script. If they are supposed to support climate change, or vaccinations, or sell expensive watches they will do so, for a price. That is how they got to where they are today. If you think that these glamorous people who show up at the Oscars and Golden Globes, don't know what they are doing, who they are really working for or what is really going on behind the scenes, think again! Admire them for their acting abilities but think twice before making them your role models, spiritual leaders, heroes, or saviors. They are just minstrels for hire, reading words that are part of a scripted story. Their allegiance goes to the highest bidder. They are paid to distract you from what is really going on. This occurs on screen and off. So enjoy the popcorn!

How could humanity be so blind when the truth has been parading in front of their "Eyes Wide Shut" for decades? While missing children's faces line the milk cartons, the truth has been hidden in plain sight. Let's take the movie *Hocus Pocus,* a fun-filled Halloween movie with Bette Midler and Jessica Parker, right? Witches who come back from the dead on All Halo's Eve, flying around on broomsticks! Great costumes, "enchanting" music, and what special effects! Destined to become a children's classic! But let's look closer at the underlying story line. This is a story about three witches who round up children to suck the life force from them so they can stay young forever. All the while the parents are "spellbound" dancing to the musical incantation, *"I put a Spell on You and Now You're Mine!"* Even when the children come to their parents for help, they are too mind-controlled to help them. Cute? Not when you think about our modern world where parents are so busy working, they can no longer keep a watchful eye on their own children. Or where governments can (il) legally take the children away from their biological parents. We must wake up to the fact that millions of children go missing all over the world, every day or governments take these children away from their parents for absolutely no valid reason. This happened to a friend of mine from Denmark. We must acknowledge and put an end to the child trafficking, pedophilia rings, and Satanic Ritual Abuse that has gone on in front of our eyes wide shut.

All those who rise to power and fame are subject to MK ULTRA Mind Control. This is to ensure they will not break out of the narrative and use their fame and power to expose the truth. It also explains the weird and bizarre behaviors so many Hollywood Icons exhibit along with their black eyes and illuminati hand gestures. Many of them have multiple alter personalities. Perhaps your favorite talk show host, rock star, politician or movie star is charming, funny, charismatic," and a champion of the people on stage. This is their "front" personality that surfaces when the cameras are rolling, but underneath lies rumors of addiction, deviant behavior, and violent stories of spouse abuse or other self-destructive patterns. Many times, these celebrities try to free themselves from the spell of MK ULTRA mind control only to have one of their sub-personalities rat them out. The punishment for trying to escape your mind control is to shave your head or worse. Perhaps we need to have compassion for these mind-controlled victims who are demonically possessed and who have lost all touch with their true selves. Although they may look successful and be one of the "beautiful" people, in truth, they are prisoners in a labyrinth of illusion, subject to whatever altar is called upon to serve their handlers. They have lost the greatest gift of all, Free Will and even their soul! We need to look at the real enemy, these parasitic "controllers" who do not possess one bit of creativity or original thought. Therefore, they must vicariously live through creative people, co-opting their talents to serve their dark agenda, and controlling everything with their black magic money cruses.

There is a long, long list of many courageous souls who have broken free from their mind control or tried to. They used their power and influence to make major positive changes in the consciousness of our planet. These souls, tired of the corruption and deceit tried to expose it. As a result, they have had their characters assassinated or worse, they themselves, assassinated, or their internal suicide program of self-destruction activated. The untimely deaths of many famous people are becoming more obvious every day. We can pay tribute to a few but there are many more unsung heroes and many more each day. John Lennon, Prince, Michael Jackson, Whitney Houston, Robin Williams, Princess Di, Bob Marley, Jim Hendrix, and the list goes on and on as many great souls are taken from us. But take a moment to reflect on all the wonderful people who were a light on this planet and the wonderful gifts they left us. John Lennon finally broke free of his satanic programming and gifted us with songs like: *Imagine, Give Peace a Chance* and marched through the streets singing *Power to the People*. His activism for PEACE brought a tremendous shift in consciousness.

> *"Death is only changing vehicles."*
> JOHN LENNON

HOW PREEMPTIVE HOLLYWOOD STOLE OUR FUTURE:

Hollywood has defined our concept of everything from romantic relationships, family life, money, war, food, poverty, injustices, and even our concept of God. Hollywood uses the power of symbols of ascension and inverts them into satanic occult symbols to subconsciously control us. They misrepresent our true history and herd us toward their prepackaged Orwellian future. They create confusion and fear using trauma-based mind control by creating disaster films that "trigger" our past trauma from the first human holocaust. They cause us to dread our intuitive abilities by depicting everything "supernatural" as evil, hideous, or something to be feared. The subliminal message being anyone possessing these abilities is cursed and must be hunted down and destroyed. They have depicted nature as our enemy and the organic human body as something frail, weak, and powerless, while placing value on AI androids or bionic humans as something to be envied and emulated! If you pay attention, even the most uplifting Hollywood films, have hidden witch messages that push forward the dark agenda of disempowering organic human beings.

The *Star Trek* franchise was monumental in programming our minds as to what the future of humanity should be like. In 1966, the original *Star Trek* series was born. It was born when the powerful waves of ascension frequencies began streaming into our planet during the sixties. This awakened the "hippy movement" as they began to embrace peace and love, and their anti-establishment ideals attacking the social structures and institutions that had been mind-controlling us. For the first time, awakening "star seeds" had their deep unrequited longings for the stars ignited by a starship boldly going where "no "man" has gone before", traveling at warp speed discovering "Alien" life throughout our galaxy.

Despite the fact that this metal ship carried men and beautiful women wearing mini shirts, voyaging throughout a galaxy filled with planets inhabited by more beautiful women, of all shapes, sizes, and colors, who wanted nothing more than to make passionate love to our three leading heroes Kirk, Spock, and Bones, there were some powerful kernels of truth behind the stories. Many of the early episodes exposed mind control tactics, androids taking over human bodies, entity possession, and the existence of highly evolved non-corporal beings. And, of course, there was the age-old struggle represented through the character of Spock, the human's dilemma of head over heart. Should logic and reason rule over intuition, love, and passion? I believe the most positive message to come from the original *Star Trek* series and films that followed was the transformation of Spock from a cold, emotionless logic-driven Vulcan into a loving, compassionate human being who used both heart and mind and was the embodiment of the unification of both the Divine Masculine and the Divine Feminine.

In a few short years, *Star Trek* had implanted in humanity's consciousness a fascination of a world where human beings were completely dependent on technology. Where a "computer" controlled every aspect of human life, from the air people breathed to the "replicated" food they ate. Doctors used the miracles of technology to replace organic body parts with artificial ones, or concocted miraculous vaccinations for every deadly virus imaginable! We were glamoured into believing technologically could "heal" us and take care of our every need. It could send us to the stars and "free" us from our backwards planet. Technology was progress, ascension, the tool that unified our planets and liberated us from our earth prison!

We humans were convinced that the only way to travel to the stars was through artificial technology. This SCAM duped us into believing our own inner divine technology our true multidimensional nature was "less than" "artificial" technology. It taught us that our consciousness was confined to our physical bodies co-opting our infinite nature and creating a dependency on AI technology. We were never told the truth, that our divine technology was far superior to the artificial bad copy they were pawning off on us.

While under the hypnotic spell of space adventures, we were programmed to believe technology had a solution for everything. If we were in a bad situation, we only needed to say, "Beam me up, Scottie!" In one of the last episodes of the original *Star Trek* Series after we had grown to trust James T. Kirk, Spock, and Bones implicitly as our heroes, they aired an episode where they picked up a group of space hippies who had stolen a starship and were on their way to find "Eden." This episode aired in 1968 as the sixties was culminating. These space hippies held their hands up, forming a circle and would chant, "WE ARE ONE." They called uptight, mind-controlled people "Herberts." For example, Kirk was a Herbert. However, they could relate to Spock, who was sympathetic to their mission. They had grown tired of a world dominated by technology under the control of the "Federation of Planets." They longed to find "Eden" where they could live a simple life in harmony with nature and the "ONE."

Of course, they were depicted as crazy kids, and their leader deemed insane by Bones who said he was a "carrier of a deadly virus" and had to be "quarantined." I kid you not. However, they did manage to commandeer the Enterprise and find "Eden". Kirk, Bones, and Spock followed them and found these poor, reckless, hippie kids dead or injured. All the life forms on the planet were filled with a deadly acidic substance according to Dr. McCoy's "technological readings". The message was loud and clear. Don't trust nature, God, or the ONE. Organic life is deadly; only technology can save you. *Star Trek* had completed its mission and was canceled shortly after that. The world of *Star Trek* and its vision of technology had infiltrated the human psyche so completely that when "cell phones" were introduced to humanity, the most popular model was the model resembling the "*Star Trek* Communicator".

Star Trek was resurrected ten years later as humanity was rapidly advancing into the birth of its Age of Technology. *Star Trek*, "The Movie", was about the body of a beautiful woman taken over by A.I. parasites so much so that she became a "mechanism" as Bones put it. She longed to be joined in "Alchemical Union" with a human being, which she did, creating a new hybridized "life form". In the New Generations Series, Spock was replaced by Data, an android, and we saw our characters' bodies become more and more overrun by technology culminating in Captain Picard being assimilated into the "Borg" by having his organic body fused with technological overlays and his mind absorbed into a collective technologically controlled hive-mind.

The construct of technology and space continued to unfold in *Star Wars,* where Darth Vader became "more machine than man", and in the *Terminator Series* where SKYNET becomes self-aware and takes over the Earth, and then, of course, there was the *Matrix Series* broadcasting in plain sight that human beings are enslaved in a prison of the mind and used as energy sources. In truth, there is no such thing as science "fiction." If you see it on the screen or read it in a book, it exists somewhere in our infinite multiverse. "Sci-fi" films over the past thirty years have begun depicting a very dark future world run by negative Alien Entities and A.I. Tyrannical Control. In the film *Minority Report* we are introduced to a future world of total technological tyranny with retinal scan recognition, pre-crime justice, and twenty-four-hour surveillance. If you think this preemptive programming has no effect on humanity, think again. Sci-fi films have been paving the way for cell phones, talking computers, cashless societies, androids, driverless cars, twenty-four-hour surveillance, replicated food, AI life forms and the assimilation and replacement of our organic body parts with artificial ones for decades. Even God has been depicted as a computer in movies like *Logan's Run.* If you want to see the future the Dark Side has in store for you, simply turn on your tell-a-lie-vision.

So, why would Hollywood expose their agenda? Remember the subconscious or "the part of the mind which one is not fully aware of but influences one's actions and feelings,"does not question or argue but simply accepts the "program". So, the real power is not in telling you what to do but in showing you or planting subconscious messages into your mind that influence your feelings and actions. In short, casting a spell over you. This ancient practice is called by many names in our modern world, such as entertainment, marketing, hypnosis, Neuro-linguistic Programming, MK Ultra mind control, mirroring, et cetera! The subliminal messages are carefully hidden in symbols or subtle signs that go undetected by our conscious minds. When you are seduced into a passive trance-like state, anything can be implanted in your mind. As you awaken, you begin to use more of your brain capacity and no longer have a "sub" conscious but become "fully" conscious.

Most films run for about ninety minutes. So for eighty of those minutes, images of a dark futuristic world are flashed across the screen taking root in your brain, as you are lulled into a passive trance-like state in a dark theatre enjoying the popcorn. It is only in the last few minutes of the movie, that the hero appears and "saves the day again." Your brain, like a computer, does not argue; it simply accepts the program. So, for most of the movie, you are being programmed to accept this dark future world as your reality. Your brain is acclimating to the preemptive programming of the future they want you to accept. Human nature does not permit us to accept something that is inharmonious with our fundamental organic nature, values, desires, and our true divine essence. It just feels wrong for most human beings to accept these futuristic nightmares of a dark, anti-life world controlled by technological tyranny. But if they repeatedly feed this to your subconscious, your mind becomes accustomed to it and you eventually accept it as your reality. Who would have thought a year ago people would passively walk into a store and allow some stranger to point a gun at their head and pull the trigger, or walk around with muzzles unable to breath fresh air, or see friends and families only on computer screens? Every day people are being forced to participate in these insane satanic rituals that further bind them to these dark forces and take away their freedom. So people will eventually give in. This is trauma-based mind control programming. As you slowly get accustomed to this new "normal," your subconscious eventually accepts it as your reality.

This is how they are now herding humanity into the great reset of the New World Order of Technological Tyranny. They seduce and glamour you with your favorite celebrities, then they SHOW you what they plan to do, so you eventually accept it as the inevitable "future." That has been the "soul" purpose of Hollywood and all media. As the years progressed, the entertainment industry perfected the "Art" of massive mind control and merged it into the "real" world. Reality Shows became entertainment. "Actors" became presidents. Comedy shows became sources of "daily news" More and more staged events became the "news" as "crisis actors" were engaged to "portray" roles as disaster victims in " real" newscasts. Have no doubt there is no "real news" anymore since the Magic of Hollywood has now found its way into all media, yes even alternative media!

Perhaps there is one Director who because of his keen intellect and unique status left behind a trail of breadcrumbs leading to the truth hidden in plain sight throughout his films. His name was Stanley Kubrick. Early in his career Kubrick asked the US military if he could use their facilities to film a scene in one of his movies. They denied him access of course, but he went on to create such a realistic imitation that he caught the attention of "the powers that be." He was asked to use his skills to stage the moon landing. Why would they do that? Did we not go to the moon? Of course we did. But they knew if they really showed a live broadcast of a moon landing, their Secret Space Program and the multiple off planet cultures who have colonized the moon as well as Mars would be revealed. So, it had to be staged. Kubrick used the same techniques he later used in his film *2001 A Space Odyssey.*

Because of his "big secret", Kubrick enjoyed a unique status in Hollywood that no other director had. All his movies were green-lighted and he gleaned a certain pleasure in exposing the truth by hiding it in plain sight. In his film *Clock Work Orange,* he hints about Adrenochrome and exposes the technique of MK Ultra mind control. In *The Shining,* hidden symbols referring to the Apollo moon landing are abundantly placed throughout the film. Kubrick continued to feel the weight of his deceptions and a need to reveal the truth. His attempts became bolder. In *Eyes Wide Shut*, he exposed the Satanic Rituals of the elite even filming in the home of the Rothschilds. Many believe it was this film that got him "killed." It is true that after his death, many of the scenes he had filmed were edited out and replaced with a more "vanilla" version that was later released. However, I believe it was the film he was working on at the time of his death, A.I., that caused him to mysteriously die of a "heart attack" in the middle of filming. After his "death" Steven Spielberg or "Spell Borg" took over and metaphorically drew on the classic story of Pinocchio, used frequently in MK ULTRA mind control for children, to depict a poor little "A.I." robot boy living in a world where evil human beings were bullies and who had abandoned him and tried to destroy him for being "artificial." And like Pinocchio, all this poor little robot boy longed for was his mother's love and the chance to become "real." I believe had Kubrick lived, the direction of the movie A.I. would have been much different. I think he would have exposed the "Dark" agenda of trans-humanizing organic human beings into A.I. slaves using technology as a weapon against humanity. He already sent us a strong warning in his movie *2001* when "Hal" destroys his human hosts. But the world will never SEE what he wanted to reveal to us because, like so many, he died in the middle of his project.

If you still believe Hollywood has no effect on the future of humanity just open your eyes and look at the children, the future of humanity. Most of them are muzzled with their eyes glued to their cell phone. Many have completely lost the ability to connect socially with other human beings. Now we are swiftly being herded into a false AI Ascension Matrix as Hollywood's pre-emptive programming infects the" spiritual" world with New Age Guru celebrities. They use paltering techniques designed to seduce you with kernels of truth, tagged in words to trigger your deep desire for reconnection with Infinite Source. They herd you into their finite controlled techno spiritual "awakening" and a false AI ascension matrix. They seductively co-op your inner power by placing the power outside of you and keeping you spell bound, poised awaiting for the next " event, happening, solar flash, political hero, the second coming of Christ, the return of the good aliens, or the "creator gods", the next live stream activation to save us. They have humanity looking into their black mirror for every need; to eat, to travel, to work, to connect, to heal, to unite us, to transmute us rather than to nature, our Mother Earth and the Great Spirit of Infinite God Source within!

With the creation of Blue Beam Steering and the Satellite Cage now surrounding our Earth we are now living in a holographic theater similar to the fabricated reality depicted in the film *The Truman Show*. Coming Soon!

We will soon see projected in our skies through the Magic of Holographic Technology shows like: The Second Coming of Christ, Alien Invasions and a whole host of "super natural events" artificially fabricated to distract and coerce you into giving your power away to something or someone outside of yourself. All designed to stop you from connecting to your own inner infinite power, and from realizing you are a Divine Infinite Human Being. You have the power, and it is within! This is an inside job. If humanity would only awaken to their Inner Infinite Power, game over. We could co-create a free world! Storytellers, Journalists, Filmmakers, Musicians, Artists et cetera would be free to express their voices of truth and create from their souls without interference. We could break the spell of Hollywood and give birth to a New Consciousness Renaissance!

CHAPTER 15

FAMILY

I drove back from California to Kentucky to find my mother living alone in our two hundred-and fifty-year-old Log Cabin Home with six fireplaces, a swimming pool, and a smaller cabin which we called the slave quarters. She was eating her dinner out of tin cans with food rotting in the refrigerator. Her dementia was increasing daily, and she was having trouble walking, driving, and even making it up the stairs at night. It was that difficult time in life when the children SEE that their parents are no longer the ones in charge and the roles have been reversed. Or can they? Needless to say, it was not an easy transition for what was left of our family. We had not faced the tremendous loss of our father and to make matters worse, although I always loved my brothers, it was as if we inhabited two separate universes. My perspective, in fact, my very presence seemed to anger them. I moved in with my mother since she was not ready to move into a retirement community and could not live alone. I had no income, so I began working as an intuitive life coach in the office where my family had set up a family therapy practice. I had a Masters in Mental Health Counseling and incorporated "alternative" therapies such as Reiki Crystal healing, hypnotherapy, art therapy, and tarot coaching into my practice. I used the holistic co-healing model Peter and I wrote about in our book, *The Pathway Home*. I started a talk show with local guests who were holistic practitioners, healthfood store owners, intuitive healers and psychics. I also began working in festivals of healing and spiritual awareness or psychic fairs which helped me fine tune my intuitive abilities.

That Christmas I took the opportunity to clean out my dad's old cabin that was filled with mice crap. I cleared away tons of old stuff from the attic. The place was a mess but I moved in so I could have my own space and be with my fahter's energy. My mother had not wanted a dog in the main house I asked her if she minded if I could get one, now that I lived in the cabin. She agreed and magically Kiki appeared the timing was perfect!

I really needed a good friend. Four years prior I had a vision of me living in Florence with a blonde Pomeranian that I named Kiki. I had been looking for her for years. When I found her she was a small grey pom. I almost didn't get her because she did not look like the big "blonde" pom I had seen in my vision. But she just kept clawing at me through the glass. I knew she was the one. But then, the owner said another family had first choice and they had chosen my Kiki! However, when they turned her over and saw she was a girl they passed her onto me and I got my Kiki! I could not imagine my life without her. Not since I lost Peter have I had such a loyal, faithful, loving friend and ally. Dog spelled backwards is God and in this inverted, backwards, insane world, these little pieces of God are gifts to us all. I made Kiki my "service" dog and we embarked on our Service to Humanity together. Ki , like Rei-ki or Chi means Divine energy which is why I was guided to name her Ki-Ki. She is pure divine love incarnate and whenever she walks into a room she fills it up with her playful, loving energy! She has been my greatest spiritual teacher reminding me always to love people unconditionally and play with life! She too is a grid worker and together, we travel the Earth transmuting it into 5D!

I lived in my Dad's cabin, or man cave, as he called it. He used it as his office to see clients, do group therapy and write his many books. The walls of the cabin were crammed with shelves of books ranging from Jung, Freud, Milton Erickson, Erick Erickson and other topics such as psychotherapy, religion, philosophy and of course there was the old dragon king, Puff which I had made for him many years ago. I could feel his presence all around me. He was guiding me. Many evenings when Kiki and I were watching T.V. Kiki would jump up and start barking at the air. Now, we have many ghosts in both the big house and the cabin since it is over 250 years old but I knew my Dad's energy signature! My Dad would guide me to certain books he wanted me to read. I would lie in bed at night and look around the room at all the gifts I had sent him from all my travels around the world. He had found a cherished place for each one in some corner of his Cabin Kingdom. I would reflect on how many people had been within these walls. How many lives had been changed by his gentle voice, positive hypnotic suggestions and wise words.

Once when we were kids Dad told us he would reveal to us magic words he had learned in the boy scouts He told us that if we repeated these magic words over and over again, all the wisdom of the Universe would be ours. We leaned in closely and listened as he whispered these sacred words, "OH WA SAI GOO I AM", then he told us to repeat them over and over again as we kneeled and bowed, waving our arms over our heads. We did so immediately anticipating all the wisdom of the Universe to be ours! After a while, he looked at us and broke into laughter as he watched us religiously chanting, "Oh What a Goose I am!" I think that explains why my Dad turned his energy towards helping people help themselves rather than preaching at them.

Once someone told me how David Steere had taken a gun from his hand. A gun he was going to use to commit suicide. Another time I was at the train station in Rome, Italy where I met a woman who shouted, "You're David Steere's daughter," after I had told her my last name. I often lamented about the years I was not able to sit by my father's side at our kitchen table discussing the true meaning of life, his favorite topic. I left home at seventeen. I believe my youngest brother felt I abandoned him. I had looked over him like a treasure. Once when we were playing at a construction site he fell and cut his knee open. I picked him up and carried his bloody body to a neighbor's house, banging on the glass door covered in blood! Later, our neighbor gifted me the record, *"He ain't heavy he's my brother"* I used to cry every time I heard it.

Although my father and I had been very close spiritually, my brothers did not share the same interest in spirituality, and were none too quiet about it. I would burn sage after a Reiki healing session to clear the space, and my brother asked what that horrible smell was. I told him it was something to clear the bacteria from the air, and the next day I found a can of Lysol on my desk! Ha! Like Joseph and his technicolored dream coat, my brothers did not appreciate my "visionary" abilities and a rift was growing between us daily. Unfortunately, this is a familiar story that often happens among the black sheep of the family, the divine dreamers, those who dare to see the world from a different perspective and break free from their ancestral chains.

Because we are deeply sensitive, empathic souls who came here with a desire to heal, this often leaves a deep wound that must be healed. Secretly all children have a desire to heal their parents. I had tried to do whatever I could to heal my mother by performing crystal Reiki, sneaking coconut oil into her coffee for her dementia, and reading tarot cards to give her a sense of purpose in her life. One day, when I was reading her Tarot cards, my cousin, who is a minister, came into the house, uninvited and began to exorcise me!

I had taken my mother to the hospital countless times, cleaned up her diarrhea and vomit, begged her to take her medications, and in the end, my brother accused me of trying to kill her. Yes, it hurt deeply, I must confess. It has been one the greatest pains in my life to realize that those you love most will never accept all you so want to give them! Whenever I tried to reach out, to communicate, to share my perspectives, I was met with bitter contempt and aggression in no uncertain terms. For example, "That is the stupidest thing I ever heard, you idiot." You get my point. The Divine Dreamers in the families too often become the scape goats . Instead of *sororicide*, my brothers released me, and my divine dreams, from all my duties concerning my mother in no uncertain terms. I was banished from the kingdom, cut off from the family wealth, and even lost the right to see my own mother. I was sad having lost the only family I had. But I also knew that I had done everything in my power to help awaken, heal, and evolve my family. I had to come to grips with the truth that they did not want me to be part of their lives, not the real me. They have never reached out to me and quite frankly would not know whether I was alive or dead, save my attempts to reach out to them. It is still something I cannot fully comprehend. But it is what it is.

Because of my mother's dementia, she would burst into my room in the middle of the night, and tell me to leave and then not even remember it the next morning, and beg me to stay. One day she told me in anger, "I wish you had never been born." My great grandmother had tried to abort my grandmother, her own child, by sticking a coat hanger inside her own uterus. My grandmother held the scar on the heel of her right foot from this attempt on her life by her own mother until the day she died. Then when my grandmother was a little girl, her parents had tried to give her away, but her older sister begged them not to. So, how could I be upset with my mother? You can see this ancestral miasma is passed down from generation to generation and it is up to us to heal it within ourselves to end the karmic chain. I think this may be a familiar story for many Star Seeds who choose families with difficult lineages.

Why would we do that? The reason is because by freeing yourself you change the ancestral miasma of your entire family! The real reason your family members spurn you is because they fear you. They are terrified of your bold actions that go against all that is familiar to them. You are the embodiment of the most terrifying thing that could ever happen to them, change. You are not playing by their rules, living within their lies, following in the footsteps, traditions, or legacies of the family and continuing to define your reality as finite. They see you as a threat and want you gone. The truth is that despite their hateful actions and total rejection of you, your family is secretly cheering you on. Especially your parents, who deep down, want you to break the ancestral curses that have bound them for generations. They long to see you break the chains, hoping that your courage will give them the courage to go against the grain, to free themselves and rewrite a new story.

In reality, my brother whom I thought was my greatest enemy, turned out to be my greatest ally. He released me from all my responsibilities towards my family, freeing me to at last heal myself and find my power within. I know many of you have lost loved ones, friends, family members or partners on your spiritual quest. I recall my favorite movie, *Brother Sun and Sister Moon*, by Franco Zeffirelli. In this film, Saint Francis removes all his clothes and gives them back to his father. As he stands naked before his mother and father, in the town square he says, "What is born of the flesh is flesh. What is born of the spirit is spirit. I am now born again." As much as we love our families, our parents, our siblings, our spouses, our children, our friends, our freedom and theirs, must be honored. They may or may not choose to come with you on your journey home or even want to be around you. They may not choose to ascend becoming Infinite Human Beings, now. Your ascension may even irk them because of their fears. But you must know beyond a shadow of a doubt that your true Star Family awaits you as you return home to them. Do not be afraid to "go it alone" for a while as you transit out of the broken relationships and biological families of 3D Earth. Know that they have served their purpose to help you break karmic patterns and pay karmic debts. In our imperfect fallen Earth nobody is perfect so forgive them and do your best to love them unconditionally. Your true Star family who will celebrate you not tolerate you, is awaiting your return!

Ultimately, it all begins and ends with you. All relationships are ultimately about you learning about yourself. If you are seeking love from someone else, where are you not loving yourself? If you are longing for a supportive community, how are you not supporting yourself? If you want someone to take care of you, where are you not taking care of yourself? When you do these things for yourself, you will find that your external world mirrors your inner reality. You will draw to you people that love, support, and truly care about you. The first relationship is to love yourself. Every relationship blooms out of the one you have with yourself and the way you feel about others reflects how you feel about yourself. When you can stop looking to a partner, a parent, a child, a family member, a friend, a boss, a spiritual teacher, to others for validation, you will be free! You are the one creating your own life story. If you walk around angry at people because they are stupid sheeple, then you are giving away your power. True, we may be witnessing (m)asses of mind-controlled sheeple who refuse to think for themselves, but don't let that take away your own peace of mind. They have free will and are choosing to create that reality for themselves even if it is a passive choice. Getting angry is not going to wake them up just as shouting at a frightened child does not help them.

We are all part of the collective human consciousness. Since the first human holocaust down through the eons we humans have been ridiculed, shunned persecuted and crucified for stepping out from the herd. We have been burnt at the stake for speaking the truth, for stepping out of line. So, of course, there is a deep seated fear that each human being must overcome in their own time. All we can do is be role models of how to live in love rather than fear. We have reached a point on our Earth where those of us who are awakening need to be the patient loving parents that humanity never had. This is our own test to move beyond our own emotions of fear, anger, hurt and grief so we can stand in the stillness and power of love and truth. We need to speak with wisdom which is knowledge administered with love. If you can do that, watch what an amazing effect you will have on others. Ascension is not a religion where you have to convert people. Your ascension, awakening or freedom is not dependent on others. Yes, it would be wonderful if one morning the entire planet woke from the nightmare spell and no longer let the controllers control them, but everyone has free will and is learning their lessons at their own pace. We need to patiently be available for those who awaken from the nightmare and choose to heal themselves.

Actions speak louder than words. Rather than running around trying to "red pill" those who don't want to hear what you have to say, become the embodiment of Truth. TRUTH IS A FREQUENCY, something you embody and constantly transmit without saying a word. It moves beyond the barriers of the brain and is absorbed into the energetic field of all those around you. If you do this from a place of love you may find people are much more receptive. The other night I spoke with my brother by phone. During the conversation about our mother he mentioned vaccinations several times. At the end of our conversation he urged me to get vaccinated to which I responded, "I love you brother". Ironically at the heart of this vax, anti-vax war that seems to have broken out there is love. Behind the urges of each person is a sincere concern for their well-being. We all want the same things for one and other; to be healthy, happy, to live long and prosper!

HOW DID WE GET HERE?

The birth of a child is a miraculous event to be celebrated and cherished! The human child needs to feel welcomed and mid-wifed into the world with loving tenderness. Yet it has become standard medical procedure to do so in such a harsh manner that it creates deep wounds of birth trauma. Most children are birthed into a sterile world of bright lights and loud noises. The umbilical cord is severed immediately, and the child is smacked on the rear to start them breathing. For male children shortly after their arrival, the most delicate part of their anatomy is mutilated. Most children are injected with toxins, nanobots, and tracking devices shortly after their arrival into this world. Then registered as property to be bought, sold and traded. It is up to us to change this now.

Our parents or surrogate parents have been through the same indoctrination that has existed on Earth for eons. They naturally pass this on to their children both consciously and subconsciously. Because of our dependent state at birth and as a child growing up, we are in need of others for our survival. This need is equated with love, and unfortunately, in most cultures, the child is taught that love is something that must be earned, won, or bought. If you are a good little boy or girl and behave the way mommy wants you to, I will love you. If you make good grades or succeed in a certain career, I will show you my approval (love). And if I don't love you, even if I can't, it means you are bad. So, children quickly learn how to adapt in order to survive. The child learns which behaviors and actions illicit love and which actions do not. This is taught to the child by the parents who themselves were taught by their parents and so on, to mold them into the insanity of humanity.

Once the child has been properly conditioned by the family unit, the child is sent to school where the social conditioning and indoctrination can be fully implemented at an early age. This is where the child learns everything it needs to know about how to fit into a dis-eased society. They learn that every thought, feeling, instinct, creative impulse, or intuitive knowingness they have is bad and must be repressed. They are taught that the only way to survive on planet Earth is to adapt to the insanity of humanity. They are NOT taught that they are Divine Infinite Human Beings who are a precious gift to our planet and need to be loved and cherished and that their thoughts, dreams, and aspirations are vitally important to our dying world. Rather they are taught they are not enough and must abandon who they are in order to "fit" into this broken Earth. They are taught that they "know" nothing and must learn everything from scratch. They are conditioned to believe being different is bad and their unique and special gifts and talents have no place in the world. They are taught to never question authority but blindly obey rules. This programming is then reinforced by society at large and the role models who surround the child. So, like a rat in a maze, the child is given love and positive feedback every time they appropriately respond to the external world with their indoctrinated programming. They are punished when they respond using their own independent thought, creativity, discernment and intuitive knowingness.

By the time most children reach puberty they have had their "spirit" broken to fit into our broken world or they have rebelled and become a "problem" child. Many of these problem children are simply angry that they came here with such amazing gifts and talents to help fix this broken planet, but no one wants to hear, see or acknowledge their authentic selves. They just want them to learn how to adapt to a broken world by doing the "same things over and over again and expecting things to change", which by the way is the definition of insanity! So, these teenagers, the sane ones living in a mad, mad world, rebel. And what happens to young people who rebel in an insane world? They are the ones diagnosed as insane, mentally ill, or sick because they cannot adapt to the insanity of humanity! So, their parents take their "disturbed" sons and daughters to the doctor, the therapist, the school counselor, and the psychiatrists to help the child "adjust" to our insane world. But since it is an impossible task to make a sane person insane, they have to numb them to the pain of going against the grain of their soul, their own personal truth and authenticity. Pain is an indication that something is terribly wrong which is why God gave us the gift of pain. So, we can heal. But instead of looking at the underlying cause of the pain these Doctors of Medicine give them drugs so they will not FEEL their pain. For those kids not prescribed drugs by the medical community, they find their own drugs. But for many, the pain becomes unbearable. The only thing left for them to do is to end it all by taking their own life. This explains why there is so much drug addiction and teen suicide. These sensitive souls could no longer adapt to the insanity of our broken world, so they left. Many of those who have survived learned how to tolerate their pain and paid the price by sacrificing who they truly were to "fit" in.

So, let's look at the family unit where our foundation for relationships began. Let's see how societal norms promote this co-dependency. Let's examine just a few of the beliefs we were raised with. Family units are taught they belong to each other like possessions or extensions of one another. Relationships are riddled with co-dependency and ownership.

For example, "my" children, my husband, my wife, my mother, my father. This is ridiculous you may say these are just terms of endearment. Let's look closer at the premise of "thought directs energy" in statements like, "No son, daughter, wife, mother of mine is going to do such and such..." Or ancestral curses like, "No one in our family has ever done that!" What family ancestral curses may still be haunting you? This is perhaps why many of you have distanced yourself from family abstain from family gatherings or are considered the black sheep of the family! However, the next time you find yourself surrounded by family, rather than judge, observe. Observe the things that trigger you because, most likely, these are the things that have been passed down from generation to generation. It is your job to uncover these family skeletons, beliefs, traditions, and curses and take them out of the closet to be healed, and love them to death. This is the way you can best serve your own family of origin by transmuting these ancestral curses through self-love.

As you ascend in frequency letting go of that which no longer serves you, you heal not only your present self but the past and future versions of you. So if you get triggered instead of blaming your parents or feeling victimized by others, begin to see it as an opportunity to heal. Own your pain, suffering, shame and guilt but realize it was not your fault. The Universe has given you the opportunity to heal your dis-ease once and for all, clearing up lifetimes in a single moment! You do this by first opening the closet door and allowing yourself to feel the pain. You must "feel to heal"! Then embrace these experiences with self-love. Knowing it was never your fault, you were simply born into a fallen planet. This is how you transmute the pain of the old finite Earth leaving your baggage behind and freeing yourself to step onto the New Infinite Earth! This is a process that may take linear time as you learn to change your programming and react differently to trigger events. But with loving patience, one day you can see the pain and suffering as a gift, that made you who you are. Your pain served an invaluable purpose along your life journey, but you no longer need it! Every person who enters your life is a gift to you. It may not always be pleasant and often, the most powerful life-changing lessons are indeed the most painful ones, but, nonetheless, they are all gifts to help bring you closer to the true essence of who you are... Infinite.

ELIZABETH MONROY M.S. & PETER MONROY M.D.

CHAPTER 16

THE TRUTH ABOUT SPIRITUAL TEACHERS

"When the student is ready the teacher will appear. When the student is truly ready, the teacher will Disappear."
LAO TZU

I left Kentucky and moved to Pawley's Island, South Carolina, in search of Paradise. I hoped a bit of the old world I had known as a kid growing up in the seventies still existed in America. I had fond memories of childhood vacations to both Florida and Pawley's Island. But things were much changed. Thirty years earlier, I remember having delicious fresh seafood pulled from the Ocean and wonderful locally grown produce. Now the "fresh" seafood was trucked in, and locally grown produce was non-existent. What had passed the test of time was the remnants of what had been the largest plantation in the South. I visited this plantation now made into a private park that had once housed over two thousand slaves. I followed the narrated tour around the planation. It was a story of a poor slave boy who died of an appendicitis because no doctor was ever called to attend to him. I had several past-life memories while walking the grounds. One of being a slave and another as the wife of a wealthy plantation owner. Both were forms of slavery. Funny, not much had changed in South Carolina, although the civil war was over, the black community remained in much the same conditions that existed over three hundred years ago: no health care to speak of, same working conditions, and run-down homes. On the plantation each slave had a long list of chores they had to complete before they could go to sleep each night. Their food was of a very poor quality. They were kept illiterate. They had to have written permission to travel, and were often muzzled. Wait. Doesn't that sound remarkably like our world today? In fact, it has become apparent now that slavery did not end in the South it just expanded to include everyone.

I had planned on renting out my place for an income and visiting my mother once a month but those plans went south when I found out I wasn't permitted to rent my own home out under the "home owners'" association rules and I was banned from visiting my mother! I found myself alone, broke and getting sicker every day with no health care! I didn't know it then but, my condo fees had gone to having surveillance cameras with "high speed" internet (5G) installed at my "resort". I am extremely sensitive to EMF waves and I was getting sicker and sicker each day. The skies were filled with chem-trails and after enduring five geo-engineered hurricanes, and eating expensive fake food, I realized Pawley's Island wasn't the Paradise I had sought and I was again a slave! My health was so bad I was declared legally disabled by social security but the Judge did so in a way that I was not able to receive one penny of all the money Peter and I had paid into the social security system. But all these were lessons I had to learn, pushing me to reclaim my power within!

After Patrick my spiritual teacher's husband, had died, Peter chose to distance himself from Sharon and the group. Our lives took us out of the US and globetrotting across Asia and Europe. During this time Peter would drop little hints to me like, "Do you believe everything Sharon says?" Upon Peter's death bed, he told me that if Sharon said that he "wanted" to leave me it was a lie. After Peter's death, I returned to seek solace in Sharon and the group, but things had changed, mostly inside of me. Sharon casually told me as I stood sobbing in front of her that, "Peter was always going to leave at this time." Which only added insult to my deep sense of grief and abandonment. Like my family of origin, I no longer resonated with my "spiritual" family. I had to pay huge sums of money to fly across the country to take workshops, then stand in line to ask my spiritual teacher a "question" which began to just feel wrong. It wasn't until one day when I missed three flights trying to attend a workshop, that I got the message loud and clear. I had outgrown my spiritual teacher and my spiritual family. It was time for me to move beyond them and start finding my own answers within. This was terrifying. I felt utterly alone. Peter was gone, my father was gone, my friends had dropped along the waste side as I continued to travel the globe and evolve. I had no family to speak of and now no spiritual family and no spiritual teacher. I was completely and utterly alone except for Kiki, my little fur baby who loved me unconditionally! This was one of the most difficult periods of my life. It was in my darkest hour that my "dark" mentor appeared.

Gene was married and had been part of our spiritual group. He had met Peter and me casually at some of the retreats and I had a vague recollection of him. He began talking to me about things our spiritual teachers had only eluded to. He showed me just how deep the rabbit hole goes and to what extent the Dark Side commanded our planet. All our conversations were by phone. At first, I thought the guy was nuts! I just wanted to hang up and forget about him. But it became clear that Peter was working through Gene and I had something to learn from him. It was like in the movie *Ghost*. Gene kept telling me things that only Peter and I knew. He spoke for Peter because I was too ill to raise my frequency enough to communicate with him. At first, I didn't want to believe all the horrible things he was saying. They seemed crazy! But I was known to be a little crazy. Certainly my brothers thought so. They called me their "crazy" sister. I even had a psychiatric label to support this. Was I crazy? But then I could see the patterns emerging. Like *Alice Through the Looking Glass*, I was seeing the mirror opposite of what I had perceived as reality. Still, I refused to accept the degree to which darkness ruled our planet. I didn't want to hear all of this "negativity"! However, something inside me kept pushing me on! I could no longer ignore the truth staring me in the face! The deeper I dug in, the more I researched, the more I pushed aside the veneer of the "accepted" reality, the more I could see that our world really was all a put-up job. Patrick had been telling us this for years, Sharon had dropped hints under her breath, and Peter had tried to tell me the world wasn't what I thought it was and now my own life experiences had been proof! But nobody wants to hear that! I just wanted to let all the darkness around me remain in the shadows. I was afraid to look deeper because that meant I would have to look at the darkness within me. It meant I had to face my own pain, sorrow, fears and the deep wounds of my past. I would have to begin the painful process of healing myself. I would have to forgive myself and yes finally love myself. I have found that those who refuse to SEE the darkness in the world around them, also refuse to SEE the darkness inside of themselves. But you cannot heal in lies!

Gene told me books to read, films and videos to watch, and practices to perform. He spent long hours on the phone helping me to get off my meds, balance my chakras, change my diet which he said was the cause of bipolarity. He educated me about the Dark Side that had been on this planet for eons. I soaked it all up like a sponge. This was the missing piece of the puzzle that would make sense out of my life experiences. I was beginning to think I was a failure and didn't have what it takes to get ahead in life, and would never succeed at anything. At last, I realized my life, thus far, had been a tour to show me the shadows that were ever-present in every aspect of our finite 3D Earth. I began putting together the true history of our planet. I began to heal my past lives. I began to retrieve parts of my soul identities that had been fragmented by trauma and journey toward wholeness. I began to remember where Peter and I came from and have a much clearer understanding of my mission here on Earth. I lost my fear of SEEING the dark side and how completely corrupt and inverted this fallen earth is. I began to let myself FEEL the deep grief, pain, and loss of Peter, to let go of the world and how I imagined it to be, and everything that I had held so dear. As I detoxed my emotions my body began to heal! I got off all my meds! I began to activate my pineal gland and accrue more genetic strands. I was understanding books and texts I had previously been unable to decipher. My pineal gland was clearing, and my third eye was opening. At last, I was able to SEE and raise my frequency enough to join Peter.

I visited Peter on our future/past Earth of Tara in Andromeda. Funny, on the eve of our wedding, Peter and I had a big fight because I wanted to have a child. He already had five children but he agreed to have one more child for me. I wanted to name our child Tara, if she was a girl. But as fate would have it, we couldn't have children. Peter was so angry at his second wife he had asked his friend and colleague to give him a vasectomy that could never be reversed. Well, it worked. Even though Peter underwent a painful operation for me to reverse it, it did not take. It became obvious a child was not in the cards for us. It was then I realized that the child that we were giving birth to was not "Tara", a human child, but Tara, the future 5D Earth. We were working together to create a rainbow bridge from 3D Earth to 5D Tara. I would serve as an anchor on the 3D Earth and across the rainbow bridge in Andromeda Peter, the Rock would anchor me into the future timelines of 5D Tara. This was the mission we had agreed upon before our incarnation and why Peter had to leave or "die" to change form to live on the fragmented piece of Tara or Urtha in Andromeda. We were, through our love, anchoring in the higher frequencies and helping 3D Earth ascend. As I began to embody more of Peter's masculine energy it was balancing my feminine side and my "bi" polarities began to stabilize. I began to ascend beyond duality and more fully have access to the fifth dimension.

Peter built me a beautiful home on Tara that sat upon a cliff overlooking a velvet purple sea. Our home sang when the wind blew through it and we spent most of our time swinging in our hammocks overlooking the Sea, or flying around in the starry sky. Peter always loved flying. There was a star gate by our home, and I would accompany Peter on his assignments throughout the galaxy. It was just like old times! I wrote our adventures down in a children's book entitled: *The Chronicles of Andromeda*. So, instead of buying a ticket and flying halfway around the world to stand in line to ask my spiritual teacher a question, I would go to Infinite Source for my answers. Infinite Source would speak through whomever was needed at the time! I would meet with the Guardians, the Andromeda Council and my star family and receive my assignments and the necessary training.

But I began to wonder if I was just imagining all this. I had written long ago in one of my books that our imagination is our passport into the higher dimensions. But was this true? Could this really be happening, or was I just making it up? Gene used his remote viewing skills to confirm what I saw and reminded me that our "imagined" world was the true reality, and what we humans called "reality" was the dream world or what the Hindus called Maya, the world of illusion.

Then Gene told me the most frightening thing of all. He talked about our spiritual teachers and said Patrick was, as Sharon had confirmed, a "hooligan" from the Dark Side. He had chosen to return to the true light, which is why he left. But Sharon had never revealed to us her story to us. In fact Sharon had always been shrouded in Mystery and I remembered the night before I met her, the fear I had felt deep within my belly. According to Gene she was from the Dark Side and had not decided to return to the true light. For twenty years, whenever anyone questioned Sharon or said anything bad about her I would always rush to her defense. Gene was now telling me things about her that I didn't want to hear but I listened. Why? Because I knew I had to find the courage to question EVERYTHING! To see the dark as well as the light in our fallen world of duality. That my search for truth could not be confined only to what I felt comfortable exploring. I had to prepare myself for the fact that like everything in this fallen world, was not what it seemed, which meant I also had to question my "spiritual" teacher.

She had always invoked a great fear inside of me. The things she "told" me to do often led me to the most difficult challenges in my life. Now I needed to have the courage to look behind the veil and trust my own ability to discern the truth. I began to reflect over the past twenty-five years of my life under her guidance. I had learned so very much and experienced many great initiations and spiritual highs. But I had never really been given full disclosure of the Dark Side. It had only been hinted. Many times when I asked her to expand she would respond by saying, "You don't want to know!" Perhaps the "group" wasn't ready to face the truth but the mere fact that I was asking these questions meant I was ready for this knowledge. So why was I flying all over the world, paying huge sums of money to be part of a group where she was shutting me down? And why had Peter left the group several years before his death?

As Peter evolved he began asking the Universe for more awareness. Once Peter asked Sharon how far she took us, to which she responded, "All the way Home." That just didn't resonate with me. How could anyone take another person Home? It's an inside job. Not even the most evolved Guru or "Christ" being, not even your twin soul can take you "Home". But what is Home"? Home is breaking free from the illusion. Home is achieving the higher perspective of SEEING beyond duality. HOME is reclaiming your own inner power and not looking to anything or anyone outside yourself for answers. Home is knowing beyond a shadow of a doubt that you are infinite and can call upon the power of the Infinite to take care of your every need. Home is reconnecting your twelve-stranded diamond DNA to Infinite Source and healing all your fragmented identities back into Holiness. Home is ascension through the Alchemical Synthesis of transmuting the polarities of duality through self-love which enables you to break free from the barriers of illusion into the inner knowing that the external world is the illusion and the "real" world is Infinite, accessed by the power of your imagination! Home is being at ONE with all Creation. How could anyone take another soul Home? True a soul who has been of service can be hosted out of the prison matrix but their spiritual journey is their own unique experience.

As I began distancing myself from the group, many of my old friends reached out to pull me back into the herd. I took a closer look at these friends and questioned them. Some had been with Sharon for over fifty years in this life time alone! Many of them had grown old and died still fighting over front row seats to the Sharon Show. When someone in our group died, Sharon would tell us if they had "ascended" or not. One friend told me she was riding Sharon's coat tails "all the way" home! As part of Sharon's workshops I had glimpses into many of my past lives, with the other group members. We had all incarnated together lifetime after lifetime. We were the "clump" that Patrick had mentioned. We had created karmic debts and entanglements between each other that needed to be paid. But in all those years I had never gone deep into my own personal pain and trauma and healed it. Once I asked Sharon about my painful trauma with my mother to which she responded, "visulaize something positive." I had fallen into the consciousness trap of believing that because of all my profound spiritual experiences, combined with my masters in Mental Health Counseling and my parents being "family" therapists I was beyond all this shadow work! Because I hadn't healed my mother wound I was still desperately seeking love and validation outside myself from a mother figure and Sharon fit the bill. I slowly became more and more dependent on Sharon. I began to trust her words more than my own inner intuitive voice. I found I had reached a point where every other word out of my mouth was, "Sharon says".

For years I had been mesmerized by her supernatural stories about how spiritually evolved she was. After all nobody in the "real" world talks about these things. At first, they had helped me SEE things from a different perspective and notice how the super natural played a hand in my daily life. But after twenty years of listening to "her" story and "her" experiences they began to over shadow the supernatural experiences occurring daily in my own life. Sharon's story was over powering my story. She had always said we were supposed to go beyond her but no one seemed to. I just kept repeating the same workshops hearing her same tired old stories over and over. The time had come to write my own new story!

How did I get there? Gene encouraged me to look back over the teachings I had received and unplug anything that no longer resonated. As I reviewed my life I noticed while much of the information she gave me rang true to my soul, there were also things that simply did not resonate anymore. Perhaps they had served me at one time but I was evolving beyond her. Patrick always said, "Don't believe us, check it out yourself." But Sharon had never said that. She had a very subtle way of making you feel like everyone else had it wrong and only she held the truth. I can't quite put my finger on it but as a result I never looked outside her for my information. I never validated or cross referenced it. Much of her information would contradict what was said by outside sources, her own husband or even what she had previously told us before. Over the years the more I attended her workshops the more confused I became. At first I thought it was just because I wasn't evolved enough to "understand" my spiritual teacher who was so beyond everyone. When I asked the other group members if they understood what we had done in a retreat or in a workshop, I realized that no one did and no one even cared. We all just felt a wonderful high from her amazing meditations and figured we had absorbed whatever information we needed to at a soul level that was beyond our comprehension.

The group let Sharon "lead" them wherever she wanted to because, after all, she was God-Realized. She would always begin every session by taking us under into a deep trancelike state of meditation. I also began to notice that Sharon's manner of speaking to the group was as if they were little children or "nursery schoolers" as she called them. She had her own vocabulary of "Sharon Speak" which the group would pick up and use as group speak. I once asked Sharon how many of the people in the group had contracted to go "home" in this lifetime and she told me about half. If half of her followers were choosing to continue on the merry-go-round of reincarnation watching the Sharon Show, why was I being taught the same thing as them? The last time I checked in on her agenda, she was leading her followers into the Galactic Federation of Fallen Angelics!

Peter and I have had many wonderful incarnations and experiences traveling the world with our spiritual family. Peter even rose from his death bed flew half way around the world, and attended his last retreat in a wheelchair with an oxygen mask two weeks before his death, to bid farewell to this beloved group of mighty souls. But now Peter wanted me to look deeper and move beyond Sharon and the group, as he had. The more I began to raise questions, the more my spiritual family shunned me. Gene was the only person who answered the many questions that had been left unanswered for all those years. He told me I would never be able to understand Sharon because she used what he called "double speak". He also asked me if in all the years I had known Sharon had she ever offered me a viable solution for all the karmic patterns she so carefully pointed out? All I knew was after spending over twenty years following her, I found myself alone, sick, broke, and totally depressed. I am not blaming anyone for my situation. I had chosen to follow this path as part of my education. This was exactly where I needed to be to finally break free from the old world "spiritual teacher" paradigm and the illusions that had been binding me on 3D Earth. She had taught me the greatest lesson of all of my lifetimes go to Infinite Source within for everything!

I am now filled with love and gratitude for both my spiritual family and all my spiritual teachers who were the best possible teachers one could have had in the finite 3D world of illusion! They both served as mirrors of the polarities existent within the 3D world and within me. One black, one white, one "lunar" female, one solar male, one hidden, one exposed. One who ascended into the light of Oneness. One who worked within the 3D finite world of darkness. I SEE now that Sharon like most spiritual teachers serves as the "Daring Wolf" archetype, a gate keeper threshold guardian, the one the adept must pass to have full knowledge and access to the higher dimensions. She is akin to a software program, like the character of the Oracle in the film the *Matrix*. Her program is to keep the balance within the prison matrix's world of duality. She serves as a handler to manage awakening souls from lifetime to lifetime. Her job is to keep souls recycling within the matrix until they have proven their worth enough to challenge her and break free from the matrix. Like the ancient statues of the Griffins used to guard the palaces of kings, she scares people away. But like all things in this world of illusion, she is not real and crumbles when you find the courage to challenge her authority.

Historically, all gurus have functioned as "product managers" who will not release the product until it has passed inspection. Peter had helped me receive all the necessary training, as all good mentors do, but it had been up to me to pass the final test to prove my own worth or worthiness! Souls must have the courage and inner confidence to challenge authority so they can become their own inner authority. Thus the saying, "When the student is ready the Teacher appears, when the student is really ready the teacher disappears". But most adepts are too fearful to look beyond the veil of illusion and are recycled back into the prison matrix, life time after life time often returning to point zero with the same teachers! I had been given the gift of knowledge! Knowledge about our fallen earth, about the Dark Side and about spiritual teachers. I had drunk from the fountain of Truth. I had received the elixir of life! Peter had reached this epiphany before his death. He knew that the truth cannot be told but it must be remembered. He had been trying to guide me to the truth but I had become so utterly lost in my own grief that I had become prey to dark entities who were attacking me and keeping me trapped in the lower densities unable to communicate with him. It was Gene who had answered Peter's call and brought me back from the dead. He served as a liaison between Peter and me. He confirmed my experiences with Peter were real until I had enough faith to fully navigate the higher frequencies myself. Then Gene disappeared.

I felt so freed! I felt so wonderful I wanted to share the truth with the world! I gave free talks at the local public libraries, psychic fairs or on any platform where people may have ears to hear and eyes to see the TRUTH! But I discovered that most people did not want the truth. They did not want to have their illusions shattered. They were too frightened to look behind the veil of their illusions and just wanted to blindly follow authority. They wanted me to "tell" them what to do. To lead them in comfy cozy spiritual practices, meditations, and other spiritual "fluff" that would make them "feel" better for that moment rather than helping them take responsibility for their own inner healing and their own lives. They wanted me to become like the "spiritual" teacher that I had left behind and were willing to pay me lots of money to do so! I knew that this was a karmic trap that I did not want to fall into.

This karmic pattern has infected our planet for far too long and is being exposed as we see religious leaders like the Pope telling people to be injected. Or the Dalai Lama appearing on camera muzzled receiving his injections. The old world leaders are herding their followers into a false ascension matrix because that is the only place they can exist. As are the New Age religions where people pray to fallen Archangels like Michael or Metatron while branding themselves with the fallen sacred geometric patterns such as the bloom of doom, (false flower of life) The Cabala Tree of Death rather the Kathara Tree of Life and the Fib-a-not-CHI anit-Krystala spiral of death, or bind themselves to Thoth and channel aliens from the Fallen Galactic Federation like the fallen Anunnaki Pleiadeans.

In the higher dimensions of 5D Earth and beyond, there are no spiritual practices because people do not need to "practice" their spirituality. They ARE spiritual beings. Because of this, there is no need for spiritual teachers because spirituality does not need to be taught! There is no religion, only the Law of One. Everyone comes together as equals, sharing their unique gifts and intuitive abilities for the benefit of all connected by the Law of One and Infinite Source within them.

Just as Peter could not tell me the truth, I had to come to realize the truth in my own divine timing. And so it is with the World. Many people will need to follow speakers, spiritual leaders, religions and groups as crutches until they are able to walk on their own. We cannot deny a crippled person a crutch. Nor can we judge them.

I was left alone in my spiritual journey and began to explore many sources of disclosure, one of them being Ashyanna Dean's work in Voyager II and her live-stream videos. I found her work to have the highest frequency encryptions I had yet encountered. But difficult to decipher. I was alone in my pursuit and followed her video streams, which were spaced out sometimes years at a time, or when the "guardians" said she could break "radio" silence. I kept asking for more. Finally I found Lisa Renee's Energy Synthesis online. Lisa Renee filled in many of the gaps I had been missing. When I joined her group I naively thought she worked with Ashyanna Dean

ELIZABETH MONROY M.S. & PETER MONROY M.D.

author of Voyager II, because after all, don't we all want the same thing? Ascension, evolution and freedom for all by sharing the truth? I found out there was a bitter war raging between the two and she warned us not to try to put her teachings together with Ashyanna or speaker 1 as she is known or we may end up being attacked and dying like her other followers! Wow fear! At first I remember thinking oh I better stop following speaker 1, but then I realized how ridiculous that sounded. Soon Lisa's level of disclosure ran thin and I wanted more. Lisa is an excellent researcher and I have used much of her work in this book as well as that of speaker 1. So I guess I broke the curse! I began to look for higher levels of disclosure and found out speaker 1 had years and years of videos called The Freedom Teachings. Her office did not tell me about these in all the years I called them asking for more information. I also found out that she was hunting down and removing all these videos so people would not have access to them. When I listened to them I found a wealth of information! Everything seemed to click into place and I realized why I had not understood her recent work. But why was she withholding this information? So much resonated and awakened deep memories within me but there were many parts that did not resonate. These two women and many others have shared pieces of information from the Maharata Texts, CDT plates or Emerald records. This is the Truth about the hidden history of our planet, ascension, the true science of creation and much more. This was the information written down by Jesheua 12 and given to the twelve Essene tribes to be hidden around the world. This is the truth that these people were hunted down and murdered for and now lies in a 53 mile long hermetically sealed library beneath the Vatican! This Truth is our birthright! No one should own it! The time has come for us to become the speakers, the guardians and to share this knowledge freely with humanity!

I have never identified with any teacher, speaker entity or prophecy that promotes the destruction of our earth and evacuation of humans from their Mother Earth. I strongly believe we all need to freely share our puzzle pieces of truth with one another this is why I created The Infinite Human Talk Show to discuss these concepts that co create our a New Consciousness Renaissance and our collective reality. The idea that one person owns the rights to our hidden history and these records that people died for is ludicrous! But we must also pay respects to those who came before us. That is what bibliographies are for! I honor both of these women who have been sign posts pointing to the ultimate truth which lies within! I do not agree with everything they say but I appreciate them for saying it. We all must learn to discern and stay humble remembering "the more I learn the more I realize I know nothing." Socrates. This is my motto. So only take what resonates from my words and know that you too will grow beyond them as will I because we are all INFINITE!

I am grateful to ALL speakers who have sparked memories that have helped me heal my past or alternative identities. I do believe there is as always an attack to stop the truth held in the Emerald records from coming forth. But I love the dark side because there are always bits of truth in their lies and if you listen with keen awareness you can learn decipher what they are trying so desperately to hide! This is a reminder for us to stop going to a middle man and go directly to infinite source. Speaker 1 declared herself the one and only true speaker to "the guardians" But we are the Guardians! It is time for us all to begin to speak the truth and share it freely! But we must also do more than speak! We must walk the walk and integrate this information into your daily lives! We must integrate these spiritual principals into our physical, emotional, mental and spiritual bodies. We must bring them into our relationships practice what we preach and BE THE CHANGE by putting our words into action. All you ever do is really only for you and your own self discovery. It matters not if you do it alone or have millions of people watching you. It is ultimately all about you! Many who hide behind computer screens or speaker platforms and only answer questions in "controlled" situations, have placed themselves above others as the one and only authority. Many say do not listen to the other sides version for they are evil. I always listen to everything I am guided to. I find that many times I learn much more about the dark side from the dark side! The dark side uses the truth to tell lies so the more I have come to trust myself the more I know I am able to see the truth through the lies. The only power the dark side has is in making you believe they are more powerful than you.

What many Krystic people fail to realize is that the parasites have been in control of our planet for a long time. They have successfully down graded our DNA, so we do not have the twelve strands needed to connect directly to Infinite Source. In fact the ones who have the higher genetic packages sometimes as high as eleven strands are the fallen angelics. Many times these have been the "spiritual" teachers we have flocked to. When these fallen angelics enter a contract for bioregenesis they must pay back the harm they have caused. So since they were masters at embroiling humans they must teach them the truth, hence they become spiritual teachers/ speakers. But too often their arrogant nature begins to shine forth and they see krystic humans as stupid and gullible and they begin to use their knowledge for their own selfish motives to enslave others. They may say they are working for the good guys and even believe it but they are over souled by parasites from parallel realities who are often getting the better of them without them even knowing it! Hence we see the battle of light and dark playing out in most spiritual communities. This is why it is imperative to learn to think and feel for yourself and going directly to Infinite Source.

Once you can successfully do that you need to break the cycle of following and become a leader who creates other leaders. You must integrate these lessons into your life and share them through your unique soul mission. I see so very folks who have studied advanced teachings for years but they do nothing with them. Like a student who has five Phd.s and is applying for grants. They have not integrated their knowledge into their daily lives. They are sick, lacking in abundance, fearful and critical of others. They are afraid to step out of the herd to express their uniqueness and claim their own inner power. When you truly begin to live as your true authentic Infinite self you will be able to go to Infinite Source for ALL your needs and you will lack nothing! But so many are too afraid to step out and be themselves for fear of what the others think or to be shunned by the group. I have been privy to some very high levels of information, which by the way every group I participated in believed their level of truth to be the highest and their teachers would always tell them that they were very highly evolved souls. It may be true but don't use it to separate yourself from others. We are now entering a time when as infinite human beings you can be the co-creator of your own holographic reality. You can manifest anything in alignment with Infinite Source. I always say investigate everything and don't just follow one true teacher connect the dots tuning into many different speakers, spiritual teachings, philosophies and groups. In this book I have referenced many different sources. This is our way of bringing into wholeness all the scattered splintered parts of ourselves. Now through the magic of cyberspace we can listen to everything! We can pick and choose, discern, integrate and think for ourselves. Then you will cease to identify with any finite construction of yourself or those around you and begin to identify with your infinite self. At that moment you will step into your infinite power as a manifestor and begin to co create your optimal reality. You will come together with others not under finite containers of: Christians, Americans, Women, or anything other than Infinite Source. This loving infinite energy will be the cosmic glue that binds you and brings you together in deep connective ways beyond the confines of 3D models. You will come together both inside and outside of time for the purpose of expressing your unique gifts and talents. These moments will be perfect as you begin to surrender your finite concept of self or ego surrendering into the unity of Oneness consciousness. When we can continuously see all people places,and things as simply sign posts pointing us towards Infinite Source within then we will be free to properly access the wealth of knowledge without having to stop and worship the sign posts or worse take it with us.

SPIRITUAL TEACHERS

Since the Fall of humanity when the Divine Holographic Architecture of our Earth was severed from Infinite God Source and all truth was carefully hidden we have looked outside ourselves for answers. We have looked to Spiritual Teachers, Priests, Priestesses, Shamans, Witch Doctors, Sorcerers, Magicians, Witches, Warlocks, Ministers, Preachers, Pastors, Rabbis, Gurus, Mystics, Swamis, Psychics, Therapists, Fortune Tellers, Seers, Healers, Life Coaches, T.V. Evangelists, Celebrities, Newscasters, Icons, Presidents, Speakers, Experts and the list goes on. Like cell phones without a sim cards, we have been rendered non-functional, unable to go to Infinite Source for our information. Thus, we have become dependent on external sources of information that may or may not be reliable.

Many highly evolved ChristPlayers incarnated into bodies containing higher genetics to write down and preserve the Truth and to serve as guides to steer us through the maze of deception back towards Infinite God Source. However in this fallen world of deception those who retained these higher genetics and sacred documents were hunted down and killed their sacred text stolen. They were replaced by imposters who intentionally led humanity astray, serving the dark agenda of false light rather than the eternal living light of Truth and Infinite Source. Many of us who came to help humanity ascend have ourselves become blinded by the false light and embroiled in the Matrix of deception. So rather than empowering people, misguided leaders have created a dependency loop. These self-appointed middlemen and women claim to know more about God than you do. Human beings often fall prey to this kind of deception because we have been genetically downgraded, hard-wired and mind-controlled to constantly seek the truth outside of ourselves. When the Word WAS God the word or vibrational frequency of truth was within us ALL and there was no need to seek the truth or even speak the truth. It was simply known, held within our genetics. We all just knew WE are ALL ONE! However when the word became separated from God Source as we did, we were taught to look outside ourselves for our answers, our salvation, our savior, our redeemer, our healer, our spiritual teachers.

After our fall, many great souls chose to remain on our planet as it plummeted into darkness to serve as a source of eternal living light and truth. Many of these great souls have also incarnated throughout history as "Christ players" to help humanity return to its true Infinite Human State of Being before the Fall. Some of these great souls fell and were assimilated into the dark collective and became known as fallen angels. Then there are those who completed their mission and ascended back to the God Source Worlds. There were also those who were captured by the dark side and have remained inprisioned in the phantom worlds. Many of these are being resurrected from the phantom worlds now. Then, there are souls who have recently incarnated as well as old souls, who have reincarnated throughout the ages and forgotten who they are, why they came here and what they came here to do. Many of these Krystos Star Seed Souls, were sent from the "stars" or God Source Worlds long ago, for this very time, we have now entered for the Krystos Reconnaissance Mission. Many of these Star Seeds are now awakening to their true identity at this very moment. Many of these Star Seeds are reading these words right now. Like in the *Never Ending Story* you are awakening to your true identity with each word you read. And as you do this, you are rewriting your current life story and our collective Earth Story.

A True SEE-ER possesses the "gift" to see beyond the veil of illusion of our put-up world, to read between the lines, to properly interpret the signs, symbols, and omens that are the reflection of the true hidden world behind the veil. This is why, throughout the ages, Mystics have used soft eyes or their third eye to reach beyond the veil of illusion. They have possessed the "second sight" to see both worlds and served as guides to those who heeded their wisdom. This ability was often passed down through the genetics of the female Celtic-Druid lineages. Throughout the ages, many resorted to tools for divination such as the Tarot, Tea leaves, Runes, Palms, Bones, Crystal Balls, and anything that augmented a deeper trance-like state and provided a portal into the higher dimensions of truth. As our Earth fell into lower frequencies, these "tools" were hijacked and people began placing their power on the tools rather than themselves. Many of these tools were infiltrated and seeded with portals into the lower demonic dimensions and those with gifts of true sight were hunted down and had to go into hiding, often in remote forests or caves, while deceivers took their places. Throughout history this lineage of gifted people with higher genetics have almost all been eradicated. Many of these souls desperately tried to carry the light of eternal truth in their hearts during humanity's darkest night of the soul. Many of these souls are reading these words now.

THE TRUTH ABOUT MAGIC

Before the Fall and the downgrading of our twelve-stranded silicon-based genetics we all possessed magic or innate divine technology. This is the language of our soul and the ability to communicate with all of creation, the Consciousness of the Earth, her deva and nature spirits, the elementals as well as the cosmic energy of the stars. We inherently had the ability of immediate manifestation to perform what now would seem like miracles or things we rely upon "artificial" technologically to do for us. Our power, our magic, our divine technology was never used to harm others nor for self-serving motives but only for the good of all concerned because we knew we were ALL ONE. These inherent gifts were part of our royal birthright as Cosmic Krystic Beings.

As the human being digressed into the fallen universe of duality, the integrity of our DNA was lost causing us to loose our inherent "magic" or divine abilities. But there were a few who retained these higher strands of DNA and were born of "magic". They had supernatural powers, "extrasensory" gifts, or powerful medicine, as the Shamans called it. They possessed a "sixth sense." They retained the memories of our true racial history. These were the Krystos Avatars, the "Christ Players", whose births were arranged by manipulating the bloodlines so a great soul could incarnate into a twelve-stranded "Krystos" body and retain the memories and powers of the original Krystic Infinite Human Beings. These people were looked upon as gods, messiahs, saints, magicians, gurus, etcetera. They were the true grail kings and queens sent to be Guardians of our Earth. These Krystic Beings incarnated throughout history during pivotal times with specific missions to help in the "Krystos Mission" or the mission of helping Earth and humanity return to its original divine place in the Cosmos.

They have played powerful roles in our Earth's history, both behind the scenes and in the limelight. These avatars have had many jobs. Some *Kokopelli*(s) served to "seed" humanity with their higher DNA genetic codes to allow the Star Seeds born in this pivotal time frame to activate their dormant twelve-stranded genetics now hidden, in what science calls our "junk" DNA. Many guarded and translated the Emerald records and the star gates which were portals that connected us to the God Source Worlds. Throughout history, many of their offspring retained much of these advanced genetics and were born with "intuitive" gifts, while others remained dormant to be fully activated during this time of ascension. These gifted people practiced their innate divine technology or magic, to counter balance the darkness within our fallen world of duality. As a result, they used the power of thoughts, their words, tones and incantations as tools to help overcome the dark side. They understood the connectedness of all living consciousness, of nature and her earth spirits. They would use nature, the cycles of the seasons, plants, herbs, crystals, stones, ley lines, energetic portals, star gates, et cetera to help them to effect a positive change in the holographic fabric of creation. They also retained much of the true ancient knowledge which they passed down from mother to daughter or father to son. Throughout history, the dark side has sought out these "gifted" humans and the knowledge they had recorded. When they found them, they condemned them as heretics and killed them in painful and humiliating ways to frighten people from practicing "magic" or using the power of their inner divine technology.

During the Inquisition, they were depicted as evil and in league with the devil, while in truth it was those who condemned them who were doing the "devil's" work. They confiscated their work, the true records of our history and ascension mechanics and used it against humanity. They created diluted, inverted, weaponized versions of the truth mixed with lies to create narratives to enslave rather than empower people. They used this knowledge to create the dark arts of black magic to serve themselves and their dark agenda. They confiscated ALL TRUTH held by these evolved Krystos Avatars and twisted and corrupted it and replaced them with false icons in their false stories. This sacred knowledge was weaponized to pull us further away from the fabric of all creation and distorted, to bring its users further away from the eternal light of Infinite Source into the false Luciferian Light of occultism and into a false ascension matrix that uses A.I. black magic against us to serve their Satanic Gestalt.

These Negative Satanic intruders infiltrated the "pagan" groups who worshipped or worked in harmony with our Life giving Sun, Nature and the Deva Kingdom and served as Guardians of our Mother Earth. They contorted these into Saturnian practices of the dark arts. They corrupted sacred festivals honoring the natural rhythms of our Mother Earth, turning them into satanic blood rituals. Over the centuries, they have confiscated our star gates and infected our ley lines. They have inverted our creator codes, enslaving the Divine Feminine energy and degrading it into the dark mother goddess, Baphomet. They enslaved the elementals and deva nature spirits, turning them into shadow creatures such as goblins, banshees, ghouls, and hungry ghosts unleashed on this earth to do the dark side's bidding and feed upon human souls. They tricked us into believing our natural, inherent divine technology was evil and persecuted anyone who used their intuitive gifts. They murdered the true grail kings, like King Arthur, to stop the Albion light body from rising on the Island of Great Britain and degraded his sacred marriage with Guinevere into lies of infidelity. Likewise, they corrupted the true teachings of Yesuah 12 and imprisoned his twin soul Sophia Maria Magdalena. They replaced the true Krystos Avatars with their fake cloned versions repackaging them as the "Ascended Masters" or Archangels, as icons to be worshipped, to distract you from the true Christ which lies within you. In many poor countries, starving people die in the streets while temples to the "gods" are filled with tasty delicacies rotting before stone statues. This is not what these true Krystic Beings taught, nor what they want for you. They do not want you to worship them. They wanted you to BECOME them. Christ is the door! You do not stop at a door, fall to your knees and worship it! You go through it! No Christ ever said, "I am the only son of God" and you are supposed to WAIT for me to return to SAVE you. All this has been done with one purpose in mind -to cheat you out of your ascension.

The entire history of our planet has been an ongoing war between good and evil that is culminating now. Everything has been pre-planned to deceive, mislead and throw you off the scent of the true power of Infinite God Source which lies within you! When you can, at last, see with your "one eye" through the world of illusion and know that the "the Kingdom of Heaven is within" and know the truth through the living language of knowledge, the true organic word which IS God, not the weaponized half-truths and lies spelled out in a bible, then you can reclaim your inner divine technology and the magic within you!

As I mentioned before, India retained much of the spiritual knowledge and ascension mechanics that were confiscated by the Catholic Church in the West. The guru-disciple construct served as the only means that this esoteric knowledge could be imparted during these dark times on our finite 3D Earth. Adepts needed to prove themselves trustworthy of the knowledge their gurus imparted and tradition required them to surrender their ego totally to their guru's wisdom. This model was used throughout history at a time when the frequencies were extremely low and adepts needed someone who could SEE through the world of illusion and guide them. Many of us have held this model sacred and have served as both guru and disciple throughout the ages but this model has deteriorated. Unfortunately, much of the rituals, ancient texts, and knowledge these holy men imparted has been diluted, misdirected and hijacked as well as their genetics. Many of the modern-day ashrams have become havens for tyrannical dictators who control every aspect of their followers' lives, never allowing them to think freely for themselves or have the free will to make their own choices. They dictate what people should eat, think, do, and even whom they should marry. Many have taken advantage of their followers financially, sexually and energetically. Many New Age people have found their way into these cults and communities because they do not want to take responsibility for their own lives. They are spiritually bypassing, and if you question any aspect of their "faith" their mind-control mechanisms kick in, causing them to dismiss any type of independent thought.

A TRUE LEADER CREATES LEADERS NOT FOLLOWERS.

The truth is the mark of a great spiritual leader. It is not by how many followers they have but by how many leaders they have inspired. A true spiritual teacher's job is to help the adept find their way back to Divine Infinite Source (within them). Once this occurs, their job is done and they self-extinguish. Spiritual leaders who have hordes of followers lining up to ask them questions, seek approval, or receive their blessings are not doing their job. Like the wise bird that pushes its young out of the nest when they are ready to fly, a wise spiritual teacher must teach their adepts to fly! A teacher helps their students to go beyond them and find their own answers.

In all Hero's Journeys, the Mentor Archetype serves as a teacher at the beginning of the Hero's Journey to prepare the Hero for what lies ahead. He or She gives them tools to face the "Dark Side" When our hero leaves behind the Ordinary World and steps into the Supernatural World, the mentor disappears, remaining with our hero only in spirit and often sacrificing himself to allow the adept to move beyond him. Look at mythic stories like *Star Wars,* where Obi-Wan is cut down by Darth Vader; or in *The Matrix* when Morpheus is captured and Neo is forced to step into his own power, realizing that he is the ONE; or in *The Lord of the Rings* when

Gandalf falls into the Abyss and Frodo must "go it alone" As a child, I remember riding around with training wheels on my bicycle until one day my Dad took the training wheels off my bike and cheered me on! I peddled out of our driveway never looking back! What a freeing experience! True spiritual teachers, like good parents, are there for their adepts in the early stages but joyfully embrace their own demise and celebrate their student's graduation!

True spiritual teachers who empower others to trust their inner intuitive voice and reclaim their infinite power are the most precious commodity on earth. They deserve to be respected, celebrated, and rewarded for their services. They may create the space, intention, and appropriate environment for people to do their own inner work. They embody such high frequencies that just being in their presence can serve as a catalyst to raise your vibration. They initiate inner healing in the people and the world around them. They shine their light on the areas of your life that need to be brought out of the darkness and healed. They serve as coaches, guides and mirrors, never taking away your power but rather offering provoking questions from a place of unconditional love and expanded awareness. They prepare you to face your own inner demons and triumph! They can serve as catalysts that help people awaken and begin their own inner spiritual journey. Now, as the energetic frequencies of our Earth rise, many do not need a teacher in physical form.

But there will be many who still need the crutch of seeking their own answers from people in the physical. Unfortunately, this sacred relationship has become tarnished in our modern day world tainted by the Black Magic Money Curse of enslavement. In ancient times, a patient would pay their doctor when they were healthy because the doctor had done his job keeping them in health. Now because people seek out help when they feel bad, it is good business to keep people in a perpetual state of dis-ease, so they keep coming back. Like the pharmaceutical companies who create customers instead of cures, many spiritual teachers, gurus, therapists, life coaches, healers, psychics, etcetera want to keep their clients coming back for more rather than empowering them to heal themselves.

If a person seeks help for a problem and is given the tools to heal themselves and resolve their problem but keeps coming back with the same "problem," it means they like their problem. You are not serving them but helping them feed their problem by allowing them to continuously return to ruminate over the same problem never resolving it. Nor are you serving yourself for they can drain the precious time and energy that could be used for the "right" people who truly want to use your gifts and talents to grow! But that is good business, to create returning clients! Likewise, many people when they feel bad, confused, upset, or dis-eased seek out their spiritual teacher for their "guru heroine" which makes them feel temporarily better. However, this stops them from going deeper into the root of their dis-ease and healing it. Like the physician who gives a shot, a pill, or removes a body part, never addressing the underlying cause of the dis-ease so the soul can be properly healed, they are simply masking or covering up the signs and symptoms that something is profoundly out of balance in the person's life. This may serve as a crutch temporarily, but the student, client, or patient who temporarily feels better may get caught up in a dependency loop never ever addressing the underlying issue but simply returning over and over again to have their "feel good" therapy by placing a bandaid over a deep wound or what I call smearing honey over pus.

Since it is good business for a Spiritual teacher to create dependency in their followers to keep them coming back for more, they must give you what you want but not always what you need. They must be careful not to offend you with the truth, or tell you the whole story. After all, why would you pay to come back for more? They must give you just enough nuggets of truth to keep you dangling, waiting for the next workshop, retreat, video, staying tuned in for more to come. Likewise, they cannot focus on making you feel: enough, complete, powerful or independent of them. Like any narcissistic relationship, they need you more than you need them. They need your energy, your money, your praise, your devotion. They must continuously convince you that they "know" more than you do, otherwise, why would you keep coming? This means they can never say to you, "You are Infinite, you are God! Go to Divine Infinite God Source within where you can get all your own answers for free!" They can never be a leader who creates other leaders that would outshine them. That would be creating competition and bad for business. Instead, they must continuously lead you back into a blind alley of dependence deeper and deeper into the maze of illusion and false ascension.

GROUP THINK

Many groups use common terminology and offer support, fellowship, even love. Before you know it, you are in a cult but of course you don't believe you are in a cult. You look to others to see how to react, what to accept as truth. You use the vocabulary, the terminology your spiritual leader has given to you. Your appropriate behavior is reinforced through acknowledgments and compliments to those who demonstrate the accepted thought, actions, and speech of the group think while ignoring or even ridiculing those who question or step out of line. The Spiritual Teacher makes those who follow them believe they are "special," superior, more advanced, more "aware" than other people. They hint that they are part of a special group of "evolved beings," the "spiritually elite," who are privy to esoteric knowledge that only their Teacher can give. They look at all other teachings, beliefs, and practices as inferior to theirs. The Spiritual Teacher insidiously presents themselves as the only "all knowing" wise person while quietly discounting any other Sources of information. They erect themselves as the sole source of all reliable information. In short, everyone else has it wrong and only they hold the truth. "They do not speak the truth, they are the truth!" Never reminding you that Truth is a frequency all can attain!

Spiritual commercialism has overrun the good intent of grounding spirituality into the physical world! I see "spiritual" people paying all kinds of money to attend the latest spiritual retreat, workshop, or cyber event! Many blindly and obediently follow their "marching orders" without any clue as to what they are doing. They are no different than the churchgoers who obediently recite creeds, sing songs, partake in rituals, or quote scriptures without fully understanding the true meaning behind these "spells." They do so because their friends, partners, family members or parents did so, because it is easier to follow than to lead.

On my Esoteric Renaissance Tour, I had three people from India tell me how the Brahmin Priests of Hinduism realized that if they told the people the truth, that they could go directly to God themselves, the priests would lose their power and position. So, they began to tell people that only through them could they reach God. Likewise, the Catholic Priests set up the same pyramid of power with themselves as the "emissaries" to God and only by donating to the Church or buying indulgences could you secure your spot in "heaven" or buy your loved ones out of purgatory. All religions are based on the premise that you must go through someone or something else to reach God or they would not have any "products" to sell. Tithing, indulgences, retreats, pilgrimages, religious icons, T-shirts, etcetera. History is filled with wealthy patrons who gave fortunes for their salvation! If you choose to participate in these activities, that's fine, but be sure you are fully aware of what you are doing and what these people are "selling" you. Is it helping you connect to the true power of Infinite God Source within you and true ascension or is it putting you into a false ascension matrix?

Here in Italy, I visited a church in a small village where the bones of a pilgrim were displayed. Apparently, he had walked all the way from Turkey to Lucca, collapsed there and died due to exhaustion. If your journey as an Alchemist is bringing you closer to the Word Frequency, which is God, inside of you, to the truth that you are Infinite Source, then the journey is well worth the effort. Like Dorothy in *The Wizard of OZ* you may have to travel that yellow brick road to far and distant lands to finally discover that the Infinite has always been within and that there is no place like home!

After years of investment with your chosen teacher, are you closer to KNOWING who you are? Where you came from and what you are here to do? Are you God-Realized, knowing you are a unique expression of God incarnate? Are you fulfilling YOUR unique soul mission? Do you trust yourself to find your own answers within? Are you transmuting physically, emotionally, mentally spiritually, financially and socially? Is your third eye open and are you SEEING the duality of our 3D world and ascending in frequency? Are you able to find your own answers within, SEE the truth for yourself? Can you SEE both the darkness and the light in the 3D world of duality and rise above it? Can you maintain your own high frequency? Have you faced your shadow self? Healed your own wounds, traumas and pain? Transmuted your fears, insecurities, anger and self-doubt? Are you being honest with yourself? Are you just talking the talk or are you walking the walk? These are all personal questions that only you can answer and may continue to ask yourself no matter how "evolved" you think you are. Let's face the truth. Everyone on 3D earth has an ego to some degree. To put it more bluntly, everyone's "shit" stinks, pardon the expression. Some of us have more awareness than others. If you find yourself in a group, learn what you need to learn and move on. "Don't let the group or the "teacher" hold you back".

We are in a time frame where just being "spiritual," is not enough. Being curious about past lives, aliens, prophecies et cetera won't get you home nor to the true freedom only organic ascension offers. We have lived in an upside-down, fake, finite earth for far too long. Fake spiritual teachers, false gurus and phony healers have made lots of money scamming those who have come to them for help. But the truth is, they have been scamming themselves. They have been the architects of this fake, finite earth and now they must live in it. They have missed the greatest gift of all which only comes from being truly of service to others and knowing that WE ARE ALL ONE! The truth is that every client, student, and patient that comes to you is there for you! They are a gift and have an important message for you. Their problem represents something you also need to pay attention to or heal within your own life. As you help them to heal you, also help yourself and this allows you the opportunity to help heal all Creation. This is because when you become God-realized, you realize you are God, your client is God, we are all God. In helping another you are helping yourself. It's always a win-win situation. There is no need to take something from someone else to have. No need to set yourself up as better than another. True you may have certain gifts people want and there needs to be a fair exchange of energy. But it needs to be a win-win situation on both sides. When Infinite Human Beings become leaders, they will create a world full of Infinite Humans Being Leaders and everyone will win! If you are not being "supported" in tuning into your own inner power and clearing away blocks by doing your own inner work and deep healing, then you are being led into a false ascension matrix. So know where you are being "led". Is it into true freedom and union with Infinite God Source, embracing your own inner power as an Infinite Human Being? Or are you being led deeper into the labyrinth of false light and faux ascension, to be fed upon by narcissists and parasites?

We Infinite Human Beings need to own our greatness with humility! We need to stop apologizing for our expanded awareness, unique gifts, talents, innate power and for speaking the truth! We need to stop hiding who we are and the gifts we have brought to heal, liberate and evolve our Earth! We need to stop masking ourselves, our abilities and that of our children! We need to stop dowsing our brilliant light so as not to offend the broken people of this fallen world. No longer do we need to try to fit into a broken planet! No longer do we need to hide in the shadows, afraid we will be found out, ridiculed, persecuted, martyred, burnt at the stake for being different as we have in so many past life times! The tides have now turned! We are in an Ascension Cycle! A Shift into 5D! You are the Light of Truth that has come here to lead those who are willing, out of the shadows of darkness and into the living light of their own true Infinite Nature. You are Earth's most precious resource! YOUR coming has been foretold. Stop walking on eggshells, afraid that your power and brilliant light will offend someone or aggravate their demons, which it will. Stop following spiritual teachers that are functioning within the Old 3D Earth paradigms! Stop trying to fit into a system that no longer wants you! Stop looking for someone else to be your light. You are it! This is your time. Rise and shine and you shall be richly rewarded for all your gifts and talents, with the true abundance that the Multi Universe has been waiting to bestow upon you!

SELF LEADERSHIP:

We are all Works of Art in Progress! Perfection perfecting itself. True leadership does not come from those who place themselves above others pretending to be better or know more than others. Nor by those who tell you how you should live and what you should do, think and feel. True leadership comes from those who have a deep desire to serve humanity, our Mother Earth and all Creation and to share their unique gifts and talent, making the world a better place. It comes from people who are humble enough to admit they do not have all the answers and are willing to go to Infinite Source for their answers. True Leaders respect others opinions and input as fellow co-creators. They are constantly reinventing themselves and engaging in self-reflection, observing both their strengths and weaknesses and are continuously working to communicate honestly with themselves first and foremost and with others. They are always striving to align themselves to the highest expression of their authentic self. They don't "need" people to need them. They don't "need" followers to feel complete. They don't need people to fall silent when they enter a room, bow to them, compliment them, line up for their blessing, advice or guidance. Their joy comes from expressing their unique soul mission. True power is not power over others! The true Grail Kings or Christ Beings did not come here to be the King of Kings and rule over humanity. They came as guardians to serve Mother Earth and all Creation.

"Stop trusting in mere humans, who have but a breath in their nostrils. Why hold them in esteem?"
ISAIAH 2:22

Just as all religions, including the New Age Religion have been corrupted and their spiritual foundations based on half-truths, falsehoods and lies, likewise much of the so-called "channelled" information has also been from beings of false light who are deceiving their channelers. Those who are unaware of these deceptions are leading their followers deeper into the finite world of deception and a false ascension matrix. Many who are now awakening are being herded from one finite reality into another. By continually giving your power away to someone or something outside of you, you are being deceived. Be (A) ware! I do not sit in the judgment of any spiritual teacher today. That is not my job. But we have entered into a cycle of ascension where the higher frequencies are helping more and more people awaken and break free of the old finite systems. So, the need for the guru-disciple relationship is ending.

To ascend you must reattach your own inner organic divine technology and go directly to the SOURCE for your own answers. Once this is done, you do not need to go to any human being for your answers. Source is the only place where you will receive, "The Truth, the Whole Truth, and nothing but the Truth, so help me God!" Go to the Source. When you have awakened to your true nature as an Infinite Human Being, you will realize you have the wisdom of Infinite God Source at your beckoning.

Once you can reactivate your divine organic microchip within your brain and use your God-given divine technology you can escape the "net" and surf the INFINITE gaining whatever information you need to accomplish your soul mission. You will reclaim your multidimensional abilities! You will never be alone, but ALL ONE. All truth will be revealed to you for you will reside within the higher frequencies of the Truth Vibration. It may take some time before you can digest all the information of your Cosmic downloads but you will have access to it when the time is right.

THE HELP

As you are able to move beyond the old paradigm of "spiritual teachers," your internal bond with Divine Infinite Source eventually consumes all else and you will find yourself getting help from everywhere. After all, Infinite Source is omnipresent and omnipotent! I was conversing with a "spiritual" friend who still saw my old spiritual teacher. I was explaining how I found my own answers from Infinite Source. She then asked me, "Other than Source, who do you go to for help?" Clearly, she was not ready to embrace the Infiniteness of Source. Infinite Source is "All that is, ever has been and ever shall be... it is YOU!" All you need do is, "ask and you shall receive". But you must be open to receive. It may not come the way you expect. When you stop making the Infinite into a specific person, place or thing, you will find the entire multiverse is conspiring to HELP YOU! The answers may not come from a swami wearing robes but a bum on the street or a line in a movie or a jingle in a song! But the help is always there!

Once you activate your pineal and open your third eye you can reclaim your multidimensional nature, you gain the power to navigate the Infinite! You surf the cosmos gaining unlimited, uncensored infinite knowledge, love, guidance and abundance. You hold the magic key that unlocks the door to the Infinite Multiverse. You no longer have to look to someone outside of you to save you, enlighten you, love you, or heal you. You do not have to put your name on a waiting list for a workshop in order to "ascend" or get a permission slip from some Guru to know you are God! You can do it yourself. You are Infinite! You can receive infinite cosmic downloads on any chosen topic. All you need do, is ask. But be careful what you ask for, you just may get it!

As the frequencies on our Earth rise and the need for a middle man or woman is eliminated, you must learn how to successfully navigate through the lower astral plane of illusion and false light beings and into the higher frequencies of eternal living truth. Do not get hijacked by the entities of false light or A.I. projections masquerading as ascended masters, archangels or benevolent aliens, et cetera. This is why opening your third eye and developing the intuitive ability is key to navigate beyond the artificial frequencies and dark entities of false light. Highly advanced artificial technology that you could not even fathom has existed and has been used by the controllers for eons to create consciousness traps such as synthetic telepathy, holographic inserts, "Voice of God" technology and blue beam steering. This has been used throughout history to lead key "religious" figures astray and change our Earth's history. The A.I. Artificial "Voice of God" can create voices, words, and images of "God," inside the mind of the recipient. These holographic inserts and images have been used throughout time to create projections of "angels" "ascended masters" who have visited "biblical" figures or ordinary folks and given them messages from "god". These false messages have created artificial timelines, conflict and war. History is littered with people who have heard or seen God, the Virgin Mary, Angels, or Aliens that were not authentic. Now, with blue beam steering, they can project anything they want onto the skies of our Earth, herding people into a false ascension matrix of a One World Order Religion, completing their false preemptive "revelations" narrative.

So how do you know if you are attuned to the organic higher frequencies of the God Source Worlds or being tricked by the false light entities and dark A.I. technological traps? This is a very good question and will become increasingly more and more important as technology advances and the holographic web of illusion is spun around us. Those who are not willing to open their own wounds and bring them into the light to heal are giving their power away to someone or something outside of themselves. They tend to be part of groups that look to spiritual teachers, political leaders, new age gurus, or good aliens to fix the problems of the old 3D Earth rather than rolling up their sleeves and creating their own reality and the future they want to live in. Like small children they are often waiting for something or someone to make the bad guys go away. They look to technology as their new "god" to heal them, inform them, enlighten them. They take the easy way out wanting the world around them to change rather than changing themselves. They refuse to take responsibility for their own lives and current situations tending to blame others. They are giving their power away to external sources waiting for someone or something to change things for them rather than them changing. These type of people are prey for the entities of false light.

As you take more responsibility for your life you will ascend in frequency. The higher your organic frequency, the less these A.I. frequencies will have a hold on you and the more easily you will be able to spot their deceptions. These AI frequencies will begin to feel wrong to your organic body. They will just not be compatible with your high energetic signature. As you raise your frequency, you will also develop the ability to discern and navigate through the vast sea of deception. You may be like a newborn child at first, so do not be upset with yourself for being tricked at times. The Finite Artificial Dark Side has created elaborate campaigns to trick you into accepting their artificial bad copies but it is only a test so you can prove your own worth. If you can remain centered in your own Infinite inner power and pass the tests, the illusion will disintegrate since ALL the Dark Side tactics are ultimately illusions. Hint: (If it seems too good to be true and the masses are running towards it, chances are it's one of the Dark Sides' illusions.) As you grow in your spiritual maturity, you will realize the real deal does not have to put on bells and whistles, have an enormous marketing campaign, or be something you feel like you "have" to have or do. The information will not be "channeled from aliens through a "vessel" which speaks in a dramatic voice." It may come, "out of the mouth of babes". Or as a simple whisper of inner knowing. In fact, it will most likely be something very simple that you do not have to "buy" and most people won't even want.

If you have spectacular experiences, are taken up into spaceships or see projections of angels and ascended masters who "tell" you what to do, chances are you are under the spell of Luciferian mind magic and A.I. manipulation. In my personal experience, subtle signs and symbols are placed along my path, requiring my awareness, deep contemplation and introspection to decipher the profundity of their meaning. This can happen anywhere. In a crowded room with only those AWARE enough to SEE what is really happening. Or it may come all at once as an inner knowing. I can't explain it, but you just know beyond a shadow of doubt the truth of it. Then there are those concepts I must sit with, perhaps even for years. But I find if I sit with something, if it is of the world of illusion, it disintegrates, the narrative unravels. Like a magic act, when the smoke clears, you can SEE through the illusion. True, when I first began my journey I had some very "dramatic" experiences. Why? Because I needed them and sometimes I still do. Sometimes the "help" has to go to extremes to get the message through! Sometimes, a person will appear in my life and will "tell" me, in no uncertain terms something that I need to hear but I have not been listening to my guides, because I didn't want to hear it! But as I attune to the higher frequencies, I find many times I just have to ask to clarify something and eventually I get the "ah ha".

Many of you may be finding yourself alone now. Friends and family members may have dropped by the wayside. When you find the courage to "go it alone" for a while, you will realize that you have never been alone and have always had help. Even if you didn't know it or ask for it. Maybe you are alone now so you can better attune to "the help". Whether you call them angels, guides, soul friends, soul family, spirit guides etcetera you are always receiving help along your spiritual journey. They may be loved ones who have crossed over or beings from higher dimensions. As you raise your frequency some of your guides may leave giving way to new ones much the same way as when you graduate from one grade and go into the next, you change your teachers. But you also have life guides who never leave you. As you graduate and climb in frequency, you are at last reunited with your true spiritual family. You can, at any time along the way ask to meet your guides. This may occur in the dream state especially if you have lucid dreams.

As you reach spiritual maturity and surrender the finite will of your ego to the Will of Infinite Source your inner dialogue may change from, "oh God please help me!" to, "I surrender my will to you Infinite Source, please show me how I can be of the highest service to you and all creation?" (Although during these frequency wars you may need to evoke god for help! Which is really you!) As you do this you will find your every need will be met. I did not say your egotistical whims, I said your needs. You will be funded, supported, the Universe will have your back! As you move into the higher frequencies and begin your Soul Mission here on Earth your desires will shift. You will begin to crave simplicity and your abilities to manifest will increase. Things may not happen the way you envisioned. They may begin with small steps, humble beginnings. They may not appear to be what they seem at first or not happen when you want but in Divine Time. You may have to do things outside of the money system. But if you need money, money will appear. Why? Because you have stopped being self-absorbed in your own petty egotistical desires and dedicated yourself to serving the Universe, so the Universe will serve you! You are all ONE!

Throughout this dark cycle, we have been severed from our Mother Earth, Mother Universe, and the True Mother /Father God aspects of Infinite God Source. The good news is that the finite architecture created to imprison you has been dismantled and the true divine infinite architecture restored. Earth has returned to its true place in the higher harmonic Universe. The 5D Earth is here now! God has never abandoned you! The Guardians have always been with you patiently waiting for this ascension period so the artificial prison encasing that held you could be dismantled. The pathway has been cleared but another AI prison matrix has been installed. You have free will, no one can choose for you. So you must choose. Nobody can "save" you and you can't ascend into the higher frequencies until you are ready. This is just plain logic. You cannot bring the baggage from 3D earth with you. It is an inside job that takes work. This is something that, quite honestly, most humans may not choose now. They may choose the easy path, continuing to want to have things "done" for them. They do not want change, to create a new world from the ground up. They just want to step into the prefabricated artificial world the controllers have prepared for them. They will continue playing the victim, passively consenting and feeding these dark forces. Only you can choose to free yourself from the prison matrix.

THE GREATEST STORY NEVER TOLD!

This brings us to where we are now: The Greatest Story Never Told! Groups of away teams made up of great souls have incarnated on Earth to serve as guides to help humanity break free from the spell they have been under for so long and create a New Infinite Earth. These souls are undercover agents, part of an inside jailbreak. They are highly evolved souls who have had their memories erased and incarnated in bodies with dormant royal DNA that has been" offline" and live lives as ordinary inhabitants of Earth until their time of awakening. They would not know anything about their soul mission or their true origins. They would be living time capsules with a preordained time to awaken to the truth about who they really are and their soul mission. This preordained time of awakening could be triggered by certain life events. It could happen from reading a book(this one), seeing a movie, meeting a person, etcetera. Or it could be one big trigger such as an Earth Event that causes masses of people to awaken all at once. These beings are often referred to as away teams, wanderers, plants, earth angels, light workers, indigos, rainbow warriors, Aquafarians or star seeds. I have been using the word Star Seed because I think of us as "seeds of change" from the God Source Worlds, here to plant ourselves in the fertile soil of the fifth dimension, blossom and be the change we want to see the world. If you are reading these words, chances are you are one.

Upon realizing this, you may feel a deep sense of sorrow, abandonment, feelings of loss, and being left alone in a hostile environment to fend for yourself. You may recall all the years of suffering, feeling different, trying so desperately to fit in, but only making things worse. You may have even felt like you were adopted, an outsider, or the black sheep of the family. Like E.T. you longed for home, but you must remember ... you are home. Home is ascension and you volunteered to be here now! This is your job! Everything you have done in all your life times has led up to this very moment. So don't blow it now! You agreed to incarnate now because you are a highly evolved soul that needs only to remember you are a Divine Infinite Multidimensional Being and a host of Great Ones are now assisting you. You need not be distracted by the external world and the desperate attempts of the Dark Side to maintain its control. You need not wait for someone else to make things right! You are supported by your true star brethren--your star family, and Infinite Source! They love you unconditionally, with no agendas attached. They only want to see you complete your soul mission and return home to them. Although this journey has been a difficult one, it has been a very productive one. You may have suffered greatly and learned many lessons along the way, but you have begun to break free from the dream spell that binds you. You are important, vital, and making a difference with every breath you take! Do not lose heart now. This is the time you have been waiting for, the time to reach deep inside yourself and show the World what you got! It is time to remember who you are, where you came from and what you came here to do! You are the Spiritual Leader you have been seeking!

STAR SEEDS AWAKEN!

CHAPTER 17

CYCLES OF CREATION, ASCENSION AND THE GREAT YEAR

Over two thousand years ago, Plato spoke about what he called "The Great Year." NASA now refers to it as the Platonic Year. Just as our Earth rotates around our Sun, taking approximately 365 days for one complete revolution, our Solar System rotates around the Galactic Sun, taking approximately 26,800 years. This Galactic Year is also referred to as the Procession of the Equinox. Like our Earth's rotation, it contains a descending cycle, winter or a Dark Age as well as an ascending cycle, summer or a Golden Age of high frequencies. The Galactic Year is made up of ages, epochs, or eons which last approximately two thousand years and corresponds with the houses of our "known" zodiac. In the Ancient Hindu Religion and in Swami Sri Yukteswar's book called *The Holy Science,* the time spans are referred to as the "Yugas".

WHAT ARE THE YUGAS?

We are used to thinking of time as linear, with the future being more evolved than the past. However, time spirals, which includes cycles of ascension and cycles of descension or devolution. These cycles are called Yugas and are divided into four: Satya, Treta, Dwapara and Kali. The Satya Yuga is of the highest frequency, known as the golden age, when the Earth is closet to our Galactic Sun. The Kali Yuga is of the lowest frequency and the furthest away from our Galactic Central Sun. We have now entered the ascending cycle, moving closer to the Great Galactic Sun, and the vibrational frequencies of our planet are rising. We are aligning our sun with other "suns" as we ascend into the Golden Age. In the Dwapara cycle, the Yugas do not last the same amount of time, and according to ancient texts, the orbit around the Galactic Sun is not Circular but elliptical. This elliptical orbit creates a slig shot affect accelerating the ascension process when our Earth reaches a point of critical mass. This manifests as a radical shift in consciousness or a quickening.

Unfortunately due to black hole technology from Fallen Angelics in the Parralle Time Matrixes our past natural cycles have been altered and co-opted to keep us stuck in an AI time loop matrix which has caused us to become a race with amnesia. Certain measures have been taken to assure that during this Ascension Cycle, humanity will experience a rise in vibrational frequency, conscious awareness, clarity and enlightenment. We wake up from the Dream Spell. We move into the higher frequencies.

Sri Yukteswar writes this about the Golden Age or Satya Yuga in his book *The Holy Science*, "The human intellect can comprehend all, even God the Spirit beyond this visible world." This concept of a "Golden Age" exists in the ancient myths and memories of many cultures. Some of the aspects of the Golden Age are, "people look young their entire lives. They do not age or get dis-eases. People communicate with animals and live in harmony with nature and one another. The weather is perfect and there is an abundance of everything you need. Nature is pure and pristine. Everyone communicates in one language of the soul. Love is the currency and people can fly at will."

The last Golden age on Earth was the time before the Fall of Lemuria and Atlantis. This was a golden age where spiritual enlightenment and advanced crystalline technology were harmoniously aligned. After Earth reached its zenith during the Golden Age, it began its descending cycle. This is a natural process that follows God's Natural Laws. It follows the Divine Krystal Spiral of Creation, allowing lessons to be fully learned and integrated as the collective spirals upwards rather than simply moving forward in a linear fashion. However, invading intruders took advantage of this natural descending cycle and augmented it by using Artificial Technology, creating reverse polarities and plunging us deeper into the unnatural lower frequencies of duality. The two great civilizations of Atlantis and Lemuria became polarized between their masculine and feminine qualities. Atlantis began abusing their Crystalline technology, causing the poles to shift and the two great continents sank into the Ocean. This is how the Intruders engineered their first Human Holocaust with AI technology which humanity has been repeating over and over since we have been caught in an artificial time loop. The spiraling descent continued until it reached its Nadir during the Dark Ages, our lowest point on the descending cycle. We are now on the ascending cycle, approaching our zenith. According to popular astrology, we have entered a "new age" or a new zodiac, leaving behind the old house of Pisces and moving into what the musical group *The Fifth Dimension* heralded as the "The Dawning of the Age of Aquarius". A time for "no more falsehoods or derisions, golden living dreams of visions, mystic crystal revelations, and the mind's true liberation!" However, there is another zodiac which has been hidden from us and forms the thirteen house or constellation of the Zodiac. The house we have now entered is called *Ophiscuis*.

THE SUN AND ASCENSION

In the 1920s, a French Alchemist and esoteric author, who was known as *Fulcanelli*, although his true identity is still debated, wrote a book entitled, *Le Mystère des Cathédrales (The Mystery of the Cathedrals)* in 1922, which was published in Paris in 1926. His book was about a simple cross in the courtyard of St. Vincent's Church, located in the town square of Hendaye in south western France, and its message for our age. There are many symbols carved into the cross and the pedestal on which it rests. The cross is supposed to symbolize the procession of the equinox and the arrival of the Golden Age. There is also an angry sun on the pedestal, which represents how the old world will be "destroyed" giving way to the new one. The Cross at Hendaye is a physical representation of the belief held by ancient Christians, Rosicrucian's, and Alchemists that the world's end is rapidly approaching and will occur in the midst of fire. Prophecies from Nostradamus, the Bible, Mayan calendars, NASA, and many other sources have depicted this ending of our world as a time of great destruction and something to be feared. Many believe that the Cross at Hendaye is just one more reminder that the end is near. Or could it be the beginning? Could it be that all these prophecies and revelations of end times have been positioned to make us afraid of the very energy that is transmuting our bodies and our organic earth, restoring us to our rightful position in the Cosmos? Could it be that the end of the world is simply the shedding of our finite earth to give way for the beginning of a New Infinite Earth in the higher dimensions?

The role of our Sun and its alignment to the other suns is paramount in the ascension process. If you observe our sun, it has changed greatly in the past several years. The color has gone from a warm yellow to a white-hot glow at times, filling up the entire sky. Many photographs have revealed pink and blue orb overlays around the sun. These are light body activation codes being emitted from the Sun activating our dormant twelve strands of Kystraline DNA. The activities of our Sun have been off the chart. There are solar winds, solar flares, solar storms, solar flashes, even solar sneezes that have been prophesied for eons. But this is not an event to be feared as the wrath of an angry God but as the normal organic process of ascension. Nor is it one cataclysmic event, but an ongoing process that increases as our Earth acclimates to each higher frequency. Certainly there will be milestones as more and more critical mass is reached. The Sun is breaking everything down. In alchemical terms, it is burning away the dross of our carbon bodies and applying the necessary heat and pressure to turn a lump of coal or "carbon" into a radiant diamond. Likewise, the iron in our blood is transmuting into a silicon base. It is purging away the lower densities and infusing us with the higher plasma light rainbow frequencies. Perhaps this explains the desperate attempts being made to block out our sun?

THE PHOTON BELT

In 1961, astronomers utilizing satellite instrumentation discovered what appeared to be an unusual nebula. We normally understand the nebula phenomenon as a vast cloud-like mass of gas or dust. This one, however, appeared to have anomalous properties and was named the Golden Nebula. What is this electromagnetic cloud, this golden nebula? Its more universal definition is 'photon belt' or 'photon band' consisting of many bands. Any encounter with this band or belt is recognized as of great importance. The Photon Belt is the Galactic Plane of alignment of solar system orbits across this Photon Belt which occurs twice in approximately 26,000 years during the Precession of the Equinox. It is referred to as the 'Great Crossing' which occurs every 13,000 years. This brilliant protonic light from the Great Central Sun radiates out through the conduit of the

Galactic Plane Photon Belt. The time in which our Solar System sits either partly or fully within the Photon Belt is referred to as periods of "Light." When our Solar System is not within this Photon Belt, it is referred to as periods of Darkness. Every 13,000 years we reach the PEAK central region of the photon belt of light which coincides with the yearly Stellar Cycle of our Sun. On the December Solstice of 2012, "the end of the world" according to the Mayan Calendar, our Solar System fully entered this Photon Belt field. Earth is now entirely within the photon belt. On the December Solstice of 2020 during the conjunction of Saturn and Jupiter, we reached our zenith of this photopic energy, the highest form of light that is known.

This light of Source carries a sentient supra-conscious intelligence, coded into the frequencies just as laser light encoded into fiber optics can carry thousands of videos and phone conversations encoded within the light. Modern science has only recently 'rediscovered' what the ancients already knew. This understanding of 'Galactic Light' was known to the Gnostics: The 2000-year-old Gnostic text, discovered in Nag Hammadi, Egypt in 1945, reveals the cosmic understanding that the brilliant plasma light at the central core of our Galaxy is actually a sentient intelligence. Furthermore, these Gnostic texts tell us that the physical world we inhabit came into form as the intelligent expression of the plasma light spiraling outwards. Leading experts of both quantum science and the Mayan Calendar say that our DNA is being "upgraded" or encoded with intelligence from the center of our Galaxy. As our galactic sun aligns with the Great Central Sun, and other suns, these alignments of suns reach far beyond our galaxy, even beyond our Universe and into the Higher Harmonic Universes to call us home.

STELLAR ACTIVATION CYCLE

Our Time matrix as well as our Earth has an intricate system of Star Gates or Holy Grails that were Guarded and energized by the true Magi Grail Lines of Royal Dragon King and Queen Lineages. There were twelve major star gates guarded by the twelve tribes of these Magi Grail lines whose genetics corresponded with the gate they guarded and served as keys to unlock them. When attuned to the Krystala Spiral these star gates allowed humans with the proper genetic coding to travel the multiverse. These Guardians also worked with the Dragon ley lines and Dragon Nods or the energetic Template of our Mother Earth. Malta holds the Key or passcode to the energetic template of our Earth which is why it has been fought over throughout time and was held by the Knights "Templar" and all that remains of the Goddess Dragon Queens who Guarded it are a few Goddess Temple ruins with the Krystala Spiral encrypted in their massive limestones. This was at one time on Tara a vast network of Ancient Goddesses in the Land of MU which kept our Earth and our time matrix in alignment with the organic timelines of the Krystala Spiral of Life and Divine Infinite Source through rituals of toning conducted in Goddess temples both above ground and within the womb of our Mother Earth. Krystal Spirals were etched into the massive limestones or painted in red ochre on the walls and ceilings of these temples to hold the Krystala frequencies.

Stellar activation occurs every two thousand years when our solar system aligns with the higher frequency bands such as those found in the Pleiades, Sirius, Arcturus, Orion, and Andromeda systems. To understand the alignment, one could think of circles within circles (cycles within cycles) turning at different rates which are attached magnetically periodically aligning to form one long and powerful magnet. This would act like a powerful current, or holographic beam containing the fundamental energy of all these systems. When Earth is in alignment, it merges with the higher dimensional parallel or future Earths of Tara, and Gaia. During this process, the particles and antiparticles of these planets and their antiparallel planets are unified in certain specific ways. When these particles and antiparticles come together, they create intense photonic activity, which we know as the Photon Belt.

FAIL-SAFE

The true history of our earth has been an ongoing war between the light and the dark, the finite and the infinite, those who feed from Source and those who parasitically feed off of others. This battle has been waging for over 260 Billion years ever since our time matrix was infiltered by black hole entities who indirectly caused the 12th star gate to be blown up causing our entire time matrix to fall. These fallen entities from the Parallel Time matrixes have been vying to pull our time matrix into theirs through the fallen Fibonacci spiraling down into their dark universe. The truth is The Guardians who are connected to Infinite Source have been check mated on every play and our time matrix would have been lost. But the Guardians would not allow our entire time matrix to be lost because of its vital position. Like wise Earth had lost its ascension ability. But in 2012, this entire Time Matrix was reset to return in alignment with Infinite Source. A Fail Safe program had been activated. Our Mother Earth has chosen Ascension and she and our entire time Matrix are being hosted by another highly evolved time matrix called Aquino. Aquino is creating a Krystal River of extremely high plasma rainbow frequencies to serve as a bridge to pull us out of the collapsing the fallen angelics AI technology and Downward Fibonacci spirals freeing us to ride the Krystala Spiral home. Many evolved souls came from this advanced time matrix taking on human form becoming Aquaferians to be the change now on Earth. This is the true meaning of The Age of Aquarius! These humans are encrypted with very high genetic coding to help them to accomplish their missions. The game is over and we are free! However it is up to each individual to choose to return home on the Krystala Spiral of life or go into fall into fallen parallel universes with the Fibonacci Spiral of Death.

The hideous atrocities against humanity and our Earth we are now witnessing are the parasites last attempts to retain as many souls as possible as their source of energy. They are trying to scam people into investing their consciousness and energy into their fake AI death cult of Crypt-o-currencies, Corp-o-rations, and inject their consciousness into their Metaverse to serve as TAKE AWAY FOOD when they are evicted from our Earth since they will no longer be able to reside in the higher frequencies. In fact these higher frequencies are now here. The New Infinite Earth is here! We just need to allow it to penetrate our consciousness and not remain asleep in the dream spell lulled back into the artificial time loop of their AI finite technology. It is time to "bio-cync" with our organic Mother Earth. This is what our wise indigenous brothers and sisters have been telling us for eons. This is the message of the Hopi Prophecy Rock being fulfilled. Ascension is not escaping our Earth like so much predictive programming has told us or even evacuating though the nearest star gate. It is not artificial technology but in getting back to nature to our organic Earth and listening to spirit and our inner organic technology! The good news is Fail Safe has been activated and the Krystal River is taking us in a more direct pathway HOME!

WHAT DOES THIS ALL MEAN?

This means that these high frequencies of supra-conscious plasma intelligence from the photon belt and the Krystal River Host are activating our Plasma Light Body which acts an ascending vehicle for humanity and earth. These frequencies are merging and synthesizing with the lower dimensional particle rays infusing them with the higher dimensional frequencies. Our Earth coalescing her fragmented parts and returning to wholeness of holiness in her proper position in the Cosmic God Source Worlds and the higher parallels of our harmonic mother Universe in Andromeda. We are now able to break free from the time loop of a 225-million-year cycle and free ourselves through ascension.

OUR BODIES AND THE BODY OF OUR MOTHER EARTH ARE INTRICATELY CONNECTED. WE ARE ONE.

Because we live in an Infinite Multiverse, anything you can imagine exists in Infinite Creation. All these sci-fi stories exist within the mind of the Divine Story Teller. Your job is to determine which story you want to be a part of. Which story brings you closer to the Word which IS God and back into the higher vibrational frequencies of what is organic, authentic, true, and in alignment with Infinite God Source. Just as an organic spherical Earth exists so does an A.I. Flat Earth. In fact, there are many other Earths existing in various dimensions and densities. I suggest you choose wisely which Earth you want to live on since only one is an ascension planet. In ancient cultures it was believed that if one sailed past the Straits of Gibraltar they would fall off the face of the Earth and be eaten by horrible Sea monsters. This fear based belief was created by the Intruders to stop Europeans from passing beyond the Strait of Gibraltar and finding evidence of the Lost Continent of Atlantis. At that time the waters were still turbulent from the cataclysm and many activated crystals were causing worm holes like the one in the Bermuda Triangle. Many of those who did try were indeed consumed by the Sea.

The Flat Earth theory was reintroduced by the C.I. A. to misdirect and divide the awakening Earth community and discredit "conspiracy theorists". The Flat Earth program depicts a chunk of Earth cut off from the rest of the multiverse encapsulated in a dome where nothing else exists, save some hand moving a spot light. There is no Space, no planets, no extraterrestrials, etcetera. Make no doubt the Flat Earth does exist within the A.I. architecture. It is there to misdirect you away from our true organic Mother Earth. So be wise in choosing the Earth you make your reality. Our spherical Earth was at one time knocked off its axis ages ago, which is why we now have a wobble and the poles shifted. So, like everything on our inverted upside-down Earth, the North Pole is really the South. This has thrown everything out of alignment and distorted the natural flow of the horizontal female staff energy harmonizing with the vertical masculine rod energy of our planet. This has affected our own physical body and the sacred union of the masculine and feminine energies. This distortion of how our earth sits on its axis has also created many spinal problems in human beings ability to align their spine with the divine, especially in their occipital lobe where the skull and neck meet. Now, thanks to Elon Musk we have the Space X cage of low orbiting satellites distorting Earth's natural electromagnetic spin which in turn affects our body's electromagnetic balance. This is combined with the geo engineering designed to transhumanize us, our Earth and block out our Sun's powerful ascension energy. These are all direct attacks to halt the ascension of our Earth and our organic bodies.

We now live in a war zone over frequencies on our Earth, and our bodies are the battleground. Many of the ascension symptoms you are experiencing go beyond just purging out the lower densities and acclimating to the higher frequencies. Every day you are dealing with a new layer of toxins and increasing radiation levels bombarding our planet. This is the real reason why so many people are sick and dying and Covid is the cover up. It is very important to do whatever resonates with you to upgrade and safeguard your health in these times. Through consciousness sweeping technology, many of you are being targeted for AI attacks and don't even know it. However, you can transmute whatever the Dark Side throws at you and like everything else concerning the Dark Side, if it doesn't kill you, it makes you stronger. In fact, you can even use it for your shadow clearing.

The Infinite is infinitely more powerful than the finite. The river eventually wears down the rock and returns to the Ocean. Your power is in your softness. Your strength is in your love. My favorite tarot card is the card of "Strength", often depicted as a beautiful woman gently taming a lion with her love. Through the power of love all can be transmuted. Take actions that resonate with you to protect, heal and clear yourself during these challenging times. Hint, not breathing properly, staying out of the sun and away from nature, and injecting yourself with toxins "may" not be the healthiest solutions. Eventually, your frequency will rise to the point where you will become an untouchable Infinite Human Being. The frequency wars we are now all living through are putting additional "pressure" on your carbon-based body to return to its true crystal diamond matrix. Or, in "alchemical" terms transmuting your carbon body into a diamond body. Diamonds are the hardest substances known on Earth. Stay centered in Divine Infinite Source and you cannot be broken!!! You have been wearing winter coats, stuck in the winter of your soul. It is now time to slough these over coats and dawn your radiant summer garments!

All Reality is Divided into levels of awareness, frequencies, dimensions, or densities.

DENSITIES OF CONSCIOUSNESS:

The first density is the density of the elements Earth, Water, Air, Fire and the mysterious Fifth Element of Aether, or in scientific terms: solids, liquids, gases, and plasma. The second density is the density of organic life: plants, animals, bacteria, etc. The third density is the density which human beings inhabit. It is the density of self-awareness. It is the density where free will exists and humans have the right to make choices and decisions regarding dualistic beliefs. It is also the density of duality, through which the individual chooses their polarity of service. The fourth density is the density of love or understanding. And like all subsequent densities, is inhabited by those of a higher level of spiritual evolution. The fifth density is the density of light and wisdom wherein long and deep contemplation and introspection are practiced so that one's own wisdom may spring forth and the entity may become refined to an even higher degree. The sixth density is the density of unity consciousness, where love and wisdom are united and where all other polarities are united. The seventh density is the gateway density, the last density before mind/body/spirit merge. The eighth density is the beginning of the next octave which is made of yet another seven higher densities and the journey continues into the Infinite.

Many of the Great Ones from the Founder Races who are working with us on the Christos Mission are from the 16D, 17D, and 18D non-corporal God Source domain fields and beyond! Their mission is to help you return to your Divine Infinite Human State of Being. They have no other hidden agenda. Their only desire is for you to have what was originally gifted you: free will, God sovereign freedom, and your divine right to freely express Infinite Source within you however you choose. This is why I encourage people to seek the highest frequencies or dimensions for "help" rather than blindly following anyone in physical or etheric form including "good" aliens from surrounding galactic federations who may or may not have hidden agendas. They may offer assistance in our ascension process, but it may come with a price.

In order to progress from third density to fourth density, individuals must choose between two polarities of service: Service to others or service to self: or in ordinary language, between altruism and selfishness. The purpose of third density is to make this choice.

WHAT ARE DIMENSIONS?

We live in a Time matrix composed of Five harmonic Universes and fifteen dimensions. These are different planes of existence each consisting of a different vibratory frequency or flash sequences. Each dimension has certain sets of laws and principles that are specific to the frequency of that dimension. Each dimension vibrates at a higher rate or frequency than the one below it. In each higher dimension, there exists a clearer, wider perspective of reality, a greater level of knowing where we experience more freedom, greater power, and more opportunity to create reality.

THE THIRD DIMENSION

The Third Dimension often called 3D earth is locked in a time/space, cause/effect duality paradigm. This dimension is a schoolroom that souls attend by inhabiting humanoid physical bodies to learn more about creation. In the Third Dimension our life experiences are but reflections or mirrors of a greater reality and we are seeking to understand all we see. Therefore, the process of creating via our thoughts and feelings is slowed down so that we can track the circumstances of what we hold in our consciousness. The Third Dimension is a state of consciousness that is very limited and restricted. Third-dimensional society and science seek to prove that the only reality that exists is the one we perceive with our five physical senses and urges us to believe that our 3D perceptions of reality are the only reality. Because we have been living in this third-dimensional reality for so many lifetimes, we tend to assume that this is the only reality available to live in.

The third dimensional "operating system" runs on rigid beliefs and a fairly inflexible set of rules and limitations. For example, in the Third Dimension, we learn to believe that our bodies are solid, that they can't merge with each other or walk through walls. Everything is subject to gravity. Physical objects cannot disappear, and we cannot read each other's mind. There's a solid belief that we have to "work hard" to accomplish our goals. Fear, judgment, and separation from the whole are pervasive. We are taught to not value the imagination and conditioned to view people who do as frivolous, irresponsible, worthless, crazy day dreamers.

THE FOURTH DIMENSION

This is the "bridge" between the third and the fifth dimension. Many of you are traveling through the Fourth Dimension, preparing yourselves for the Fifth. Many of you have had experiences of the Fourth Dimension for a number of years now without even realizing it. You are experiencing this dimension when you have moments of spiritual awakening and experiences of opening your heart. Other times, it can happen when we're simply feeling clear, quiet inside or in the "zone." Everything within and around us feels lighter and less rigid. There's an elasticity to time and space and a sense of infinite expansion and upliftment. Time is no longer linear in the Fourth Dimension. Fourth-dimensional perception of past, present, and future is more fluid, as the laws of time and space change. You discover that time is malleable that you can actually stretch or condense it, much to your third-dimensional surprise. Because of the fluid nature of time and space in the Fourth Dimension, your astral forms naturally morph. Hence, there is a huge mobility of form. A shaman or holy person who can shape shift has learned to ground their astral form upon the fourth dimension so completely that they can temporarily change their third-dimensional form. Manifestation is much faster in the Fourth Dimension. Thoughts and feelings create reality much more quickly than upon the third dimension. In general, when you are experiencing love, joy, and gratitude, you're glimpsing fourth-dimensional consciousness. Many of us are serving as bridges now in the fourth dimension between 3D and 5D Earth.

THE FIFTH DIMENSION

All life upon the Fifth Dimension lives in the Unity Consciousness of Spirit, but there is still an experience of "I am" as an individual. Linear time and space do not bind consciousness here, and there is NO illusion of separation or limitation. Instead, there is a constant experience of the Oneness of ALL. In order to enter the Fifth Dimension and stay there, all mental and emotional baggage must be left at the door. No fear, suffering, anger, hostility, guilt, or sense of separation can exist there. Mastery over thought is a prerequisite. All actions on this plane are based upon love because fear cannot survive in the higher vibration of the fifth dimension. If we were to experience fear while in the Fifth Dimension, our vibration would drop and our consciousness would instantly be lowered to the sub-planes of the Fourth Dimension. On the Fifth Dimension, we live in unconditional love, unconditional forgiveness, and unconditional acceptance. Manifestation in the Fifth Dimension is instantaneous. You think about something, it becomes present. People generally communicate through telepathy and have the ability to read each other's thoughts and feelings with ease. The experience of time is radically different: some describe it as "everything happening at once." There is no distinction between past, present, or future.

Many of you may be having experiences or dreams that feel like visits to the Fifth Dimension. These are exhilarating, tremendously exciting, and hopeful. They keep you moving on through the difficulties that arise as we deal with the finite broken 3D earth and travel through the Fourth Dimension and into the Fifth. The Fifth Dimension is the beginning of Ascension therefore, all consciousness there is naturally multidimensional. Many worry that communities on the New Infinite Earth will experience the disharmony and ruin of previous communities. But these communities will be in the fifth dimension, and you cannot exist on the fifth dimension with baggage from the lower dimensions. As you ascend in frequency and reconnect with the Infinite, you begin to transcend time and space. You will realize time is an illusion created to make sense of your 3D existence. As you ascend, you will wake up from the dream spell and reclaim your status as a multidimensional Infinite Human Being. You will have the ability to project your consciousness to any part of Creation at will at any given moment! As you escape the illusions of your lower vibratory prison this will become more and more part of your life! The illusion of time will melt away as days may seem like minutes or minutes weeks, or sometimes you will even forget what time, day, or year it is!

Time is governed by Saturn or Cronus, Father Time, or the Grim Reaper, and has been created as a prison. As you drop densities and free yourself from the illusion of time, you may become more aware of the Infinite number of parallel universes, parallel realities, and parallel yous! For every choice you make, there is another you, who has made an infinite number of other choices. Therefore, as you move through your daily life, you are moving in and out of parallel realities. It could be useful to ask for "help" to make wise choices that pull you into your optimal temporal reality, on the highest organic timeline, becoming the highest organic version of you. You may want to continuously ask yourself these questions: Am I living my optimal reality? Am I blissfully being of the highest service to humanity, Mother Earth and all creation? Many times, you may still need to learn something or experience the lower frequencies to heal yourself or motivate yourself to keep moving onward and upward. Have you ever had a bad day that was totally off, then suddenly everything shifted? Perhaps you had to revisit something from the past even for a moment just to heal. Perhaps you had to feel "out of sync" with the Universe to motivate yourself to more fully align with Infinite Source? Sometimes you need to take a few steps backward to more fully forward move. This is why the Universe moves in spirals.

Check off your bucket list! Even if you just need to see a movie or read a book instead of physically doing it. Why? Because your desires, your "wish I had ofs" can pull you back into the lower frequencies of 3D Earth and the lowers versions of you. The more you align yourself with the Divine Will of Infinite God Source and let go of the egotistic desires of your finite self, the more you will have access to the higher frequencies of the fifth dimension. The more bliss, peace, creativity and expansiveness you will feel and things will easily manifest for you. Perhaps the world lockdowns have been giving people an opportunity to stop running around focusing on the 3D physical world of illusion and tune inward to the 5D reality? Many of us have found ourselves alone and unable to travel so we could stop running away from ourselves. We have found ourselves with the most difficult task of all, facing our inner demons. Perhaps all that is happening in the world around us is to change our focus, heighten our perspective and curb our appetite for the familiar 3D world. Nowadays, when I think of going out into the 3D world, I intuitively ask myself if it is worth the effort. Am I going to be of service? If so, then, of course, I show up. But often I think of what we used to say as children, "Let's say we did and don't!" It is becoming increasingly more difficult for many of us to enter the 3D World. I steer clear of places that require me to wear a mask. At this moment in Italy's "his" tory, I can no longer participate in 3D Earth without a green pass which requires me to be fully "vaccinated". No cafes restaurants, hair salons, health clubs, supermarkets, travel... no nothing! It has not been easy and has tested my faith. But I have found all my needs provided for and it has pushed me further out of the fake finite 3D paradigm of illusion and more and more into nature and the true reality of 5D bliss.

CHAPTER 18

THE FALSE ASCENSION MATRIX

I still had no idea of the many influential lifetimes Peter and I had, and the powerful role I was to play in Earth's future. This is a familiar story for many Star Seeds because the Dark Side knows more about us than we do about ourselves and strikes at a time in our lives when we are unaware and most vulnerable. Although I have always been protected, if not I would not be here and have finished this book, the Dark Side continued its attempts to seduce me and when that failed they would wage a full scale war. I still had many lessons to learn and shadows to release. I was getting sicker everyday with headaches, vertigo, and I had to have an infected tooth pulled. So, I sold my condo in South Carolina and moved back to Italy in the spring of 2018. I immediately felt much better with no 5G, eating healthy food and walking several miles daily. Florence was alive at that time with international tourists, musical groups, street performers, artists, craftspeople, and outdoor cinemas. I lived right beside *Ponte Vecchio*, and in the evenings Kiki and I would walk across the old bridge so she could be "adored" by her fans. A psychic had once told me that Kiki would be adored by millions. Sure enough whenever Kiki walked into a piazza droves of tourists would drop to their knees to adore her, and Kiki loved it! I had sought out my old friends, but again, it was as if I existed in another universe. I began to shrink away from the phoniness of social life and focus on my soul mission. I decided I wanted to dedicate all my energy to helping students expand their awareness, ascend in frequencies and create conscious media. I reopened my film school as the New Consciousness Renaissance School and created an Infinite Human Retreat.

My first student was French. She was very enthusiastic and loved the program. I should have left well enough alone, but I decided to hand her over to the other mentors I had hired. One was a performance artist who had studied under Marina Abramović and opened an Art studio in what used to be Machiavelli's kitchen. Marina Abramović, is considered the grandmother of performance art but is also rumored to be a high level witch and satanic high priestess since the 1970's. She is now 70+ years old but looks much younger supposedly because of all of blood sacrifices she has been apart of and all of the Adrenochrome she has consumed from children along with the dark magick rituals she performs daily. She was having a month-long exhibition in Florence, so Kiki and I went to check it out. The rooms of her Performance Art were filled with countless images of pain and torture. In one room there were two naked people you had to walk between, and in another room, there was a pile of bones, (which Kiki loved). I kept thinking how wonderful it would be to take performance art in the direction of creating visions of a New Infinite Earth in the Fifth Dimension. I had wanted to offer that in my school. I also read that Bill Gates was going to sponsor Marina so she could take her performance "art" into the virtual world. I had been toying with the idea of turning my film school into a 3D virtual art school since I knew it was the future. So I went to a Fantasy Fair held in Florence to meet with some people to discuss it. I tried on a headset and entered the Virtual World! I was amazed! "How cool". I thought. But suddenly, I had a panic attack. I ripped the mask from my face. The whole thing just felt wrong to my organic body. I remember being so glad I could tear the mask off. I had a flash of a memory in a parallel universe where I could not tear the mask off since it had become fused with my organic body. It was terrifying!

My student did not want to continue with the performance artist so I sent her to my other mentor. He was a Film Director who loved to make horror films, hang out in graveyards abandoned insane asylums, and sleep with snakes. I should have known better! The beautiful story my student had written with me as her mentor, about stepping into higher vibratory parallel versions of herself, turned into a dark, bloody horror film of suicide after spending a few weeks with this satanic director. I felt so bad about handing her over to this dark soul, but I realize now I offered her a choice. She had chosen to give her power over to this dark director and I could not usurp her freedom of expression nor her free will. My student told me she loved the "Dark Arts" and wanted to remain there. So we parted ways.

I could sense something big was on the horizon and the timelines of our Earth were separating. It was the time I had intuitively known about all of my life. One of my first children's stories was called *The Tribe of Uno*. It was the story of a tribe of people who suffered a cataclysmic disaster that split their tribe into two, forcing each one to choose between two worlds. I saw this playing out before my own eyes and knew I had to choose wisely and let go of everything that was not true. I began to sense that there would be those who wanted to ascend into the higher "organic" frequencies and those who would choose to remain locked in the artificial time loop of the lower frequencies repeating the past over and over and over. I decided I would no longer waste my precious time, energy and talents on people who did not desire to ascend. Instead I would dedicate all my energy to helping those who wanted to awaken from the dream spell. I realized that a Consciousness Renaissance could not occur until the world got its wake up all. So I dedicated myself to helping people wake up!

I offered a free Guru Walking Tour entitled The Esoteric Renaissance Walking Tour. Every day, Kiki and I would meet people from all around the world under the Statue of Dante in Piazza Santa Croce. I would take them around Florence, telling them about the "true" history of our planet, and what really went on during the Renaissance. I met some amazing folks who enjoyed my tour and Kiki! I felt alive! I was waking people up from all over the world, exposing the dark One World Order Agenda! A New Renaissance Consciousness was growing! One day, I had a strange couple from Los Angeles appear out of nowhere. They seemed to know more about the esoteric workings than I did but only from a certain perspective. She told me she was a student of John Dee, the purported Alchemist who served Queen Elizabeth I. After the tour, they tipped me extremely well and took me out to dinner. The woman offered to read tarot cards for me instead of me for her. She pulled out a "Thoth" Tarot deck. She kept mentioning that I was of the royal bloodlines, flattering me and encouraging me to do things that didn't feel right. After that, they just fell off the face of the Earth.

I didn't heed any of their advice. But I did realize that once again, I was being courted by the Dark Side, and had refused. At that time, I had not yet understood how Thoth had falsified the Emerald Tablets and led the Renaissance into a false ascension matrix and that I had unknowingly played a major role in that dark agenda. After that, I was once again energetically attacked and my health began to suffer greatly. I got the familiar symptoms of vertigo, nausea, and diarrhea and once again had to have an infected tooth pulled. As a result, I spent most of my time grounding myself in nature. I began communing with the deva spirits and my best friends became the trees in the gardens around Florence. I had seen workmen putting wires into the manholes around Florence. One day, I asked what they were doing, and finally, one workman admitted that they were installing 5G. My intuitive friend from England called and screamed, "Get out of Florence!" But I wasn't sure where to go! I had no money, but I started getting signs to move to Sicily. Another friend from the States came to visit me and reminded me that I had told her I wanted to move to Sicily. So I decided on Sicily. But how? I had no money! Suddenly, money miraculously appeared and Kiki and I took the next flight to Palermo. But where in Sicily was I to go? I searched for beaches in Sicily that accepted dogs and I found a *"Bau-Bau"* Beach, the name children call doggies in Italian. This was in Castellammare del Golfo. Next to it was the "Neverland" lido. Oh, I thought I'm getting warm. Then a few feet from that, there it was, the "Peter Pan Lido". Bingo! And what do you think was right next to it? A beach called "Elisabetta", Sara and Elisabetta! "Peter Pan Sara Elisabetta!" Which translates to Peter Pan will be Elizabeth. I knew this was the place. After I moved there, a reporter from the local magazine interviewed me and wrote an article about my story entitled, "The return!"

THE FALSE ASCENSION MATRIX

Currently, the collective stories running on planet Earth read like some kind of *Sci-Fi* novel. Earth's population infected with deadly virus, World Wide Lock Downs, 5G and Space X encapsulate planet, Vaccines mandated, Green Pass required for all activities on Earth! If you want to follow the Dark Side's Script, you need only look at the preemptive Hollywood movies which include the cataclysmic destruction of Earth and a great "reset" into a fake technological tyrannical AI world where humans are trans-humanized into A.I. slaves! What a story! What story are you creating? Are you passively being swept into the dark agenda's story? Moment to moment you are writing your own reality, creating your future with the two most powerful words ever uttered: I AM. Are you writing:

I am fearful, I am powerless, I am weak, I am confused, I am angry, I am apathetic, I am sad, I am insignificant, I am not enough, I am finite? Or are you writing I am infinite, I am powerful, I am love, I am God, I am Sovereign, I am Free? Your words are portals that beam steer you to the future Earth you are creating. Will you be "led" by others? Spiritual Teachers, the herd mentality, the collective of humanity? Or will you LEAD humanity? If you are unaware of what words you are writing into reality, you are allowing someone else to hold your magic pen. Someone or something outside of you is creating your future. But if you can mindfully take back the pen and write the words you choose wisely, you will create the reality YOU want. If not, you will passively accept the fake finite artificial AI web of a world void of all freedom that is presently being spun around you as you remain asleep in the dream spell.

Many are refusing to wake up and smell the Tyranny. Or they are waiting for someone to do something about it. To perform a miracle, to take out the "bad" guys so the world can go back to normal. They are waiting for others to do it for them rather than standing up for themselves and creating a world they want to live in. These souls will find it easier to simply accept the New AI World Order that is being spoon-fed, or injected into them. Their souls are not ready to be independent and still "need" to be told what to do, think and beleive. They welcome the day when the burden of thinking is lifted and the internet does it for them. Unfortunately, the majority of these souls will passively consent to this AI future world where their consciousness will be uploaded into their digital twin in the AI world of false ascension. They will be scammed into thinking it is freedom, expansive consciousness and the new Meta Verse. But they will become a prisoner in a finite fake AI reality even more fallen than 3D Earth.

True freedom only comes through organic Ascension. Because we are on the verge of the Greatest Story "Never" Told of Organic Ascension, of reactivating our divine DNA and organic technology, the Dark Side is seducing us with the forbidden fruit of AI technology. Technology above and beyond what has ever been seen on Earth is now entering the market place. Free highly advanced Tartarian technology has existed for eons, but was erased from his-tory in the last Great Reset. Now weaponized technology is carefully being released at this pre-ordained time to inspire an AI technological Renaissance. This Technological Renaissance is being diabolically masterminded to hijack the Divine Consciousness Renaissance of true ascension into the Infinite 5D world, and redirect humanity into a finite 5G World.5D or 5G? It is a distraction to throw us off the scent of our expanding infinite consciousness and herd us into a finite hiveminded consciousness. This technology is being dangled before humanity like candy before a baby, luring us deeper and deeper into their AI web. Like children following a trail of gum drops we are becoming more and more addicted day by day as we enter their Artificial AI Candy land. Certainly in this ever-expanding AI web around us we all need to use technology to serve us in our soul mission. This means using it with the maturity of an adult. Turning it on when necessary to function in the 3D Earth and turning it off and putting it away when it is not needed. But the minute you allow AI in any form to enter your body, which is your temple, you have become a servant to it. You cannot turn it off, disconnect and like all parasites it begins to take over its host, which is you! Slowly and insidiously at first, until one day, like in the movie *The Body Snatchers* you fall asleep in the AI dream and wake up a hive minded drone.

SPIRITUAL BYPASSING

If you are giving your power in any way to external narratives such as people, institutions, jobs, events, aliens, an external God or Christ, technology, money etcetera you are being led into a False Ascension Matrix. This is something that often occurs in people who spiritually by pass. Spiritual bypassing is generally an ego defense mechanism used by people who believe something or someone else will take care of them like the Government, Modern Medicine, God, Jesus, Potus, good aliens, spiritual speakers, spiritual leaders, angels et cetera, so they do not have to take responsibility for their own lives or make their own decisions. They spend much of their time reacting to what is going on around them, lost in the plot and staying within the confines of the accepted story. They are afraid to dig deeper and see the negativity of the unpleasant truths happening around them. They consider these unpleasant truths to be negative energy that will lower their vibration, so they choose to ignore it. They label these events or classify people who seek truth as fostering negativity and fear.

As a result, they tend to be apathetic people easily manipulated by dark forces, with a weakened moral character, lower ethical standards and are ineffective at leading or even helping their fellow human beings. In fact, their cognitive dissonance often makes them servants of Satan, functioning as the diabolical hand of the controllers to carry out their crimes against humanity.

Because their version of reality is selective or even delusional, they are very ineffective in making positive changes in the world and are being used as pawns to fabricate a false AI prison. Spiritual Bypassing is an act of pure egoistic selfishness in the guise of projecting oneself as an evolved, pious, or higher consciousness person. The profile of this person is that they ignore or downplay certain events they consider negative in order to protect themselves from being mentally or emotionally triggered. The danger of this Pollyanna approach is that those who continue to see the positive in everything and follow the herd may be culled, trans-humanized or worse incur the karma of serving satanic forces. Even if you claim ignorance or believe that you were doing it for the good of humanity, you can never escape the natural laws of Cosmic Karma. Like children claiming exemption with the excuse, "He told me to!" This does not hold water under the Law of One. All karmic debts must be paid. This is why good Christians can never answer the age old questions, "Why do bad things happen to good people?"

Since we live in a time where the energies on our planet are augmenting daily, all karmic debts are coming up for payment in full. Refusing to pay, heal and evolve will cause you to once again miss the boat of ascension and be trapped in a false ascension time matrix prison never even knowing what you missed. And believe me, ignorance is not bliss! Many have been doing this for millions, upon millions of earth years without even knowing it. If that is your choice, fine. But many of you have grown soul weary of this never-ending time loop of slavery and are choosing to return home. You must wake up to reclaim your God Sovereign Freedom. You must wake up to the truth of what is going on around you and stop participating in the dream spell. That is key. It is not just enough to wake up and try to wake others up but you must do your own inner work. Only then will you not leave dark portals open in your auric body for dark forces to take hold of your consciousness. We attract to us what we need to experience. Make changes in yourself, then your outer world will follow. Free yourself and you will step out of the finite 3D world of illusion and into the divine light of your soul mission.

Since the Harmonic Convergence in 1987, there has been a specific space task force assembled by *Thothian Luciferians* and the members of the Galactic Federation to fully control the information given to the awakening population for the purpose of the complete takeover of the New Age, Ascension, and Disclosure movement. A comprehensive multiple-pronged militarized approach was organized in order to gather and collect all of the technological and human resources that would be necessary to build an extensive artificial neurological network with silent-sound technology. This would be used to target awakening souls or Star Seeds and control all transmissions of "channeled" material that would be sent to the awakening population in the guise of "friendly" ET's, Ascended Masters, The (fallen) Galactic Federation, Archangels, and even deceased famous figures in human history.

As the Ascension cycle intensified, many people on earth were contacted by human and non-human imposters, comprised from these operations and military alliances to gaslight and lie to the earth people about many ongoing themes of global concern, for the purpose of the intelligence "handling" of controlled opposition and disclosure containment. These operatives have infiltrated many areas of the New Age, Ascension, Awakened, or Woke Disclosure Communities. They are on the ground and in space, hidden behind the many false-front organizations in which their primary job is to attack, dismiss, misdirect and debunk unapproved topics through mass propaganda and character assassination schemes. The purpose is to take over any truthful information about the planetary ascension or full disclosure that happens to seep through the multidimensional communication gateways when awakening people start to more easily receive telepathic transmissions directly from Infinite Source. Even reasonably benevolent entities or aliens that were in communication with assorted channelers, purposely lied to the New Age Population out of fear that our spiritually immature, violent, warring civilization would infect and harm their civilizations. As a result, they were distressed enough to keep earth humans in a "consciousness pen," afraid of what would happen if we were to be let out of the frequency fences into the higher dimensions as a collective race consciousness.

Like in the game 'telephone,' by the time the original off-planet transmission from the higher dimensions was received by the person being contacted on earth, that intelligence had gone through multiple filters and fences on several dimensions, along with several alien handlers decoding the acceptable content and deleting or manipulating many of the truthful facts. By the time the information made it to the telepathic human that was channeling it on the earth plane, the information had been tampered with by several intermediaries. This has given way to many New Age gurus dispersing incorrect or watered-down information within the New Age movement.

NEW AGE ASTRAL BLISS

One of the most appealing ways the *Thothian* Groups have found to manipulate the New Age Ascension communities is to promote the states of astral bliss through the slick marketing of spiritual consumerism. People line up like astral junkies to get a hit of false love transmissions from the astral plane while participating in events, retreats, workshops, and gatherings. There is a manipulated state of astral bliss which is a type of euphoria or emotional conditioning to activate addictive response patterns while participating with many of the New Age Group modalities that are hijacked by Thothian entities. Retreats that scratch the surface and allow you to feel a blissful high only to return home to have it wear off and find yourself in the same situation as before allows you to check off a box that later gets turned into, "I'm beyond all that shadow work because I've dealt with that already." Thus, the setup is to ignore red flags and emotional weakness in everyday life, because the fear of actually facing deeper issues and having to make changes in one's lifestyle is too overwhelming.

Spiritual bypassing also occurs in individuals who have disconnected their heart from their mind and severed their masculine from their feminine. Spiritual followers are taught that because the world is so heartless and controlled only by the brains of aggressive "masculine" people and not the heart, they should only love and not think. So, the

Luciferians who are masters at only thinking, are always misdirecting the good loving intentions of these people. Like innocent children they have never grown up, accessed their inner power and learned to discern and think for themselves. Followers are taught to have blind faith. Many are simply blindly carrying out the dark agenda, creating their own hell here on Earth while all the while praying for a miracle from God. You are that miracle! God is within you! You must use both the amazing heart and mind God gave you. You must use both your intuitive, receptive divine feminine side balanced with your logical discerning divine masculine side of action. You must stop waiting for God to create a miracle and save you! You must have the courage to question and examine everything, even your own dark side, with self-love and compassion while being honest with yourself. If you are really being honest with yourself, you will heal your wounds, learn your lessons, pass your tests, and make the necessary changes in yourself so you can become the "Natural Born Leader" you are destined to be!

In the spiritual consumer market, we can transfer that responsibility onto someone or something else and pretend that we are actually doing the spiritual work, because we paid for an event, workshop, video, or retreat. Spiritual astral bliss narratives are filled with fantastical illusions, wishful and magical thinking, self-deception, and escapist fantasies that always point to someone or something else taking care of things while you just have to patiently wait and have faith! Severely emotionally wounded people are led into these "spiritual" traps, where they are not interested in healing themselves or taking responsibility for their own behavior or thinking independently. They instead seek further excuses to continue co-dependent irresponsible behaviors letting others tell them what to think and do, all the while being deceived by themselves and others, in an accepted social setting.

The Spiritual hijack has created groups of people who refuse to grow up or to be held accountable for their actions, who follow orders without questioning authority or taking responsibility for their lives. This explains why so many "spiritual" people refuse to SEE what is really going on in the world around us today and as a result, become used as pawns in the dark agendas. Why so many kindhearted, well-meaning "spiritual" people pour their heart felt good intentions and energy into the furthering the One

World Order Satanic agendas simply because they did not KNOW what they were doing and refused to SEE the Truth.

Since the dark side has no real power, the only power it has over you is the magic of illusion. Like modern magicians who have no real magic, they must put on a great show. They must distract you away from the truth that true power lies within. This is why they wear long sleeves, have attractive assistants, and work in the dark with smoke and mirrors. Because in truth, it is ALL SMOKE AND MIRRORS. While you are being distracted, while your attention, your consciousness, and your focus is drawn elsewhere they silently work their magic, performing their "trick" to trick you! And the trick is to get you to "pay" attention to all the external shows that keep you distracted from Infinite God Source within. Energy goes where attention flows. Every time you "pay" with your attention, your energy, you empower their show. Whether you are enjoying the "popcorn" or reacting in fear to the three-ring circus of our crazy world, you are empowering this fake finite world rather than empowering yourself and creating your own show. Who's running the show???And what is more distracting than fear? So, as they trick you, fool you, glamour you, scam you, you applaud their skillful deceptions, and passively accept their faux solutions, leading you deeper into their false ascension matrix where the power is always outside of you!

Under Cosmic Law, you reap what you sow, so how can anyone who is constantly giving away their power to another ever gain freedom. As above so below. Like a child who has been constantly provided for by a parent and never learned how to provide for themselves is incapable of living on their own, so too are the "children" of God. We are all being asked to grow up! And it is time to grow up! Time to stop being the "children" of God waiting for a miracle or to be told what to do by God the Father Almighty or waiting for his son to return and "save" you! You are the Christ! You are Infinite God Source incarnate. Many souls have come from the highest God Source Worlds of the Founder Races now, with very specific "Soul Missions" in this pivotal time we have now entered to lead the way to true organic ascension. Many of these Christs, these Divine Infinite Human Beings are you! You are the solution to the world's problems. You have the power because you are Infinite!

Unfortunately, in this war of duality the dark side has cleverly constructed, with diabolical precision a plan that uses our human weaknesses against us. Like Narcissistic Handlers, the Dark side knows our fears, traumas and our deep seated desire to be saved and taken care of. They know how to use these weaknesses to control the masses. They have set up their "good cop, bad cop" narratives. After they have traumatized humanity and accomplished their goals of activating their AI networks of Space X and 5G and injecting all those who hold positions of power in their finite prison matrix our hero will emerge! I can read the script from here. "Having dismantled the One World Order satanic systems and made technology safe, our hero has cleared the way for the free world." These false champions of the people, many who are rising in popularity now will claim that technology is safe and the answer to all our woes! The bad guys have been dealt with. Vaccinated people can now be healed through technology!At last the savior "We the People" have been awaiting with bated breath has come! Hallelujah! Praise our Lord God in Heaven!" The Miracle humanity has long awaited is here! God has answered our prayers! And he, the Messiah, is here to lead his people into the false light of his AI Kingdom of Heaven on Earth! We must remember the Hopi Prophecy, "A leader will not be the one that talks the loudest, boasts of successes, or has the support of the elite." And there will be "a choice between two roads. One road is the road of greed and technology without wisdom or respect for life. This road represents a rush to destruction. The other road is spirituality, a slower path that includes respect for all living things."

REVELATIONS IS ARMAGEDDON SOFTWARE

The Chapter of Revelations in the Christian Bible contains zero content from the original Founder Records, nor the *Yeshua 12* manuscripts. The Chapter of Revelations in the Bible outlines in warped details the pre-planned Armageddon program to be installed at the "end times" of the Ascension cycle, in which assorted negative alien technologies are sequentially implemented to wreak destruction upon the earth's surface in order to serve the New World Order's objectives. The Chapter of Revelations is a blueprint that outlines each step of the intended Negative Alien's takeover of the earth surface, in which the New World Order "reset" is put into place through A.I. technological tyranny. The Four Beasts, the Four Living Creatures (Lion, Eagle, Ox, Man), kneeling before the throne mentioned in Revelations are the most powerful Founder Guardian Consciousness Networks that are interconnected within the entire Planetary Grid and Star gate system. They are the Great White Lion, Sacred Blue Cow, Golden Eagle Grid, and the Four Pillars of Man. Through the intended gradual conquering and domination of these specific four guardian planetary grid networks during the Dark Age, the intention was to "slay" and serve up these four beasts to worship at the Throne of Jehovah, the false God of Tyranny, on their knees and totally take over Earth. The content recorded in Revelations in the Bible text is coded for installing collective consciousness trigger overlays to incite fear and instigate the Armageddon Software of cataclysm, pestilence to wreak havoc on earth in order to fully control the end timelines during the Ascension Cycle.

LET US LOOK AT THE PREEMPTIVE PROGRAMMING IN THIS BIBLE PASSAGE:

A New Heaven and a New Earth.
REVELATIONS: 21

"Then I saw a new heaven and a new earth," for the first heaven and the first earth had passed away, and there was no longer any sea. (After the "Great Reset" the new heaven is the Artificial constellations of Space X now encaging our Earth and their New Earth is an Inorganic Planetoid infested with A. I. life forms so of course, there can be no Organic Ocean since it is a living entity.) I saw the Holy City, the new Jerusalem, coming down out of heaven from God, (Space Craft? Blue Beam Steering?) prepared as a bride beautifully dressed for her husband. And I heard a loud voice from the throne (Voice of God Technology? Blue Been Steering?) saying, "Look! God's dwelling place is now among the people, and he will dwell with them. They will be "his" people, and "God" himself will be with them and be their God. (Now that the Earth has been completely conquered and terraformed into a lifeless A.I. planetoid, the frequencies lowered and the real estate cleared by human holocaust the Impostor god(s) can lay claim to OUR Earth and BE the GOD of their Artificial AI Hive minded drones.) He will wipe every tear from their eyes. There will be no more death or mourning or crying or pain, for the old order of things has passed (the great reset) away and everything is new!" (Of course there'll be no pain, no sorrow, no crying, no death because everything is anew as an A.I. Artificial life form. Trans-humanized droids have no emotions, no feelings, no tears, no heart and they never die.) Then he said, "Write this down, for these words are trustworthy and true." He said to me: "It is done. (Our Organic World has been destroyed) I am the Alpha and the Omega, the Beginning and the End. (The Finite God has replaced Infinite God Source and has closed all exit points in his AI prison Matrix)) To the thirsty, I will give water without cost from the spring of the water of life. (Water is Life so your existence is dependent upon this "imposter god" who controls the currency or the "water of life" itself, which you will receive (as downloaded credits) Those who are victorious will inherit all this, (only those who obey the commands of this impostor god will receive the "water of life" or credits) and I will be their God and they will be my children."(This finite Imposter God will rule over the AI hive minded Meta verse!)

Does this sound like the future you choose to create? Do you want to have your Organic Earth Destroyed and have a False Imposter God of AI technology "rule" over you like children? Do you want to never die because you are an A.I. slave trapped in the Alpha Omega of a never ending time loop matrix of a false ascension in an AI META VERSE? The "voice of God" coming down from heaven sounds like *The Truman Show* and have no doubt this "show" will come to pass since we are now living in a Holovision Theater thanks to blue beam steering. Let no man or woman write YOUR future. Likewise, do not allow any New Age Guru to glamor you into their virtual world of emerging A.I. technology. Do not give away the power of your divine magic pen to any prophecy, oracle, soothsayer, fortune teller, spell caster or A.I. God who writes words that are "from" a false God and not the word which IS of the vibrational frequency of Infinite God Source, written in your own heart! You are a Divine Infinite Human Being, Infinite God Source is within you and you are writing your own future!

CHAPTER 19

THE GREAT WORK OF ASCENSION

After leaving Florence, Italy, and moving to Sicily, I felt great once again! My health improved immensely. I knew I was going to Sicily to complete my *"magnum opus"* or the Great Work and finish this book. The two seemed to be deeply tied into one another. Sicily was like a trip back in time. Food growing in the fields, brought to market daily, children playing in the streets and riding bikes until dark, people socializing in the piazzas and young lovers necking on the park benches! The air was fresh and clean with very few chem-trails so I could soak up the sun's regenerating rays every day. I could hardly even get Wi-Fi, which was wonderful! I was activating my 12 stranded DNA my body was healing and transmuting daily. I found it so easy to upgrade my body by performing simple ascension practices, eating clean fresh food, breathing clean air, and bathing in the Sea daily or in the natural volcanic hot springs near my home.

When summer came, tourists from all around the world flooded into the small fishing village of Castellammare. I set up a small Tarot card stand and did readings for people, mostly in Italian. It was something new! I loved being of service to others, observing my intuitive abilities growing daily as I helped people gain more clarity and insight into their lives. My third eye was opening more and more each day and I was, at last, able to piece together the puzzle from my years of research, spiritual teachers, and my own cosmic downloads. It was then I finally deciphered the mystery of the magic triangle of Sicily that had been haunting me since I arrived. Besides the ley lines running through it, I realized its chakra system began at Mount Etna as the root and ended at the apex with *Erice* being the crown chakra. I had been sent to the third-eye chakra of the island.

The symbols of Sicily are the Pinecone and the *Trinaga, Trinacria* or the *Triskelion* which is one of the most ancient and sacred symbols on this Earth. Its roots are mysterious with ties to the Celts, Greeks, Sicilians, Portuguese, and other more ancient cultures. Although the origins of this symbol are elusive, the powerful meaning can be harnessed by all. When you align yourself with the Triskelion, you are saying that you are ready to work with the Universe. You are sending out the message that you are listening, ready to communicate, ready to connect, and ready to serve and create within the higher frequencies. This is an amazing tool for manifestation and tuning into the divinity that surrounds you and is within you. It is said that when you wear this symbol, you gain access to the secrets within nature, the deva kingdom and the cosmos itself. The Triskelion is a key that unlocks the power of your own personal creation, which is deeply unique to you. It mixes your energy with the energy of nature, the Cosmos, and the Divine to produce your own individual experience. This will bring you opportunities that only you need. The three spirals are said to represent motion and movement, and the symbolism behind the number three has many meanings: mind-body-soul; earth-cosmos-you; past-present-future, ascension-love-evolution, creation-preservation-destruction; etcetera. While different, they all represent moving or spiraling through cycles of creation, which is what the Triskelion was designed to connect you to.

I recognized it as an ancient symbol from the Golden Age of Atlantis. The trifold wave, the original spark of creation, the true trinity which set into motion all life emanating from Divine Infinite Source. This powerful symbol frees you from the *vesica piscis* harness which traps us in duality. This powerful *Trinaga* symbol has been co-opted by placing the face of Medusa, a Gorgon with her snake hair draping her face and covers this trifold wave of the *Trinaga*. This is the way the symbol appears on the Sicilian Flag and most all other *Trinaga's* found in Sicily. However, on one of my trips around Sicily, I found a ceramic *Trinaga* that did not have the head of the Medusa but instead the face of a pretty woman with rosy cheeks and blonde curls! I sent a picture of it to an aware friend who exclaimed, "That's you Elizabeth!"

WHAT IS THE GREAT WORK OR ASCENSION?

Ascension has been called many things throughout history such as attaining Enlightenment, God-Realization, reaching Nirvana, Christ Consciousness, becoming a Yogi, (Yoga means union with God) and so on. In Alchemy, this process is referred to as Transmutation, the Magnum

Opus or the Great Work. It is defined as "to perfect any substance, creation or situation through its transformation back into its essential divinity." Many ancient texts speak of striving to attain this perfected state of being but few are credited with achieving this exalted state. Christ, the Buddha and Krishna are the iconic examples. Many Yogis have followed rigorous disciplines to attain enlightenment. However, the Alchemical approach is similar to the method Michelangelo, an alchemist, used when he sculpted his masterpiece the David. He found the perfect stone and knew his David was inside. His task then was simply to carve away everything that was not the perfect essence of the David. That is the task at hand. We must purge, purify, detox, and release everything that is not true to our pure divine essence. We must remove all that is finite to free the Infinite within!

This Great Work of transmutation or ascension includes the detoxing of all our bodies, physical, emotional, mental and spiritual and the releasing of our shadow body. This becomes highly important as ancestral miasma and past traumas surface to be released and purified. We must release and heal old wounds and traumas, correct misalignments and dispel inorganic attachments in all our bodies. We must release the pain body and dis-ease from ALL our bodies. We must end the mind control programming, limiting belief systems and artificial timelines which have imprisoned us in a dream spell of spiritual misconceptions from our rewritten history and false tyrannical gods. We must purge limiting beliefs and practices that have kept us enslaved in the victim, victimizer's roles and end sexual misery programming. We must end the misogyny and the division of our own inner masculine and feminine which has kept us locked in duality. We must embrace all life, our mother Earth as a living consciousness and her deva spirits and surrender our will to the Divine Will of God's Natural Laws, the Law of One and the Oneness of All Creation. We must integrate our brain and our heart to be of service to others rather than egotistical service to self. We must become ONE!

As the frequencies increase making ascension more readily accessible, your life may become more and more challenging because all of your underlying issues, shadows and dis-ease will surface for examination, healing and transmutation. But isn't it much better to free yourself from this darkness once and for all, rather than smearing honey over pus and limping through life? The truth is if you are not consciously choosing ascension you are passively consenting to descension. The choice is yours. Choose wisely.

"Who hath ascended up into heaven, or descended?"
PROVERBS 30:4

IN-CENSION

Ascension has often been depicted as some blissful place in paradise where you go when you die or drop your body. You get to hang out with the "Ascended Masters" and everything is perfect. All you have to do is just "wait" for Judgement Day and the second coming of Christ, and then, "poof", you are raptured into paradise. The truth is the kingdom of heaven is within. You actually in-scend or inwardly ascend by becoming the embodiment of these higher frequencies of the love and the eternal living light of Infinite Source. You do not have to die and drop your body. The only thing that needs to die is your finite identity or ego. It is not a place you are taken up to. It is the penetration of eternal rainbow light frequencies that infiltrate every cell of your being, transmuting you or making you inwardly-lightened, or enlightened! You do not have to go to a church, synagogue or temple to receive this. You are the temple, the House of God's light.

Your DNA is an important factor in your ascension and was purposely left out of all the spiritual texts. The fact is that all the Krystos Avatars incarnated into "Christ Bodies" or bodies that held 12 strands of Krystala DNA. This gave them the divine technology to perform "miracles" and their direct connection to Infinite Source. So it is key to your ascension to maintain your pure organic genetics so you can evolve and not allow the AI Crisper gene "therapy" injections to enter your bloodstream where they fuse with your organic genome and mutate you.

There are many ascension tools available to assist you in this "inward" ascension process of allowing more light to enter your cells and accruing more silicone-based genetic material, building your rainbow plasma light-body vehicle, and becoming your own star gate into the higher dimensions. There are disciplines, practices and meditations which can help you activate the frequencies of your rainbow plasma light body and your twelve-stranded silicone-based genetics, open your third eye, build your Torrid field, and build your *MerKaBa* et cetera. You can spend timeless time meditating in the Void which is the purest essence of Divine Infinite Source from which all creation sprang where there is no thought, no sound, no light. By simply spending time in the Void will help you release the dream spell of duality and identify more with this pure state of infinite love and Oneness releasing your finite ego self. There are also many breathing techniques such as the *Lotus Breath*, *Prana Yama*, *Ouija breathing* or the *Breath of Fire*, which can take you into deeper states of consciousness, purify and unify your body, mind and spirit and help ease the flow of energy throughout your body. There are high vibratory diets that can support you in your ascension. Choose the ones that resonate with you and keep charging things up. Nature abhors a vacuum. Use your intuition and feel free to ask your guides to help you find the right practices for you. Above all, you must learn to listen to your body(s) and give all four of your bodies what they need moment to moment. However, all these meditations and spiritual practices are nil if you do not heal and transmute your own inner shadows.

In this time frame, higher frequencies are entering our planet with such force it is impossible to avoid them. These energies are displacing the lower densities and toxins inherent in your 3D body. So, the task at hand is to make the transition as smoothly as possible by releasing, purging, and detoxing physically, mentally, emotionally and spiritually. This often causes what is known as ascension symptoms. This is your body, mind and spirit's way of naturally throwing off your lower densities and synthesizing the higher frequencies. This will require you to constantly upgrade your life, your diet, your environment, your thoughts, your practices as you outgrow your finite container and expand into infinite consciousness. I want to take a moment to stress the point that everyone's body is unique just like your thumbprint and "one person's medicine may be another person's poison"! So tune into "your" body to see what "you" need in terms of food, supplements, exercise, environments, etcetera moment by moment. Being a vegetarian and doing Yoga may be one way for a beginner to initiate their spiritual journey, but it is not for everyone. When I taught Yoga, I called it Yoga Therapy before anyone used that term and for the first thirty minutes all I taught was breathing! Then I helped people to learn to listen to their bodies. You need to constantly tune into your body, mind and soul to see what works best for you! Adjust your diet depending on what is going on in your life day by day. Adhering to rigid diets, exercise routines and dogmas about ascension is not the true pathway Home. Learning to access your intuition is! You may require more rest or grounding by being in nature and walking barefoot. You may require more meditation, mindfulness and holistic healing practices another day. You may need to be in the world observing your thought processes and triggers or in isolation and quiet contemplation. The Art of Ascension is deeply personal and intuitive. Don't be thrown off by appearances. Wearing long robes, living on bean sprouts or being able to contort your body into a pretzel does not make you an ascended master! I have known breatharians who were clueless.

As your own frequencies become more refined, you may become increasingly more sensitive to harsh environments, foods, products and people. You may need to remove yourself from toxic people, places and things as you climb in frequency. You may find people, jobs and environments releasing automatically from your life. Let them go, knowing that when the time is right they will be replaced with something much better. Some suggestions to support your ascension process: BREATH! Continuously BREATH in the Breath of Life, pure, clean fresh air and exhale out your toxins unhindered! Do not breathe back in your own toxins. Drink lots of pure, clean fresh water daily. I recommend distilled or alkalized water but determine what is best for your body. Eat clean wholesome organic locally grown food not genetically modified or processed food with artificial ingredients. If it comes from the back of a truck you do not know where it comes from. Do not trust lables "corp"orations place on your food. This is why I recommend growing your own or knowing your local farmers or co opts if possible. Learn how to Alkalize the PH balance of your body and about herbs and nutritional supplements. You may want to intuitively work with Crystals and other stones as well as the deva kingdom to support your healing journey. You may be guided to use tones, frequency, sounds or music to support your healing. You may draw to you a team to support your ascension both in the physical and non-physical. You may be guided to holistic practitioners, chiropractors, massage therapists and energy workers. Be in the natural sunlight as much as possible. These are all some of the practices I have used to aid me in my own ascension. But I would never tell you what to do. We need to move away from the paradigm of going to an expert and having someone else tell you what you should do. You are your own expert and the owner of your body! You must ultimately decide what is right for you. You may decide you need an operation, a therapy, or a treatment, but whatever you do, take full responsibility for your health and ascension. Begin to research, experiment and find out what is right for you! It's your job and the most important one you have!

I recommend what Dr. Klinghardt a German Physician suggested to parents of autistic children. Create a sleep sanctuary and unplug everything. I too have noticed a dramatic increase in my health by unplugging everything and creating a sacred regenerative sleeping space at night. If you have Wifi, unplug the modem, turn off cell phones and even unplug lights. Use technology responsibly. It is becoming increasingly important that we protect ourselves and our children from the toxic radiation of EMF waves. If your environment is becoming increasingly more toxic and affecting the health of you and your family MOVE! Leave the big cities and BE IN NATURE! Ground yourself by walking barefoot or lying on Mother Earth heart down, hug trees, walk through forests, beaches, parks, swim seas, love, live and commune with nature and her deva kingdom. Rejoice with your fellow human beings. Laugh, sing, dance, and celebrate life! Let your food be your medicine and detox your body with natural herbs, home grown if possible. GET THE METALS OUT OF YOUR BODY! I use the powder for of Zeolite which comes from Volcanic Ash, but there are many ways to do this find what works best for you! This is crucial. Everyday people's bodies and brains are bombarded with nanobots. It's in the food, the water and the air we breathe. More and more people are experiencing brain fog and losing their ability to focus and even think. If possible, live in non-toxic areas that have natural blocks to radiation like trees, volcanos, mountains et cetera. Release high maintenance life styles so you can experience the joy of living simply! Give yourself lots of downtime to relax, repair and rejuvenate! Sleep, meditate and heal because your body is morphing and assimilating higher frequencies. So, like the caterpillar, you may need long periods of cocooning. Here in Sicily everything closes down at one p.m. and doesn't really get going until around five p.m.! People go home, have lunch and take a siesta!Lock Downs were a breeze for these ancient people. It drove me crazy at first but I slowly learned how very healing and relaxing it is and I gave myself the gift of rest, reflection and regeneration!

On my Esoteric Renaissance Tour of Florence, Italy, I explain to my adepts that Michelangelo, Leonardo da Vinci, Botticelli, and other Alchemists of the Renaissance, who studied under Marsilio Ficino, a man of my own heart and soul, met in secret at the Medici Villa in *Careggi*. Much of the genius of these Renaissance Men lies in the fact that they had found the revered philosopher's stone and hid clues of its whereabouts in their artwork. Dan Brown only scratched the surface of Leonardo da Vinci's encoded messages in his book. I wrote an article entitled *Leonardo's Third Eye* to commemorate the five-hundred-year anniversary of his death which explored many of these secret messages and exposed the source of his genius. Michelangelo also left many esoteric symbols in his Artwork. I always give numerous hints to help my adepts uncover the location of this precious jewel. One such symbol is in Michelangelo's greatest masterpiece, found on the ceiling of the Sistine chapel. Most everyone is familiar with his image of God, reaching out and touching the finger of Adam. But what you may not have noticed is what in 1990, physician Frank Meshberger noted and published in a paper in the *Journal of the American Medical Association*, deciphering Michelangelo's imagery was the stunning recognition that the depiction of God in the central panel was inside a perfect anatomical illustration of a cross-section of the human brain. Why would Michelangelo place God inside the human brain? What did he know from his esoteric studies with Marsilio Ficino, the head of the Neo-Platonic Academy founded by Cosimo the Elder, that he was inadvertently trying to share with the world?

The Philosopher's Stone is the most sought after possession in all of human history. This is the precious stone that many seek but few find. Its symbol is the Pinecone. Throughout history, Pinecones have served as a symbolic representation of Human Enlightenment. The Egyptian Staff of Osiris, dating back to approximately 1224 BC, depicts two intertwining serpents rising up to meet at a pinecone. In addition to spiritual consciousness and enlightenment, pinecones have also historically been used as symbols of everlasting or eternal life. Ancient Assyrian palace carvings, dating back to 713-716 BC depict four-winged God-like figures holding aloft pinecones, or in some cases, using a pinecone to pollinate their depiction of the Tree of Life—a tribute, perhaps, to both the pinecone's immortality symbolism and its role as an icon of enlightenment.

In other ancient cultures, the Pinecone is a symbol of spiritual ascension and immortality. The statue of the Mexican god *"Chicomecóatl"* ("Seven Snakes") depicts the deity offering forth pinecones in one hand and an evergreen tree in the other. The Greeks and Romans also incorporated the Pinecone into their elaborate systems of religious belief and mythology. The Romans later built an enormous bronze sculpture, the *Pigna*, in the shape of a huge pinecone three stories tall. According to a popular medieval legend, the sculpture stood on top of the Pantheon as a lid for the round opening in the center of the building's vault. The *Pigna* is confirmed to have served as a large fountain overflowing with water next to the Temple of Isis in Ancient Rome, however, the gigantic statue now sits directly in front of the Vatican in the "Court of the Pinecone." Dionysus, later known as Bacchus to the Romans, was continually depicted carrying a *"Thyrsus,"* or a fennel staff woven with ivy and leaves topped with a pinecone. The *Thyrsus* purported to drip with honey, was regularly used as a sacred instrument at religious rituals and festivals. In a small fishing village here in Sicily a group of fishermen pulled a two thousand and five-hundred-year old statue of a dancing *Satiro* out of the Sea. Though badly damaged, you can see that the *Satiro* has his head flung back in ecstasy with one leg up, showing he is dancing in a spinning motion much the same way the whirling dervishes do to align their chakras. He was believed to be holding a thyrsus, the pinecone staff. The Pinecone is the sacred symbol of Sicily, along with the Trinacria, another powerful symbol that pulls us out of duality.

Hence the secret of the Magic triangle is the ability to rise above the duality and the world of illusion. This can only occur by gaining the second sight and SEEING both the light and the dark and transmuting them. Have you guessed what it is yet? The Pineal gland! Also called conarium, epiphysis cerebri, pineal organ, or pineal body. In health, it is a small fluid-filled gland the size of a grain of rice, covered with tiny crystals and resembling a pine cone in shape. Throughout history it has been highly coveted. However, most humans do not process a healthy pineal gland anymore. It has been reduced to a clarified-hardened stone that sits in the centre of the brain. It has been rendered inoperative throughout the years by an onslaught of calculated poisonings: Fluoride put into our water, toxic aluminum and other artificial ingredients in our food, and our metals put in chem-trails in our air, and glyphosate from pesticides sprayed on our produce, along with a host of other ingredients which are found in prescription drugs, and vaccinations. This is all being cooked on or radiated with increasing toxic 5G Wi-Fi frequencies. To top all this, the Covid tests require swabs containing an assortment of A.I. parasites and other toxins such as graphite, ethylene oxide, to be shoved deep into the nasal canal, penetrating the blood-brain barrier and directly infecting our pineal cavity, further contaminating our pineal glands.

But why has this highly sought-after gem been so purposely hijacked? What is the power behind this tiny gland? The Pineal is the source of melatonin, a hormone derived from tryptophan that plays a central role in the regulation of circadian rhythm (the roughly twenty-four-hour cycle of biological activities associated with natural periods of light and darkness). The separation of Darkness into Light? Ancient Rituals and secret societies would enclose initiates in the dark for long periods of time then suddenly expose them to the light to aid in opening their third eye. This ritual is still performed by secret societies today. The Catholic religious tradition is intricately interwoven with pinecones, perhaps most prominently atop the sacred staff carried by the Pope himself. The Coat of Arms of the Holy See, found on the Vatican flag among other places, features a stacking of three crowns suspiciously similar in shape to a pinecone. The very name, "Holy See" appears to be a direct reference to the Third Eye. The pineal gland has long been an enigmatic structure. The seventeenth-century French philosopher René Descartes wrote that the pineal gland is the seat of the soul. When Michelangelo placed the almighty inside an anatomical replication of the human brain, he was not stating that our brain was god but, as an Alchemist, he was alluding to the fact that our pineal gland, in the center of our brain, is a radio to God, our direct communication with

Infinite GOD Source. Could our pineal be the magic key to ascension, to becoming a Christ Being?

Let's look at the true meaning of the word "Christ" and what the "Christ" meant when he said, "Seek the kingdom of heaven within." In ancient Greek, the word Christ means the anointed one. The Pineal, is a pine cone-shaped gland which secretes a yellow or golden fluid, like honey. Let us look at the symbolism behind the crucifixion of Christ and its correlation to what goes on inside our body during transmutation. According to the Bible, Christ was crucified, died and was buried, and on the third day, he ascended. He was crucified at a place outside of Jerusalem called Calvary, which in Latin means skull. Protruding from the Skull is the Vagus nerve, also known as the Tree of Life which is also depicted in Michelangelo's Creation of Adam and is attached to the brain where God is seated. The word crucify comes from the Greek word Stauros, which also means "to fortify" or make stronger. So, this sacred secretion of our pineal gland, this "Christ" oil, is being fortified in the skull so we can see or touch God. Therefore, the true meaning of the crucifixion is to become Christ, not to kill our inner Christ!

The Pituitary gland, opposite the pineal, is ellipsoid in shape and contains a whitish secretion, like milk. Both these bodies come from the Claustrum. The Claustrum, a word originally described as "an enclosed space in medieval European monasteries", but in the mammalian brain, it refers to, "a small sheet of neurons just below the cortex". It is the seat of all consciousness in the body. The Claustrum signals the secretion of the Christ Oil or CFS cerebral spinal fluid into the spinal column. This precious fluid that flows down from the Claustrum separates, part going into the Pineal gland and part to the Pituitary body; as these differentiate from the Claustrum the Pineal Gland becomes yellow and has electric properties, while the Pituitary Body, becomes milk-like fluid, having magnetic properties.

"If the Lord is pleased with us, he will lead us into that land, a land flowing with milk and honey, and will give it to us."

NUMBERS 14:8 8

"Whoever believes in me, rivers of living water will flow from within them."
JOHN 7:38 38

The pineal gland which secrets the golden melatonin honey is surrounded and bathed in cerebral spinal fluid or milk. Melatonin which affects the immune system and mood and is anti-aging, and stress-reducing is called the Living Water or milk. The milk and the honey are produced by the pineal gland and the pituitary gland. This process of refining and raising the milk and honey is referred to as the crucifixion or the "Raising of the Chrism." When this oil (ointment) is crucified (to increase in power a thousand fold) it remains two days and a half in the tomb (cerebellum) and on the third day ascends to the Pineal Gland that connects the cerebellum with the Optic Thalamus, the Central Eye in the Throne of God that is the chamber overtopped by the hollow (hallowed) caused by the curve of the cerebrum (the "Most-High" of the body) which is the "Temple of the Living God" the living vital substance.

"And Jacob called the name of the place Peniel: for I have seen God face to face, and my life is preserved."
GENESIS 32:30

"The light of the body is the eye: if therefore when thine eye be single, thy whole body shall be full of light."
MATTHEW 6:22-23 22

"As for you, the anointing you received from him remains in you, and you do not need anyone to teach you. But as his anointing teaches you about all things and as that anointing is real, not coun-terfeit—just as it has taught you, remain in him."
JOHN 2:27

"There is no name under Heaven whereby ye may be saved except by Christ and then crucified."
ACTS 4:12

So the true crucifixion is the activation of your pineal gland, your third eye, not a Satanic blood ritual under a half-naked bloody body hanging from a cross designed to make you worship the crucifixion of your own inner

Christ! We can now SEE how the true Ascension mechanics taken from the Emerald Records have been weaponized into words separated from God whose shadowy reflections convert the truth away from the Word, which IS God. The early Christians knew that the Scriptures, written in ancient Hebrew or Greek, contained bread crumbs of truth hidden in the allegories, parables, or fables of the ascension mechanics hidden in plain sight. The Essenes fully realized and taught the great truth that Christ "the anointed one" was a substance, an oil contained within the Spinal Cord, or a "River that flows out of Eden (the upper brain) to water the garden. This fluid, oil, or marrow which flows down the spinal cord, comes from the upper brain, the Creator, or Father, the "Most-High," and is known in physiology as ovum, or the generative seed of life essence. When the Christ oil is refined, transmuted, lifted up, raised, and crucified it becomes so highly vitalized that it regenerates the body and "overcomes" the last enemy, death.

Could you image if the Church, Spiritual Leaders or the" New Age" community taught this? They would have no followers, no clients, no customers! All efforts have been made to keep you looking outside yourself to someone or something that will save you when the truth is within!

In truth, all those collecting crystals are really seeking their own philosopher's stone within! When the third eye is open, We See All. The Pinnacle of the Temple! The Apex of the Triangle. The true eye of Horus, the true inner All-Seeing Eye on top of the missing capstone of the pyramid.

Can you now SEE how the true nature of our body, the true earth history, and truth about religion has been co-opted to keep you a slave? Whether you believe these biblical interpretations or not is of course up to you. I am only stating my findings to drive home the point of how incredibly important your organic body is! This is why your divine technology has been sabotaged throughout the ages! Because it has been hijacked, most of humanity is walking around blind. In the world of the blind, the One-Eyed woman is Queen or man, King! If humanity only could open its "singular eye," game over. The controllers can no longer hide in the shadows and cast their spells into your subconscious, controlling you. Our pineal gland and third eye are the magic pair of sunglasses in the John Carpenter film *They Live*. Put them on and you can SEE all!

Before the Plandemic of 2020, I was guided to send out a symbol of a triangle with a third eye in the middle of it asking everyone, "Do you have 2020 Vision?" At that time, I was just following my inner guidance, not really knowing why I flooded the earth's energetic fields and cyberspace with this symbol, asking people if they had 2020 Vision. Soon it became quite clear why I had been guided to do this. For years, I had been trying to wake people up! I realized that nothing was going to change unless people woke up from the dream spell. Most of humanity was too caught up in the web of deception having lost their third eye vision. All their desires, actions, and manifestations were contained within the finite earth's scheme of things, and they were pre-programmed to simply be a cog in a wheel pushing forward the dark agenda. In short, they were like good little sheeple doing just what the dark side wanted them to do and changing nothing!! Nothing is going to change until enough people fully awaken and create something new outside the prison matrix.

If you have not activated your third eye you are not ascending. You can meditate, eat high vibrational food, chant mantras until you are blue in the face but to be truly enlightened, God Realized, or Infinite, you must be able to SEE and communicate directly with Infinite God Source. You must SEE through the veils of illusion that masquerade as truth in our world of Maya. If you cannot do that then you are the blind leading the blind, or worse, you are following a spiritual teacher who may be blind themselves or blinding you! In truth the only esoteric knowledge that ever needs to be taught is how to activate your pineal. Then you can find all your own answers from within and know what you are looking at. The only way you can do this is to reconnect your divine technology, activate your pineal gland and open your third eye. Only then will you cease to be food for the entities of false light, pawns in their false ascension matrix looking to someone or something outside of yourself for answers. When your third eye truly opens you cease stumbling along the path in darkness, being a lamb led to slaughter, a cog in the great wheel of deception. You will cease seeking and begin KNOWING. You will just KNOW, why you came here to Earth and that things are unfolding as they should and you will be guided to make any of the necessary course corrections along your path. Your faith will be grounded in yourself and the deep inner, knowing that the World is an illusion and you can manifest anything you need to fulfill your soul mission. Then, and only then, can you do something that will really affect a change on our planet. Only the fully awakened will be the true leaders, the true builders of the New Infinite Earth. The rest will just be rearranging the shit which they live in.

The real lockdown on planet Earth has been the caging of the pineal gland and disconnecting humanity from Infinite Source. They have robbed you of your most precious jewel, your divine organic microchip, your philosopher's stone! You have been taken offline and convinced that your organic body, your divine technology is defective. Now they want to offer you a bad copy, an A.I. artificial biochip or microchipped nanobotted brain so Google can think for you and you can only surf within their "NET" held captive in a finite hive mind. Don't be scammed! You are an Infinite, multidimensional human being. You have the God-given right to surf the Infinite by activating your third eye, connecting to who you truly are: all that is, ever has been, and ever shall be!!! You have the power; you have always had the power within you and your third eye is the key to your ascension and your true freedom!

SO HOW DO YOU ACTIVATE YOUR PINEAL GLAND?

There are many who have had their kundalini rise and their third eye open spontaneously, even prematurely or before they had acquired enough spiritual maturity to assimilate this rapid change in perspective. They could instantaneously SEE auras, hear people's thoughts, know things before they happened and were told they were insane. We have been taught to fear being different, fear our power, fear being awake because it is equated with being crazy. In a crazy world, it will always be the sane ones who are considered crazy. These abilities are the real norm. This is the way Infinite Source created you to be. I have a friend from Iceland who possessed this second sight when she was young and without knowing what to do with it, she became frightened by her own power. She wanted to be "normal." So, she went to a woman who "turned off" her psychic abilities. Of course, there is fear around owning our divine technology, our infinite multidimensional abilities and many of us have turned them off without even knowing it. And understandably so. Historically, those who possessed these abilities were hunted down and murdered in horrible ways. But we are in an ascension cycle. Being an Infinite Human is our natural state. More and more of us are standing up every day, reclaiming and owning our true power. There is emerging on the face of the Earth, a new human, an Infinite Human, and that Human is you!

Many people today are engaging in practices to cleanse their pineal and force open their third eye. I too took this route by forcing the rise of my kundalini though the *breath of fire*. This is a very challenging path. This is what you need to be aware of if you feel called to do that. Like many, I had not completely healed from my trauma and inner wounds which caused me to feel fear, sadness, anger etcetera which sometimes pulled me into the lower frequencies of the astral plane as I purged these emotions. This is much like sinking into the deepest fathoms of the Ocean and then opening your eyes and looking around. If you do, you may see hideous glowing fish with huge monstrous teeth swimming around you. Whereas on the surface in the higher frequencies you may see dolphins playing in the sunshine. My point is that opening your third eye allows you to SEE the world around you; the good, the bad, and the ugly of where you are vibrationally. Which many do not want to do. Having the "second" sight also means you can only SEE or access the dimensions or frequencies you are attuned to. For example, at many "psychic fairs" and in the New Age communities I encountered "psychics" who were ghost hunters, read the Akashic records or communicated with angels. This is all good for them to develop their skills but who are they communicating with? What radio frequency or channel are they tuning into? Being "psychic" does not necessarily mean you are evolved enough to ascend to the God Source Frequencies of Truth, or raise your vibrational frequency enough to pierce the veil of illusion by transmuting your own inner wounds. This does not mean you are attuned to the higher dimensions of the God Source Worlds. If you still have shadows that open portals in your aura, then you are tapping into the astral plane of illusion and are being manipulated by demonic entities. So the question remains, from whom or what are you receiving your guidance?

Many who are afraid to see the "bad" we are now witnessing in the world are also afraid to see the "bad" inside of themselves. As a result, they remain locked in this world of illusion, comfortable in the finite limits of their ego and false spirituality. I have known many psychics like this who possess uncanny abilities, but have not triumphed over their own inner shadows nor humbled their ego to the Divine Will of Infinite God Source. As a result, their motives are self-serving and manipulative. This is why traditionally the opening of the third eye occurs gradually as the adept rises in frequency transmuting the astral world of illusion. Then and only then can you reside in the higher frequencies of the Truth found only in the God Source Worlds. Many people use drugs and alcohol to open their third eye. But even natural substances like ayahuasca, mushrooms, marihuana, etcetera may temporarily augment your psychic abilities but they will not sustain you to the higher frequencies. That requires inner work. This is why when people go to psychedelics they may have a good trip or a bad trip depending on where they are at vibrationally!

Earth's history is filled with Oracles, Soothsayers, Witches, Witch Doctors, Psychic Readers etcetera who could not tune into the higher frequency of Infinite Source. Thus their guidance came from false light entities or demonic forces of the Astral World. Their advice often given to powerful leaders served to push forward the dark agendas. This is why I recommend a holistic or holy approach to the holy SEE or third eye opening. It is important to heal and raise your frequency first. Then the opening of your third eye is a natural part of activating your DNA and your light body. In this way, you will SEE ALL from a higher perspective, above the astral sea of deception and your guidance will come from Infinite Source.

We have been spiritually conditioned to believe that our physical bodies are "Mortal Coils" unholy vessels, and when we are "freed" from them, we will ascend to "paradise". This sin or "missing the mark" has kept many people in-prisoned in their genetically downgraded and physically impaired carbon bodies without ever knowing that our bodies are divine holographic software programs that contain our consciousness. Enslave the body and you enslave the mind, enslave the mind and you enslave the soul. Lose freedom over your body and you lose your freedom of mind and soul. Ascension is transmuting or upgrading all your bodies thus freeing your consciousness and escaping the prison matrix. But we have been conditioned to believe this is either unattainable or reserved for only a privileged few like Christ, the Buddha. This an inside job, accomplished day by day, moment by moment which requires the mindful practice of continuously shifting your perceptions of reality which can only be accomplished by freeing your infinite self from your finite self. You have to do your own inner work. No one else can do it for you. But nobody wants to hear that! We live in a world where everyone is lining up for the next shot, pill or cure. Or in spiritual communities where everyone flocks to the latest leaders or speakers who are talking about something outside of them, some new activaton that will do it for them. Of course we all need hope, inspiration and information to spark our inner flame. But the Truth is the Truth is simple. It is a Vibrational Frequency. As you ascend in frequency you may have dramatic ahah moments or revelations as the puzzle pieces fall into place and you obtain more clarity but, "As above so below". Like everything in life worth having it requires work, effort and dedication. In order to ascend, you must drop your lower densities. Lighten up! Laugh, have fun (in) joy life! Then there is a quickening, an acceleration of your cells into a higher frequency. This can feel like a rapture or a feeling of ecstasy. But this is your natural state! You just have to learn to maintain that frequency and not be pulled back down into the lower frequencies of duality by your triggers. Rather, become a compassionate observer of the crazy world around you! This is the gift of the dark side, to test you. If you pass all the tests, you get the reward-ecstasy...not the drug. The truth is all "addictions" are simply our search for that natural state of joy within, that only our connection to Divine Infinite Source can give us.

As our Organic Earth goes through its ascension, you too will raise your frequencies, and your divine organic DNA will be activated. Which explains why the dark side is testing you now to see if you will take the easy path of the masses into a false AI ascension or if you have what it takes to take the road less traveled. True Freedom is the Journey of the Hero! Unfortunately, most of the New Age Gurus and their channeled messages of love and false light skim over the "darkness" leaving people trapped in an astral bubble of bliss, too afraid to SEE or do anything lest they burst their bubble and their world comes crashing down around them. Earth is overrun with "spiritual" people putting on their fake "love and false light" faces, pretending to be "highly evolved" beings, hiding their festering wounds and deep pain for fear of what others may think. The more others poke at their wounds the more aggressive they become. Like a wounded animal, they attack those who seek to help heal them. I say pull out your wounds and scars, your broken hearts, for all the world to see so you can rejoice in the lessons you have learned and your authenticity!

True ascension or transmutation requires you to face your shadow self so you can finally love it to death and rise above duality. Any ascension practice that does not take you on the inner hero's journey of facing your shadow self... all your fear, pain, sorrow, grief, guilt, shame, anger, hatred, etcetera and transmute it is leading you into a false ascension matrix. All of the traumas buried deep within your soul must be brought into the light and transmuted with love. This does not mean you need to overindulge in shadow work, lingering in self-pity or self-hatred. But you must uncover the underlying root of the viruses running in your subconscious, that are continuously corrupting your divine program, stealing your bliss, stopping you from flowing with Source, and creating dis-ease. Ignoring it will only cause it to grow and fester. When you find it, you must forgive yourself and those who have "trespassed against you." Forgiveness is the key to freedom. Forgive others not for them, but for you, and most importantly forgive yourself. As you begin to have past-life recall, you may discover you, too, have been part of the dark agenda. Forgive yourself for falling from the Grace of God and from the Christ of Light Infinite Human being you were. Forgive yourself for not being able to heal or "save" those you love! Forgive yourself for becoming lost in the false light of deception. Know that all of your experiences, even things you would consider "bad", were part of your magnificent story, of learning about yourself as part of the Infinite. Accept responsibility for everything that has happened to you... even your "fall" into the lower densities of a fallen world and know it was all supposed to be! It was all part of a grand story in the mind of God, The Divine Dreamer! It all happened just as it was supposed to happen. Your story has simply been a learning experience, a journey into the darkness of false light so you could better appreciate and serve the True Light! All these aspects of you the good, the bad, and the ugly, have made you the unique human being you are to date.

When all your traumas, past, present, and future, have been forced out into the light, this is often seen as the "dark night of the soul." But instead of getting upset, embrace it for what it is, the darkness at long last releasing and purging itself from your soul. If you can learn to love your dark nights of the soul and see them as an opportunity to shed that which has been holding you back and keeping you out of the "ZONE" of true bliss, then you can truly grow from this gift. As you begin to accept yourself for who you truly are with all your wounds and battle scars, you will learn to love yourself. You can embrace all of you, even the "defects" of your dark side, and learn to love them to death. By loving and no longer resisting your darkness, it will no longer have any hold over you. You will no longer be locked into the conflict of duality but move into the higher frequencies of true love and pure light. You will cease judging yourself and others. This is the key to true ascension, turning the baser metals into gold or the lower frequencies into the higher frequencies of love. This is the real gold within you, not the fool's gold you seek in the outside world of illusion. Once you are able to LOVE yourself with all your flaws, imperfections, and scars, they will melt away and whenever the dark side rears its ugly head, you will not fear it but SEE it as an old friend come to teach you yet another lesson. When the lessons are learned, the teacher disappears, and you will truly transcend the darkness within yourself and the world around you. The dark side will no longer have any hold on you.

Grief is also a very important part of the ascension process and far too often, it is swept under the carpet. Your own individual grief process must be honored. We live in a time where our old world as we knew it is gone. All the world is grieving. The first stage is denial, then anger and under mad is always sad. We have lost the old Earth. It is never coming back. I know this is very difficult to accept, like the death of a loved one. And believe me, I have done my own share of grieving. There are those literally holding their breath, waiting for things to return to "normal." The good old days are gone. But were they really that good? I have spent most of this book pointing out how broken our old Earth was. True, it holds our memories, our old-time religions, our traditions! But like the Stockholm Syndrome or a child of an abusive parent, we have fallen in love with our captors, our abusers because we are loving creatures, and this has been all we have known! Like many slaves set free during the civil war we refuse to leave the plantation because it has been our home. We cling to a broken world and the remnants of what was familiar. But like Plato's cave, these are but shadowy reflections of the true light of Infinite 5D Earth. As you ascend and begin to awaken from the dream spell your memories of your true home will begin to return. Like someone awaking from a coma you will reawaken to your rightful place in the God Source Worlds and wonder what on Earth you have been doing down here for so long living in squalor!

Like all heroes, you are reaching the top of the mountain. As you gaze down on the path you have climbed, you see it has been a long and treacherous one. You have lost many companions along the way. You have suffered many injuries and have many battle scars. But as you gaze out into the horizon you can SEE the world below you from a new perspective! A higher perspective you gained with each step you took on this climb. You feel a deep inner peace, a blissful ecstasy as you gaze down upon the world you left. A world filled with busy people rushing around going nowhere. And you realize how silly it all was. You rejoice in your new awareness and all you have achieved by breaking away from the illusion and taking the road less travelled! At long last, it is time to claim your reward! The Elixir of Life! This is all the wisdom you have acquired from all your soul's experiences, journeys, and life stories. You have learned so much!

Ascension is the journey of the Hero, Heroine, the Alchemist, the Fool, the Adept, those brave souls who have the courage to leave behind the herd and all that is familiar and journey into the supernatural realms, face their dark nights of the soul, their pain, fear, isolation, despair, and grief as they battle their inner demons and emerge victorious, with the elixir of life in hand as Infinite Human Beings! Where are you in your Soul's Journey?

Stages of Ascension & The Hero's Journey

1. ORDINARY WORLD: We find our hero or heroine in their everyday life. But there is a growing dissatisfaction. There is a longing for something new, but most likely you do not know exactly what it is you are longing for you just know that the things that once held your interest and fulfilled you no longer do and there is a desire to explore new territories both inside and outside of you.

2. CALL TO ADVENTURE. There is a call deep within your soul to step out of this ordinary world and begin your adventure. This call comes from a herald of something new that enters your life. It may be a person, a new job, a new project or a world event. It may be a droid that lands on your planet with a holographic message from a captured Princess, or a twister that pulls your home into the Land of Oz.

3. REFUSAL OF THE CALL: The next phase is the refusal. You get scared, cold feet. You begin to think about what would happen if you actually stepped out of your comfort zone and began to strive for these longings within, to reach for the stars and live your dreams.

4. MEETING WITH THE MENTOR: It is at this point you meet your mentor. This can be an internal Mentor or guide i.e. your higher self, spirit guides. Or it could be a person, a spiritual teacher, a soul mate, a coach, a book, a wise old wizard, a Fairy God Mother or just a friend. These mentors prepare you for your adventure. They impart wisdom, teach you skills, and give you tools with which to face your enemies and the dark side. Some tools are internal and some may be external. Like a magical book or talisman

5. CROSSING THE FIRST THRESHOLD: You buy that plane ticket, leave that farm, cross that bridge, go out on that date. You take that daring action to leave behind the familiar.

6. TESTS, ALLIES, ENEMIES: Once you take off on your journey, leaving the familiar or the ordinary world behind, you enter into the world of the extra-ordinary or supernatural. This may be as bizarre as falling into the Land of Oz or as simple as opening a book. This is where you meet both friends and foes. Those who support you in your soul mission and those who may oppose you. Hint: You will learn that those who oppose you maybe your greatest allies because they teach you the most valuable lessons, mostly about the dark side both around you and inside you.

7. APPROACH TO THE INMOST CAVE: Eventually, your journey will lead you to face what you fear most: your dark side. Your inner demons.

8. ORDEAL: The ordeal is where the Kiss of Death occurs. This is where our hero dies. This may be symbolic or not. When Neo gets shot in the

Matrix and dies, he then realizes the truth that death is an illusion and is reborn as the One. The hero must let their finite self die so they can be reborn as Infinite!

9. REWARD (The Elixir of Life): Once you have faced and overcome your dark side, your inner demons, you will be rewarded with your personal epiphany. This is a deeper understanding into the true nature of reality and who you really are. This knowledge will free you. This may come as a revelation of your Soul Mission, the reason you incarnated here on Earth, or as a deeper understanding as to the nature of reality.

10. THE ROAD BACK: As you journey back home with your reward in hand, tests still await you. These tests are there for you to solidify what you have learned from your ordeal and put them to practice.

11. REBIRTH: This is the moment the hero crosses the final threshold— the final test of the hero's true growth to demonstrate their mastery and step into their power. This battle pushes the hero to defeat their limitations and release their old finite self, once and for all. They return home as the Infinite Human Hero.

12. RETURN WITH THE ELIXER: You have faced your dark side, learned your lessons and obtained the Elixir of Life. Now it is time to share your wisdom with your home tribe. This is when you begin your Soul Mission!

Are you being called to an adventure? Are you in the Dark Night of your Soul? Do you know your Soul Mission? Have you met your Soul Tribe? True to the nature of our Spiraling Universe, these stories continue repeating themselves, each time teaching us new lessons.

CHAPTER 20

LOCKDOWN IN ITALY
2020 VISION

At the end of all Hero's Journeys, after you have obtained the elixir of life, you must return to the world and share that wisdom with your tribe...but will they listen? On March of 2020, Italy went into lockdown and the rest of the free world watched. Soon, the same Draconian Mandates implemented in China were put into place here in Italy. It didn't take long for me to fit the pieces of the puzzle together in my own isolation, from people and mainstream media. Most of my information was intuitive. I then followed up with concrete proof, that I gathered first hand, or from reliable sources and trusted friends. That's the way I like to work. I intuit my information first from Infinite Source then I look to the external world to SEE how it is playing itself out. I had already done my own research, and knew the "script" so I watched as the New World Order carried out each "plot point" of their story.

I was not surprised at what they were doing but, I was surprised at the speed to which they so swiftly took tyrannical control over our planet, with virtually no opposition. I observed as everyone here in Sicily obediently put on their masks, meticulously washed their hands and closed their businesses in accordance with the MK Ultra Trauma-Based Mind-Control bilge that poured out of their tel-a lie-visions. However, my first reaction was excitement. Yes, I was elated! For years, I had been passionately telling anyone who would listen about the One World Order Negative Alien Agenda that existed on our earth for eons. I had become fed up with people's apathy, ignorance and arrogance! I had done what any self-respecting alchemist would do and entered into my hermit phase, renouncing the world and humanity. I had self-isolated myself in my villa in Sicily long before the lock downs to finish this book. I sought my sustenance from the nature spirits and my spiritual family in the higher dimensions. I tuned out the insanity of humanity, and resided in my own world of inner peace, love, and harmony and seldom left my Villa. One day I remember wandering out and seeing everyone wearing masks. I wondered what was going on now in this crazy 3D world and why couldn't I have my daily cappuccino at my favorite cafe. I watched as the New World Order came out of the shadows, exposing themselves to carry out their tyrannical takeover of the Earth. Finally, I thought to myself, the whole world will have to awaken from the dream spell and SEE the dark side! How can they continue to ignore this blatant tyranny? No longer could their insidious trickery overpower humanity! I watched as more and more people's freedom was taken away daily! There was nowhere else to run, no place for humanity to go! At last, people would stand up for themselves and stop passively consenting to their own genocide and enslavement! The day had finally come when humanity would get up off their knees and just say NO! I do not consent! I'm not going to take it anymore and end the rule of the one percent! I waited with great anticipation for this monumental moment! And waited, and waited, and waited...

I don't have a tel-a-lie-vision so I didn't know what magic mind control words they were feeding the Italians but it must have been good! I watched as everyone religiously followed the Draconian mandates without ever questioning them. I watched as these satanic practices found their way into the Italian culture as easily as their Catholic rituals. They would religiously wash their hands, put on masks and line up for their covid tests and vaccinations in the same obedient manner of mind control submission that they dipped their fingers into holy water, crossed themselves and lined up for "communion"!My international life style had given me the gift of observing many cultures around the world and choosing how I wanted to participate. As a "foreigner" in Italy, I amused myself by watching their customs and rituals. I laughed at their phobias of never walking around with bare feet, never putting parmesan cheese on Seafood, or never having a cappuccino after dinner. Then there was this mysterious disease every Italian gets when cold air hits the back of their neck! Once in a while when I visited a historic Cathedral I would pay one euro for a thin frock to cover up my "unholy" bare arms, but I was never forced to dip my fingers into "holy" water, drop to my knees and cross myself! I always had my choice as to whether I wanted to play the "Italiana" or the "Americana". Now their irrational fears were forcing me to participate in their silly rituals. I refused. I rebelled. I never wore a mask, washed my hands or respected the illegal lockdowns!

My computer mysteriously broke…again, after having been in the apple store for one month so I could not write, and I had no means of communicating with the outside world except by making live-stream videos on social media, trying to tell people the truth about what was really happening here in Italy. After China, Italy was the next place in the spot light. I had cultivated many friends around the world who trusted me and were looking to me for answers. I kept getting messages like, "Elizabeth are you okay?" Apparently the media made it look like we were dropping dead like flies here in Italy! So I wanted to shed some light on what was really happening. The truth is very few people died or even became ill at the beginning of the 2020 lock downs. In fact, the death rate dropped. I know this because within every village, there exists networks of old women whose system of surveillance is far superior to any high tech surveillance cameras. Nothing slips past them. You can see them peeking out of their windows, relentlessly keeping a watchful eye on everything that happens and sharing this information with their neighbor, who shares it with her neighbor and so on. Then the word is made public by the old men who gather in front of the cafes and *Tabacchi* shops. It was only in the North of Italy that there were many sick people and a large number of deaths.

It was then I began to feel that familiar feeling. Terrible headaches in the center of my brain, vertigo, fatigue, nausea, and diarrhea. This time the gums around the metal bridge in my mouth became infected. I became very, very ill. One day when I "escaped" my lockdown on my daily trip to the local hot springs, I realized why they had locked us in our homes. I saw that almost overnight 5G towers had been secretly erected all over Sicily! While we were under house arrest and were being told to stay home and stay "safe" they had blanketed my little area of western Sicily with 5G weaponry. I felt called to share this information with the world! My blogs were deleted, my videos censored, and my social media groups hijacked. Even the name Infinite Human had been co-opted by two x-military women a few months prior. So this "planned" demic had all been carefully orchestrated. I watched as all truth was censored and banned.

People like David Icke, who had been writing books about this for years, had their voices silenced, their videos replaced with bogus propaganda videos explaining why everything he had said was false. I am so thrilled to have him as a guest on my Infinite Human Talk Show on the Voice America Empowerment Channel to give his truth frequency a voice! I watched as more and more mandates were issued robbing us of our freedom and forcing humanity to stay home. We were only allowed to leave with a written permission slip once a day to buy food, wearing a muzzle. I tried everything I could to wake up the world, to warn people! I believed that if the truth could be told, we could nip this in the bud and We the People could take back our planet!

My friends and family in the States asked me what was happening and I told them my experiences. Then many "spiritual" people whom I had thought to be "awakened" asked me what they should do? I told them "I can't tell you what to do! Go to Infinite Source for your answers!" So I watched as they went to their "source", spiritual teachers, friends, family, the Medical Community and the Media! As the Plandemic hit the US, I saw all my supposedly "spiritually evolved" friends proudly donning masks and gleefully following the Draconian Mandates like good little brainwashed boys and girls. I even saw one of the leading figures in my "spiritual family" get injected and tell everyone how SAFE she now felt! Now I am not judging anyone in their choices, but I would hope those who choose this path would do so from a place of being fully informed. At that time, those who were making these choices did not have a clue as to what was going on. They were just following the crowd. I watched as the entire world complied. I felt called to stand up, speak out and speak the truth no matter what the cost! I was bullied, ridiculed, mocked, unfriended, and worse. I was attacked both physically and energetically. But I continued to shout out in Italian, English, French, Spanish or in any way I could to anyone who could hear! My words fell upon deaf ears, but there were very few who heard me, supported me and with whom I have formed deep lasting friendships and who have become powerful allies. As masks became part of people's daily costumes I refused to wear them. Once inside a store I was assaulted and thrown out and the police chased me. Another time on Liberation Day which was also Global 5G protest day I left my lockdown to protest. I encountered a garrison of Italian Soldiers who tried to stop me but I just shouted, "Liberta! Liberta!" and put my petal to the metal!

Every time I connected the dots of Covid 19, 5G and vaccinations, all my posts were deleted. However, one day, out of the blue, I was invited to appear on a talk show by a film Director from New York. I was so thrilled that, at long last, I could tell the world what was really happening! When we began the interview, Lee Adams, the director, told me that they were having "technical" problems and sat there staring at me with his soulless black eyes while I passed the time making small talk. Then, when I told him "on the air" about the Italian Doctors who were speaking up about the fact that all those fatalities in Northern Italy had only occurred to people who had received a new "flu" vaccination in September 2019 or when I mentioned the medical findings of the University of Rome connecting 5G to the corona virus and the fact that 5G radiation causes the same symptoms as the corona virus he edited it all out and replaced it with our meaningless conversation when he had told me the camera wasn't rolling. Then he brought in several experts each explaining why 5G could NOT be the cause of the virus. The whole interview had been orchestrated to discredit me!

All intelligent professionals, who had not been bought out, had opposed 5G technology and most world governments prior to 2020 had agreed to NOT roll out 5G. Now, with the Covid coverup, they had cast their magic act by distracting everyone with a highly contagious deadly virus so they could carry out their dark New World Order Agenda rolling out 5G with absolutely no respect for Humanity's choice to NOT CONSENT to 5G. While people were forced to stay locked inside their homes, believing they were safe, the real weapon, the silent killer, the "frequency" virus was being installed in every corner of our globe. While people were being terrorized by MK Ultra mind control bilge about a "contagious" deadly virus, isolated and muzzled so they could not communicate with one another or see what was happening in their own towns and cities, the foundation for the genocide and trans-humanization of the human race known as the "great global reset" into a New World Order of technological tyranny, was being laid in secret. How diabolical! I began to message my friends all around the world, from Australia to Spain, from South America to Norway. I learned that as each country went into lock down everywhere, even in the remotest villages, 5G towers were being laid.

To see the full picture, you must put all the puzzle pieces together. 5G is just the visible portion of a much broader takeover of our planet, which became very obvious to me one night, during the first month of lockdown, when I was unable to see the stars from my terrace in Sicily, because a new artificial "star" had appeared in the night sky. The glare was so bright I had to dim my eyes! Through my research, I found out about Stefano Gallozzi, and his Italian colleagues, who had been trying to halt the deployment of mega-constellations by suing the US government in the International Court of Justice for economic damages caused by Starlink, what is now known as Space X, under the UN Liability Convention, which states that it is legally responsible for damages caused by these space objects. In spite of the Covid-19 "plandemic" that hit Italy, Gallozzi and his colleagues managed to launch an appeal by astronomers, "Safeguarding the Astronomical Sky," asking governments and international institutions (such as the UN) not to support the deployment of these mega-constellations of Space X. It has been signed by more than 2,000 astronomers and astrophysicists around the world. During the "plandemic", Space X did not slow down its activities. Workers at its Hawthorne facility in California were required to go to work since the company is a government contractor. Elon Musk tweeted, "The coronavirus panic is dumb," in March 2020. So, why the rush to build satellites and rockets in the middle of a pandemic?" "Their only purpose was to turn on the service and secure a monopoly," Gallozzi says "In the telecommunications field, when you turn on a service... you actually acquire the right, and once you have managed to provide a service to someone, it is difficult to rescind."

CURRENT PLAYERS IN SPACEX AND THEIR PLANS.

Here is a list of companies that are known to have actively launched or are planning to operate large constellations of satellites in low orbit around the earth. The purpose of these satellite networks is to shoot focused beams of radiation at the earth from phased array antennas. Space X based in the United States, at the time this article was written gained approval to operate 12,000 satellites and had been granted 30,000 more applications which have been filed. Just the beginning. Companies such as Amazon had their applications to operate 3,236 satellites, approved by the FCC last July 2020. Facebook is planning to launch a constellation of small, 50-pound satellites called CubeSats. It too, has an experimental license from the FCC and has not revealed how many satellites it plans to operate. Telesat, based in Canada, has increased its planned number of satellites from 117 to 1,671. Omnispace is honored to have been selected to work with the "U.S. Navy" and the Marines to demonstrate 5G capability from space," said Campbell Marshall, Vice President for Government and International Markets in a March 15, 2021 interview. And of course, there is Elon Musk's company Space X and its Starlink constellation."

Truthfully, we really have no idea what they are and have been putting around us in their current space cage. These satellites are launched into a low earth orbit to achieve a global wireless network. This infrastructure will significantly alter the world's electromagnetic environment to unprecedented levels and may cause unknown consequences to the entire biosphere of both the Earth, human beings and all organic life. NASA has satellites that can now control the weather from space. And as JFK warned us in one of his historic televised speeches, "He who controls the Weather controls the Earth!" In August 2021 Space X officially went live, securing its legal right to operate. My body went through a major adjustment. Many of my aware friends all over the planet communicated similar experiences.

WHAT EXACTLY IS 5G?

5G is a military weapon developed by the US military in the 1950s. It has been used in warfare to burn the flesh from victims, sear people's eyeballs, burn the lining of their lungs. It has been used for crowd dispersal; it can change the algorithms of your brain for mind control. It can pull both oxygen and water molecules from the air, it can start fires, penetrate walls. There are a multitude of other "patented" applications. This was taken from an article by Beverly Rubik and Robert R. Brown, College of Integrative Medicine & Health Sciences, Saybrook University, Pasadena, CA; Institute for Frontier Science Oakland, CA, USA Evidence for a Connection between COVID19 and "Exposure to Radio Frequency Radiation from Wireless Telecommunications Including Microwaves and Millimeter Waves. I have paraphrased some of the findings: 5G: impairs microcirculation and reduces erythrocyte and hemoglobin levels exacerbating hypoxia; amplifies immune system dysfunction, including immunosuppression, autoimmunity, and hyper inflammation; increases cellular oxidative stress and the production of free radicals exacerbating vascular injury and organ damage; augmenting intracellular viral entry, replication, and release, in addition to promoting pro-inflammatory pathways; and worsening heart arrhythmias and cardiac disorders. In short, RFR is a ubiquitous environmental stressor that older populations and those with comorbidities, such as hypertension, diabetes, and obesity, creates a greater risk for severe disease. Acute respiratory distress syndrome and the cause of severe shortness of breath as endothelial cells lining blood vessels and epithelial cells lining airways lose their integrity, and protein-rich fluid leaks into adjacent air sacs. 5G can cause insufficient oxygen levels (hypoxia) that has been seen in up to 80% of intensive care unit (ICU) patients (Gattinoni, 2020) exhibiting respiratory distress. Decreased oxygenation and elevated carbon dioxide levels in patients' blood have been observed. Massive oxidative damage to the lungs has been observed in areas of consolidation documented on lung radiographs and CT scans in patients with COVID 19. The disease can spread and damage organs and soft tissues throughout the body, including the lungs, heart, intestines, kidneys, blood vessels, fat, testes, and ovaries, among others. The disease can increase systemic inflammation and induce a hyper coagulable state. It has also been known to produce suicidal thoughts in people. That was from California.

Below is an excerpt from a study done by the Department of Nuclear, Sub-nuclear, and Radiation Physics, at the University of Rome, Italy. Received May 13, 2020 – Accepted June 9, 2020. "In this research, we show that 5G millimeter waves could be absorbed by dermatologic cells acting like antennas, transferred to other cells and play the main role in producing Coronaviruses in biological cells." DNA is built from charged electrons and atoms and has an inductor-like structure. This structure could be divided into linear, toroid, and round inductors. Inductors interact with external electromagnetic waves, move and produce some extra waves within the cells. The shapes of these waves are similar to the shapes of hexagonal and pentagonal bases of their DNA source. These waves produce some holes in liquids within the nucleus. To fill these holes, some extra hexagonal and pentagonal bases are produced. These bases could join to each other and form virus-like structures such as Coronavirus. To produce these viruses within a cell, it is necessary that the wavelength of external waves be shorter than the size of the cell. Thus, 5G millimeter waves could be good candidates for applying in constructing virus-like structures (spike proteins?) such as Coronaviruses (COVID-19) within cells."

WHAT DOES ALL THIS MEAN???

The Truth is people are being exposed to a sophisticated form of bio weaponry never before known to humankind. Our Earth is being continuously bathed with toxic levels of radiation that are increasing daily. Oxygen levels are also decreasing daily as our planet is being terraformed into something that will no longer sustain organic life. They are testing the capabilities of this highly advanced technological bio-weaponry on unsuspecting populations. This strategically positioned "silent enemy" is emitting 5G millimeter waves from towers blanketing our Earth's surface, beam steering these frequencies from the low orbiting satellites positioned in the Space X cage now encircling us, which is also throwing off the delicate electromagnetic balance of our planet. These top-secret applications are now being tested on the unsuspecting world population and being covered up as "covid" casualties of a deadly organic virus. Each of these frequencies has specific functions and holds a patent that can be bought and sold. Some of these patented frequencies can burst organs, stop hearts, kill bees, disperse crowds, start fires and the list goes on. Through 5G beam-steering, these frequencies can be directed to very specific areas such as a city, a town center, a place of business or residence, even to a specific individual. They can be directed into people's devices such as cell phones and computers, to affect them. 5G does not penetrate through trees, which explains the massive destruction of our Earth's magnificent Forests. Since the plandemic of 2020, this 5G network of antennas, towers, fiber optics, routers, reflective attachments on poles, etcetera now completely dominates the Earth's surface. It is the deadly silent virus among us now. It is the FREQUENCY VIRUS, tagged as Covid 19, a name created years before the 2020 "outbreak". Sadly, the people of Earth are blindly going to their governments and weaponized medical communities for cures which further augment their own demise.

The symptoms of Covid are the same symptoms of radiation poisoning. According to the Mayo Clinic early signs of radiation poisoning are: nausea and vomiting, diarrhea, headache, fever, dizziness, disorientation, weakness, fatigue and hair loss. As it progresses, it causes bloody vomit and bloody stools from internal bleeding, infections, low blood pressure, skin rash and other disturbances. What most people don't understand is that 5G strikes at the Mitochondria. These double membrane-bound cell organelles power the cell's biochemical reactions whose purpose is to create the energy that powers the body. If you have a defect in the pathways of the Mitochondria you are going to have symptoms in the muscles, the brain, the liver, et cetera. Modern medicine admits that it does not know all the dis-eases weakened Mitochondria can create but it, along with RNA and DNA are the building blocks of our body and the foundation for our health. When these are compromised, our body is weakened and underlying health issues can resurface and become deadly. Basically, we are now living in an invisible deadly soup of radiation with a silent enemy unbeknownst to us that is making us sicker and sicker every day! And their solution is to modify our DNA so we become an alternate Artificial life form that can survive in their toxic inorganic environment. It is happening so slowly and so insidiously that people are not noticing it and all their symptoms are being blamed on an organic contagious "covert" virus. But have no doubt this "frequency" virus IS killing people by destroying the natural abilities of their bodies to heal. We are seeing people sick and dying from an assortment of dis-eases because 5G radiation destroys our cell health, the very building blocks of our organic bodies!

THE EFFECTS OF RADIATION POISONING

"Clinical and experimental data used to describe the acute and late reactions of the lungs to both external and internal radiation, including pneumonitis, fibrosis, and carcinogenesis. Acute radiation pneumonitis, which can be fatal. Longer exposure can damage the brain. Nerve cells die, which can cause seizures; cataracts can form in the eyes; the thyroid loses function, which affects normal metabolism; risk of lung cancer is increased; blood vessel cells near the heart are damaged, which increases the risk of cardiac failure; the cells in the GI tract are damaged, leading to indigestion, nausea, vomiting, and diarrhea; eggs and sperm in the ovaries and testes die; skin cells become burnt and damaged; and the cells of the immune system are not adequately replenished, leading to increased risk of infection."

I have been following the health complaints in social media groups from people all over the world. There is an unprecedented rise in the number of strange skin diseases, redness or irritations, thyroid diseases, diabetes, infertility, cancer, arthritis, fibromyalgia, heart attacks, muscle and joint pain and deterioration. In short, people's health is being greatly affected and will continue to deteriorate. The body's coping mechanism to deal with the increasing toxicity of our environment due to radiation poisoning is to flood your body with toxins, looking for a pathway to exit. This causes your body to detox at an alarming rate, creating flu-like symptoms such as fever, cold sweats, and also flushing out underlying infections that may have remained dormant. If you have too many built-up toxins and underlying health issues, this can overload the body to the point where your body cannot regain balance and can cause death.

WHY THE MEDICAL COMMUNITY WILL NEVER BE ABLE TO CURE COVID.

Can you imagine what it would be like if your brain couldn't tell your leg muscles to contract so you could walk? Or your bladder couldn't tell your brain that you had to use the bathroom? Or what if you contracted an infection and your immune system could not tell your body how to heal from it? Cells need to be able to communicate with each other to do these things, and so much more! In biology, depolarization is a change within a cell, during which the cell undergoes a shift in electric charge distribution, resulting in a less negative charge inside the cell compared to the outside. Depolarization is essential to the function of many cells, communication between cells, and the overall physiology of an organism. Hyper-polarization is a change in a cell's membrane potential that makes it more negative. It is the opposite of a depolarization. Depolarization is essential to the function of many cells, communication between cells, and the overall physiology of an organism. Chloride salts such as sodium chloride are often very soluble in water. It is an essential electrolyte located in all body liquids responsible for maintaining acid/base balance, transmitting nerve impulses and regulating liquid flow in and out of cells. The binding pushes the channels open, which increases the flow of chloride ions and hyper-polarizes the cell membranes. Chloride salts such as sodium chloride are essential electrolytes located in all body liquids responsible for maintaining acid/base balance, transmitting nerve impulses and regulating liquid flow in and out of cells. Exocytosis is a process used by one cell of your body to tell another cell in your body what to do. For example, to take out its trash (toxins) and to incorporate proteins (food) into the cell membrane. There are three different styles of endocytosis: 1) phagocytosis, which is the process similar to eating, where the cell engulfs a molecule in order to move it to the interior of the cell; pinocytosis, is how the cell drinks; and receptor-mediated endocytosis which is a bit like a lock-and-key system.

WHAT IF A CELL FAILS TO SEND OUT A SIGNAL AT THE PROPER TIME?

What if the insulin cell's signal is lost? As a result, sugar accumulates to toxic levels in the blood causing diabetes which can lead to kidney failure, blindness and heart disease. What if nerve cells can no longer transmit signals from one area of the brain to another? This could cause nerve damage for example like what we see in multiple sclerosis which leads to many problems, including muscle weakness, blurred or double vision, difficulty with balance, uncontrolled movements, and depression. Or, what if our brain cells cannot do their job? This can cause a stroke, which occurs when a blockage forms in a blood vessel, cutting off the blood flow to part of the brain. The immediate result is the death of nearby brain cells.

Many mechanisms maintain appropriate cell growth: Cell division occurs in response to external signals. Enzymes repair damaged DNA. Cells make connections with their neighbors. If these connections suddenly change, neighboring cells send out an alert. Cells respect and stay within tissue boundaries. If the plasma membrane ruptures or breaks down, the cell will not be able to exchange material from its surroundings by diffusion or osmosis because it acts as a mechanical barrier. Thereafter, the protoplasmic material will disappear and the cell will die. If a cell is beyond repair, it initiates its own death. If a cell has an error in its DNA that cannot be repaired, it may undergo self-destruction (apoptosis). Apoptosis is a common process throughout life that helps the body get rid of cells that no longer work or that it doesn't need. But what happens if we cannot create healthy cells to replace the dead ones?

The COVID phenomenon is linked to oxygen shortage (aka hypoxia or under oxygenation) perpetuating the misconception that it is a contagious disease substantiating the mask mandates which only augment the problem. Dr Robert Young refers to it as Pathological Blood Coagulation and Systemic Acidosis. Dr. Young explains that COVID is actually blood coagulation, created by the 5G 60GHz effect on oxygen molecules. Lactic acidosis is a medical condition characterized by the buildup of lactate acid in the body, with the formation of an excessively low pH in the bloodstream. It is a form of metabolic acidosis, in which excessive acid accumulates due to a problem with the body's oxidative metabolism or under utilizes lactic acid, and the body is not able to adjust to these changes. Lactic acidosis is typically the result of an underlying acute or chronic medical condition, medication, or "poisoning". In acute cases it prevents the lungs cells from absorbing oxygen, causing asphyxiation. Chronic lactic acidosis may cause mitochondrial disease. The mitochondrial dysfunction has been involved in: diabetes, Huntington's disease, cancer, Alzheimer's disease, bipolar disorder, schizophrenia, aging, anxiety disorders, cardiovascular disease, sarcopenia, chronic fatigue syndrome, and many more.

Mitochondrial disorders may be caused by mutations (acquired or inherited), in mitochondrial DNA (mDNA), or in nuclear genes that code for mitochondrial components. They may also be the result of acquired mitochondrial dysfunction due to adverse effects of drugs, infections, or other "environmental causes". The prognosis of lactic acidosis depends largely on the underlying cause; in some situations (such as severe infections), it indicates an increased risk of death.

SYMPTOMS OF LACTIC ACIDOSIS:

- Rapid and shallow breathing
- fatigue headache
- sleepiness
- lack of appetite
- increased heart rate
- The breath smells fruity, which is a sign of diabetic acidosis (ketoacidosis) In short, these lactic build ups occur because of an unacceptable level of a probable carcinogen which creates inflammation as an early warning sign of this carcinogenic build up. Inflammation is the body's natural defense mechanism against foreign invaders, foreign organisms, such as bacteria and (frequency) viruses and our toxic environment that increases daily. Inflammation of the taste buds and olfactory (nose/smell) causes the "loss of smell" associated with Covid. It also causes redness, pain, tenderness, swelling, bumps, rashes, puffiness, bruising, stiffness, loss of mobility, fever, nausea, lethargy, sleepiness, irritability, runny nose, sore throat, stuffy nose and headache. Chronic inflammation is a sign that something is terribly wrong in your body and needs your attention.

Three years ago when I came to Sicily I was amazed to find a world much like the one I had grown up in during the Seventies in America! In only three short years these same people no longer laugh, play and many don't even leave their homes. They have stopped living, even breathing! The young people now huddled together with masked faces, glued to their cells phone oblivious to the world and other human beings around them. Many family businesses, shops, and restaurants that produced high-quality food products for centuries have gone belly up. Open-air markets, festivals, and celebrations died out. Artists, actors, and craftspeople were out of work. Tourists, which are the lifeblood of Italy were banned. I watched as the once "Dolce Vita" of Italy turned sour. Old people were separated from their families, isolated and died alone. I watched the warm, fun-loving Italian people no longer gather in the streets for their family dinners. I saw these loving passionate people stop smiling, kissing, and touching one another. I quickly realized why these extremely passionate, childlike people were being hit so hard by the "virus." They were one of the few remaining cultures on this earth who were still "human"

For years I watched the people of my own country become more and more robotic, becoming servants to technology. I had grown accustomed to my nieces and nephews glued to their cell phones during family get-togethers. In fact, this was the very reason I came to Italy seeking something that had all but been extinguished from our planet... human beings. Now they were becoming conditioned to be something they were not, by being forced to wear muzzles, not being permitted to touch one another, go into cafes, restaurants or congregate in the piazzas, which has always been at the core of the Italian culture. I saw a video where a woman was walking her dog in front of the Hard Rock Cafe in Florence where I had my film school and fifteen policemen attacked this woman and her dog. One grabbed her around the throat. They arrested her because she had no mask. This is something that could happen in the U.S, but never in the Italy I knew.

Ironically, Italians, being ancient people, intuitively held the knowledge that most leaders and their governments were corrupt. They adapted to these tyrannical laws handed down throughout the centuries by simply not following them. But now their irrational fears were causing them to stop being the compassionate, heart based Italians I had come to know and love! The Police, Military, *Carabinieri*, Doctors, Health Care Workers, Educators, Store Owners, etcetera need to stop supporting this New World Order Agenda out of fear. They need to choose to support their fellow human beings and human rights, not help bring about the technological tyranny which is only leading to their own demise. Illegal laws, passes and fines need to stop being given power. Store owners need to stop putting themselves out of business by enforcing lock downs , mask wearing and green passes, which drive their customers to shop on Amazon! All Tourists, Italy's life blood, need to be welcomed back to Italy. All GREEN PASS restrictions need to be obliterated! Physicians need to remember their sacred Hippocratic Oath of "First Do No Harm" and leave the weaponized health care system to create alternative healing centers rather than centers of death. In Italy, and around the world as well, hospitals receive three thousand euros for any death that is tagged as Covid as well as being well paid for all government "authorized" procedures for treating Covid. Families take their loved ones to the hospital and once there, the patient cannot leave and the family is not allowed to see them. I met a young man who checked his mother into a hospital because she had a slight fever and was told the next day that she had died of Covid.

Most Sicilians have little understanding of advanced technology, including the Medical Community. In fact, most of the World's population has no knowledge of the sophisticated technological weaponry developed by DARPA, the Defense Advanced Research Projects Agency a branch of the US Military responsible for the development of emerging technologies for military use, now being used against humanity. This is bad enough, but the bigger picture is even worse. The tiny waves of 5G can accomplish what other EMF technology (4G and below) cannot, by penetrating the cell membrane and interacting with our DNA inductors. We're talking about the power to influence and manipulate our very DNA here. The current injections contain mRNA (CRISPR gene editing) designed to mutate the human DNA into something that is not human, nor organic.

It is no coincidence that since the fifties humans have been poisoned with heavy metals. Our produce has been coated with glyphosate found in pesticides, artificial ingredients filled with aluminum, and other metals have been added to our food. Our water is contaminated with Fluoride and arsenic, and as if that isn't enough, chem-trails containing smart dust are dropped on us daily so we can't help but breathe in nanobot technology. This micro computer technology is in the smart dust we breathe, the food we eat, and the water we drink. Anything ingested can eventually be removed from our bodies. But when this nanotechnology is injected into the bloodstream through what is being passed off as "vaccinations" they fuse with the RNA and become part of genetic cellular make-up of whomever is injected. These nanobots are patented. So, when they meld with the building blocks of your body, you become the property of whoever holds the patent. I recently saw on the BBC a documentary of a nanotechnology demonstration revealing how these tiny nanobots, or microcomputers can waltz or move in harmony with the "frequencies" of music. These tiny nanobots, once inside your body, replicate inside your organic tissue eventually taking it over. Allowing you to be controlled by the frequencies sent out from 5G, Space X and beyond. So, you can imagine how easy it is to silently control a person who is infested with A.I. They will no longer be human, but an artificial or A.I. life form controlled by whoever is pulling the strings or operating the technological frequencies that control them. These frequencies can control the mind and the bodily functions of those injected with this technology. So euthanasia or genocide on a massive scale can silently and insidiously be carried out without the masses ever knowing. It is no coincidence that one of the names of these "vaccines" is Astra Zeneca which literally means star (seed) killer in Latin.

During the lock down when the world was at a standstill and when planes stopped flying, people stayed at home and whenever we were allowed out we had to stay six feet apart. They were creating a digital twin of our organic Earth or a "Holo Vision" of our Earth. This is the AI Meta Verse they are herding us into. Because this fake reality feels "wrong" to organic human beings they must acclimate our bodies, our minds and our souls to accept their bad copy. The continuous injections or boosters are overrunning peoples' organic bodies with AI biotechnology. This perpetuates cognitive dissonance and assimilates their consciousness into the AI New World Order World they are constructing around us daily. Don't believe me? Take a look around you and SEE how many people are glued to their cell phones now.

We are being herded into their (inter) "NET" for our every need. Our cell phones are rapidly becoming mandatory to survive in the New World Order of AI. Green pass restrictions are required now to move about in the 3D world freely and people are required to demonstrate that they are marked by the beast via an app on their smart phone which is scanned the same way merchandize is scanned in a checkout line. It is no coincidence that Apple's latest IPhone's sim card is called a "bio" chip. We are being herded into a New AI World Order where "Bio" chips implanted inside our bodies will be mandatory for anyone to participate in the New World Order of banking, traveling, working, shopping, even breathing! Everyone will be required to be hooked up to the Hive Mind SKY NET created by DARPA via biotechnology.

We are being filtered into two opposing groups. Weaponizing us against each other as the controllers meticulously carry out their dark agenda never missing a beat. Their brilliant Luciferian tactics have created a world that fills us with fear of our fellow human beings. These divide and conquer techniques have created World War III, where we are fighting one another instead of the real enemy! We the People are Not the enemy!

BELOW IS A BRIEF OVERVIEW OF A 5G PROMO PIECE FOR 5G ROLL OUT IN JAPAN:

BEYOND 5G PROMOTING STRATEGY (OVERVIEW)

5G, which is rolling out worldwide, will develop an infrastructure *expected to be the backbone of Society by integrating cyberspace with physical space.* Amidst an explosive and global COVID-19 (planned demic), there is no choice but to fully rely on ICT capabilities, such as telework, due to restrictive measures preventing people from traveling to work. 5G has been formulated as an *emergency measure for constructing a new social system* a (New World Order), against current global challenges after the COVID-19 disaster.

EXPECTATIONS FOR SOCIETY IN THE 2030S

Cyber-Physical Systems (CPSs), whereby *cyberspace is integrated with physical space*, (that means you in a Meta Verse Digital Twin of Earth) will have come to fruition, alongside the widespread use of 5G in daily life, resulting in a transition into a data-driven society (You are the Data!) By the 2030s, we will create a society where our daily lives and economic activities are fully maintained within cyber-space-to "safe guard" against unexpected crises in the physical world (No more privacy). This will form the formation of a sustainable global environment (transition of all organic life into an A.I. Meta Verse) and the international community as the common foundation for mankind. Creating an INCLUSIVE SOCIETY where you can be in constant contact without having to leave your own home and *"super cybernetic technologies that expand physical and cognitive abilities by real-time support of cyberspace to people's thoughts and actions through wearable devices,* "etc." (Your brain will be connected to a Hive Mind) A TRUSTFUL SOCIETY with super-autonomous security technologies that are able to *protect security and privacy, without the user being aware of it,* (cyber spying) by utilizing AI for automatic detection, automatic defense and automatic restoration, and super fail-safe network technologies (Skynet) that do not lose connectivity even during disasters due to their ability to flexibly and autonomously change their network structures, and levels of power consumption and transmission methods. (Skynet that can never turn it off.)

OBJECTIVES FOR DESIRABLE BEYOND 5G:

In order to realize the above vision for society in the 2030s, it will be essential to gather detailed data about trends in physical spaces, accumulate and analyze it in cyberspace, and achieve the "advanced synchronization" of CPSs to enable instantaneous feedback into physical space. (Create a Meta Verse holographic reality) Consequently, it is vital that even faster communications, infrastructure, more so than even 5G, are developed that are able to safely (We will be told it is SAFE when it really IS NOT and people will believe it because they want to) and accurately transmit vast amounts of information across land, sea, sky, space, and more. (Your data is now a commodity that is being bought and sold by the elites.) The new system also needs *"structural reform"* in order to make full use of real-time data securely with less load to the environment. (*The Great Reset*) By around the year 2030. Beyond 5G can be implemented freely and flexibly proactively utilizing National Strategic Special Zones such as the "Super City" concept. (Smart Cities)

So we are now in a pivotal time where everyone on our Earth is creating their reality and choosing 5G or 5D. Yes, that is the fundamental question. Of course, we need technology to SERVE US, not for us to become its servants with our consciousness controlled by a hive mind. Whoever controls the mind commands the soul. You do not want technology in or even on your body. It must be put in its place, a safe place where its micro waves cannot infect you, others or the environment after it has served its function. You can best respect others, our Mother Earth and all Creation and stop the spread of "COVID " by only using cell phones when necessary and keeping the EMF radiation contained!

Aldous Huxley depicted a future world whose citizens are environmentally engineered into an intelligence-based social hierarchy or hive mind. Let's take a moment to examine a hive-minded society. In the beehive, the Queen Bee is born into her position. Upon her birth, the first thing she does is to kill off all of her sisters to secure her throne. She reproduces in a mating flight where the drones that manage to mate with her are killed by having their sexual organs ripped away after they have supplied the necessary sperm. The other female worker bees, when young, perform the duties of undertaker bees that clean the hive by removing dead bodies and killing any "weak" bees. When they are older, they work outside the hive, normally dropping dead after one month because they put in over five hundred miles of flight time and their wings are torn apart. All this is for the good of the hive. This is how the hive mind operates. We are being socially and genetically engineered to operate as a hive mind.

Years ago, the anthropologist Margaret Mead was asked by a student what she considered to be the first signs of civilization in a culture. The student expected Mead to talk about fishhooks, or clay pots, or grinding stones. But no, Margaret Mead said that the first sign of civilization in an ancient culture was a femur (thighbone) that had been broken and then healed. Mead explained that in the animal kingdom, if you break your leg, you die. You cannot run from danger, get to the river for water, or hunt for food. You are meat for prowling beasts. No animal survives a broken leg long enough for the bone to heal. A broken femur that has healed is evidence that someone has taken the time to stay with the one who fell, has bound up the wound, has carried the person to safety, and has tended the person through recovery. Helping someone else through difficulty is where civilization starts," Margaret Mead said. Each of us is facing a choice whether to become a hive minded A.I. Drone or to be a civilized Infinite Human Being. Progress is not sophisticated new technological toys rather it is being humane and caring for your fellow human being.

THE PERFECT STORM!

In summary the diabolical Covid 19 plan behind the Plandemic is so evil that it is beyond most decent folk's ability to comprehend. It is the sheer genius that only satanic pathological minds could concoct. But it is what it is and we must know what we are looking at so we no longer play into the hands of the evil controllers.

This perfect Plandemic Storm has been in the making for a very long time as our Earth's environment, food, water, medicine, and technology has over the years insidiously been weaponized to harm rather than heal us. Toxins have been implemented to create underlying health problems and to instill addictions to foods and drugs that harm rather than heal. So basically, human bodies have been prepped for this perfect storm with toxic levels of carcinogens that have created underlying health problems. An accident waiting to happen.

In 2020, the first blow was rendered when Earth's population was terrorized by the threat of a deadly contagious virus. While we were forced to stay home terrorized by MK Ultra Trauma based mind control and thinking we were "safe" 5G weaponry was being positioned around the planet and the toxic levels of radiation were increased daily. Draconian mandates were issued to purposely destroy healthful habits and stop human's natural ability to detox themselves. People were not allowed to be in nature, to breath properly, exhaling toxins breathing in fresh clean air. They were terrorized with fear which weakens the immune system and separated from their loved ones. As more and more people became "ill", lies about a deadly "contagious" virus justified more mandates and the complete takeover of Earth, clearing the way for their AI injections. The 5G weaponry DARPA had developed was now being tested on the world population causing more and more deaths and illnesses that were easily covered up as "Covid 19" casualties feeding the fear that allowed them to easily remove any last remnants of freedom. To keep people from catching onto their evil plan they kept everyone distracted with racial riots, political races, and other divide and conquer tactics. While misdirecting the awakening communities with a three ring circus show by dropping Q bombs of contrived "disclosure", controlled opposition and misinformation about vaccines and Covid.

While we were "paying" our attention to all the distractions, 5G towers and all their apparatus were installed and Space X went live acquiring its legal right to exist. All the while people were under house arrest, wearing muzzles, staying six feet apart, communicating on DARPA's inter (NET) where we were spied on, censored, controlled and attacked. Meanwhile bought and paid for Scientists created bogus cures in test tubes rather than looking at the ever growing toxicity of our environment. Green Passes requiring multiple injections were enforced for most commerce, travel, and pseudo freedoms. Physicians trashed their Hippocratic oath of "First do no harm"by blindly giving vaccinations to the world's population, without ever questioning the narrative or standing up for their patient's rights. Like a boiling frog, humanity is being cooked alive in a microwave but now there is no place to jump out!

CHAPTER 21

SMEARING HONEY OVER PUS

I can't begin to express the overwhelming frustration one feels when they know the road ahead is leading towards a cliff and as drawn on the Hopi Prophecy Rock, the majority of Earth's population, the two-hearted people, are blindly running towards this "dead" end. Perhaps this is what they mean by the saying, "knowledge is both a blessing and a curse." Perhaps you know the feeling and you are a bit like me. I am the kind of person who screams, "don't do it!" at the characters in a movie I have seen a hundred times at the precise moment they are about to make that fatal choice that leads to their downfall. You know the road ahead is laden with tragedy and you long to ease people's pain and suffering. So you stand by the road side screaming at the top of your lungs, "don't go down this road!" But nobody listens. Alas, the truth is we cannot rob another person of their life lessons. This is all part of their own soul growth and I was about to learn that very painful lesson which nearly cost me my life.

On Christmas Eve of 2020, I found myself alone and very frustrated with the world. Even though my dream had come true and I had finally found a beautiful Villa very isolated from the problems of the world, that I had seen in a vision when I first came to Sicily. It was exactly what I wanted but instead of being grateful for all my blessings, I just saw what was lacking. I arrived home late that night and did not have a chance to work with the energy of the house as I do with all my living environments. That evening Kiki stood up and barked at some energetic being that entered our bed room. The next day, I went outside early to open the gate for a technician and the door slammed and locked behind me. I had only been given one key which was locked inside the door. I was locked out, without a phone, in the middle of nowhere. The door was glass, so I kicked it gently, but it didn't break. "Oh God," I thought, "here I am locked out of my new home in my pajamas in the cold, on Christmas Eve!" All the deep unresolved wounds I had festering within, along with the frustration of being alone, again, on Christmas surfaced. No Peter, no family and what's worse it didn't look like the people of Planet Earth were going to wake up any time soon...if ever! In angry desperation, I kicked the glass again harder this time and it broke. I pulled my foot out and there was a gash on my leg. "Oh God," I thought, "I hope I don't bleed to death!" I grabbed a sock from my car and made a tourniquet. Then reached in the opened the door. I found my phone, and called an ambulance which passed by three times trying to find the house. Thus began a nightmare.

All my worst fears were suddenly in my face. I found myself at the mercy of the weaponized healthcare system and to make matters worse it was in Sicily (which has the worst healthcare in Italy) on the onset of their very long Christmas Holiday, during a total lock down! The ambulance took me to the hospital. I had to leave Kiki alone in a strange house, with no one to take care of her. Under the Covid protocol I had to get "Covid tested" before being admitted and could not leave the hospital once admitted and no one could come in! I had no phone and no means of communication with the outside world! I had fallen into the broken health care system surrounded by people who were more concerned with pulling a mask over my face so that I could not breathe and finding out if I had "covid" than the fact that I was bleeding to death. Unfortunately, my tendons were severed and I was told I needed to have surgery. I was transferred to another hospital where I waited most of the day and into the night until they finally told me they could not operate until January fourth, when the holiday season ended and I had to stay in the hospital until then. I had no phone, no possessions and no one to take care of Kiki so I signed myself out and talked the realtor who found me the Villa into driving me home on Christmas Day so I could take care of Kiki! She was furious. Suddenly, I was a small wounded child again with some crazy narcissistic woman screaming at me about how I had ruined her Christmas!

My father's wise words keep ringing in my ears, "Rescuers become victims." We cannot SAVE anyone. We cannot make people SEE what they do not want to see. We cannot learn their lessons and take their tests for them. We cannot give them the courage they lack. If we did, we would rob them of their God given Free Will. Like loving parents, we can only offer guidance and if they do not heed our wisdom they must learn these hard lessons for themselves. All we can do is love them unconditionally and be there when and if they are ready to accept our help. But we must take care of ourselves first. This was probably the hardest lesson for me and perhaps for many Star Seeds since we are loving, heart-based souls who came here to help humanity into the freedom that only comes through ascension. It hurts us deeply when our hands are tied and we can do nothing but watch them struggle through their mistakes and like innocent lambs be led to slaughter.

THE WEAPONIZATION OF HEALTH CARE

The definition of Medicine is, "the science and art of diagnosing and treating disease or injury and maintaining health." For many years, Peter and I had tried to work within the medical system to change the current course of modern medicine. We watched daily as the Art of Healing, and the dedication and devotion doctors felt for their patients gave way to greed, lawsuits and professional protocols that weaponized healthcare. As the direction of medicine and science deviated more and more from God's Natural Laws of restoring health, harmony and balance, doctors were reduced to the status of drug pushers or mechanics who replaced faulty body parts. Big Pharm, the New England Journal of Medicine and other ivy league schools bought and paid for by the Rockefellers were redefining Medicine and Science. Anyone who deviated from their accepted "medical" protocol was open to law suits and ridicule from the medical profession. I know I stood by Peter as he navigated the treacherous waters of the medical/ legal system.

I had been forewarned by an orthopaedic surgeon from Scotland who told me how he could not give patients the necessary care they needed because the Covid protocols were gumming up everything. Since I had been told I needed an operation and no one would do it, I waited in bed for a week trying to find someone who would operate so I would not be crippled. At last, I found a private clinic in Palermo and on New Year's Eve I was operated on by a doctor whose name was DARPA. I kid you not! The same name as the US military agency behind weaponized biotechnology. Coincidence? There are none.

I should have known better but I still clung to the belief that traditional medicine could heal me! True to his name, he butchered my poor little ankle and I contracted sepsis during the procedure, a serious infection. When I finally went home my wound became very infected. When I returned to see this doctor of death, my wound was full of pus. He told me that this was a good sign! He took me off all antibiotics and told me to just "smear honey over the pus" and it would go away. I was not able to walk or drive and was stuck at home in bed in the middle of nowhere, smearing honey on my leg and watching my wound fester more and more each day. If I had not received divine intervention by way of some many amazing souls who came to my rescue I would have lost my leg and probably my life. I finally found a good doc who properly diagnosed my infection and prescribed the proper antibiotics. A dear friend named Serena volunteered to come and take care of Kiki and me. She drove us everywhere and gave me the daily injections I needed to overcome my infection and gave Kiki all the love, affection and security she had lost due to my near death!

I am telling you this story because you cannot smear honey over pus. You must weed out the root cause of the "infection", and express the pus out. Modern Medicine has been purposely redirected to no longer cure. Physicians have been systematically conditioned to stop looking at the root cause of dis-ease and devout their entire practice into finding ways to "mask" the symptoms that indicate something is seriously wrong. For example, if someone has high blood pressure, diabetes, or chronic inflammation these are warning signs that something is seriously wrong. Something in that person's diet and/or environment is toxic to them and must be eliminated to restore balance and health, defined as "a condition of optimal well-being". But instead the Doctor gives a pill, injection or operation so the person will not have the warning signs any more. This is like a car with a busted tire and the mechanic simply patches it up and sends the driver back onto the highway knowing full well they are an accident waiting to happen. But doctors can never admit that we live in a world that is becoming more and more toxic by the day and preventive healthcare is key because there is no money in it. Likewise, they cannot admit there will never be a "cure" for Covid, since COVID IS OUR BODIES WAY OF WARNING US THAT SOMETHING IS TERRIBLY TOXIC IN OUR

ENVIRONMENT. That the levels of toxicity are reaching lethal levels. Our bodies are screaming this to us! But modern medicine's solution is to ignore the dead elephant of toxicity in the middle of the room and modify our bodies into something other than human that will acclimate to the new anti-life AI world. The medical community has sworn their allegiance to Big Pharm and the rich elites to push their bogus solutions.

With the hind sight of 20/20 vision I realize now I should have never let Dr. DARPA operate on me. I should have known that all his medical procedures and COVID tests did nothing to help me but only harm me. My accident was minimal but it took me over a year to recover from his surgery and "modern medicine". The operation did not repair my severed tendons but made them worse since he cut another even deeper incision. In short, he did not follow his sacred Hippocratic Oath of "First Do no Harm" He was a private Doctor and operated on me because of money even though he did not have the skills required for the job. The black magic money curse has poisoned the practice of Medicine. We now live in a world where it is more profitable to kill patients than cure them. Where Hospitals are paid for everyone that dies from "covid" but not for those who recover. So hospitals have become morgues paid to kill rather than heal! These doctors who hide behind their masks following their pseudo-science protocols are bought and paid for by the elites. While all those upholding their sacred oath and speaking the truth are silenced. I saw first-hand how so many doctors have lost their souls and no longer follow even their common sense. But this incurs a very heavy karmic debt. I know because I was paying mine!

Karma exists even if you do not believe it does. This is why Christianity will never be able to explain why children are born with disabilities, why "accidents" occur or why, no matter what we do, some people just die. Everyone must have the right to pay back their karma. This is why we cannot save others. So in truth I begged for this operation from Dr. DARPA, to pay back my past life karma of being a Nazi Nurse. I had assisted in genetic experiments on Jewish women. I had silently suffered knowing that what I was doing was wrong but had not spoken out until it was too late! It was in this lifetime I decided to stop letting fear control me.

All my life I was the lone rebel who always spoke out anytime I witnessed injustice. History repeats itself until you change your karma!

This karmic lesson also forced me to stop smearing honey over the pus of deep patterns that had infected me life time after life time. Patterns that I thought I had healed but only glazed over were resurfacing for further examination. If you do not get to the root of the dis-ease and take the appropriate action to heal yourself, you are leaving energetic portals open for dark entities to enter. Which is what I did! I had honey glazed over many of my early childhood traumas that were also deeply related to past life wounds which led to the volcanic eruption of emotion that had resulted in my "accident". I was taking a great leap of faith into the higher dimensions and in one moment of emotion all the deep unhealed wounds of my past had surfaced throwing me off balance and causing me to fall into the rude reality of 3D earth. There are no "accidents". This event forced me to do some deep soul searching and revisit things I thought I had finished. I realized I had a deep underlying cesspool of infected pus that had to be cleaned out, old baggage that had to be released before I could embody the higher frequencies of the higher dimensions. I took a long hard look at the areas in my life where old wounds hurts and blames hadn't been healed And boy, did I find them!

I realized I had not fully addressed my Mother Wound, the Mother of all wounds! I had written about the extremely miasmic ancestry inherit on my mother's side, but I had not fully healed it. This wound exists in everyone but is more pronounced in the mother/daughter relationship. It is the wound of being born female in a world dominated by the Dark Masculine. It stems from what I call the woman wound. Because of the world's imbalanced patriarchal structure and the suppression of women's natural divine feminine energy, women have traditionally been reduced to subservient roles. The Mother Wound is, in a sense, the hurt of being born a woman in a world that oppresses and undervalues women. It is the tragedy of the unlived life of the mother which passes onto the daughter who in turn finds her own life hemmed in and unconsciously hands her unexpressed pain down to her daughter. This karmic load is passed down through the generations. We can see how this process results in generations of un-mothered children, carrying stories of loss, rage, jealousy, shame, stifled creativity, and grief in their souls. This trauma extends to the deep-seated spiritual trauma of what we have all felt by being cut off from the Mother aspect of God, the Divine Feminine aspect of Creation, that has been replaced with a tyrannical male imposter god. We women who have the courage to address and heal this mother wound are clearing the karmic path not just for ourselves but for future generations.

All this past pain is here in our present lives to uncover and heal. Fairy tales are good indicators of the type of mother archetype your personal story may follow. I always saw my mother as an angry wicked witch or a jealous step mother. I felt she was a jealous, insecure, unhappy, unappreciated woman who attacked me, forcing me to join her in her own misery. But most of all, because she had not been properly mothered herself, she was the absent mother. The story that always haunted me most was Hans Christian Anderson's story of *The Poor Little Match Girl.* This is the story of a poor little match girl who leaves home one bitter cold New Year's Eve wearing the shoes of her mother that are too big for her feet and loses them. Barefoot, she wanders through the town trying to sell her matches but no one buys them. She spends the entire day in the cold but no one gives her even a farthing. She knows if she goes home with no money she will be beaten so she stays on into the night. Because she is so cold she strikes one match. The light from the match transcends her into a beautiful space where she sees all kinds of wonderful things. A beautiful feast and a Christmas Tree with presents under it! But the light burns out, bringing her back to her brutal physical reality. She keeps lighting matches until she sees her grandmother coming towards her. Her grandmother was the only one who had ever really loved her and who had died several years ago. Not wanting her grandmother to fade away she lights the entire bundle and begs her grandmother to take her with her. Her grandmother does. On New Year's Day, when the towns people return to the town square they find the Poor Little Match Girl, frozen to death, with all her matches burnt out and a smile on her face.

It is no coincidence that this" accident" occurred on Christmas Eve and I was operated on New Year's Eve by Dr. DARPA! I had felt totally abandoned by my mother and my family. I have never received a phone call from my mother nor any family members to say Happy Birthday, Merry

Christmas, how are you doing, are you still alive, or I love you! I felt like my family had basically left me for dead and would perhaps even be happy if I were dead! I had subconsciously felt that I deserved this treatment because I was bad and unworthy of love. This deep-seated pain had erupted inside me like a volcano in a violent action that I had committed against myself. I realized I had been limping through life like an abandoned, hurt child, with my adult self completely absent. My inner child had been doing the best she could to survive in a grown up world. It was time to rejoin my inner adult and inner child. I had to become my own Divine Mother and begin to love and care for my divine inner child. As I freed my Divine Feminine within, I was able to provide for my divine inner child the things I had lacked growing up. My fears began to subside and I began to feel safe, wanted, seen, heard, loved, worthy and enough! It was a long process but I had set myself on the right road to recovery and stopped smearing honey over my pus!

I had done this to my right side my masculine side, and after I had freed my Divine Feminine side I had to address my masculine side. My spine was completely out of alignment since I had been dragging around a heavy boot prescribed by the doctor. So, there was a great schism within my spine and my inner Hara line where my masculine and feminine side join. I had been relying on Peter's masculinity to navigate the world. I had been very angry at Peter for having abandoned me! Because of my anger I had cut myself off from him and my Divine Masculinity. I was misusing my own masculine power by being angry, aggressive and forceful! My healing now lay in realizing that Peter had never left and becoming the embodiment of his Divine Masculinity.

The operation had also weakened my energetic body, lowered my vibration and the repeated covid tests had shut down my third eye and closed off my crown chakra. I use my intuition one hundred per cent of the time to navigate the world around me, but now I was blind as a bat. It was then the Universe gifted me an amazing soul named Susan. She came into my life and began helping me restore my inner balance. She was incredibly intuitive and like Gene my Dark Mentor she could communicate with Peter. I hadn't realized that I still had unresolved feelings around his death. She told me what Peter had been shouting at me but I had refused to hear. She told me he did not want to leave me but he had to go so I could become the embodiment of both of us here on Earth. She told me I had to stop feeling guilty because I could not "heal" Peter. He "died healed"! Those simple words cleared away years of pain and guilt. My healing now lay in my ability to know that Peter and I were ONE and I was to embody my divine femininity and his divine masculinity, becoming the heirogamic union of our twin souls incarnate on Earth.

After I had healed my mother wound I called my mother and told her I forgave her and asked her to forgive me. Although she could not really follow because of her dementia, I felt I needed to say this. I realized my mother was just following the karmic pattern of her mother that had been passed down through the generations. She had done the best she could to love me to the best of her ability. I also know she loves me now very much. Then, an incredible thing happened that night while I was talking to Susan. She told me she was getting a message from someone named Margaret. She did not know Margaret was my mother's name. She told me that Margaret wanted to thank me for doing what I did. I needed to hear it from another person. I also had my grandmother and great-grandmother come to me and thank me for setting them free through my own inner healing.

THE WOMAN WOUND

During the reign the Dragon Queen Goddess Guardians our planet maintained its connection to Infinite Source through the Krystala spiral. The frequencies of Oneness, unity and love prevailed and it was heaven! But the raider races of men desecrated the Goddesses' temples both externally and internally forcing them to breed their leviathan races, harnessing them with lunar overlays and banishing them to the shadowy recesses of home and hearth. If my destiny had been different and I had a husband, children and grandchildren I would probably be doing the same. But destiny took a hand and as that crazy drunken man shouted at me years ago in California, "you have no husband, no father, no son! You answer to no man!" Life has pushed me down a lonesome road to uncover my inner infinite power and true freedom as a Goddess (the embodiment of the inner hierogamic union of divine feminine and divine masculine)! I have found woman are often afraid of their power. Not just because, throughout the eons, we have been raped, burned, drowned, stoned etcetera. "If it doesn't kill you it makes you stronger" is our motto and most women are incredibly strong! I believe our woman wounds go deeper. I believe it stems from a deep seated unconscious fear of our own power. I think we women KNOW how very powerful we truly are and that if we were to unleash our power it may destroy the world! We would tumble the Dark Masculine's little man made world. Perhaps we believe that men, afraid of our power, are right in keeping us "in our place". I think this fear is subconsciously hidden behind a mother's desire to clip her daughter's wings, for fear that she like in the Greek Myth of Icarus, will fly too high and have her wings melted by the Sun.

When I visited the ancient Goddess Temples of Malta and touched the stones I became aware of a deep sense of guilt I had carried for an eternity. I had felt responsible for our planet's destruction. I believed I had let down humanity and our Mother Earth! I also carried an deep anger at myself for having failed and at my fellow sister Goddesses. I had to forgive myself, the men who had destroyed our world and my divine sisters. I had to realize it was all just part of our planet's story. I had learned much from this fall and now I was given the opportunity to reset our Planet's energetic template to the Krystala Spiral of life, which I did and reclaimed my position as a Dragon Queen Goddess Guardian of our planet's Template!

All women know that we have the ability to change the world but are we afraid of what would happen if we did? We know that as intuitive creatures, our power comes from opening ourselves as a portal to allow Infinite God Source to flow through us, to permit the Divine Feminine Force to return to its rightful place as the Goddess Guardians. Like sleeping goddesses, we have allowed our power to lie dormant and allowed ourselves to be used and abused by the misguided male energy on our fallen Earth. We have martyred ourselves lifetime after lifetime patiently waiting and hoping our male counterparts, would get it and wake up from the spell. That they would love us the way they once did and heed our wise words of council.

THE COUNCIL OF MU

Before the destruction of Tara the Council of Mu was created to restore the balance of the rift occurring between the masculine and feminine energies on our planet. The masculine energy was going down the rabbit hole experimenting outside the Law of One and God's Natural Laws due to its infection from a fallen Universe. The Wise Women of the Council of Mu tried to prevent this. We failed. This created a time loop where history continued to repeat itself each time reseting us further and further away from our true divine essence. This created a sense of guilt many women carry below the veil of consciousness which has been weaponized by the Eve Myth. The Fall of Atlantis threw and the Luciferian Rebellion that followed reset us into a dark masculine world void of the Divine Feminine. All evidence Reign of Goddess was destroyed and like sleeping beauty the Goddesses fell into a deep slumber as our world was reset into a world where the female was not permitted to fully express herself. She could not do what she does best heal, nurture and rebalance the male energy and maintain the energetic frequencies of our Mother Earth which plummeted our world into fear, despair and isolation from all that was holy. This sense of guilt and frustration caused the female energy to fragment. Women become enslaved by the moon's lunar harness forced to seek their power only through procreation or outside themselves in the men who now ruled Earth. Stripped of our solar feminine and reduced to only a lunar reflection of the masculine power we were confined to seductive, manipulative means to gain power.

But the truth is we did not fail! It was all just a divine lesson we needed to learn to better serve Infinite Source. The masculine aspect of ourselves needed to fall, to experience these lower densities and to learn what it feels like to live outside of God's Nature Laws. We needed to write our story away from the word vibration of Infinite God Source. Now, we are collectively choosing to return home to Infinite God Source. Since there is no time, then all is happening exactly as it should be, in Divine Time.

It wasn't until I made my pilgrimage to Malta and received the Dragon Key Codes (the pass key to Earth's Template) that I was able to fully heal myself and rewrite my story. Malta or Melita as it was known in Goddess times is the Isle of Honey, or Divine Plasma. This is the very heart center of the divine feminine node or dragon nodes of our Mother Earth. It is here all the Dragon Ley lines of Earth's template converge to form the Mother Dragon Egg. It is through this point the energetic template of Earth is controlled and he who controls the energetic template controls the Earth! The Parasites knew this hence the reign of Malta's Knight's Templar and its violent history: bad against bad trying always to gain control of our Earth! But the Earth's Template has been realigned to the Krystala Spiral of Life and is back in the hands of the Dragon Queen Goddess linage even though the One World Order is doing everything they can to destroy the island and its people. This was to date one of the most difficult assignment of my life times!

It is the era of the Divine Feminine! The Return of the Dragon Queen Goddesses in 2024 the Year of the Dragon! Those who can restore the balance of their divine feminine and masculine within and reclaim their dragon key codes will be the creators of the New 5D Earth. When the inner masculine and inner feminine are in energetic balance within the female part pulls in the energetic frequencies (magnetic), while the masculine part transmitts the frequencies (electric). When the divine male and divine female come together the energetic power of receiving and transmitting is amplified into the solar frequencies of a third creation or tri-wave field. (The two become three become ONE) This is a secret in successful manifestation on the matter plane, the inner male and inner female energies must be balanced, then manifestations are greatly amplified in spiritual power.

Woman are now shedding their Lunar harnesses stepping into their Solar Krystos power. We are stepping out of the old fallen dark masculine 3D Earth. It is the era of the Solar Dragon Queen Goddess the co- creators of the New Infinite Earth.

Many women have lost husbands, partners, and lovers to death or separation. They find themselves alone now because they are coming into their own power as this inner divine union of feminine and masculine and healing from the women wounds of surviving in a dark masculine world. Because it will be totally foreign to many males who have successfully navigated the old 3D Earth and are not in touch with their feminine, much less their divine feminine, this may be very frightening.

They may have trouble releasing their masculine control to their feminine side. Because of this, healed women must lead the way. Women must stop trying to fix the broken masculine world and its men. We have reached a time when ALL relationships must be for free if they are to survive. Then, watch out world! We shall see an amazing shift. This is what the dark side has feared most. Women shedding their "lunar" shackles as the reflection of men and stepping into their own power. Woman standing their ground as the Protectors of the Children, Guardians of our Mother Earth and all Creation, the True Leaders of Humanity. As we women heal the woman wound and expand our power and go beyond the finite confines of home and hearth, we will create a New Earth as Divine Infinite Feminine Energy incarnate! Our love can expand beyond family, to all humanity. We will cease looking for "equal" rights, stop waiting for male counterparts or male leaders, to resolve the problems of our planet. How can they? They are part of the fallen system that they created. They are waiting for you! You are the missing link, the fifth element. You are the Divine Feminine made Manifest! You are Infinite. Your time has come to command the Earth through the power of love! Rise and Shine Feminine Christs! Solar Females!

THE NEW CO-HEALER

"An evolved healer is the first step in restoring spiritual wellness to a dis-eased society."
PETER MONROY M.D.

Physician Heal Thyself! We cannot expect healors who have not healed themselves to heal us. This is the title of the first chapter in our book *The Pathway Home.* It is illogical to think medicine administered by wounded healers in a weaponized health care system can heal humanity. Only healed healers can "assist" others in their own healing. These will be the new "co-healers" of the Infinite Earth. In order to ascend to the fifth dimension, Star Seeds must heal all their traumas, wounds, collective miasma and shadows present in all four natures. We must clear away the pus of the pain and suffering we have experienced during our many lifetimes on this fallen 3D Earth. We cannot expect any true healing to come within the corrupted finite systems of modern medicine, where the patient passively submits to its tyrannical mandates administered by wounded healers. True healing can only occur when each individual takes full responsibility for his or her own body, mind and soul.

DEATH

Death is merely a transformation from one form into another. When this time comes and it will come to all, it needs to be done in a loving and peaceful way as possible. The individual needs to be given the opportunity to finish up any unfinished business, say good bye to loved ones, and begin the transition which may take several weeks. There are many souls who assist each person as they release their life force through the process of death. This process includes severing the silver cords and collecting the soul parts to free the soul in their passage through Mother Arch. When a soul experiences trauma it fragments the soul and binds them to the lower planes. This is why the Birth and Death environments of transition are so key and you want to make them as peaceful, nurturing and loving as possible. Currently most health care systems do not even allow loved ones to visit the patient or be present at the moment of death. Patients are often in a very cold, harsh environment sedated on drugs and hooked up to machines. I understand that death is a very emotionally charged area in all our lives but we need to begin to release the finite belief around it and shift the paradigm. This can only happen as we learn to face our own death and fully release all the fear which has been conjured up around it. Peter was helping me do that.

THE ASCENSION OF MY MOTHER

You died on a Sunday, August 14, 2022, at 3:33 a.m. You were alone in your room but I WAS THERE WITH YOU! Peter and I were on either side and we shared our plasma bodies with you building up yours for the journey HOME. When you were ready we boarded the "limo" and Peter drove us. I held your hand as we arrived at the spiral crystal rainbow bridge LEADING BACK HOME. I bid you farewell and Peter drove off escorting you through the Arc back Home. In my bedroom in Sicily I had been holding your life essence in my hand all during this and at the moment you crossed over I felt your faint life pulse dim then extinguish and I knew you were gone. I knew I would never see you alive again although I had been waiting five years for that moment. I had hoped to embrace you one more time and gaze on your loving face. But suddenly I know it was ok. Everything had happened just as it was supposed to. I called the nursing home and the nurse on the floor confirmed the time of your death as being when you crossed over with Peter. My dear friend Susan remotely viewed your arrival on Tara. She told me you were dancing with Peter and wearing a purple dress. I didn't get to say good bye to you in the physical but when I finally arrived in the US and made my way into the funeral parlor I stood before the casket gazing down at the empty vessel that had contained your gentle spirit and saw you were wearing a purple sweater and I knew that your soul at long last had been freed from this prison matrix! Hallelujah!

Although our relationship like many mother daughter relationships had been tainted with the ancestral miasma of what I call the Thothian Curse. I had managed to heal that right before your death freeing our royal grail lineage which enabled your ascension. It was extremely painful and deep work going to the root of the pain and sexual misery that has cursed the sacred angelic celtic druid female grail lines who held the higher genetics. These women were then raped and forced to bear children an offspring engineered to destroy the angelic human race like Rosemary's baby these woemn knew that they held a demonic seed within their womb. Even when they hoped to love their children into holiness they found that their sons were taken from them at birth and raised to be warriors and to hate their own mothers. This broke the woman's heart and soul causing them to become dominated by the fallen dark masculine. But perhaps the worst curse was that we began to hate our own children and even worse our own inner divine child and our inner masculine side. All this must be healed so we can take our place as true royalty and return ourselves to our place of power within!

I had spent 2020 doing everything humanly possible to be a truth sayer, and to expose the Satanic One World Order Agenda. I had suffered greatly. One day, while I was hobbling around on my crutches with a mask on so I could go inside a store and buy something I needed, a fat Sicilian woman accosted me because my mask was not covering my nose. I began fighting back with my crutch! My dear friend, Serena, came to my rescue and laughed as she told me I reminded her of "Enrico Totti", an Italian War Hero who led his troops into battle with one leg and a raised crutch! Sometimes, you just have to stand up for yourself... even if you only have one crutch.

My injury was teaching me to stand my ground and to stay grounded moving forward very slowly by carefully placing one foot in front of the other. This simple act is something I had never done! It also made me realize I couldn't change people. I couldn't "red" pill people who did not want to see the truth even if it was staring them in the face. It was not worth my own inner peace to try and wake people up who didn't want to be awakened. I realized the only person I can change is me and I would change my world by changing myself. As children we did what our parents taught us to do. As teenagers, we rebelled against our parents by doing the opposite. As adults we must discover our own unique way of being. Then we must have the courage to be our authentic selves and stand our ground no matter what. We must become Alchemists transmuting everything around us, through the power of love. I had developed the ability to SEE through the scams of our times and passed the tests by overcoming my fears and having the courage to speak out and live my truth. I was free! I could stand my ground when needed and become an alchemist, transmuting the world of illusion with the inner light of truth.

MY MALTESE MISSION: RETURN OF THE DRAGON QUEEN GODDESS TO MALTA

In 2024 Kiki and I set sail for Malta. I had been "sent" there and was none to happy about it. I would much rather have gone back to the warm beaches of the Yucatan to co create New Earth Communities but there I was with my car in the belly of a great ship on my way to Valletta! When I arrived I was ecstatic about reawakening the Goddess within me! I was thrilled to reclaim my "home turf"! I first visited the Hypogeum an ancient subterranean honeycomb complex which contained acoustic healing chambers mysteriously carved out of ancient limestones. One of the chambers was called the Oracle Room where a voice set in a certain tone would carry that vibration throughout the entire honey comb structure. Another chamber called the Holiest of Holies had (Krystala) Spirals painted in red orchid on the ceiling, a theme which was repeated throughout all the Goddess temples. I toned my KRYSTALA Spiral in the Hypogeum chambers to the shock of the Maltese staff. This sacred space is heavily guarded and must be booked months in advance. A propaganda narration is given throughout the entire trip into the caves which covers up the mysterious findings and events surrounding this ancient archeological site. The priest who originally began the excavation mysteriously died and all his work was confiscated. He was replaced by a British Archaeologist. Countless stories were fabricated to deny any "alien" skulls that were rumored to have been found there. When I asked the staff when were they would excavate the rest of the site they looked at me shocked emphatically denying the existence of any other chambers. I think we both knew that further excavation would reveal to the world the true cosmic history of our Earth.

I visited other amazing Goddess temples on Malta and Gozo where I found massive limestone megaliths creating framed doorways with Krystala Spirals carved deeply into the stones. These massive limestone megaliths hold frequencies. There were also massive sculptures of Goddesses that had shattered to pieces. One of the most famous artifacts was called "The Sleeping Goddess" which was thrown into a pit at the Hypogeum. As I touched the stones of these ancient temples memories poured into my mind. Visions of the "good ol' days" when the Goddesses maintained the energetic frequencies and connection of our Earth in alignment with Divine Infinite Source through devotional toning rituals . Each of these megalithic temples held a multitude of doorways and chambers which served as portals into the higher dimensions of the God Source Worlds. The Goddess would enter these worlds through these carefully positioned chambers that held the perfect "arch angle" allowing encrypted live streams of energetic information to be downloaded.

THE TRUE HIDDEN HISTORY OF MALTA

Malta is a portal or entry point where the ley lines of our earth's template all converge. This Portal gives those who control it access to Earth's template or the energetic field of our planet. Hence The Knight's Templar were one of the many factions that controlled the Earth by taking control of Malta. This is why every power on Earth has tried to conquer Malta. Malta now a tiny little rock in the middle of the Mediterranean, is all that remains of The Land of MU a vast continent on pre- Earth Tara. With the destruction of Tara and it's fragmentation this power point became part of Lemuria. It was once again held by the Goddesses the true Guardians of our planet who did their best to keep the eternal flame of divinity sparked by maintaining the ley line grid structure or template of our planet in alignment with Infinite God Source and all the fragmented parts of Tara. This helped to heal and maintain the resonance of Earth in the high frequencies of unity consciousness. But the raider races came and destroyed the Goddess temples and statues and raped the women guardians creating their Leviathan Annunaki offspring to serve as raider races. Malta fell and our earth's ley lines were polluted with negativity. Fear, grief death and powerlessness infected our planets energetic template. Dead bodies were thrown into these sacred chambers to promote the death cults control. This is how the parasites maintained their control over our planet. He who controls the energetic holographic template of a thing controls that thing.

It was then my pilgrimage turned into a nightmare. I began to recall all the pain, grief, sorrow and guilt I had hidden deep within my soul about losing our Mother Earth and watching her desecrated by the fallen angelics and their raider races. I began to feel this in my body as a deep dark emptiness took hold. I had only felt this once before when I lost Peter. I was severely attached and became very ill. A Maltese Doctor to whom I had given a copy of our book The Pathway Home came to visit me. He had wanted to discuss the book but found me in bed too ill to even sit up. He checked me out and said that I was being attacked energetically! To which I responded, " Ya think?"

I began to see the very dark side of Malta which had become a "smart" island overcrowded with foreigners from third world countries there only to make money. The island had been destroyed by concrete jungles covering up the archeological evidence of our true history. There was barely a patch of green left on the entire island. The island had become a death trap with very little alternative healing solutions or nature to ground yourself from the 5G matrix. Kiki and I were under the most massive attack I have ever experiences. A.I. mixed with black magic rituals forced me into my bed every time I had completed a key part of my mission. Factions of those who still served the parasites continued to perform their dark rituals in these sacred sites at night. Now their rituals were directed at the new intruder...me! Their black magic laced with A.I. was used to launch a full blown attack on my third eye complex.

At last I managed to reconnect and reboot up all the ancient KRYSTALA Spirals in the Goddess temples and charge them up inside the hypogeum. After I did that I fell ill again and it wasn't until I was watching the Movie Billy Jack and listening to the song "One Tin Solider" that I finally had my cathartic release. I sat up in bed and let out a loud deep pain ridden scream from the depths of my soul. I don't know how long I screamed I was outside my body observing myself . All the aeons of pain, guilt, and sorrow were pouring out. I had been alchemizing all the trauma held in Earth's ley lines. I felt it purging from my body. Then I was able to finally complete my mission.

I had been renting a huge ancient limestone palace and lived mostly in the underground section. I needed to be there to connect the dots in the Earth's subterranean ley lines. During a profound meditation I felt the Krystal River Rainbow plasma pour through my body into Earth's ley lines from Aquinos. I anchored them into Earth's template clearing out the toxicity. Then Earth's ley lines were superimposed with the fragmented piece of Tara in Andromeda called Urtha which still held the divine holographic blueprint of our true Mother Earth. This divine blueprint melded into Earth's ley lines imprinting her divine structure into our Earth's Grids. This moment was monumental and Peter's brilliant smile shone through! I knew then I had accomplished my mission here in Malta! Our Earth's template had been restored to its divine holographic blueprint. It would take linear time but Earth would regather her fragmented pieces and resurrect herself as whole or the holy embodiment of her true divine essence! It had almost killed me and Kiki but we had done our small part! Earth's energetic template was fully positioned onto the Krystal Organic timeline of ascension back home to Infinite God Source!

MY REWRITTEN STORY

Peter and I came to this time matrix on assignment long long ago from another Time Matrix. We became embroiled in the story here, lost in the plot. We suffered greatly but learned so very much about the fallen aspect of creation. I FORGIVE all who have played the roles of persecutor and I FORGIVE myself! Forgiveness is such a blessing and only through forgiveness can we experience true freedom. I release all hurt, guilt, blame, shame, pain, fear and unworthiness. I LOVE MYSELF! I no longer play the victim, the martyr, the rescuer, the persecutor! I AM FREE! I AM INFINITE! I free myself from the shackles the lunar female and restore my inner GOD-DESS. My twin soul and I are ONE, the eternal embodiment of Divine Masculine and Divine Feminine. I celebrate my life here and now grounded in my Mother Earth! My power is in my love. I live my soul mission with passion every moment! My words are healing, transmuting and activating souls to embrace their soul mission and BE THE CHANGE. The New Consciousness Renaissance has begun! When I have finished my soul mission here on Earth I will rejoin Peter where we shall step through the portal of no time and return HOME!

CHAPTER 22

THE NEW INFINITE EARTH

There is emerging on the face of the Earth a New Human ...an INFINITE HUMAN and the human is YOU!

THE NEW CONSCIOUSNESS RENAISSANCE

Over five hundred years ago, painters, poets, writers, philosophers, humanitarians and alchemists steered our world out of the Dark Ages and into the Light of the Renaissance. This "rebirth" of classical wisdom gave way to Neoplatonic thought. In Ancient Greece, Plato taught that the purpose of all Art was to reflect infinite beauty, truth, and wisdom. That all artists should first seek to attain this world of perfection within, then transmit it through their Art. This age was filled with beauty, creativity, and the idea that each human possesses a divine spark of the Infinite Creator within. Great Artists expressed this divine creative spark through their artwork, literature, science, architecture, inventions which they left for all the world to behold. Love, freedom, and the search for the Infinite were the defining values of the Renaissance. Love was understood primarily as a platonic way to rise to the perfection and contemplation of God. According to Marsilio Ficino, "Love is the Work of God in the World." These were the ideals striving to break through the Dark Machiavellian World of conspiracies, and blood baths. Likewise, in our world today, the Light of Truth is breaking through the lies and deceptions that have held humanity hostage. The power goes to those who awaken from the dream spell. Those who first awaken will be the Creators of the New Consciousness Renaissance and will co create our future.

The New Infinite Earth Builders will be the artists, painters, poets, writers, healers, inventors and visionaries who are not distracted by the current narratives running on our finite 3D Earth. These spiritually mature Infinite Human Beings will not wait for someone or something outside of themselves to take care of things, but will roll up their sleeves and create a world they want to live in! The New 5D Earth will be populated by Infinite Human Beings who have freed themselves from the scripted dramas and finite illusions of the 3D World and can focus on their creations! This New Consciousness Renaissance, unlike the past one, will not be based on ancient scriptures, documents, bibles, tablets and external sources of information which can be co-opted to misdirect individuals from the Truth. Rather, it will be founded on each person's direct connection to Infinite God Source within. The information will come from INFINITE SOURCE born from the soul, the heart and every Infinite Human Being who has ascended to their own freedom within. They will be, as Plato wrote, "individuals who attain this world of perfection within." One by one, as each human awakens to the Infinite within themselves, this expanded awareness will pick up speed like a massive snowball! There will be no stopping it! This time the Dark Side will not be able to corrupt that which is pure and created in the higher frequencies of truth.

As you awaken from the Dream Spell and have the courage to face and transmute your deepest fears, wounds, traumas, and the Cosmic Rage of your shadow self, you will clear the way for the power of Infinite Source to flow through you! You will be victorious over the Dark Side! This is the only battle that needs to be fought, the battle within. As you transform your inner world, your outer world will also transform. You do not have to fight your fellow human beings, the cabal, demons or the Dark Side! The only demons you need to face are those within you. You must overcome them through the power of love, by loving them ...to death. Once you are free from the shadows that pull you into the lower density of the World of Illusion and Duality you can reclaim your infinite power! You have the ability to create your optimal self and your optimal future. You can take back the magic pen and write your own life story.

Perhaps all your life, you have felt like an outcast, a misplaced person, a misfit, an ugly duckling? Perhaps you have hidden your special gifts and talents even your supernatural abilities for fear of persecution, ridicule or just being "different"? You may now find yourself alone having drifted away from partners, friends, colleagues and family. This is because you have outgrown them and like the ugly duckling it is time to become a Swan! You have been a caterpillar scaling the caterpillar pitter-patter ladder leading nowhere. Now you may find yourself alone, cocooning into the beautiful butterfly you were created to be! Many of the caterpillars you know will choose to remain caterpillars, but you, Great Infinite One, are morphing into that beautiful butterfly that embraces its freedom! As you identify more and more with the Infinite, the false timelines will collapse around you and your past as well as your future will change. Your memories about people, places even events may also change. You may begin to identify more with your future self that exists in higher dimensional worlds and beyond! You may be morphing so rapidly your appearance may change drastically from one moment to the next. You may not even recognize yourself. Not to worry, you are not losing yourself. You are finding yourself, the true authentic you! You may need time alone to develop your supernatural gifts and multidimensional nature that has lain dormant or been repressed by you. As you uncover your divine creative sparkle within, everything you create will come from your soul and be birthed with love. As you embody more and more of the Infinite God Source Frequencies you will create a ripple of change around you. All who come in contact with you will be uplifted. You will be a pebble of truth and your ripples will affect great change in the World. You will be the change you want to see in the world! You will be a beacon of truth an eternal living light. You will be Cosmic Sovereign Law made manifest! You will be part of the solution rather than the problem.

As you awaken from the Dream Spell you will regain full memory of all your past lives or your alternate identities. You will recall the Golden Age of Atlantis and Lemuria before the Fall. You may remember lifetimes on other planets, in other star systems! You will have future memories of what it is like to live in a world of harmony and unity based on the Law of One. You can use those future memories to beam steer yourself and humanity out of the rumble of the collapsing 3D Earth and beyond the seduction of the AI false ascension matrix. You can remember a time when the Divine Masculine and Divine Feminine resided in perfect harmony within us all, a time when human beings lived in harmony with Mother Earth, one another, and respected the God Sovereign Freedom of all Creation. A time when Crystalline Consciousness Technology worked in accordance with God's Natural Laws and served our own inner divine technology. When Infinite

Human Beings co-created with other Infinite Human Beings, empowering the creativity and unique expression of one another. You can follow the beam Home to a place where love is the currency and self-discovery the motive for all commerce. Where inter galactic commerce and cultural exchange thrive. Where love, joy and bliss are our natural state of being. Where we are both grounded in the soil of our Mother Earth yet fully realized in our multidimensional nature. This is not a fairytale. This is the true reality. These visions are past and future memories. Now it is up to you to remember your future and make it so.

Many of you may be creating a future based on FEAR. Fear of losing your job, your livelihood. Many of these jobs that you have slaved away day and night do not honor your passion, creativity, uniqueness or your soul's purpose. You have been selling your soul for a few pieces of silver, betraying the Christ within you. Each day the broken finite 3D Earth created by demonic forces to enslave the Christ within us demands more and more ownership over you to participate in it. You may want to ask yourself this question... which Earth do I want to be a part of? Do you want to continue to be part of the old broken Earth that has enslaved you? How much more freedom are you willing to give away to continue to fit into this ever increasingly finite cage? Is it worth it? Will you choose to feel stuck, trapped and give away your power simply out of fear? Or will you find the courage, creativity and faith it takes to step out of this finite story? Will you choose to be the Hero in your own life story? Will you be a lion among the sheep and awaken to your power within? Will you reclaim your royalty! It is time to stop living the lie and subsisting within finite societal structures of tyranny that limit your infiniteness and douse your brilliant divine creative sparkle. Why would you want to give up all rights over your body, mind and soul to subsist within these broken structures? If you have learned anything from this journey dear reader and from the full disclosure which I have bestowed upon you, I hope you have begun to realize that the world you previously thought of as reality is a put-up job created to contain your infinite consciousness in a finite prison. I hope the tyrannical events taking place on our Earth now serve as a wake-up call to inspire you to free yourself from this prison matrix by refusing to comply, participate and feed the controllers' dark agenda. I hope my words will awaken you to the

Infinite God Source that lies within you and to use your power to become the hand of Infinite God Source and co-create a New Infinite Earth, where dreams do come true!

The definition of insanity is doing the same thing over and over and expecting a different result. If we want things to go back to normal so we can do what we did before, how will anything ever change? What would happen if people stopped feeding these finite Earth systems? What if you began withdrawing your energy from a world that no longer wants you? This is where your true power lies. What if you got small, lived simply, became self-sufficient and autonomous so you could hear the whispers of Divine Infinite Source in your ear? What if this whisper guided you to true abundance, the true riches of the soul? This may not happen overnight. You may need to pass small tests of faith slowly extinguishing your inner demons as you extract yourself day by day from the prison matrix. Fear is the mind killer and the controllers' means of exerting power over you. Faith is the bridge that carries you to the inner knowingness of Truth! " Oh Ye of little Faith!" It will be those who have faith, faith in themselves, faith in Divine Infinite Source and faith in the Divine Plan that will become the Founders of the New Infinite Earth.

Do not give your power to any future that has been "spelled" out to create an artificial reality of dependency, doom and disaster. Do not write any words in your story that do not enlighten, uplift, and bring you closer to the Word Frequency which IS God, the power of Infinite God Source within you! You are creating our own reality! You are writing your own story word by word! You are bringing into manifestation the word which IS God with the two most powerful words ever uttered: I AM. Are you writing I am afraid, I am powerless, I am worthless or are you writing, I am powerful, I am love, I am Infinite?

If the doors to the finite broken world are closing there are better ones opening. Stop banging on closed doors demanding that they open. Follow your inner guidance to a new door that is opening into the higher dimensions. Stop wasting your precious time and energy trying to be part of a world that you have outgrown. You are Infinite! Use your infinite creativity to create a better world! You are a Swan! Why do you want to

at you, knowing your own inner power comes from your connection to Infinite Source! You will cease to fall prey to the consciousness trap of "Problem/ Reaction/ Solution" created by the controllers to herd the masses into their "pre-packaged" solutions. So take a moment to ask yourself these questions: Are you reacting to the world around you from a place of fear, blindly obeying illogical laws? Are you afraid of what others think? Are you letting family, friends, employers, doctors, the government, modern medicine decide your future for you? Are you responding like a frightened child making poor choices? Or are you thinking for yourself? Are you gathering information using discernment and intuition to come to your own higher understanding and awareness? Each person must take responsibility for their own life, reclaim their own inner power, and create their own future.

What if everyone on this Earth became self-responsible? It would end the tyrannical rule of the controllers. They cannot control you if you do not give them control. So, in order to stop being scammed, you must stop giving away your power to anything outside of yourself. Once you can SEE the system is controlling you, take action to stop letting it control you. Respond by finding creative alternatives. This does not have to happen overnight but you can begin to make little changes that lead to big ones! If you realize that the food you are buying is poisoning you, grow your own, if the water you are drinking is polluted, make your own. If your home or your environment is making you sick, move! It is time we all need to take responsibility for our own health. We can no longer turn over our power blindly trusting Doctors who no longer honor their sacred Hippocratic Oath or hospitals being paid to be factories of death stamping out cures of weaponized bio-technology. We need new healed, whole or holy healers, who make others responsible for their own health. We need to take responsibility for our health by creating healthy toxic-free lifestyles in toxic free environments. Creating healthy alkalized bodies where disease cannot take hold. We need to take responsibility for our Mother Earth, by becoming the Rainbow Warriors who heal and "make her green again!" We need to take responsibility for our own organic ascension. We need to use technology responsibly and stop funding corporations that are manufacturing instruments of genocide. In the beginning, it may seem difficult to let go of old-world structures, but look at the green lights rather than the stop lights. How exciting to be part of the creation of something new, holy, sustainable and infinite! In truth, as you ascend these old broken systems that carry the low frequencies of disharmony they will no longer feel good to you or your organic body. You will long for people, places and things that are in harmony with nature, Infinite Source, the Law of One and the higher frequencies of God's Natural Laws.

THE SOLUTION

You are the solution! Like the Healer who has properly diagnosed the dis-ease, it is time to stop focusing on the problem and find the solution, the Cure. If you keep running around telling people how bad the world is, then you like the problem and you are feeding it. Those awakening to the dis-eased state of our world must find the solutions. They must be the bridge builders between the old finite 3D Earth to the New Infinite 5D Earth. Divide and Conquer is the main weapon of the controllers. Unity is their enemy; love is their poison. Love unifies. They maintain their control over humanity simply through illusion. Break through the illusion by SEEING the strings and understanding how they manipulate you. Rise above the illusion of duality and then DO THINGS DIFFERENTLY. True rebellion does not come from anger, from attacking your fellow human being, or crying like a baby wanting someone to change things for you! You create your own reality so if you want things to change, change yourself. Change your world. When you realize how powerful you are and stop giving away your energy to the wrong people, places and things, you will, like the Cherokee fable starve the "Bad Wolf and feed the Good Wolf". You will stop feeding these greedy satanic fallen systems and create new solutions. Start small by planting "seeds of change" in a small patch of Mother Earth, where you can heal and restore her soil with love, creating a garden in harmony with and all creation, including your fellow human beings. If you need to stand up for yourself in order to clear away some weeds, fine. Do so with the power of love!

TRUE LEADERS:

A particularly interesting part of the Hopi prophecy relates to the choosing of leaders. According to the story, "a leader will not be the one that talks the loudest, boasts of successes, or has the support of the elite. Leaders will be those whose actions speak the loudest, the ones that have demonstrated wisdom and courage and have proven that they work for the benefit of all." Most people who want to be leaders now are coming from a place of ego. They have not done their own inner work and just want to be in the spotlight. You must begin to trust yourself as your own authority. Do not give your power away to people who talk the good talk and say the right words but are not the real things; to aggressive charismatic speakers of the False Parent architect! Many of the champions of the people emerging now, who have the microphone and "talk loudly" are "talking the talk", but are they "walking the walk"? You must ask yourself if they have had the courage to look within? To expose the lies they have been telling themselves? Have they had the courage and the humility to fully "Know Thyself," and to "Thine Own Self Be True"? The key to a true leader is the degree to which they can be honest with themselves. To have the courage to look at themselves profoundly and heal all the lies within. To practice self-love, self-respect and self-honesty. To take responsibility for their actions and the consequences of their actions and demonstrate honesty and integrity.

"The beginning is the end, and the end is the beginning." Many great souls are here on Earth now to help with this SHIFT. But many of you may feel home sick, soul weary, and tired of the insanity of humanity. You may long to go HOME. You may be a star seed who feels like you want to "leave" the planet and return to your home in the stars. You may identify with the Sirian, Pleiadian, Arcturian, Andromedan, Lyran, Vegan, Orion, or other star systems. You may have spent life times in several of these places as well as fallen star systems or parralle time matrixes. You may be a Krystos Star Seed who has come to Earth with a unique Star Seed mission to assist in Earth's ascension. Many Krystos Star Seeds are from the higher God Sources Worlds and have experienced many incarnations both on Earth and in many different star systems. Just as I am an American living in Italy but have lived all over this Earth, in this life and other lives, you too may have traveled the Cosmos. You may be receiving help from your Star Seed families in these star systems. But the show is here on Earth. NOW! Why? Because Earth is the pivotal point that is now determining the future for everyone. All eyes are upon you! You agreed to be here now for the shift. As our Earth ascends like an axis on a great cosmic wheel we synthesize our neighboring planets and star systems. So now is not the time to wistfully gaze up at the stars, like ET longing to go Home. Nor is it a time to fantasize about traveling to Mars in a space ship or await the return of aliens who will save you! They want to be on Earth! You are an Infinite Multidimensional Human Being! Everyone has a job and everyone is depending on you to do yours!

I have lived all over the world. I did this because it was my call of service to humanity and our Earth. I did it as part of my tour of duty to SEE how truly broken the systems are in every country, every culture, every corner of this 3D Earth. As I navigated the systems penetrating the upper layers of power I always ran into the same dark cesspool of greed, ego and tyranny. Like many I was secretly searching for Shangri La, hoping the grass would be greener on the other side. But it never was. With time, each new paradise deteriorated as the corruption became exposed. I learned an important lesson, "wherever you go... there you are"! You bring yourself and all your dirty baggage! It wasn't until I hurt my foot and was unable to run away that I finally realized that true spirituality comes from healing all within! Opening up all your suitcases and airing them out in the light of day. Scrubbing what needs to be cleaned and throwing out everything that no longer serves you. Only then can you clear away your own weeds, and create a paradise within where you can then plant yourself into the fertile soil of 5D Earth. Then you can create your own Shangri La. "The Kingdom of Heaven (you seek) is within". Wherever you are it begins and ends with you!

As the Old 3D Earth crumbles giving way to the 5D Earth the Dark Finite Side is busy spinning their Artificial AI Meta verse around you daily. This is a web of AI weaponized technology now encapsulating our Organic Earth with the goal of herding society into their false finite ascension matrix to populate it. This War of Consciousness is over you! Your soul is the data they want to lay claim to and upload your consciousness into an AI (Artificial Intelligence) Digital Twin Avatar. Although the incoming artificial technology may appear to be the ascension humanity has long awaited offering interconnectedness, enhanced intelligence, biotech healing modalities, even immortality it is a false ascension matrix and a poor imitation of the true you and your divine inner technology which will activate as you ascend daily.

BIFURCATION OF TIME

Dolores Canon and many others have talked about the Earth's timelines splitting and forming two Earths. These two Earths exist now! You are choosing every day with your daily actions which Earth you give your precious energy to. The New Infinite 5D Earth by remaining organic and ascending in frequency as you assimilate more and more of the light activations from our sun(s) and the protonic belt bio- syncing as you reset to the Infinite on the Krystala Spiral of Life? Or will you cling to the past being passively herded into a false ascension matrix and a bad finite Artifical copy of the Earth? One Earth requires inner healing, transmutation from the lower densities into the higher 5D frequencies. The other Earth requires passively allowing external forces shape your reality as you are passively transhumanized, surrendering your body, mind and soul. One Earth takes you Home to the Freedom of Infinite Source. The other pulls you down into Universes to be fed upon by parasites. One requires you to surrender your finite conception of yourself in order to realize that you are Infinite God Source, all that is, ever has been and ever shall be! The other requires you to relinquish your soul and your free will to a hive mind where your consciousness is controlled by a finite reality that has permanently closed off all exit points and trapped you into the Möbius strip of a META Verse time loop prison! These are the two choices spelled out. 5G or 5D? Choose Wisely!

The Dark Side's job is to seduce, glamour and scam you out of the real deal of organic ascension and into using your "free will" to choose their bad copy. My job is simply to give you full disclosure so you can make an informed decision. Many of you are facing the devastating realization that many of your friends, family and loved ones may not be choosing the Ascending Earth Door at this time. Because you are a heart based loving star seeds this maybe causing you great pain. You may want to follow them as they fall, sacrificing yourself for them. You have done this many, many, many times and it does not work. You cannot save anyone. You must honor their free will! But you may need to learn that for yourself... again and again and again. The choice is and always has been yours and yours ALONE!

Many of you are feeling called to move from cities due to the ever growing restrictions and toxic frequencies seeking clean pristine places in nature that are protected areas with natural buffers. This may be an oasis away from damaging radiation and bio weaponry now inside our fellow human beings. You may long to create or be part of a peaceful community on 5D Earth. Or perhaps you have found it! These are places Great Ones have set aside for us, eons ago before the Fall for the times we have now entered! Many of these Great Ones knew this time would come and this land has been protected throughout the Eons to serve as fertile soil for Star Seeds to be planted. You need only follow the bread crumbs. Ah but here's the rub. It may not look like much to you at first because it has been kept pristine for you outside of space and time. The energy will feel much different and will require you to check all your 3D baggage at the door to reside there. It will not have all the bells and whistles of the latest iPhone, smart car, smart house or smart city! It will not do everything for you. You will have to "do it yourself"! You will have to create it yourself! You will have to roll up your sleeves to create something NEW in the higher dimensions. Only those who have proven their worth will be able to BE there. They must endure the tests of faith, perseverance and the willingness to LET GO of old finite identities to reclaim the rewards of their birth right as Infinite Human Beings. *The Path Way Home* is always the road less traveled. Only the few who are called to be the builders of the New Infinite 5D Earth, who have faith, vision, and perseverance, will heed the call. Those who do may have to go it alone for a while...until they realize they have never been alone but ALLONE! There is always HELP! And IF YOU BUILD IT THEY WILL COME! If you can let go of the relationships that are no longer serving you, you will clear away the dead space for your new family, your soul tribe who will resonate with your higher frequency. You will find a place where you are celebrated, not tolerated!

I have spent my life trying to change the course of history, standing up against Tyranny, speaking the truth and trying to stop the weaponization of modern medicine. I believe it was a necessary karmic step that we all have to go through. I regret nothing because I know in my soul I did everything in my power to "awaken" others and serve as a catalyst for change. But many souls are not ready for ascension. They will need a crutch to limp along until they are ready to "walk the walk". All souls eventually return HOME like a river to the Sea. In their own divine time. As of 2023 the Fibonnacci 3D Earth timeline has spilt from the Krystala Spiral of 5D Earth which takes us back home into alignment with Infinite Source. Like two horses some of us have a foot on one horse and a foot on the other as we serve as a bridge between the two Earths. But every day you will be choosing more and more which reality you will feed by doing your inner healing and building your foundation on truth, love and unity consciousness. Those who build on the Krystala Spiral time line as inscribed on the Hopi Prophecy Rock will experience eternal life, true abundance, and bliss. Those who continue to hold onto the old Fibonnacci Spiral will experience povery of mind, soul and material. Their lives will become more and more bleak void of life, love and spiritual fullfillment. I do not know how much longer these two Earths will continue to exist side by side. But the time has come to populate the new 5D Earth and create infrastructures outside the old 3D paradigms. To create counter cultures free from the parasites of the Old World. Many of the builders of the New Infinite 5D Earth are being called to provide the foundation on the New 5D Earth to serve as a place where souls can come to heal, recharge and recalibrate and eventually populate as they transmute.

When the shift is finished and the split occurs the controllers will be evicted because Earth's Frequency will be too high for them to maintain their parasitic hold. Then 5D Earth will shed the parasitic AI web like a snake sheds its skin. The Artificial Web will take with them all the souls they have laid claim to who have not healed themselves of their patented genetic Bio-technological 666 Mark of the Beast, Enki overlays and Metatronic reversals. Those who choose greed and technology over spirit our Mother Earth and respect for all life. Those who choose the artificial AI replica of 3D Earth in a fallen Meta Verse will slowly lose all touch with anything outside of their "meta" experience. They will think they are in the "real" world but they will be asleep in an AI virtual dream. Perhaps they will believe they have been raptured as their consciousness is uploaded into their new (AI) heaven on earth where "There will be no more death, no mourning, no pain, for the old order of things has passed away and everything is made new," in an AI META verse!

The good news is that as the 5D Earth is released from the hold of the parasitic AI controllers we will experience an enormous acceleration of in ascension consciousness. This is why it is important to prepare by purifying your body, mind and spirit. At that point our Divine technology will come online. The Golden Age will begin! It will be a time of great celebration. I do not tell you these things to incite fear or so you will wait for this day like some great event whose coming is foretold. I tell you this so you can begin to prepare yourself NOW! There is much to do! So do not waste your precious energy being distracted by the show or mourning that which is no more. Our Mother Earth needs you to assist in her ascension seeds of change need to be planted, self-sufficient homes and communities in harmony with the Law of One need to be created! Don't remain stuck like crabs in a barrel. You must climb out of the matrix and find the higher ground so you can serve as an anchor for those trying to climb onto the New 5D Earth! This is your Mission should you decide to accept it!

Now it is up to you to choose what kind of world you want to create. As each of you come into your own personal consciousness renaissance, you will lay claim to your birthright as the Guardians and Sacred Keepers of our planet, our Mother Earth, and all her creation. You will be the pioneers, the vanguard, the Founders, the key builders, the Rainbow Warriors of the New Infinite Earth. You will be the leaders of the New Consciousness Renaissance who will in turn create more leaders!

I have pointed out how clever these Archon masters of trickery are and how they have scammed you in the past into living their story. Knowledge is power. Freedom is using it. My job is not to tell you what to do. Then, I would be no better than those who seek to control you. Your job now is to take only what resonates and use what knowledge serves you best to set yourself free, reclaim your power, your birthright, and your rightful place in the cosmos and as Guardians of our Mother Earth. As you do so, others will follow, and like the hundredth monkey syndrome, when one monkey starts washing their fruit, so does another, and another, and all over the planet we will have fruit washing monkeys! What if every human being finally realized their infinite power within? It all starts and ends with you. Every Star Seed comes to Earth with a Star Seed Mission encoded within their DNA. As you awaken and activate your twelve strands of DNA you recover your memories and your mission here on Earth. As you do this you are funded by the Universe! Your manifestation abilities augment and you will be unstoppable! You will remember the Divine Plan and your part in this PLAN. We will all remember our story, a script written many eons ago that we all chose to participate in. We chose our parts based on our unique gifts, talents, passions and what brought us bliss. We each have a job and as we the awakened Krystos Star Seeds come together we will be like pieces of a divine puzzle perfectly falling into place. The Divine Plan will be realized as we join together in Infinite God Source. It is time to activate your divine blueprint and embrace your soul mission! You star seeds are premium divine seeds! You are the true gold, the real wealth, the richest resource of our Earth! You are so incredibly powerful! I know this and the dark side knows this too, which is why they are doing everything in their power to distract you from becoming what they fear most, fully realized Infinite Human Beings! Your coming together to form projects, create communities, solve problems, educate others, reclaim the spiritual sciences will bring about their demise. All the Multiverse is looking to you! Powerful change always begins small. One step at a time.

> " If you want your dream to grow take your time go slowly. Small beginnings, greater endings, heart-felt work is holy."
> DONOVAN. BROTHER SUN SISTER MOON

Do not let your consciousness be trapped by the black-magic money curse. Ask Infinite Source to help you to be of the highest service in the ascension of yourself, humanity, Mother Earth, and all Creation and to provide you with whatever you need to complete your soul mission, then follow the directions you are given. Take the help! As you develop faith, trust, and dedicate yourself more and more to Infinite Source miracles will happen and you will truly be taken care of. As you allow Infinite Source to guide you no matter how crazy or scary, or unfamiliar, it may seem you will reap rewards beyond the banksters' finite fake-monetary system of scarcity! As you follow this extraordinary path, life becomes amazing, fun, comical, and challenging at times, but never boring. So, stop playing it safe! Safe is boring. Stretch your wings and fly and let the winds of spirit carry you into the higher dimensions! Do not be afraid to embrace your uniqueness and speak your truth in a world gone mad or to be perceived as the crazy one. In an insane asylum, it is the sane one who seems crazy. Stop taking your cues from the outside world. Stop listening to spiritual teachers, gurus, politicians, world leaders, media icons, religious texts, and prophecies. They are all part of the fallen system. Go to the Source! Get your information by turning inward and connecting directly with Infinite Source within. If you are attacked, shunned, evicted or cast out, great! Stop wasting your precious energy on the wrong people! Stop fighting! Only children who do not know their own power fight. You are Infinite! The dark side is helping you by expelling you from its broken systems so you can create your own! If you have to inject yourself with toxic substances to travel, find alternative means of travel, to work or find a better job. If you have to inject your children to send them to be indoctrinated by the public school system, un-school them! Come together in communities where highly evolved and gifted individuals will migrate and bring with them their amazing gifts and talents. New healed healers with integrity will come to assist others in their own self-healing physically, mentally, emotionally and spiritually. Creative, talented individuals who will create art, media, events and adventures that inspire others to more fully know themselves, the Infinite and develop their unique gifts and talents will come. Souls that create free clean technology that works in harmony with nature and our Mother Earth and serves our Divine Inner Technology will gravitate towards these communities. IF YOU BUILD IT THEY WILL COME!

FREEING OURSELVES FROM THE BLACK MAGIC MONEY CURSE

"*For the love of money is the root of all evil*"
I TIMOTHY 6:10

"No man can serve two masters: for either he will hate the one, and love the other; or else he will hold to the one, and despise the other. Ye cannot serve God and money."
MATTHEW 6:24-34

"Therefore take no thought, saying, what shall we eat? or, what shall we drink? or, Wherewithal shall we be clothed? But seek ye first the kingdom of God, and his righteousness; and all these things shall be added unto you."
MATTHEW 6:31 - 6:33

Money has been the curse of humanity since it was created with that intention in Ancient Babylon. Ancient Egyptian curses are embedded on the American dollar bill. The words "In God We Trust" refers to the money God. This curse is so subtle it seeps into your very core without you even being aware of it. Until slowly, you begin to trust the "money god" more than Infinite God Source. And there you are, stuck waiting...and waiting for the money to come so you can live. You have forgotten you are Infinite and thought directs energy. You must first begin to move your energy in the direction you want it to go by visualizing your project, feeding your dreams and taking some kind of action no matter how small. Stay focused on what you want, never letting doubt enter the picture and you will accomplish your goals and the money will come when you need it.

Our history is one of piracy where human beings have been branded as merchandize and sold into slavery. The Money Spell serves as the invisible chains that bind us to a fictitious monetary system. Humanity has been scammed into slaving away their lives in drudgery to pay to live on our own planet. Now they are requiring complete and total ownership of our body, mind and soul to live in their finite world. We have been giving up our most precious commodities our God-given sovereign Freedom for fictitious ones and zeros, created out of thin air in the bankster's computers. Why are we continually giving away our power to these banksters? Why are we paying them to live on our planet? The only power they have is the power you give them. It is time to stop empowering their fictitious world of Maritime law, ownership, and greed. We must return money to its true state of balanced energy exchange. To its rightful and lawful place of integrity where humanity has the right to live freely as the Guardians of our Mother Earth. Where everyone has the freedom to pursue their passions, interests, professions, crafts, trades, and happiness making this world a better place. It is so simple. Because the truth is simple. God's natural laws are simple. Cosmic Sovereign Law is simple. You serve up your best to me and I serve up my best to you out of love, and we are both the richer for it! This is the Law of One. We need to return to our divine simple state where core love is the underlying currency. We need to create a world free of the parasitic tyranny that stops the free flow of loving humans being of service to one another and sharing their amazing gifts and talents with the world. Imagine if everyone on earth lived independently in self-sufficient homes and communities where they generated their own power, produced their own food, made their own clothing, unschooled their own children, created their own art, entertainment, and events that unified, inspired, and uplifted everyone. What if we could create clean energy, safe technology, grew food and herbs that healed and regenerated people. What if we embraced our children as unique gifts from Infinite Source and empowered them on their journey of self-discovery? What if we empowered one another to discover our unique gifts and talents and share them? What power would the black-magic banksters have over us then? None. Game over. What a wonderful World it would be! Can you imagine? It's easy if you try!

"Blessed are the meek for they shall inherit the Earth
MATHEW 5:5

In Greek literature, the proper translation of meek is gentle or soft. The Divine Feminine energy reminds us that our power is in our softness. After the aggressive, dark masculine forces have destroyed themselves these gentle ones, these "meek" ones will inherit the Earth. They will be the key builders of the New Infinite Earth. Those who work within the frequencies of love and eternal light will lay a foundation built on God's Sovereign Laws where love, compassion, and consciousness rule supreme.

LOVE

"Self-Love is the Best Medicine"
PETER MONROY M.D.

The truth is that love is not an emotion. It is not a commodity. It is not something limited to being given and or received from one person to another. Love is a frequency. Love is the Cosmic glue that binds everything together. As you forgive, accept and love yourself, you drop densities and ascend into the vibrational frequencies of love and pure light. You need only maintain the power of pure love in your heart to ascend into the God Source Worlds. So, forgive yourself and forgive others, for they know not what they do and neither do you! You have been encapsulated in a spell, living in a dream, doing the best you knew how to do. We all have! Let bygones be bygones and let us move onward and upward. If you can truly remain focused on the ever-expanding love filling your heart and your entire being and release the wounds of the past, then you can truly love yourself and others no matter what is going on around you even if they do not have your level of awareness. You will become invincible! As you harmonize with these frequencies you will realize that love is all around you, and inside of you. As you do this you rise above the lower polarities of duality and become untouchable. All the manipulation of the dark side has no hold on you because their false light cannot survive in your brilliant light of everlasting love and truth! This explains their desperate attempts to keep you trapped in the lower frequencies of fear, anger and hate. This is why I began this story with the concept that we are all just stories in the mind of God. The power to write yourself closer to the Word (frequency) which IS God is through love.

Many of you are being called to stand up for freedom and speak out to expose the evil agendas being carried out in front of your very eyes. This is the lesson now of the spiritual warrior of love. You can do so from a place of peace and love. True courage is love. It means you care about people so much you cannot turn your back on them. Your love for humanity is so great you cannot turn a blind eye to their suffering, even if they are doing it to themselves. It means you love others enough to tell them the truth but you also have the wisdom to know how much they can handle. Your love for humanity, Mother Earth, and all creation has brought you to this fallen planet and sparks your passion for freedom and your desire to speak the truth, even when those you are trying to help get angry at you. Even if they do not take your help and harm themselves you must continue to love them unconditionally honoring their free will. This perhaps is one of the greatest challenges of our times. If they will not listen perhaps it is more powerful for you to remain silent and simply stand in the vibration of truth and love. Truth is a frequency. Love is a vibration. This Love Light frequency is the unspoken word, which IS God. As you merge with this frequency, love envelopes your every word, action, thought, and deed. Like a mother loving her child into existence or an artist lovingly giving birth to their master piece so too will you give birth to your soul mission and the New Infinite Earth.

As you shatter the finite cages that have encapsulated your reality, please remember that there is always another level of awakening another finite box to break free from into the infinite and beyond! That is because you are Infinite! You must embrace, honor and enjoy where you are each step along your life's journey. "The Process is the Goal and the Goal is the Process"! If you can remain free by never placing the power on things outside of yourself, you can enjoy the characters, settings and events of your life story while remaining detached. You can "be in it, but not of it." The only thing that needs your constant devotion is Infinite Source within you. Through your connection to Infinite Source ALL things are possible. This is true Freedom!

Energy flows where attention goes. Attention is the currency of our Planet. Where are you "paying" your attention? Are you "buying" into the dream spell of the oppressors? Giving away your power and freedom. Is their reality becoming your reality? Do you believe you must fit into their finite world in order to survive? Then, they have succeeded in using your infinite power against you. If you are buying the fake A.I. bad copy as your reality, then that is what you will get and "they have you just where they want you!" Be ever mindful of where and how you may be giving away your Infinite power. Have you had your subconsciousness hijacked and misdirected into creating someone else's version of your future? Have you allowed something other than Infinite God Source to hold the pen that is writing your life story? Some people are writing stories where they are waiting for someone to free them. Only slaves wait for someone to free them! These are the children of God waiting for some external imposter God the Father to tell them what to do. And because they believe this, they will believe it into their reality and it will become their "truth". Or are you creating a future where you are the embodiment of Infinite God Source. Where your will merges with the Divine Will of Infinite Source. Where you co-create a future filled with freedom, creative expression, love, unity and bliss. A future where anything is possible!

As humanity moves through its spiritual adolescence, there will be much upheaval, confusion and turmoil. As you continue to peel away the layers of truth, you will find that ultimately, there is only one truth which is Love. Infinite Love is omnipresent and omnipotent. As you write your story and observe those who are writing theirs do so with love! Love yourself for how far you have come, all that you have learned and experienced, all that you are! Love those around you and respect their journey! Cease judging yourself and others. You must stop stealing others' pens to write their story. Everyone has one pen to use however they please. May you love your story wherever you are at in it always knowing there is more to learn, more to know, and more to discover as you write each word of yourself into existence!

BECOME AN ALCHEMIST

Once you have fully mastered the lesson of unconditional love for self and others you will at last reach the apex of the Magic Triangle transcending the world of illusion and duality and you shall become an Alchemist! Your job then is to transmute the finite systems of enslavement into the Infinite architecture of freedom through love. You will reclaim your position as the true royalty, the Kings and Queens of this Earth. Not as rulers over people who are God Sovereign Free but as the Guardians entrusted to the care of our Mother Earth and her creation and as those who follow the Law of One. When you at last free yourself from the spells and curses of the dark side you can transmute all you touch from these finite systems through the Infinite Power of Love. Once you have proven your worth and your integrity by taking a leap of faith freeing yourself from the "money god" and its curses of greed and fear you are free to use whatever source of energy is available and transmute it. Whether you use paper, plastic, crypto, stones, beads it matters not! You can love the banksters and their finite money magic systems transmuting that energy into energy that flows freely to you now for your Soul Mission. But you may notice that that precious metals were used in ancient times as a means of currency and was until banksters that took us off the gold standard with the creation of the Federal Reserve Hoax. I'll let you figure it out since my job is not to give anyone financial advice. As you tap into the abundant nature of the Infinite great wealth will flow to you. You can use your wealth to invest in things that will free humanity from the finite anti-life systems that harm our Mother Earth. You can buy land, organic seeds, create healing environments, resurrect Tartarian technology, , create conscious media, self-sufficient eco homes and clean energy sources to offer people who choose to live independently from the failing systems. You will prosper as your sincere intentions pioneer new possibilities that help free and empower your fellow human beings. You will create a new economy!

As I review my life I realize I have always been an Alchemist. Going into the darkest of places working within dark systems digesting, integrating and transmuting their lower frequencies. This often manifested in various states of dis-ease within me as I assimilated the darkness of the world around me. But it is only in fully grasping the inner workings that we gain access to transmute them. This is something many star seeds have had to do. We have gone into the darkest corners of the Earth and of human consciousness to transmute it. Many star seeds have even participated in the current medical protocols, even injections to create true "herd" immunity against it. This has been part of our job on Planet Earth. But now is the time to reap the rewards of ALL our sacrifices! As more and more Star Seeds' blossom so will their enterprises and we will create a new thriving economy, community and culture no longer based on greed, power and the accumulation of wealth for control over others. Rather, a culture based on love, service to others, our Mother Earth and the celebration of each person's unique gifts and talents co creating a beautiful world we all want to live in and leave to our children. You the Royal Krystos Star Seeds will allow abundance to flow into your life and you will inherit the Earth becoming the Hand of God writing a New Infinite Earth into existence!

If you have journeyed with me this far, then you are well equipped to navigate the treacherous waters of deception our world now faces. You have learned that you cannot heal in lies and must stop smearing honey over pus in order to fully heal your own shadow self so the Dark Forces can no longer have a hold on you. You know how to spot beings of false light, double speech, half-truths, lies, mind-control tactics, and the deception perception the dark side conjures up. You can identify those who are spiritually bypassing and how to spot a scam! Take only what resonates and leave the rest! This is your elixir of life, the reward you can now claim! But the true reward is to fully realize that you are Infinite! You are all that is, ever has been, and ever shall be! You are Divine Infinite Love! You are Divine Infinite Truth! You are Divine Infinite Source! You are a Divine Infinite Human Being and live it every moment. It is with great love for you and your journey that my never-ending story now ends. Go forth Divine Infinite Storyteller and write your own!

THE END

ABOUT THE AUTHORS

Elizabeth Monroy serves as a Truth-sayer and Ascension Guide for Awakening Infinite Humans, Star Seeds, Twin Souls, and the Master Builders of the Infinite New 5D Earth. She is an International Author, Film Maker, Visionary Artist, Talk Show Host and Inspirational Speaker. She holds a Masters in Mental Health Counseling and is skilled in a number of alternative healing modalities. She traveled the World with her husband Peter Monroy, a board certified Obstetrician/Gynecologist laying a foundation for a higher form of co-healing and the energetic blueprint for the New Infinite 5D Earth. She has worked for years as an intuitive life coach and founded The New Consciousness Renaissance School in Florence, Italy for the creation of conscious media. She now travels between the world with Kiki and Peter, who is always with her in spirit, offering Infinite Human Retreats and guiding her fellow blossoming Infinite Human Beings in their Ascension process and the co-creation of the Infinite New 5D Earth.For more information about what Elizabeth is doing please go to her website:

www.infinitehuman.com
or tune into The Infinite Human Talk Show
on the Voice America Empowerment Channel :
www.voiceamerica.com/show/4180/the-infinite

REFERENCES

I would like to express a deep heartfelt gratitude to David Icke, Ashayana Deane, Lisa Renee, Jay Weidner, Sacha Stone, Edgar Cayce the Elders of the Hopi Nations and our indingenous brothers and sisters who keep the flame of truth burning and many others for the vast volumes of resources they have made available to the public over the years. The knowledge of these great souls has greatly helped humanity and me in my journey of awakening. Below, please find websites of information I have used in my research for this book and as always, take only what resonates.

Lisa Renee
https://energeticsynthesis.com

David Icke
https://davidicke.com

Ashayana Deane
https://www.arhayas.com/

Jay Weidner
http://jayweidner.com/contact/

William Henry
https://www.williamhenry/net
https://www.lisaaromano.com/

David Wilcock
https://divinecosmos.com/

Cory Goode
https://coreygoode.com/

Michael Tellinger
https://michaeltellinger.com/lies/

List of Reported UFO Sightings Wikipedia
https://en.wikipedia.org/wiki/List_of_reported_UFO_sightings
Edgar Cayce
https://www.edgarcayce.org/

Zecharia Sitchin
http://www.sitchin.com/kindle_books.htm

The Deliberate Dumbing Down of America: Charlotte Thomson
http://deliberatedumbingdown.com/ddd/

Grandfather Martin Gashweseoma
https://ministryofconsciousnessnevada.org/teachings/hopi-prophecy-rock-
with-elder-grandfather-martin-gashweseoma
https://www.ancient-origins.net/myths-legends/warriors-rainbow-
prophecy-001577

Living in Sicily
https://livinginsicily.eu/mammismo-marriage-problems/

BIBLIOGRAPHY

Anderson Hans Christian, The Little Match Girl Hans Christian Anderson, Dansk

Folkekalender, 1846

Apollonius, The Argonautica, a Greek epic poem

Aristotle. Aristotle's Poetics. New York: Hill and Wang, 1961.

Barry Niel Kaufman, Sonrise, HJ Kramer, 2011.

Charlotte Thompson Iserbyt, Deliberate Dumbing down of America,com science Press, 1999.

Corpus Hippocraticum 350 B.C.

Fulcanelli, Le Mystère des Cathédrales, Ink book, 1926 Hans,Jenny ,Cymatics,

Macromedia,1972

Huxley, Aldous, Brave New World, Tingle Books ,1931

Icke, David Human Race Get Off Your Knees: The Lion Sleeps No More, David

Icke Books, 2010

Jong, Erica Fear of Flying, Holt, Reinhardt and Winston, 1973

King James Bible (n.d) The King James Bible Online https://www. kingjamesbibleonline.org/ (original work published 1776)

Laozi, Tao Te Ching credited to the 6th-century BC sage.

Monroy, Elizabeth, The Magical Mist, Infinite Human Productions, 1995

Monory, Elizabeth, The Chronicles of MerWord: Corbin and Serena's Tale, Infinite Human Productions, 2011

Monroy Peter, Monroy Elizabeth. The Pathway Home, Infinite Human Productions 1996 Norman R. Bergun, The Ring Makers of Saturn, Pentland Press, Limited, 1986.

Omar Khayyám, Rubáiyát translated by Edward FitzGerald Bernard, Quaritch,1859 Paramahansa Yogananda, Autobiography of a Yogi, Yogoda Satsanga Society of India, 2001

Rubin Theodore Isaac, Jordi/Lisa and David,Forge Books, 1998 Salinge, J.D. Catcher in the Rye,Little, Brown and Company, 1951

Steere, David, Rediscovering Confession: The Practice of Forgiveness and Where it Leads,Routledge; 2009

Swami Sri Yukteswar, The Holy Science, Self Realization Fellowship, 2004 Waltari,

Mika, The Egyptian, G.. P. Putnam's Sons, 1945

Weidner, Jay, The Mysteries of the Great Cross of Hendaye: Alchemy and the End of Time, Destiny Books, 2003

Whiting, Jim, The Life and Times of Hippocrates, Mitchell Lane, 1943 Xaviera,

Hollander, The Happy Hooker, Harper Paper Backs, 1972

Zecharia Sitchin. The Lost Book of Enki: Memoirs and Prophecies of an Extraterrestrial god, Bear & Company, 2002

Zohar iii, 288b The Zohar

FILMOLOGY

A Space Odyssey, 2001 A.I.

Always

A Wrinkle In Time Arcanum

Billy Jack Blade Runner

Body Snatchers, The

Bride of Dracula, The Brother Sun Sister Moon Clockwork Orange Brother Sun and Sister Moon

Cosmic Disclosure Chariots of the Gods Dune

Egyptian, The

Esoteric Hollywood Gaia Field of Dreams

Ghost

Handmaiden, The, T.V. Series

Hocus Pocus

I Will Fight No More Forever Jesus Christ SuperStar

Little Dictator, The Logan's Run

Lost Horizon

Made In Heaven

Manchurian Candidate, The Matrix, The Minority Report, The

Nine

Out On A Limb

Pandora and The Flying Dutchman Peter Pan

Razor's Edge, The

Shining, The

Star Trek Original T.V. Series

Star Trek Movies Star Wars

Supernatural T.V. Series Terminator, The

Time Cop

They Live

Total Recall Truman Show, The West Side Story

SONGS

"Brother Sun and Sister Moon," Donovan "Dream," Johnny Mercer

"Hair," Musical lyrics by Gerome Ragni and James Rado and music by Galt MacDermot

"I Put a Spell On You, and Now You're Mine," Jay Hawkins

"Imagine," "Give Peace A Chance," and "Power to the People," John Lennon "Jesus Christ Super Star," Andrew Lloyd Webber and lyrics by Tim Rice "Joseph and is Amazing Technicolored Dream Coat," Andrew Lloyd Webber and lyrics by Tim Rice

"Money money money," by Benny Andersson and Björn Ulvaeus "One Hand, One Heart," Leonard Bernstein and Stephen Sondheim "Puff the Magic Dragon," Peter Yarrow

"Put the Blame on Mame Boys," Allan Roberts and Doris Fisher "Stranger on the Shore," Acker Bilk

"Sympathy to the Devil," Mick Jagger and Keith Richards

ACKNOWLEDGEMENTS

Peter and I would like to pay our respects and gratitude to those who came before us and inspired us to seek our own answers within. Everyone holds a piece of the puzzle which helps us ALL to awaken from the Dream Spell and begin to uncover the true nature of reality. It is a never-ending journey into the Infinite.

David Icke

Lisa Renee

Jorden Maxwell

Graham Hancock

Tod Adams

William Henry

Corey Goode

David Wilcox

Jay Weidner

Edgar Cayce

William Henry

Gene

Shirley McClain

Tom Laughlin and Delores Taylor

Sam Keen

My spiritual family

Susan, Serena who saved my life!

Patrick and Sharon Ohara

My Dad, David Steere, a great role model whom I found every morning in front of his computer writing away , my mother, my grandmothers, my brothers and the rest of my family, who taught me many valuable lessons.

And of course, Kiki, my spiritual teacher who teaches me to love unconditionally and to play with life!

And last but in no means least, Susan Hendy for her intuitive guidance, unconditional love and for her Mum and family who let my cyber spirit feel like part of their family just when I needed it most!

Many thanks to great souls seen and unseen who have always been there for me!

www.ingramcontent.com/pod-product-compliance
Lightning Source LLC
Chambersburg PA
CBHW051257120626
46547CB00015B/1978